Language and Learning:
What Teachers Need to Know

Language and Learning:
What Teachers Need to Know

Elise Trumbull and Beverly Farr

Christopher-Gordon Publishers
Norwood, MA

Credits

Every effort has been made to contact copyright holders for permission to reproduce borrow material where necessary. We apologize for any oversights and would be happy to rectify them in future printings.

Figures 7.1 and 7.2, "A Multi-day Performance Assessment on Volume," from Grant Wiggins, *Assessing Student Performance*, Copyright © 1993 reprinted with permission of John Wiley and Sons, Inc.

Figure 7.4, "Linguistic Modification of a Mathematics Test Question," from Abedi, Lord, & Plummer, 1997 used with permission.

Figure 7.8, sample assessment item from WASL assessment samplers used with permission of the Assessment and Research Office of the Superintendent of Public Instruction, State of Washington.

"Layers of language" concept and graphic from Henry, M. K., Calfee, R. C., & Avelar LaSalle, R. (1989). Structural approaches to decoding and spelling. In S. McCormick & J. Zutell (Eds.), *Thirty-eighth yearbook of the National Reading Conference*. Chicago: National Reading Conference. Used with permission.

Christopher-Gordon Publishers, Inc.
Bridging Theory and Practice
1502 Providence Highway, Suite 12
Norwood, MA 02062
800-934-8322
781-762-5577

www.Christopher-Gordon.com

Printed in the United States of America

10 9 8 7 6 5 4 3 2   08 07

ISBN: 1-929024-80-0

Library of Congress Catalogue Number: 2004115664

To educators everywhere who strive to learn

about the language needs of their students

Contents

Preface

Teachers play a critical role in supporting language development. Beyond teaching children to read and write in school, they need to help children learn and use aspects of language associated with the academic discourse of the various school subjects. They need to help them become more aware of how language functions in various modes of communication across the curriculum. They need to understand how language works well enough to select materials that will help expand their students' linguistic horizons and to plan instructional activities that give students opportunities to use the new forms and modes of expression to which they are being exposed. Teachers need to understand how to design the classroom language environment so as to optimize language and literacy learning and to avoid linguistic obstacles to content area learning. A basic knowledge of educational linguistics is prerequisite to promoting language development with the full array of students in today's classrooms. (Wong Fillmore & Snow, 2000, p. 7)

Motivation for Writing the Book

With this book, we hope to respond to Wong Fillmore and Snow's call for teachers to learn more about language. The book is intended to be a resource that can serve as a foundation for understanding many of the most important topics related to language and schooling. From all that we see, teachers are struggling valiantly to bootstrap their proficiency with language issues—but they need more support.

Our experience as teacher educators, applied researchers, and professional developers has repeatedly alerted us to teachers' needs and desires to learn more about language. Particularly in light of the increasing cultural and linguistic diversity of students throughout the country, teachers find that they need greater understanding of things such as how a second language is learned, what the relationship is between oral proficiency and literacy, and how to treat dialect differences that appear in students' writing or speaking.

Specialists may have deep knowledge in an area such as second-language acquisition and instruction, yet only a superficial knowledge of reading and writing processes. Teachers who have had the benefit of extensive professional development on new approaches to literacy may not have been grounded in an understanding of how English language learners acquire literacy in a second language—and of all of the factors that shape the path of that acquisition process. When one reads what experts on language and learning have to say about what teachers really need to know, one is struck with the breadth of a potential curriculum on "educational linguistics" (see Brumfit, 1997; Wong Fillmore & Snow, 2000) and the apparent impossibility of providing access to such a curriculum for both preservice and inservice teachers. Nevertheless, teachers have no choice but to do the best they can to teach the students they have. Students' needs are not going to disappear while a perfect solution is found.

We decided to do our best to provide a tool that will help to fill the gap. We have no illusions that this book can really provide *everything* teachers need to know about language, but we hope that it offers support and will stimulate interest in a complex of topics that are absolutely central to educating our current population of students. Let us say also that it is not just for teachers who have large numbers of linguistically "nonmainstream" students. We believe that what we offer in the book is basic for *all* teachers.

Who Are We?

Who are we to presume to write such a book? We can simply say that we are long-standing students of language. Both of us have professional credentials as psycholinguists—those who study language processes, such as how people learn language, how they learn to read, how the mental processes of first- and second-language acquisition differ, and the like. Elise Trumbull earned her doctorate at Boston University, and Beverly Farr earned hers at Indiana University, and both have spent several years as reading specialists, working with special-education students and those with language or reading disabilities. We have both taught college courses on psycholinguistics and have done many a professional development workshop with K–12 educators on topics related to language. In our roles as teachers and, later, as researchers and consultants, we have both worked closely with teachers and administrators in real live school systems throughout the country. Both of us have also delved deeply into the assessment arena, focusing on implications of assessment policies and practices for students learning English or straddling two or more cultures (see, e.g., Farr & Trumbull, 1997; Trumbull & Farr, 2000). We are both multilingual as well, having struggled to learn and maintain languages other than English.

Our colleagues, Katherine Bruna and Rosalinda Quintanar-Sarellana, are teacher educators who prepare students to become teachers of English language learners. Katherine Bruna did her undergraduate work in Hispanic Studies at Vassar College and her master's in Linguistics and her doctorate in Education at the University of California at Davis.While at UC-Davis, she taught courses in bilingual language development and instruction, as well as Spanish as a foreign language. She also worked for 2 years at the American Institutes for Research evaluating a California English-learner professional-development initiative before accepting an assistant professor position in Multicultural and International Curriculum Studies at Iowa State University.

Rosalinda Quintanar-Sarellana received her master's in International Education and her doctorate in Language, Literacy and Culture from Stanford University. She is an associate professor at San José State University in San José, California, where she teaches courses that address pedagogy in diverse school settings; language acquisition; and the needs of second-language learners. Her research is consistent with her teaching interests. She has published in the areas of diversity, equity, first- and second-language acquisition, and the education of linguistic minority students.

As we have acknowledged, we can't really know everything that teachers need to know, but we do have a broad base of education and experience to draw upon. We hope that we have been able to communicate what we have learned in clear but not oversimplified terms. At the same time, we invite others to try their hand at developing resources that teachers and teacher educators can use to promote the spread of educational linguistics.

The Nature of the Book

This is not a recipe book. It is more of a guide, illustrated with examples from a range of grade levels and settings. The examples are meant to be suggestive rather than comprehensive, and we have taken this approach on the basis of both pragmatics and principle: An exhaustive set of prescriptive examples would have lengthened the book intolerably. More important, however, we believe that there is a general knowledge base useful to *all* teachers, and we would like to reach that audience rather than just "early childhood educators" or "secondary-subject-matter teachers."

We also think that teaching is made easier when teachers have productive frameworks rather than prescriptive programs for pedagogy. Understanding the process of building vocabulary in a second (or first) language, for example, is likely to lead to more creative and long-term successful strategies than a preplanned program or a set of lessons for vocabulary development. This kind of understanding can also lead to intelligent and critical use of existing materials and approaches promoted by a district. This is what real accountability is about: informed choices and decision making in planning curriculum, instruction, and assessment and bringing deep knowledge to bear on the interpretation of student outcomes.

Organization of the Book

Each chapter in this book takes a major topic and presents what we judge to be the critical content within the topic. Choosing the topics was not entirely easy. We have tried to select those that are important for the greatest number of educators. We devote considerable space to topics related to English language learners and how to make classrooms work for them. We made the decision not to deal with the topics of learning disabilities and language disorders in great depth, however—as important as they are. Instead, we have merely touched on these topics in order to emphasize the fact that students often exhibit individual language differences that teachers should be aware of and address. We do believe that with an understanding of the issues in language and literacy development covered in the book, educators will have a better sense of how to determine whether a student needs to be evaluated for developmental problems.

We make an effort to point the reader to implications for practice and to offer examples from a range of instructional settings. However, teachers will have to consider what our recommendations mean for their own settings. Within the chapters, teacher research activities are suggested as ideas—seeds, if you will—that we hope will germinate into personal inquiry, collaborative research, or professional development (these are labeled as Teacher Inquiry boxes). Additional text boxes (Teacher Notes) offer illustrations or expansions of important instructional concepts or ideas.

At the end of each chapter is a list of recommended readings on topics covered in that chapter. We provide them as a selection from which readers can choose based on need and interest. We hope that readers will find that they can more critically evaluate other resources and proposed instructional strategies after reading this book. Nevertheless, we must stress that although we hope this book is both interesting and helpful, readers will still need to explore other writings on the topics we have introduced.

In chapter 1, we offer a primer on language: what it is, our philosophy about its role in teaching and learning, and how linguists describe it.

Chapter 2 takes on the all-important issue of how language and culture are related. This topic comes up in other chapters as well, and because of our sociocultural perspective on language, it is difficult to talk about any other language topic without addressing it. Many knowledgeable educators would suggest that language cannot be understood at all without reference to culture. In addition, as Wong Fillmore and Snow (2000) observe, "An understanding of linguistics can help teachers see that the discourse patterns they value are aspects of their own cultures and backgrounds; they are neither universal nor inherently more valid than other possible patterns" (p. 5). An informed approach to language differences is extremely important, in part because teachers make judgments about students' abilities on the basis of language forms and use. When a student's language sounds different, teachers may unconsciously believe that the student's intelligence is lower or that his or her potential for learning is less than that of someone who sounds "right."

Chapter 3 explains the basics of first-language acquisition, replete with many concrete examples. Chapter 4 shows the similarities and differences between first- and second-language acquisition, something any teacher with a diverse group of students will find useful.

Chapter 5 focuses on language and literacy, a topic that is difficult to cover adequately in a full-length book, much less in a chapter. We have selected what we believe to be the most important topics and tried to present them in an engaging way that will be meaningful to every teacher.

Chapter 6, a discussion of effective strategies for teaching students with language differences, especially English language learners, builds directly on what is known about how learners acquire or learn a second language. It is eminently practical, with activities that can be adapted for most grade levels.

Chapter 7 is about the role of language in assessment. We do not mean to indicate with its placement that assessment is the last thing a teacher should consider. In reality, planning for assessment needs to occur iteratively and in concert with instructional planning. Language is at the heart of assessment, and it is practically impossible to think about how one would carry out assessments without using language. Of course, this matter becomes all the more challenging when one is assessing students of many different backgrounds.

Readers will note occasional reduncancy across chapters. This feature reflects the interrelatedness of many topics and the fact that we wanted each chapter to stand on its own.

Terminology

In addressing issues of language and culture, writers are always faced with choices in terminology. So many terms are laden with unfortunate social and historical baggage that it is often hard to choose one that conveys the appropriate meaning. For example, in speaking of U.S. students and families who are members of groups other than European American, one does not want to use the term *minority* because it carries the taint of "less than." In addition, members of groups that have been labeled "minorities" are often in the majority within a particular community or school. We have sometimes used the terms *nondominant* or *underserved* to refer to students from such backgrounds. Neither is entirely satisfactory, for obvious reasons.

We generally use the term *American Indian* rather than *Native American* because our experiences with American Indian colleagues and organizations have led us to believe that more people prefer it. Likewise, *Latino* seems to be preferred over *Hispanic*. General labels obscure important differences within populations such as Latinos or American Indians, and it is always preferable to use more specific terms, such as *Mexican American* or *Hopi*. In addition, people should be characterized in ways that they themselves choose. However, a research study may or may not reveal that kind of information.

When we use the term *European American*, we are actually evoking the Western European source of the dominant cultural values in the United States. Many people from other backgrounds have assimilated: They have consciously or unconsciously adopted the cultural values of the dominant group. Thus, a teacher's ethnicity may be other than European American, but she may have incorporated Western European values in her approach to child development and teaching. Of course, it cannot be assumed that all European Americans fully identify with the dominant values. Rather, the term captures some generalizations about a set of values that tends to be replicated in U.S. schools.

In the realm of language, *English language learner* (ELL) has widely over-taken the more negative-sounding *limited English proficient* (LEP), and we use the former term except when quoting research that uses the term LEP. Neither term places emphasis on students' capabilities, as does *multilingual, bilingual,* or *developing bilingual.* We understand that even the word *dialect* has negative connotations for some people. *Standard English* is itself a troubled term; yet, like *race*, it has powerful influence as a social construct.

For all of these reasons and more, we are tempted to put all such terms in quotation marks throughout the book, to indicate how provisional and limited they are. However, to spare our readers, we have restrained our usage of quotation marks in order to improve the flow of our own language.

Extrapolating to All Age Levels

Although most of the school-based examples we offer relate to K–12 education, we believe that the ideas we address have implications for teachers of very young children all the way through college. The language-acquisition chapters should be of particular interest to early childhood educators; even those that deal more explicitly with K–12 classrooms (such as chapters 5 and 6) can be valuable for developing greater understanding of the kind of linguistic foundations necessary for school success (Bredecamp, n.d.).

From the literature on problems that nonnative English speakers have as they confront the demands of college, we know that college educators face many of the same problems as teachers of younger students. The instructional techniques discussed in chapter 6 are applicable to students at college level as well as earlier levels, and an understanding of basic educational linguistics is equally useful to the college teacher. Spelling, writing, vocabulary development, and comfort with using discourse conventions (spoken or written) continue to be concerns for second-language learners throughout the developmental spectrum. Our desire has been to provide a credible and scholarly (yet readable) summary of thinking on a wide range of issues whose common denominator is language in schooling. We have attempted to show the roots of our own thinking by citing important theorists and researchers; inevitably, we have not given credit to everyone who has influenced us, and there are undoubtedly many more whose work we ought to know. It is both exciting and terrifying to write a book of such scope. We have learned a great deal and acquired a new measure of humility in the process. We hope that readers find the book useful and that when they identify areas that we have not dealt with adequately, they will seek out some of the resources we recommend or conduct their own searches.

Acknowlegments

We thank our families for tolerating the loss of many a weekend day and evening together over the course of the last three years. We would like to thank, in particular, our daughters Caitlin and Kristin, who have served (and continue to serve) as wonderful models of language use and development. Katie Richardson Bruna and Rosalinda Quintanar-Sarellana deserve special thanks. Their expertise lends depth and breadth to second-language topics. We appreciate immensely the support of numerous colleagues who have contributed to our understanding of language issues through countless conversations and shared books and articles. Among them are Jane Braunger, Robert Calfee, Tom Crochunis, Jorge Cuevas, Richard Durán, Susana Dutro, Marian Eaton, Janet Gonzalez-Mena, Patricia Greenfield, Leanne Hinton, Nanette Koelsch, Henriette Langdon, Robert Linquanti, Sharon Nelson-Barber, Maria Pacheco, Blanca Quiroz, Carrie Rothstein-Fisch, Jerry Salzman, Janet Santos, Deborah Short, Guillermo Solano-Flores, Ursula Sexton, Carmen Martínez Sussman, David van Broekhuizen, Aída Walqui, and Marlene Zepeda.

Finally, to our editor, Susanne Canavan, many thanks for your patience and encouragement.

Chapter *1*

Introduction to Language

Elise Trumbull and Beverly Farr with
Katherine Richardson Bruna, and Rosalinda Quintanar-Sarellana

This chapter offers an overview of language as a topic of study for educators. It invites readers to step back and think of language from several different perspectives, all of which are useful in understanding the importance of language in the classroom. The human faculty of language has long been an object of fascination not only to linguists but also to philosophers, psychologists, cultural anthropologists, and educators. We hope to stimulate readers' interest in language and simultaneously offer practical suggestions related to teaching and learning that flow from the theory and research.

The Importance of Language and Knowledge About Language

Language is so automatic for most of us that much of the time we do not think about defining it or consider how remarkable and crucial a faculty it is. Of course, anyone who has suffered language loss through illness or injury is acutely aware of how limited life can become without one's full language capacity. Those of us who have worked with students who have language disorders or learning disabilities (which are usually language based) have gained respect for what it means to have complete language functioning. In cases of developmental delay, we have observed how those students who are most successful at acquiring language are most likely to be the ones to succeed socially and academically.

Students' success in school depends overwhelmingly on their ability to master oral and written language for a vast range of purposes. Increasingly, teachers are faced with students from a range of linguistic backgrounds, many of whom

1

are in the process of learning English as a second or third language. These students need the support of teachers who understand how to foster the acquisition of a new language while maintaining academic progress. These are just some of the reasons that it is so important that teachers have a basic understanding of "educational linguistics" (Wong Fillmore & Snow, 2000). Oddly enough, teacher preparation programs do not routinely offer teachers a good grounding in language study other than courses on language arts or special programs on teaching second-language learners.

A foundation in educational linguistics is something that all teachers need and can put to immediate use in the classroom. It can help teachers to make decisions about how to support students' oral and written language development, judge and describe students' language proficiency, and make choices about how language is used in instruction and assessment. It is helpful, even critical, for teachers to be informed about these issues as well as about particular instructional strategies for teaching students from a range of linguistic and cultural backgrounds. These beliefs have motivated the writing of this book.

In this book, we hope to give teachers support both in the classroom and out; not only successful teaching but also navigating the political storms that often engulf decision making about language policy depend on an informed teacher. Fortified with a good basic knowledge of the issues we address, teachers will be able to make defensible decisions about students' education and act as advocates of the best policies. We believe that there is nothing more powerful in effecting good educational decisions than an informed teacher. It seems self-evident that teachers should have access to professional development on these matters, yet districts are limited in their ability to provide the in-depth professional development necessary to build an elaborated understanding of language issues in education. Moreover, they are often beholden to policy decisions made by legislators and elected officials who may not have a deep understanding of important language topics.

This chapter provides a foundation for the rest of the book. It also serves as background for further inquiry into language as it relates to schooling. This chapter examines what language is; presents the authors' philosophy of language; explores the role of language in thought, learning, and schooling; and describes how linguists have characterized language. Formal linguistic terminology, which is introduced here, can be useful in two ways: (a) It can increase teachers' comfort with reading important literature on language, and (b) it can ensure that terms are used accurately in classroom instruction. A basic understanding of how linguists describe language will give teachers new ways of thinking about what underlies students' proficiency with listening, speaking, reading, and writing (Wong Fillmore & Snow, 2000). This chapter also debunks a few myths about language and takes a short foray into the history of the English language in order to make the spelling system more transparent. Implications of each area of inquiry for the classroom will be offered.

What Is Language?[1]

Language is, of course, the primary means of human communication. It is also the most widely used system for representing thought, whether orally or in writing. In addition, it can serve the purpose of self-expression, sometimes rising to what would be considered art—in the form of poetry, literature, or drama. At the heart of human intelligence is the underlying ability to abstract from concrete sensory and motor experience and represent that experience. Perception itself, whether visual, auditory, tactile, olfactory, or gustatory, is not pure and direct (Pinker, 1997). The brain filters out much of the sensory input (Neisser, 1967), and then even the most basic sensory experiences are mediated by mental interpretation, most often by language (Oller, 1991). For example, if we bite into an unexpectedly hot pepper in a spicy dish, we probably not only experience the burning but also think, "Hot!" We quite literally re-present an experience to ourselves through language.

Language as a System of Representation

To get real perspective on why language is unique, it is helpful to compare it with other representational systems. All reasoning involves representational, or semiotic, capacity (Oller, 1991). Oller describes three particular human semiotic systems, all of which are necessary to normal human development.[2] The first is *sensorimotor*,[3] through which we have mental images of our bodies in space, of objects around us, and of how objects can be expected to behave under certain circumstances. Sensorimotor representations are more or less directly and iconically related to the facts of experience; that is, their form is almost a "photograph" of the events they represent. Through interaction with the environment, in what Jean Piaget has called the "sensorimotor period," young children build up mental images of how objects and people operate in the physical world. Developmentally, sensorimotor images or representations are thought to be the building blocks of early cognition and language (Bialystok & Hakuta, 1994).

The second semiotic system is *kinesic*; it is gestural, as in motioning to someone to do something, pointing out someone or something, or giving so-called "deictic" (directional) information. The kinesic system is somewhat more abstract than the sensorimotor in that gestures indicate or stand for a desired action or an implied comment or request (as when an infant points to an object). Some linguists have speculated that a gestural system preceded the development of actual language in human history.[4] The visual arts and dance are other ways to represent meaning, and forms of human activity such as sumo wrestling and cooking have been analyzed by philosophers in terms of their representational status within a culture (Barthes, 1982).

The third semiotic system is *language*, which uses abstract symbols (words) to represent concepts. This is in contrast to other representational systems that use images, gesture, or artistic media. Unlike iconic representations, which either directly (as in the case of sensorimotor images) or partially (as in the case of gesture) maintain a connection to the physical experience, words bear no physical relationship to the objects or concepts for which they stand. It is by convention that speakers of a language use each word to convey a particular meaning or set of meanings.

Although a few words in any language are indeed onomatopoeic—that is, they sound like what they mean (e.g., *hiss, whoosh, bow wow, meow, ding dong*)—these words are the exception. For the vast majority of words, there is nothing in their form that would suggest the object to which they refer. There is nothing about the actual word, *book,* that suggests "something to read" or "a set of pages bound by a paper or cardboard cover." We can confirm that this is true because the word for book is different in other languages—for example, *livre* in French and *hon* in Japanese. Research shows that bilingual children are likely to recognize this arbitrariness of the code long before monolingual children do (Bialystok, 1988).

> ### Teacher Inquiry
>
>
>
> #### Language Experts
> Design some activities to expand students' awareness of the arbitrariness of language, based on learning a bit about one or more languages they do not speak. If there are speakers of languages other than English in the classroom, they can be the "linguistic authorities" on their home languages (check with such students privately to be sure they are willing to serve this role)—supplying counterparts for common English words. If you have studied another language, introduce parallel terms from that language. If neither you nor any of your students feels comfortable being the linguistic authority, check a tape out of the library and learn a few words and phrases along with your students.

This feature of arbitrariness of the relation between form and meaning makes the linguistic system flexible, productive, and powerful (Hockett, 1963). Humans are able to use a small number of elements (the sounds of a given language) to create a virtually infinite number of meaning units (words) that can be combined intentionally in particular ways (according to the commonly understood rules of grammar) to add up to larger meanings. This combinatorial power is often referred to as *generativity* (Chomsky, 1965). The flexibility of language extends to the ways in which vocabulary and even grammar can be used. Words have meaning by convention, but people constantly bend the rules in order to communicate effectively—sometimes verging on the poetic. Author Robert Penn Warren, America's first poet laureate, once described the egg that the character in his novel was eating by saying it "bled yellowly" across his plate. It is not difficult to find such examples in literature as well as in the daily speech of children as they explore ways to use language.

The three semiotic systems we discuss have a common source, something that is demonstrated by people's ability to move back and forth among them. For example, we can translate physical experience into language. We can also translate from language to visual imagery (envisioning what someone is describing) or translate language into gesture (using a motion to indicate direction). Of course, gesture and other nonverbal aspects of communication greatly enhance our linguistic messages—sometimes carrying more weight than words themselves. Think of how much a facial expression and hand gesture can add to a statement of contempt, such as "How could you do that?"

How Language Is Different from the Communication Systems of Other Animals

It has been said that one good way to learn about one's own language is to learn a new language. Suddenly there is a basis for comparison. Likewise, linguists have compared language to the communication systems of many animals to get insights into its special features. Perhaps the most important feature of human language that becomes evident in comparison to the communication systems of birds, bees, and our fellow primates is its extreme flexibility. There is no limitation to the topics that can be addressed by language or to the ways they can be talked about. "The normal use of language is . . . a creative activity. This creative aspect of normal language is one fundamental factor that distinguishes human language from any known system of animal communication" (Chomsky, 1972, p. 100).

Most animals have a restricted communication repertoire, both in terms of the topics they can address (food, mating, danger) and the forms they can use (cries, physical signs on their bodies, perhaps gestures—in the case of primates) (Tartter, 1986; Tinbergen, 1952, 1984). Even the species of birds that demonstrate creativity in their songs are extremely limited in what they can express (Tartter, 1986). Dolphins and whales, as well as the great apes, do have representational capacity, but many prominent linguists are convinced that the human language system is distinct in its power for symbolic representation (see Chomsky, 1972; Jackendoff, 1994; Pinker, 1994).[5]

The 1960s and 1970s saw a spate of efforts to teach gorillas and chimpanzees language. Some of these efforts continue in the present, but—partly because the research was so controversial (with huge, sometimes nasty arguments among researchers as to what the data really showed)—funding for

Teacher Note

Koko's Use of Humor
One sign of representational capacity is a sense of humor. It requires imagining things as other than they actually are or recognizing the ambiguity of a situation. According to ape language aficionado Eugene Linden, Koko's wit is legendary. "Most of her jokes seem to be attempts to sabotage what Koko considers to be boring drills and conversations. For instance, if Koko is bored or feeling obstreperous, she will vary the way a sign is made and, in so doing, subtly change its meaning. Once, when asked too many times to make the 'drink' sign (which is made by placing to the lips a thumb extended from a closed fist), Koko responded by making the sign in her ear. Another time, when shown bottles, she made the appropriate sign on her nose and then signed, 'Funny there.' On another occasion, when asked by an assistant whether she wanted food in her mouth, Koko replied, 'Nose,' precipitating the following conversation:
CINDY: Nose?
KOKO: Fake mouth.
CINDY: Where's your fake mouth?
KOKO: Nose."
Linden (1986, pp. 122–123)

them has dwindled (Linden, 1986). Perhaps the most famous target of these efforts is the gorilla Koko, who was taught sign language by Dr. Penny Patterson in Woodside, California. Koko's story has been popularized in the children's book *Koko's Kitten*. Many in the scientific community dismiss Patterson's research, in part because she appears to have such a personal investment in Koko's success, jeopardizing her objectivity as a researcher. However, one wonders whether a clinical laboratory-like setting is the best in which to foster language acquisition—particularly for a member of a species that quite likely does not have the proclivity for language that a human does. If Koko does use language with any success, it may be precisely because of Dr. Patterson's "inability" to maintain a scientific stance toward her.

Authors' Philosophy of Language

There are many approaches to language study, each reflecting a set of beliefs about what language is and how it is acquired. In this book, we take a heavily sociocultural perspective. Although we believe that there is a likely genetic basis for language acquisition in humans (Chomsky, 1972; Lenneberg, 1967; Pinker, 1994), we also attribute a very large role to the environment in supporting its full development. The social and cultural settings of home, school, and community are powerful influences on the shape that language will take in each individual (e.g., Cazden, 1988; Gee, 1990; Gumperz & Hymes, 1972; Heath, 1983; Michaels, 1981; Rogoff, 2003; Schieffelin & Ochs, 1986; Scollon & Scollon, 1981). Below we discuss four intertwined elements of our philosophy of language as it applies to learning and schooling.

A Focus on Language Use

Historically, the study of language has focused on its structural elements: vocabulary, grammar, and sound system (Bloomfield, 1933; Sapir, 1921; Saussure, 1916/1959). Nevertheless, one cannot understand language simply by studying its forms. Increasingly, those who study languages have looked to *language use* as an equally, if not more, important aspect. This shift represents the recognition that the meaning of language lies in the ways it is used to accomplish various purposes within a range of social contexts. Language mastery is not just about proficiency with vocabulary and grammatical rules; it "consists rather in being able to apply such

> ### Teacher Inquiry
>
> **Linguistic Comparisons**
>
> Consider interviewing one or more parents about some of the ways language is used to express different intentions in their speech communities: How does one offer condolences? How does one thank someone, depending on the other person's status or role? What nonverbal behavior accompanies such acts?
>
> Share what you learn with your whole class.
>
> Older students could conduct their own inquiries and report to the class.

fixed features in fluid situations, or, in other words, in knowing not the rules but the usage of language" (Clark & Holquist, 1984, p. 213). We discuss language usage, or "communicative competence," on page 17, particularly as it relates to the classroom.

A Sociocultural Constructivist Perspective on Learning

We view language as a complex human faculty that is acquired through the active participation of learners in interaction with their environments—particularly with more competent speakers, such as parents, older siblings, and teachers. Ours is a constructivist perspective: We believe that an individual's new learning is built on the basis of what the person already knows (Bransford, Brown, & Cocking, 2000; Bruner, 1973; Piaget, 1954). This means that instruction—whether it focuses on language development or content area knowledge (or both)—must be designed with consideration for students' current developmental levels and their existing knowledge base. We use the term *sociocultural constructivist* to indicate that this knowledge base develops within a social and cultural context. One might say that the mind itself is socially and culturally constructed (Bialystok & Hakuta, 1994; Greenfield, 1966; Rogoff, 1990; Vygotsky, 1978).

Language, Culture, and Cognition

Language, culture, and cognition are inextricably intertwined. Language is a reflection of a culture's orientation to the world, of its needs and goals. There is no way to fully understand a language without also learning about the culture or cultures in which it is spoken. Packed into the Korean language—right into the pronoun system, for example—are ideas about how people should relate to each other. In the context of family conversation, one often does not refer to oneself as "I," but rather "we," showing relatedness to the other members of the family. This is a very different "we" from the one used by the Queen of England or the Pope. The latter usages seem to reflect a presumption of status rather than the subsuming of one's own importance to a larger entity, the family. Even this tiny example illustrates the fact that we have to understand cultural context in order to understand language usage.

Cultures differ in the ways they approach teaching, learning, and knowledge. Such differences have implications, not only for vocabulary (what concepts are important) and communicative conventions (rules for interacting with others) but also for how language is used in general. Is language the primary tool for teaching (through telling and explanation), or are demonstration and modeling more prominent, for instance, as they are in many traditional American Indian and Alaskan Native communities (Lipka, 1998; Trumbull, Nelson-Barber, & Mitchell, 2002)? Are children expected to initiate conversation with adults, tell stories, or answer questions to which adults already know the answers? It all depends upon social and cultural expectations, which differ from community to community.

Respect for the Language of Individuals

Language plays a key role in one's identity development (Fishman, 1989; Hakuta, 1986; Zentella, 1997); the language we learn at home defines us, tells us where we belong. In many ways, language constitutes who we are. To devalue a person's language or dialect is to devalue the person.

Excluding students' home languages from being part of their schooling sends the message that those languages are of less value than English. Students' sense of belonging and acceptance are inevitably affected by such choices. Even when it is not possible to provide continuing education through a student's home language, positive attitudes toward that language can be communicated through the actions of school personnel. All dialects of English should be respected as well; they are equally valid linguistically and have deep personal meaning for those who speak them.

The Role of Language in Thinking, Learning, and Schooling

The Relation Between Thought and Language

For centuries, linguists, philosophers, psychologists, and educators have pondered the question of how language and thought are related. Can there be ideas without words? Is language dependent on general cognitive development, or is it a separate and different capability?

Theory 1: Thought Depends on Language

One possibility is that thought is dependent on language, that there is no thinking without language and that our thoughts are formed by the language that we learn. The view that language determines thought—linguistic determinism—is most closely associated with linguist Benjamin Lee Whorf (1956). He hypothesized that the language we learn actually dictates the ways we will look at the world. If our language makes seven color distinctions, we will see seven colors. If it distinguishes only between dark and light (and some do), we will see only two shades. Likewise, with time and space, we will perceive the world as organized in the ways our language represents.

Theory 2: Language Depends on Thought

Another possibility is that language is dependent on thought, that we have thoughts and then put them into language. In this view language is the vehicle or tool of thought (Piaget, 1967; Vygotsky, 1934, 1962). Developmentally, at least, this appears to be happening when infants and young children are growing cognitively. Theorists believe that children have "primitive notions about meaning that are not necessarily verbal but can become verbalized" (Bialystok & Hakuta, 1994, p. 94). These notions are based in sensorimotor experiences that give rise to mental images of spatial relationships and movement, for example. When an infant points to something or follows another person's gaze, those actions suggest that there must be some prelinguistic mental activity that prepares the infant for understanding how to use language to "point to" or refer to something (Bruner, 1986).

Theory 3: Language and Thought Are Independent

A third position is that language and other forms of cognition are independent of each other (Chomsky, 1993; Pinker, 1994), that language is not built upon general cognitive faculties but is a specific faculty that develops independently. Pinker (1994) uses the term *mentalese* to refer to "some silent medium of the brain—a language of thought" (p. 56) and suggests that thoughts are "merely clothed in words when we need to communicate them to a listener" (p. 71). Pinker cites the case of a young deaf immigrant man, discovered by a sign language interpreter, who knew no sign language but showed considerable knowledge of numbers and learned computation rapidly. Once he learned some sign language, he began to tell a remarkable tale of his history, showing that he had somehow mentally represented his experience to himself—and could now put it into language to share with others.

Conclusion

One's language does not constrain one's cognition in the ways Whorf claimed. For example, people are able to perceive color differences for which they have no labels; human perception is universal (Cromer, 1991; Pinker, 1994).[6] They can also learn the categorical systems of languages and cultures other than their own.

Intuitively, most people sense that some form of thinking can take place without the direct involvement of language. Humans are, it is clear, able to engage in semiotic activity (representing ideas or experience mentally) without complete dependence on language. Everyone has probably had the experience of not being able to put certain thoughts into words—or, having expressed something, feeling that it isn't exactly what one wanted to say. This would suggest that thoughts preceded the words. Physicists have described how they "see" and mentally manipulate hypothetical physical phenomena in three-dimensional space. Watson and Crick's discovery of DNA's double helix came to them as a visual image, and Michael Faraday's conceptualization of electrical and magnetic fields entailed envisioning "lines of force as narrow tubes curving through space" (Pinker, 1994, p. 71).[7]

There are observable connections between general cognitive development (particularly the ability to represent through play and gesture) and early use of language. One caution: Although sensorimotor images are described as building blocks for language, they do not map directly onto language but are, rather, filtered through the language to which the child is exposed. Language researcher Melissa Bowerman (2000) has been studying this process for many years and has shown that even such simple concepts as placement of an object "in" or "on" something is expressed differently in different languages. Figuring out when to use *in* versus *on* in English is a challenge that is notoriously difficult for native Spanish speakers because of the different conventions of the Spanish language.

Languages such as Dutch, English, and Korean represent different aspects of that basic concept of *in* and *on* (Bowerman, 2000). In English, we use the preposition *on* to express the relationship of a Lego block fitted onto a stack of blocks, a ring put on a finger, a cup put on a table, a hat put on a head, and a towel placed on a rack. In Dutch, three separate prepositions are used to represent these actions (*om*, *op*, and *aan*). *Aan*, for instance, specifies that an object is acted on by an external force (e.g., gravity) and would not stay where it is without being held in place (hence its use with the towel on the rack). In Korean, things get even more interesting. Children learn, through their language, to distinguish between things that fit tightly into or onto other things. To express that a Lego block is fitted on a stack, the verb *kkita* is used, as it also is for a book fitted into a case. To say that a hat is on someone's head, one uses the word *ssuta*. Bowerman (2000) has shown that children learn these distinctions at a very young age (certainly, by 18 months). In other words, there is no basic way of coding the relationships observed in the sensorimotor period that crosses all languages.

There is a heavy measure of interdependence between language and cognition, both during initial development and in the mature student (see Bates & Goodman, 1999; Durán, 1989; MacWhinney, 1999; Oller, 1991, 1992). Certainly most mental operations demanded by school depend to some degree on language, and the need to express new concepts promotes the expansion of language. So although the exact nature of the relationship between language and thought or cognition in early development may be disputed, during the school years it is clearly one of interdependence: Much of learning depends on language, and schooling promotes new forms and uses of language.

The Role of Language in the School

It is almost impossible to overestimate the role of language in learning and schooling. Language is the usual medium for understanding problems and solving them—even problems that appear to be visual in nature, like reading a map or taking the measurements of a room in order to purchase the right amount of carpeting. The task of reading a map, for example, requires an understanding of spatial representation, or how three-dimensional space is translated into two dimensions; understanding of the conventions for showing north, south, east, and west; and familiarity with the concept of scale, not to mention ability to read street names. To use a map, people need to formulate an idea about where they are at the moment and where they want to go (through language). Some may rely more on a mental visual map to get from point A to point B. In fact, most of us can probably mentally trace our way between work and home without using language (Crystal, 1997). However, when planning is involved, so is language, usually: "Let's see, I need to go north on Oak for a few blocks, left on Main, then take my third right onto Sunnyhills." Imagine using a map, or even learning to use one, without any reliance on language.

Students who are thought to be visual learners may have strong observational skills and the ability to illustrate what they have learned through drawings or diagrams. Nevertheless, even though their language processing is not so apparent as in highly verbal learners, it is essential to their ability to formulate and solve problems mentally (Durán, 1985; Oller, 1991, 1992). Teachers would also be hard-pressed to teach complex ideas without heavy reliance on language.

Written language is, of course, an essential tool of academic learning. It is an efficient means of constructing and passing on knowledge and of demonstrating what one has learned. Often we don't know what we think or have learned until we try to write it for someone else. As students pass through the grades, they need an increasing sophistication with language. For instance, they will require a broader and broader vocabulary for understanding literature and content area texts and a greater repertoire of oral modes. They will have to learn how to argue and persuade orally and in writing, using appropriate techniques, discourse structures, and forms of evidence.

> **Teacher Note**
>
> **Cultural Differences in Argumentation**
> What counts as an "appropriate" way to argue is quite culturally variable. Of course, it can vary simply from family to family. Whereas some people believe, as did the ancient Greeks, that mounting a good argument entails an appeal to both logic and emotion, others find emotional elements distasteful or inappropriate. Counter to what some think, emotion and logic can coexist: they are different facets of persuasion (Wollman & Estrin, 1990). Some research has pointed to sources of misunderstanding between Blacks and Whites as coming down to just this difference (Kochman, 1989). Whites tend to want to keep emotion out of an argument: "Just present the evidence." Blacks may find that practice disingenuous. "Why doesn't she just say what she feels?" they may ask.

Nearly all instructional settings require student oral and written participation; grades are often dependent on mastery of good communication skills—which, in U.S. society, means speaking out in class, defending your point of view, and writing in the forms prescribed by state and local standards (Trumbull, 2000). We may lament the dependence of education on language and seek to cultivate a more multi-intelligence approach to education (Gardner, 1983), and we should certainly expand the stock of ways in which students may represent concepts. Yet language remains our single most important medium for teaching and learning. Any student who overrelies on kinesthetic, visual, or other nonlinguistic routes to learning will likely be hampered more and more as he or she progresses through formal schooling.

The Functions of Language in the Classroom

Language is always used to accomplish something, whether to request or command, to inform or persuade. The Teacher Note on page 12 lists a few of the possible reasons people use language in the classroom.

Teacher Note

Functions of Language in the Classroom
- secure an item one needs (through a request)
- build relationships (through small talk or expressions of friendship)
- share an experience
- express an opinion
- comment on something
- plan a future action
- show the teacher that one has read the assignment
- express emotions
- regulate someone's behavior (e.g.,teacher to student)
- request or share information
- reflect (aloud or silently) on a new idea
- explain
- signal group membership (with in-group language)
- deceive (of limited use in the classroom, one hopes)
- criticize
- amuse
- analyze language itself

Readers may be able to think of yet other uses to which language can be put in the classroom, and, of course, a single communicative act can incorporate multiple uses. For example, in writing a persuasive essay, a student is attempting to influence someone else's thinking or behavior and may reflect on ideas, express opinions and emotions, explain her perspective, and demonstrate that she has read the assigned background material. She may deceive the teacher in the process, amuse her readers, and even invite them to respond to her arguments. In chapters 2 and 3, we show a useful typology of language uses, based on that created by linguist M.A.K. Halliday, into which all of the uses above can be grouped.

The Language of Math

We mention this topic here because it has often been alleged that language and mathematics are independent, or that mathematics has its own language apart from the "normal" code. However, it has been argued strongly by logicians Bertrand Russell and C. S. Peirce that "mathematics as a kind of reasoning . . . is entirely dependent upon language" (Oller, 1991, p. 22). There is, however, a specialized language of mathematics—a *mathematics register*—that is explicitly structured to express mathematics concepts (Spanos, Rhodes, Dale, & Crandall, 1988). Words that signal logical relations are frequent in mathematical problems (*if . . . then, because, for example, such that, but, either . . . or, given, therefore*). In addition, there are words that appear to be drawn from "natural" language (e.g., *root, power, diagonal, square*) that have particular meanings in a mathematics context that they do not have in general conversation. Students must learn the mathematical uses of these words. As with any kind of problem solving, students need to be able to use language to represent the problem to themselves. Research has shown that the quality of problem representation is a key to successful problem solution (Durán, 1985).

Recognition of the importance of language in mathematics is reflected in one of the standards put forth by the National Council of Teachers of Mathematics (NCTM, 1989a): "Learn to communicate mathematically."

To express and expand their understanding of mathematical ideas, students need to learn the symbols and terms of mathematics. This goal is best accomplished in the context of problem solving that involves students in reading, writing, and talking in the language of mathematics. As students strive to communicate their ideas, they will learn to clarify, refine and consolidate their thinking. (NCTM, 1989a)

This standard highlights the connections among reasoning, thinking, and communicating—all greatly dependent on language. Performance assessments[8] developed by states and other groups are often quite linguistically complex, in terms of both the text that sets out a problem and the language the student is required to produce to explain his or her procedures and solution path (Farr & Trumbull, 1997). Thus, unfortunately, it is not safe to assume that mathematics is an area in which students who are low in language skills may expect to perform at a higher level, except perhaps on straight computation (Abedi, Lord, Hofstetter, & Baker, 2000).

Characterizations of Language

There are three common ways of characterizing the components of language: the language arts view, the traditional linguistic view, and the communicative competence view (Figure 1-1). Each contributes something to our understanding of what is entailed in students' learning language.

Figure 1-1. Three Views of Language Proficiency

Language Arts View			
Listening	Speaking	Reading	Writing (Performing)
Traditional Linguistic View			
Phonology	Morphology	Syntax	Semantics	(Pragmatics)*
Communicative Competence View			
Grammatical Competence	Pragmatic Competence	Discourse Competence	Strategic Competence

* a relatively recent addition

How Teachers Characterize Language

Most teachers think of language in terms of the components of language arts: reading, writing, listening, and speaking (and sometimes " performing"). These are really language modalities. This way of organizing the elements of language is useful for thinking broadly about curriculum and instruction and forms a logical taxonomy for evaluating students' progress. Within each of these areas, teachers may well characterize their instruction as focusing on components of language as linguists define them, although they may not use the same terminology. For instance, instruction may focus on developing awareness of the segments of spoken words (an aspect of phonology), or a teacher may evaluate a student on his or her sense of story (an aspect of discourse knowledge).

How Linguists Characterize Language

Linguists have traditionally considered the aspects of language study to include phonology, syntax, morphology, semantics, and, more recently, pragmatics. Teachers implicitly use knowledge of these linguistic components to evaluate students' reading, writing, listening, and speaking development. However, an explicit awareness of these domains can be even more helpful in analyzing student development in language arts and communicating to students and parents about particular skills.

Phonology

Phonology is the study of the sounds and sound patterns of a language. Speakers of English know intuitively what sounds are "English sounds" and what combinations of sounds are "permitted" in English words. A native English-speaking kindergartener would judge that a word pronounced *grzny* is not an English word, and a reader wouldn't consider it pronounceable according to the tacit rules of English phonology. A student may not have the word *graft* in his or her vocabulary but would know that it could be an English word. (Note: A student may have oral phonological competence but not be able to apply it fully in reading and writing.)

Morphology

Morphology is the study of word structure (*morph* means "shape"). Because English has both Germanic and Romance origins, it has many ways of forming words. We can add *-ish*, *-ly*, or *–ious/ous* to the end of a noun or portion of a noun to get an adjective (*imp + ish = impish*; *leisure + ly = leisurely*; *religi[on] + ous = religious*). We can change a noun to an adjective by substituting *-ent* for *-ence* (*insolence*, *insolent*) or change a verb to a noun by adding *-ion*, sometimes with a change in the final consonant (*prevent*, *prevention*; *divert*, *diversion*). Proficient readers and writers unconsciously know many more rules such as these, apparently from exposure to more multisyllabic words than one normally hears in conversation. There is a reciprocal relationship here: Development of literacy demands application of tacit morphological (and phonological) knowledge, but it also promotes further development of such knowledge.

Syntax

Syntax is what people commonly think of as grammar. In linguists' terms, syntax is the study of the rules for how words relate to each other within a sentence and as part of the structure of sentences (Pei & Gaynor, 1969). For example, in the sentence "Carolyn hit her little brother," *Carolyn* is the subject, *hit* is the verb, and *her little brother* is the direct object (a noun with two modifiers, *her* and *little*). Word order in English is an important part of the rules because, unlike many other languages (such as Latin or German), English does not inflect its nouns. That is, there are no endings that show who or what is the subject and who or what is the direct object. For instance, in Latin, *puella* (girl) is the subject form, while *puellam* is the direct object form. Thus, no matter where we placed *puellam* in a sentence, we would know it was the direct object.[9]

Syntactic rules (which we learn but don't necessarily know consciously) reflect the permissible ways of combining words to arrive at a grammatical sentence. For example, it is fine to say, in English, "Erica planted several rosebushes in her garden" but not "Rosebushes planted several garden Erica in her," even though we might guess at the meaning on the basis of what would make sense. Similarly, "Ice cream slurped Harold" or "Slurped Harold ice cream" might work as well as "Harold slurped ice cream." What about "Introduced to Marvin Darlene Blair"? We need some clues from word order (or word endings, as in Latin) to tell us who is doing what to whom.[10]

Syntactic rules also specify how sentences can be combined to form larger sentences. We can reduce "Harold and Maude went to the movies. Harold and Maude had a wonderful time." to "Harold and Maude went to the movies and had a wonderful time." In this case, a linguist would identify rules that allow for joining these two ideas with a conjunction (*and*), while deleting the repetition of the subjects (*Harold and Maude*). Virtually all students (except for those who are seriously developmentally delayed) have mastered basic word order, the ability to combine sentences, and a great many other syntactic rules by the time they enter school (see chapter 3). Nevertheless, a teacher may notice that some students do not seem to apply their knowledge of what makes a permissible sentence when they start reading and writing. Making tacit syntactic knowledge explicit may require some direct support. A teacher may ask a student to read a sentence out loud and think about whether it's "okay" (Trumbull, 1984).

Semantics

Semantics is the branch of linguistics concerned with meaning, or "the way in which words and sentences convey meaning in the everyday situations of speech and writing" (Crystal, 1987, p. 100). The word *semantics* has its roots in the Greek words for "signify" and "significant." Discussions among linguists of what exactly is meant by "meaning" can get very deep. There are a few issues that need to be considered. First, to understand the meaning of a word, phrase, or sentence, we need to refer to the context in which it is spoken or written. A random paging through the dictionary reveals why: Most words have more than one meaning. It is the easiest (most familiar and frequent) words that tend to have two or more distinct meanings. Just think of *bill*, *buck*, *duck*, *press*, *right*, *run*, and *strike*. *Webster's Encyclopedic Unabridged Dictionary of the English Language* (1989) has 172 entries for the word *run*. Sometimes the same dictionary entry represents more than one part of speech. The word *slick*, for example, can be a noun, a verb, or an adjective.

Second, it is important to distinguish between the sense and the reference of a word or phrase. If a friend promises to bring a "basket of fruit" to a party, we know the sense, or the meaning, of her phrase—even if we don't know exactly what kinds of fruit or what size and shape of basket the speaker has in mind. The phrase does not yet have specific reference; that is, it does not refer to a specific object in the world. It is an abstraction that makes sense to us.

We use our knowledge of syntax to help us understand sentences, but sometimes a sentence can be acceptable grammatically but not semantically. "The monkey clambered over the democracy." Monkeys can clamber over things, but not democracies. On the other hand, "The saboteurs trampled democracy with their actions" is both grammatical and meaningful, though somewhat metaphoric. Students' semantic development entails acquisition not only of new vocabulary but also of elaborated meanings for words they already know (Beck, McKeown, & Kucan, 2002; Nagy & Scott, 2000). Reading comprehension depends upon matching written vocabulary to oral vocabulary and recognizing when one does not know a word or understand its use in context.

Pragmatics

Pragmatics is the branch of linguistics concerned with "the factors that govern our choice of language in social interaction and the effects of our choice on others" (Crystal, 1997, p. 120). The word *pragmatics* comes from the Greek word *pragmatikos,* meaning "practical." Pragmatic knowledge is based on social experience. Pragmatic rules influence one's choice of vocabulary and syntax—when to say, "Thanks" and when to say, "Thank you very much. I am grateful for your generosity."

Speakers of different dialects of English (or any language) in different geographical and social settings learn what is considered appropriate for those settings. We would expect to hear very different English usage in the following situations: mates tippling in a pub in Australia, a foreign diplomat greeting the Prime Minister in London, buddies participating in a weekly poker game in Brooklyn, and sixth graders engaged in a discussion of ancient Egyptian burial practices. We have to remember that what is considered appropriate may change over time:

> People are continually modifying established language practices, adapting
> them to new situations, and, at times, straightforwardly challenging and
> sabotaging established language practices. Therefore . . . it may be more
> useful to think of language practices as an evolving and dynamic set of
> social practices that are always at a nexus of social change, stability, and
> struggle. (Bloome, Champion, Katz, Morton, & Muldrow, 2000, p. 46)

A large and important part of children's language proficiency is pragmatic; students who are learning English as a new language are also learning these pragmatic norms of communication.

Communicative Competence

In recent decades, there has been a shift toward understanding people's language proficiency in terms of their "communicative competence" (Bachman & Palmer, 1982; Canale, 1983; Canale & Swain, 1980; Cummins, 1980a; Hymes, 1972a). This shift represents the recognition that language is not just a set of formal skills; rather, language is used in particular contexts to accomplish particular goals. In this view, the pragmatic aspect of language takes center stage. Communicative competence could be described as the ability to use all of one's grammatical knowledge appropriately in all kinds of situations, to generate a wide range of discourse forms (e. g., conversations, discussions, speeches), and to detect and repair problems in communication. Although the emphasis is often on interpersonal communication, the definition could include the ability to communicate in a wider societal context, such as when scientists write for other scientists or political candidates address a crowd. This perspective on language proficiency has been most useful to teachers in understanding the skills their students need to master. See chapter 4 for a more extended explanation and discussion of communicative competence.

Metalinguistic Knowledge

Another aspect of language proficiency, which is not routinely addressed in any of the usual characterizations of language proficiency, is *metalinguistic knowledge*.[11] This term refers to awareness of language itself, its forms and functions, along with knowledge about how to talk about language. This awareness is a form of metacognition through which the learner steps back from a focus on the meaning of language to look at it as an object and a set of processes (Flood & Menyuk, 1983; Rowe & Harste, 1986). Particularly as students become readers and writers, they need to be able to bring to conscious awareness their own tacit knowledge of language. For instance, they need to tap their knowledge of phonology (how sounds work in the language), syntax (what counts as a grammatical sentence), semantics (word meanings), and written discourse (what a description or a story sounds like). It will also be useful, of course, to be able to analyze what may have gone wrong in a conversation that ended badly—something that probably requires not only linguistic but social, cultural, and personal knowledge about the participants in the conversation. The Teacher's Note on page 18 gives a quick picture of children's development of grammatical awareness as they progress from tacit recognition of what is or is not grammatical to more explicit knowledge.

Phonological awareness—recognizing rhymes, isolating and matching sounds, for example—is a foundational skill in reading (Adams, 1990; Ehri & Wilce, 1985; Juel & Minden-Cupp, 2000; Liberman & Shankweiler, 1985). Chapter 5 describes these metalinguistic skills in depth.

Teacher Note

The Progression of Grammatical Awareness

In developing metalinguistic awareness of what counts as a grammatical sentence, children progress from *detection* to *self-correction* to *ability to locate* and then *explain the source* of nongrammaticality. For example, most English-speaking first graders are probably able to detect that something is wrong with a sentence like "Girl is jumping rope." Some will unconsciously correct the error if asked to repeat the sentence, by saying, "The girl is jumping rope," perhaps even emphasizing the word *the*. Some will be able to say that the sentence requires a *the* before *girl*. Of course, no 6-year-old is likely to be able to say that the original sentence is nongrammatical because the subject noun in such a sentence requires an article, since it is not a plural or a proper name.

Children's first explanations of why a sentence is not grammatical tend to focus on meaning rather than form. A 6- or 7-year-old may say, "It doesn't make sense." Others who know something is wrong but can't put their finger on the problem may simply say, "It's yucky." At the same ages, those with more metalinguistic skill may say, "It doesn't sound good" or even "You have to say *the* girl."

In response to a more confusing sentence like "The king sat on her throne," a child may suggest that the poorly formed sentence impedes communication, "If you said it that way, no one would understand you." This response represents a focus on meaning rather than grammatical form—yet in this case, meaning *is* affected by the mixed genders. A student needs to notice when she makes an error in reading that results in a nongrammatical sentence; otherwise comprehension can be affected. For instance, reading "Caroline pointed to her little brother" as "Caroline painted to her little brother" is an error that needs to be caught because it leads to a serious misunderstanding of the text.

Based on Trumbull (1984)

Speakers of a language, probably largely through schooling, acquire facility with what we might call "the language of language." Even first graders are expected to know, or at least be learning, terms like *word*, *sentence*, *syllable*, *sound*, and *letter*. They learn how to use words like *conversation*, *discussion*, and *paragraph* as well. Later on, of course, they will hear about *nouns*, *verbs*, *adjectives*, and the like. Not only do we expect students to be proficient with speaking, listening, reading, and writing; we expect them to be able to use language to talk about these activities in very specific ways.

Whereas some students acquire many aspects of metalinguistic awareness and skill without explicit instruction, or in the context of other instructional activities, some do not. Learning about what counts as a word, a syllable, or an individual sound within a word is a developmental process (Sulzby, 1986; Tunmer & Bowey, 1984). If asked to count the number of words in a sentence, many 6- and 7-year-olds count only the important content words. A sentence like "The boy ate the orange" will be judged to have three words: *The-boy*, *ate*, *the-orange*

(Papandropoulou & Sinclair, 1974). Even some 8-year-olds have difficulty reliably distinguishing word, syllable, and phrase (Downing & Oliver, 1974). Such awareness and skill can be taught through games and other activities that model ways of paying attention to the form of language (Estrin & Chaney, 1989; Trumbull, 1984) (see chapters 5 and 6).

The Units of Language

A comfortable familiarity with the units of language and terminology for them is indispensable to teachers, for communicating with students and parents and for critical reading of literature about language acquisition and reading instruction. It also fosters a healthy respect for the linguistic knowledge that students have and are continuing to develop.

Language is composed of sounds, meaning units (combinations of sounds), sentences, and discourse (series of sentences). *Phonemes* are the smallest units of sound that make a difference to meaning. For example, *fox* and *pox* are different by one phoneme: /f/ and /p/.[12] Not every little difference in sound is phonemic, however. Consider the different sound of /a/ in *apple* versus *ample*. The nasality of the /m/ seems to blend into the vowel preceding it. However, we do not consider these two versions of /a/ to be two different phonemes. In the same way, the /t/ at the beginning of a word (e.g., *Tom*) is not pronounced in exactly the same way as the /t/ in the middle of a word (*writer*) or at the end (*bat*). In the first case, most speakers of American English let a small puff of air out (aspirate) when they pronounce an initial /t/ as in *Tom*. We tend to flip our tongue a little behind our teeth to produce the /t/ in a word like *writer*, and we cut off the /t/ entirely when we say a word like *bat*. Once again, these are just variants of the same phoneme.

The *syllable* is also a unit of sound, one much easier for our brains to perceive than the phoneme in isolation (Liberman, Shankweiler, Fisher, & Carter, 1974; Morais, Cary, Alegria, & Bertelson, 1979). A syllable can be a single vowel sound (equivalent to a single phoneme) or a consonant sound plus a vowel sound (*pa, ba, go, ho, he, do, ra, bo, it*). Of course, some of these short syllables are words. A syllable can also consist of several consonant sounds plus one vowel sound. Consider the following: *scratch, whale, thread, shrink*—all one-syllable words. The defining feature of a syllable is that it has a single "vowel center."

The *morpheme* is another important unit of language, although one that many of us may not have learned about in any routine preparation as teachers. A morpheme is usually defined as "the smallest meaningful unit of language." *Unbound morphemes* function independently: they are words, like *blue, lamp, book, a, the, which*, or *calendar*. *Bound morphemes* have to be attached to other morphemes to make words: *-ful, -ly, -ious, -ing, -ity, un-, pre-, de-, im-*, and the like. Even though these morphemes cannot stand alone, each adds some meaning as well as grammatical information to a word. For instance, *-ful* changes the noun *wonder* to the adjective *wonderful*, with a concomitant change in meaning. Some traditionally bound morphemes have come to be used by themselves (such is the changing nature of language): *ex*, *anti*, *pro*, *con* (and what about *ex-con*?), to mention a few.

Linguists have struggled forever to define exactly what a *word* is, although it seems completely evident to an adult speaker of any language what a word is. We could say that a word is just an unbound morpheme, or, very practically, we might define it as any unit of language that requires spaces around it in written text. But why is *pan dowdy*, as in apple pan dowdy, two words and *pancake* one? Why isn't *a lot* one word? So many of our students think it is.

Likewise, there is controversy over whether a single form like *bank*, which has such distinct meanings (the edge of a river, a place to store money), is one word with different meanings or two words. Sometimes the decision is made on the basis of the word's history. For example, did it come from two different source words? This strategy isn't always satisfactory, however. The word *pupil* (part of the eye) seems to be entirely different from *pupil* (a student)—yet they come from the same Latin word, *pupilla*, which itself seems to have had several meanings (a little doll, an orphan, or a ward) (Crystal, 1997).

Books on language often define *word* as a unit representing a concept, but this definition isn't entirely satisfactory. What about words like *the*, *and*, *to*, *or*, *for*? Such words don't have much conceptual content. They are often called "function words" because they serve various grammatical functions—showing how words relate to each other in the context of a sentence.

Teacher Note

Word Work

Word work is a term widely used in resources for helping students to acquire awareness of the concept of *word*, of the phonological and syntactic properties of words, and of other properties of words. Games that heighten awareness of what words are as well as how they can be combined to form sentences are easy to design. Trumbull (1984) developed a game called "Silly Sentences" to help first graders become more conscious of what constitutes acceptable sentences, both in terms of grammar (syntax) and meaning (semantics). This game, which was played by pairs or triads of students, generated much discussion about language and was frequently requested by the children.

The materials were cards of three colors, representing subjects, verbs, and objects or prepositional phrases. Each child selects a card of each color and sets them up in a plastic frame. If necessary, the teacher helps the child read the words. If a child judges the resulting sentence to be acceptable, he keeps it and gets a point. If not, in successive turns he can pick cards from any category to repair the sentence. Different rules can be used: syntactically acceptable but semantically absurd ("Mother is orange juice"), both syntactically and semantically acceptable ("Children drink orange juice"). Children learned to differentiate between these two kinds of sentences, heightening their linguistic awareness.

Phrases, clauses, and sentences are combinations of words. Quite simply, a *phrase* is "a group of words not containing a subject or a predicate" (Pei & Gaynor, 1969, p. 169). Phrases modify other more important sentence elements. Examples of phrases are *of wood*, *to Jon*, *in the spring*, *as stated*, *to him*, *on the fourth of July*, *within recent memory*, *as far from here as possible*, *deliberately pronounced with a British accent*. Phrases are italicized and numbered in the following sentences: "Elizabeth's gift was made *of wood*. (1) She gave it *to Jon* (2) *in the spring*, (3) although she had planned to give it *to him* (4) *on the fourth of July*".

A *sentence* is a grammatically complete unit of thought, containing a subject and a predicate. "Joan [subject] made a lovely anniversary dinner for Don [predicate]." Although a sentence usually has two or more words, such utterances as "Hush!" or "Stop!" are also sentences. They can, in fact, stand alone. Below the surface, such commands have an implied *you* as subject ("You hush!"). A compound sentence can, of course, express more than one thought or proposition: "The Giants won, and the As lost." In working with students to understand what a sentence is, definitions are probably of less use than examples. Students need to know when they are using sentence fragments—something they can, of course, choose to do in poetry or in creative or persuasive writing to achieve an effect. In spoken language, it is often difficult to identify where sentences begin and end, and it is usually not necessary to do so in order to comprehend what is being said. Also, we often speak in fragments or *elliptical* sentences (in which core elements are left out) because they work fine:

Bob: "What are you doing this afternoon?"

Margie: "Working."

A *clause* is part of a sentence that contains a subject and a predicate. It may or may not stand on its own. Those that don't are called *dependent* or *subordinate clauses*; those that do are called *independent clauses*. Independent clauses can exist as separate sentences. In the following sentence, the first clause is dependent and the second independent: "Although he hit the ball hard [dependent clause], the batter wasn't able to make it safely to first base [independent clause]." The next sentence has two independent clauses: "Nanette went to Arizona [independent clause], and she gave a workshop on literacy" [independent clause].

Eight Myths About Language

Common sense often leads us astray. One need only think of how hard it is to shake people's beliefs about falling bodies. Intuition tells us that heavier objects plummet faster than lighter objects, but Galileo showed us that the weight of an object does not affect its acceleration, contrary to appearances. Likewise, there are many commonsense beliefs about language that should be examined. We have selected just a few of the most tenacious myths, particularly those that could have an adverse impact on educational decision making and relationships with students and parents. The first four are related but distinct.

1. Some languages are simpler and easier to learn than others.

There is no evidence that some languages are easier for children to learn. There may, however, be certain features that are easier to acquire in some languages (Slobin, 1985). Linguist Derek Bickerton (1995) notes that when a language has a great deal of complexity in one area (such as the treatment of verbs), it often has more simplicity in another area—apparently balancing the demands on human mental processing. No language is really simple; all languages that have ever been studied have evolved complex ways of representing important knowledge of the cultures in which they arise. Of course, relative to the language or languages one speaks as a native, some languages are going to be more or less difficult. Speakers of English should have less trouble learning German, Dutch, Danish, French, or Spanish than Russian or Japanese because the first five languages mentioned are more closely related to English, which is largely a Germanic language with some French and Latin influence.

Virtually all children in any language community learn the language of their parents. To an outsider, it's sometimes hard to imagine how this happens. Think of Mark Twain's visit to France, where he marveled at how smart French children were. Even 3-year-olds were speaking French! The fact is that if a language were so difficult as to be unlearnable by the children in a community, it would have to change.

2. "Primitive" people speak "primitive" languages.

As the reader will surmise from the quotation marks, we question assumptions about what "primitive" means. Usually, the term is applied to societies that are preindustrial and/or do not have Western-style systems of education. Leaving aside questions of how "advanced" it is to generate inordinate amounts of nonbiodegradable trash, pollute bodies of water, or use scientific knowledge to develop weapons of mass destruction, let's focus on language. The fact is that there are no primitive languages: "There are no 'bronze age' or 'stone age' languages" (Crystal, 1997, p. 7). Likewise, Bickerton (1995) says, "No one can claim that any one of the 5,000 human languages is more advanced or more developed or more complex than any other" (p. 67).

People who have visited Australia and heard one or more of its 250 indigenous (Aboriginal) languages may assume that because the natives of that continent did not have modern technology their language was developmentally behind, but nothing could be further from the truth (Evans, 1998). For instance, Kayardild, a language spoken on Betinck Island in the state of Queensland, has a complex system of word endings that indicate the relationships among words (e.g., subject, object, spatial relations). In Dalabon, spoken in Western Arnhem Land, pronouns carry much more information than they do in English. Not only number and gender but also what generation a person is, in relation to another person being mentioned (e.g., like brothers or like father and son), will be indicated by the form of the pronoun (Evans, 1998).

Because of the creativity of language, any language can change to adapt to new demands, such as scientific advancements, newly discovered natural phenomena, or new concepts of any kind. It is simply not accurate to think in terms of "primitive" or "advanced" languages.

3. Some languages or dialects are superior to others.

As we have discussed, all languages have the capacity to represent all the concepts and relationships among them available to humans. We may believe that languages of nonindustrial peoples are incapable of expressing advanced scientific ideas, but this is not true. As we mentioned, new words can be coined or adopted from other languages, and all of the logical relations expressible in one language are also expressible in any other. Such beliefs are, unfortunately, useful for maintaining political or social hegemony over others, but they are not founded in linguistic fact.

The topic of dialects is discussed at length in chapter 2, so we will address it only briefly here. The myth that some dialects are superior to others is so entrenched as to be almost unshakable in many people. Linguists are unanimous in their judgment that the status of a dialect has nothing to do with its linguistic validity, only with its level of social acceptance. All dialects follow their own complex rules of pronunciation and grammar. What sound like errors to speakers of one dialect are evidence of the application of a different set of rules. No dialect is superior to another. The dialect of whatever group holds the most political, social, and economic power will be the prestige dialect in that country or society. If speakers of the Appalachian dialect (like Dolly Parton) were the CEOs of Fortune 500 companies and constituted most of those elected to high offices, theirs would be the prestige dialect.

4. Some languages are more logical than others.

For an extended period of European history, Latin was regarded as the premier language for expressing logical thought. Throughout history, various groups have claimed that their language is the most logical. In the 17th and 18th centuries, French claims to such superiority abounded. Count Antoine de Rivarol wrote as follows:

> What distinguishes our language from the ancient and the modern languages is the order and structure of the sentence. This order must always be direct and necessarily clear. In French, the subject of the discourse is named first, then the verb, which is the action, and finally the object of this action: this is the natural logic present in all human beings. (Cited in Lodge, 1998, p. 24)

Of course, this "logical" order is neither the only possible "logical" order for a language, nor is it always observed in French itself. Later in the same discourse, de Rivarol comments, "French syntax is incorruptible. It is from this that results this admirable clarity which is the eternal basis of our language." Note that de Rivarol is not using the "logical order" he touted as existing in French. In his sentence, the subject (*clarity*) is placed after the verb (*results*). It is not illogical for a language to permit variation in syntactic forms. Flexibility allows for enhancing meaning—sometimes emphasizing an action over the one doing it or vice versa.

It is a natural human tendency to believe that one's own language is the most logical, but no language is logical in the sense of maintaining complete regularity or consistency or of stringently restricting word meanings. All languages have implicit grammatical rules, and in all cases there are exceptions to those rules (Crystal, 1997). Words must be somewhat flexible to account for human reality. Even a simple word like *house* can extend in meaning to a vast repertoire of living spaces (the shell that a hermit crab uses is sometimes called its *house*). No doubt, new meanings for *house* will emerge as human life changes.

Sometimes people complain that a particular feature of syntax (often from a lower status dialect) is "illogical." They may say that to use a double negative, as in "She didn't do nothing about the problem" is a failure of logic (sometimes arguing that in mathematics two negatives equal a positive—quite an extrapolation). Of course, many languages use more than one word to signal the negative. French, that ultralogical language, comes to mind: "Je ne veux pas manger ça!" ("I don't want to eat that!") has two words, *ne* and *pas*, one preceding and one following the verb, to form the negative. Spanish and other languages have similar conventions, with no threat to their logicality. Some dialects of English (as we have defined them) use two negative components in some types of sentences ("I do*n't* want *no* dessert"), and some do not, and they are equally logical.

5. Some people have an accent.

If asked to identify American accents, people would probably mention "New York," "southern," maybe "southwestern twang" (e.g., Texan), and perhaps "hillbilly" (Appalachian). Others might mention the distinctiveness of a Chicago or a Philadelphia accent. Typically, we do not hear our own accent; in fact, we all speak with an accent. Accent is composed not only of how we pronounce our consonants and vowels but also of the intonation we use—the "melody" of speech. Our accent is like an auditory map of where we were born and raised (Esling, 1998, p. 169). A linguist could analyze our pronunciation and probably determine where we grew up, and if we had lived in more than one place, the linguist would be able to identify which geographic areas had contributed to our current accent.

Many people believe that TV anchors speak with no accent, but even they have accents that betray their origins or the target regions they are imitating. Just as with dialects, no accent is superior to another. They are simply different from each other. A stranger's speech sounds different from the norm we have accepted. "We feel that we don't have an accent because of the weight of experience that tells us that we are the best possible example of the 'norm'"(Esling, 1998, p. 171).

This myth matters because, like dialects, different accents have different social value: Some are prestigious, others scorned—and what counts as prestigious varies, depending on one's geography. Teachers, like other human beings, may fall into the trap of assuming that students who speak with particular accents are linguistically superior and those who do not are linguistically inferior.

6. Correct language ought to be preserved.

Linguist David Crystal (1997) observes, "The phenomenon of language change probably attracts more public notice and criticism than any other linguistic issue. There is a widely held belief that change must mean deterioration and decay . . . but most of the criticism . . . is misconceived" (pp. 4–5). Crystal goes on to say that the main reason language changes is that society changes. To stop language change, we would have to stop society and life in general from changing.

Accepted rules of usage and pronunciation are merely shifting sand, and it is really a fool's errand to attempt to hold them constant. Here, as educators, we are in a bind. We want to help our students successfully acquire the so-called standard grammatical forms and learn to use vocabulary in the accepted ways, yet creativity in language is the rule; and to be prescriptive about usage flies in the face of linguistic reality. Within the last decade the words *notorious* and *notoriety* have begun to lose their negative connotation. It used to be that *notorious* was applied to people who had acquired fame through less than honorable means. John Wilkes Booth was a notorious criminal; he achieved notoriety through his heinous act of assassinating President Lincoln. Now these terms seem to be interchangeable with *famous* and *fame*. The word *integral*, with its links to *integrity*, *integer*, and *integrated*, is often heard in contexts where it clearly means simply "important" rather than "belonging as part of the whole . . . necessary to the completeness of the whole" (*Webster's Encyclopedic Unabridged Dictionary of the English Language*, 1989, p. 738). Some people even change the word so that the possible connection to its relatives is obliterated by rendering it as *intregal*. What about *insidious* and *invidious*? The distinction between those two words— "treacherous, creeping, and slow moving" versus "injurious, causing ill will, and hateful"—appears to be lost on a great many speakers. Quite likely, in the future their meanings will be collapsed, or *insidious* will merely replace *invidious*.

When a critical mass of speakers of a language moves to a new form, it is almost useless to dig in one's heels on the matter. It may trouble some people that many others pronounce *str-* as though it had an /h/ in it (*shtreet, shtress, reshtrict*), but their outrage is probably wasted. The pronunciation pattern appears to be here to stay, at least for a while. Even a prominent national newscaster has been heard to say "hishtory." Maybe the majority of speakers will go back to the former pronunciation in 100 years. Another example: Because English does not have a gender-neutral third person singular pronoun to refer to people (we have only *he* and *she*, *him* and *her*), and because it is no longer socially acceptable to use *he* and *him* as a universal third-person pronouns, people have moved to the use of *they* and *them* as a gender-neutral choice. Thus we hear sentences like "Everybody (a singular collective noun) says they want to go to the party," and "Any child knows they ought to obey their parents." Most English teachers cringe at such sentences, but they are already acceptable in conversation, and some would like to see them unedited in print as well.

The challenge for teachers is to teach accepted or standard usage, recognizing that it is a moving target. Perhaps as important is helping students to develop a critical ear for their own language, particularly those who speak more than one dialect, so that they can make informed choices about language usage.

7. Children learn languages more easily than adults do.

This myth might be better cast as an overgeneralization. The research has been contradictory, with some studies showing that children learn new languages more quickly and completely than adults (Johnson & Newport, 1989) and other research showing that adults have the advantage (Cummins, 1981a; Snow & Hoefnagel-Hohle, 1978). A third conclusion seems likely from a review of the research (see Bialystok & Hakuta, 1994). That is, older students and adults learn another language more quickly in the beginning, but in the long run they tend to level off in their progress, whereas children who start early (by age 5 or so) tend to keep progressing and sometimes achieve almost nativelike proficiency. In the area of pronunciation, "the younger, the better" seems to be the appropriate maxim. Children who begin to learn a new language before age 10 are more likely to speak with little or no accent compared to those who start later (Oyama, 1976; Williams, 1980). Some say that 7 or 8 is the defining age (Bialystok, 2001). What this means is that a primary school child who is newly acquiring English in school readily learns to pronounce English words virtually like her native English-speaking friend.[13] By the same token, her friend could learn Vietnamese or Spanish and sound like a native speaker.

According to McLaughlin (1992), when one looks at the bigger picture—including ability to learn a new syntactic system, new vocabulary, and appropriate ways to use the new language—adults are actually better learners. Some argue that this has to do with the way languages tend to be taught—formally, with an emphasis on grammar and vocabulary. Also, consider these facts: (a) The standards of language performance we hold young children to are likely to be lower than those we hold adults to (playground conversation versus ability to use a language to talk about politics or read literature); (b) accurate pronunciation is so impressive that we don't evaluate the more complex aspects of language acquisition when we listen to children; and (c) adults have a fully developed language system (their first language) to use as a basis for making associations and educated guesses about the way the new language works, and they have concepts (represented by vocabulary) in their first language that can be related to new vocabulary.

One risk of assuming that children will learn a new language readily is that we may not anticipate their needs for language support. We may overestimate their language proficiency. If they sound good and seem to be functioning socially in their new language, we may not look deeply enough to recognize that more advanced forms and uses are lagging behind. This would be particularly harmful to immigrant students who may be placed in programs that are not well matched to their skills or who may not continue to get English-language development instruction when they need it. One clue that additional language evaluation may be needed is if a child is performing academically below the level of his or her native English-speaking peers. It is important in such cases to rule out underdeveloped English as a source of lower performance.

8. The English spelling system is capricious.

History is full of critical commentary on the English spelling system. Perhaps the most famous critique was by the playwright George Bernard Shaw, who impugned the integrity of a spelling system that could produce words like *tough*, *bough*, *through*, and *trough* (four pronunciations for *ough*) and use the same vowel to represent the sounds in such a range of words as *toe*, *hot*, *off*, *do*, *onion*, and *women*. Shaw suggested that, given the rules of English orthography, we might as well spell *fish* as *ghoti*—*gh* as in *cough*, *o* as in *women*, and *ti* as in *nation* (http://www.your dictionary.com/library/ling 006.html). Of course, students of English are quick to point out that *-gh* would never be used at the beginning of a word to represent the */f/* sound and that *-ti* never equates to *-sh* except when followed by another vowel (*-tion, -tian, -tial*).

Teacher Inquiry

One-to-One
Write the Roman alphabet from A to Z. Place a checkmark next to each letter that stands for only one phoneme in English (remember that the variations on a sound like */t/* count as only one phoneme). Make a separate list of the two-letter combinations that represent a single sound, if you wish. Now make a list of the most common vowel and consonant sounds that can be represented by more than one letter or letter combinations, such as the */f/* sound or the sound of the letter *a* as in *snake*.

Current-day proponents of a spelling revolution include Britain's Prince Philip, who would like to see a simpler orthography with much less variation in the way sounds are represented. Presumably, *nation* would be spelled *nashun*, *tough* would be *tuf*, and words like *boat*, *row*, and *doe* would have a single vowel letter representation, according to his "sistum."

There is good reason to believe that movement to a more phonetic orthography is neither necessary nor advisable, for several reasons. First, the English system of mapping spoken sounds to written letters is not a capricious system (Chomsky & Halle, 1968). Studies show that the majority of English words (about 90%) are spelled according to a regular pattern (Berdiansky, Cronnell, & Koehler, 1969; Wijk, 1966). The problem is that there are so many patterns. This is the challenge for children learning to read and write, yet most do learn. Most of the irregular words come from Anglo-Saxon roots (*mother, father, is, was, does, come, blood, could, cough, through*, and the like), and these have to be learned as exceptions to the expected patterns.

Second, a basic understanding of the history of the language (and we do mean basic—one learnable by third graders) clears up many of the apparent inconsistencies (Calfee, 1988). Figure 1-2 shows the layers of the English language and lists the kinds of words that come from different origins. Modern English has its roots largely in the Germanic Anglo-Saxon language (the English of England before the French conquest in 1066), French (via Latin), and Greek.[14] There are also words from other European languages, Asian languages, and from many American Indian languages, but these are the major three in terms of influence. All three are from the Indo-European language family and have common roots in a single language spoken many thousands of years ago.

Figure 1-2. Layers of the English Language

GREEK
Specialized words, mostly scientific

(*telescope, phenomenon, photosynthesis, stereotaxis, psychology, phonograph, endomorphic*)

LATIN/FRENCH
"High-class" words, used in more formal settings,
such as books or formal oral language

(*explanation, derivation, omnipotence, entertainment, correspondence, evidence, corporal, potential, presumption, comparison, language, converse*)

ANGLO-SAXON
(Germanic)

Common, everyday, down-to-earth words, used frequently
in ordinary situations

(*mother, father, sister, brother, do, have, see, wicked, wild, house, be, speech, step, was, think, thank, drink, body, dog, man, woman, girl, word, wed, know, blood*)

Adapted from Calfee (1988)

Words with different language origins interact in different, but relatively predictable, ways with English orthography. Once these patterns are made evident to young readers and writers, much of the problem is addressed. It is easy to see from Figure 1-2 that readers and writers need to be sensitive to the morphemic structures of words and not just the encoding of particular sounds. A word like *blueberry* is a good example of compounding (an Anglo-Saxon strategy for word making), the combining of two or more words. Young readers need to learn to quickly recognize compounds by identifying their components. Words like *reception, division,* and *entertainment,* which have a French origin, have suffixes that will be seen in a great many words. Those suffixes, *-tion, -ion,* and *-ment,* are used to derive new words from root words, another word-forming strategy that students need to learn to recognize.

Third, were we to change the spelling system, we would lose not only our connections to existing literature in English but also clues to the relationships among many sets of related words. For example, if *muscle* were spelled *mussel* or *mussle,* it would not retain its obvious connection to *muscular.* What about *legal* and *legislate?* They have different vowel and consonant sounds (the long *e* of *legal* is short in *legislate,* and the hard *g* in *legal* changes to a soft *g* in *legislate*). What about words like *do* and *does?* Should we change them to *doo* and *duz?* Should *paradigm* be spelled *paradime* while *paradigmatic* remains as is? The substituted forms are much closer to the surface pronunciation, but they obscure important relationships among words.

English orthography is not a perfect system, but neither is it capricious. As linguist Edward Carney says:

> Like flies in amber, English spelling has preserved a continuous record of cultural activity by borrowing foreign spelling conventions along with the borrowed words. The spelling of *phlegm* tells you that it is a scientific term [the *-ph* and *-gm* digraphs show that it comes from Greek] and that it is related to *phlegmatic.* (Carney, 1998, p. 40)

Reflections

Language is humans' primary medium of communication and principal symbol system for representing thought. It is but one among several semiotic, or representational, systems but is the most useful in terms of capturing and conveying ideas reliably. Some understanding of semiotics can help readers to see a common denominator underlying the various kinds of intelligence exhibited by humans.

Language has many distinctive features, among them the ability to use a finite number of elements (sounds, words) and a set of structural rules (syntax) to create an infinite number of meanings. Rather than being limited to a fixed set of calls or sound patterns on a small number of topics, as are most other animals, humans can talk or write about virtually anything at any time. Each generation teaches its young (largely by example) to use the language or languages of the given culture.

Language can be usefully organized into the areas of phonology, morphology, syntax, and pragmatics—roughly corresponding to the systems of sounds, word formation, word combination, and conventions of use. We have discussed the units of language within the first three areas. Aspects of pragmatics and discourse, or combinations of sentences, are discussed to some degree in chapters 2 and 5. An approach to language as "communicative competence" is helpful because it situates language within the social and cultural worlds of human beings, where it takes on real meaning.

Teacher Inquiry

Language Demands in Instruction
How dependent is your instruction on language? Examine your lesson plans for a week and observe your instructional practices. Which ones require high-level language use, and which ones draw upon other skills? How might you use access to other representational systems to support students' comprehension and language development?

Teachers can benefit from a deep understanding of the fundamental role that language plays in teaching and learning. Although this role is self-evident to a degree, we believe on the basis of our own observations that in an effort to recognize different kinds of intelligence and learning styles, teachers sometimes underestimate the importance of helping students to build high-level language skills. Perhaps in the early grades it is not so evident that "critical literacy" (chapter 5), the ability to use language in all of its forms for a wide range of purposes, is crucial to academic success. However as students progress through the grades, it becomes increasingly important. Proficiency with "academic language," the language used to engage in academic learning, is critical to student success in school. Chapter 4 addresses this topic in some depth.

Language is a phenomenon about which everyone is an expert, in some sense. After all, the vast majority of human beings learn to use language, and we are all attached to our own languages and ways of speaking. Nevertheless, like any complex human phenomenon, language is subject to many persistent myths. In this chapter, we have discussed a few of these myths, particularly those that could interfere with the most constructive approaches to teaching the extremely diverse student population of the United States. Many of these myths are based on the conscious or unconscious belief in the superiority of some languages or dialects over others. From the perspective of linguists, all languages and dialects are equally valid—all evidence of the remarkable capacity of humans to symbolize their world.

We hope that after reading this chapter, teachers will have both more understanding of linguistic issues in their classrooms and the inclination to explore these issues further. With a more explicit appreciation of the role of language in learning and schooling as well as a critical eye for spotting generalizations that may, in fact, be myths, teachers can be advocates for intelligent policies and practices within their schools and districts.

Notes

1. Actually, there is no universally accepted definition for language, beyond the widespread agreement that it is an important symbol system. Scientists argue over the degree to which it is innate rather than learned and whether it is strictly a human faculty.

2. Bruner (1966) proposes three semiotic systems parallel to Oller's: enactive, iconic, and symbolic.

3. Depending upon the theorist, this word is spelled *sensorimotor*, *sensory-motor*, or *sensori-motor*.

4. Note that sign language (such as American Sign Language) has some basis in gesture but is equivalent in complexity to oral language.

5. For an excellent and readable treatment of the question "Can animals have language?" see Napoli (2003), listed in For Further Reading.

6. However, the ways we *organize* what is perceived do depend heavily on our native language (Bialystok & Hakuta, 1994).

7. Some human development researchers have stressed the importance of visual skills that have been shown to be enhanced by playing with electronic games (Subrahmanyam & Greenfield, 1994). Skills such as spatial representation, iconic representation, and comprehension of screen-based simulations have a strong visual component; and visual skills should not be overlooked as cognitively important.

8. Performance assessments in the strictest sense are those that require a student to engage in an activity directly related to the construct or criterion in question, such as to perform a task like designing and possibly even building a birdcage. In most instances, the term refers to pencil-and-paper assessments that require students to apply knowledge within a context, such as solving a multidimensional problem or writing an essay (rather than responding to multiple-choice questions).

9. This is not a trivial piece of information. It helps us to understand why younger children have trouble with passive constructions such as "The girl was hit by the boy." It is far more common to hear an active construction, "The boy hit the girl," in which the subject comes first; without the cue of a special word ending (as in Latin), a listener or reader is forced to process the whole sentence in order to understand the relationships among the words.

10. In poetry, of course, these rules of order may be defied to satisfy artistic intent.

11. Much of the earlier literature on this topic uses the term *metalinguistic awareness*. By use of the term *metalinguistic knowledge*, we want to imply in addition an ability to go beyond awareness to a set of skills and understandings that can be productively used in the process of speaking, reading, and writing.

12. Letters in brackets stand for sounds. Formal notation using the International Phonetic Alphabet would use a different set of specific symbols to indicate /a/ as in *apple* (æ) versus /a/ as in *cake* (e:l).

13. There may be slight differences in pronunciation that are not particularly noticeable (see Watson, 1991).

14. Actually, the particular Germanic language to which English is most closely related is Frisian, spoken primarily in parts of the Netherlands.

For Further Reading

Andrews, L. (2001). *Linguistics for L2 teachers*. Mahwah, NJ: Erlbaum.

Bickerton. D. (1995). *Language and human behavior*. Seattle: University of Washington Press.

Crystal, D. (1997). *The Cambridge encyclopedia of language* (2nd ed.). Cambridge, UK: Cambridge University Press.

Napoli, D. J. (2003). *Language matters*: *A guide to everyday thinking about language*. Oxford, UK: Oxford University Press.

Yule, G. (1996). *The study of language*. Cambridge, UK: Cambridge University Press.

Chapter 2

Language, Culture, and Society

Elise Trumbull

We are the only species that teaches in any significant way. Mental life is
lived with others, is shaped to be communicated, and unfolds with the aid
of cultural codes, traditions, and the like. (Bruner, 1996, p. xi)

*The language each of us speaks—the vocabulary, pronunciation, grammar,
and the way we use language for different purposes—is shaped by our sociocultural environment. Many U.S. citizens have a home language other than English. There are also many varieties of English spoken within the United States,
reflecting different social, cultural, and geographic influences. Children from
different communities may have learned different ways of telling a story or participating in a conversation with an adult. The challenge for schools is to value
all of these language varieties and tap them as resources for students' ongoing
cognitive and academic development.*

In this chapter the social and cultural underpinnings of language are considered. Language is not simply a code to express neutral information; what one
says is shaped by social and cultural expectations and reflects assumptions about
what is appropriate and meaningful. The chapter will also discuss how cultural
differences in language use can be dealt with in the classroom and between teachers and parents. Although social and cultural elements are treated separately at
the beginning of the chapter, the reader will quickly see that it is more useful to
think of language as a sociocultural phenomenon. The term *sociocultural* refers
to the interaction of social and cultural elements—elements that are deeply intertwined in language use. We chose to situate the topic of culture in chapter 2
because of our belief that it has paramount importance for providing instruction
that is based on a knowledge of language and its binding relationship to culture.

Language as a Social Phenomenon

Language is social because, for the most part, it takes place between or among human beings. Even "conversations with ourselves" (mental speech) often involve an implicit "other." Written language is also usually composed—unless it is a grocery list or the like—with at least one other reader in mind. Of course, one can think of other possible exceptions (e.g., a diary), but even private speech is influenced by the norms of language use of the group(s) to which one belongs, making it social in at least the broadest sense of the word. All of us belong to "speech communities," or groups of persons who share basic expectations of how language should be used (Wolfram, Adger, & Christian, 1999). As a member of such communities people know the implicit rules of communicating. For example, in some speech communities it is acceptable—even desirable—for children to initiate conversations with adults (Rogoff, 2003). In others, that behavior would be considered rude or impertinent (Whatley, 1981). Children rapidly learn which rule applies, although when they move from one speech community to another (as from home to school), they may not immediately grasp how the rules differ.

Talk conveys social information as well as what we think of as "content." A conversation starter such as "If I don't get a vacation soon, I'm going to blow a gasket!" suggests that the speaker is addressing a peer (a spouse or a friend), is perhaps blowing off steam (to avoid blowing the gasket), and is probably in an informal or private space. Compare it to "I know that the company needs for all of us to keep working hard to meet production demands, and I think I will be much more efficient in the long run if I take some vacation time now." This statement is quite possibly addressed to the speaker's superior, is probably serving the purpose of a request for time off, and is certainly more formal—perhaps taking place in the boss's office.

In order to know how to participate in any communication, one has to consider its purpose, the participants (what role and status each has), the setting for the communication (time and place), the topic, genre (rug meeting, formal discussion, debate), and whether the communication is in oral or written form or uses other media (Scollon & Scollon, 1995). In the example above, we have seen how differences in all of these elements are associated with differences in what gets said and how it gets said. They constitute the overall context of a communication, and understanding expectations associated with each of them is important to successful communication in the classroom. For instance, a 6-year-old in a typical U.S. first grade needs to know that when the teacher launches a discussion about "what we know about the letter B," students are most likely expected to take turns orally showing that they know what sound B represents and offering examples of words that begin with or contain a B. Offering comments about the items mentioned ("I like beanie babies, and my favorite one is the pug dog") would be considered off topic. Failing to offer a response would likely be frowned upon, particularly if that happened time after time during such lessons. Students' responding all at once may be acceptable at some times and not others; students have to learn when to respond and in which way.

The study of the social aspects of language has been variously referred to as "sociolinguistics" or "the ethnography of communication" (see Gumperz & Hymes, 1972; Scollon & Scollon, 1995). The former emphasizes the relationship between language and society, or how people use language in social situations to communicate. The latter term reflects an anthropological perspective, with an emphasis on gathering very rich contextual information to shed light on people's language use. It could be defined as "the study of language in relation to the social *and cultural* variables that influence human interaction" (Crystal, 1997, p. 426; emphasis added). Social rules for language use will vary according to cultural group, so we cannot proceed to truly understand language use without considering culture.

Language as a Cultural Phenomenon

To understand a culture fully, one must learn to speak that culture's language. Likewise, to understand a language in any deep sense, one needs to learn about the people who speak it. This would mean learning about the values that guide a culture's ways of thinking, being, and doing, as well as the historical and geographical circumstances that influence its people's experience. After all, language is motivated not just by immediate physical needs for communicating ("Watch out! That komodo dragon is about to pounce!") but by beliefs about what is important in the world and how things should be done. If parents value children who are quiet and respectful around adults, they may socialize children in ways that conflict with the school's value of self-expression (Greenfield, Quiroz, & Raeff, 2000). Children from families that believe that direct commands ("Sit down") are the way to get children to do what they are supposed to do may not respond well to the indirect requests of their teachers ("Would you like to take your seat now?") (Delpit, 1995).

What Is Culture?

Culture has almost as many definitions as there are theorists. A simple definition of *culture* is "the systems of values, beliefs, and ways of knowing that guide groups of people in their daily life." Culture, which Donald (2000) calls our "storehouse of crucial . . . information . . . without which we cannot reproduce the cognitive systems by which we now function as a species" (p. 20), is transmitted from one generation to the next through symbol systems (language, mathematics, the arts). In this book, we emphasize culture's ideational and symbolic aspects as opposed to its material aspects, such as dress, foods, holidays, and rituals. That is to say, we take a "cognitive" approach to culture (Fetterman, 1989, p. 27). Of course, it is artificial to consider any elements of culture as completely separate from others. For example, spiritual beliefs are often associated with foods, holidays, and rituals. In this chapter, however, the focus is primarily on the aspects of culture most germane to education and schooling—ways of acquiring knowledge and passing it on (learning and teaching, often accomplished through language).

Language is so essential to the continuity of culture from generation to generation that language loss is truly equivalent to cultural loss (Fishman, 1996; Hinton, 1994; Wong Fillmore, 1991). The language that has long been associated with a culture is the best language for expressing that culture's ideas, beliefs, interests, and values. "Take [that language] away from the culture, and you take away its greetings, its curses, its praises, its laws, its literature, its songs, its riddles, its proverbs, its cures, its wisdom, its prayers. The culture could not be expressed and handed on in any other way" (Fishman, 1996, p. 81).

Culture is not fixed. Cultures change to adapt to new environmental (social, political, and physical) demands and to incorporate new learning. When cultures come in contact with each other, new hybrid cultures may emerge. Some educators suggest that this is what should happen in the classroom: A new culture of the classroom that reflects students' cultures and the culture of the school should be forged (e.g., Banks, 1988; Gutiérrez, Baquedano-López, & Tejeda, 1999). Table 2-1 outlines some explicit activities that can help students explore the cultures of the classroom.

Cross-cultural contact (through immigration, for instance) can result in changes in a culture or in people's becoming bicultural. As such, they continue to embrace their culture and adopt many of the values and practices of the new culture in which they are now immersed. Within any seemingly homogeneous group is great variability. Mexican Americans, for example, who share a common national origin, may differ culturally because of the region of Mexico they came from, degree of economic security and level of formal education, religious membership, and even language. Not all Mexicans have Spanish as a home language; some 40% of the population belongs to indigenous groups—peoples who speak languages such as Nahuatl, Zapotecan, and Tzotzil.

Table 2-1. Culture Studies Activities

Culture studies (Freeman & Freeman, 1994) are studies in which the students research and share information about their own (or others') cultural history. Adrienne Herrell (2000) suggests some projects and activities that are appropriate for various grade levels as presented in the following table, adapted from Herrell's work.

Group	Projects	Activities
Kindergarten	Family portraits	• Draw a picture of your family.
		• Tell about what your family likes to do together.
	Working together	• Draw a picture of some work that your family does together.
		• Tell about how the work is divided and who does each part.
		• Tell about the things each family member can do to help the work get done.
		• Is there anyone in your family who teaches other people in the family to do things?

cont.

Primary grades	People are different, people are the same	• Group investigations of ways in which cultural groups are the same and different. Have students interview people of different cultural groups about different aspects (use of time, importance of education, regard for animals, significance of colors, role of food in celebrations, division of work, etc.).
	The way we do things changes from generation to generation	• Individual students interview and research family photo albums for examples of how things change from one generation to the next. Students ask family members how these changes have affected the use of time and value system of the family.
Upper elementary grades	Our state and nation	• Each student researches the impact of his or her own cultural group on the history of the community, state, and nation.
		• Students' family histories are examined to determine the reason for immigration, if any, or the family work history and how the occupations of generations fit in the history of the region, state, and nation. Changes in value systems, occupations, and places can be examined.
Middle school	Values and history	• Students examine their family's values in relation to how time is spent, priorities for expenditures of money, differences in expectations for male and female children, any inequalities in the past or present in the division of work or responsibilities within the family. Also examine celebrations or rituals that have continued over time and the use of language and interactions in solving problems or disputes.
High school	Nation building	• Students examine the movements in history that affect the building of nations and how cultures have followed or differed from the general trend. The contribution of women, minorities, and the effect of world events are all considered in light of the building of nations across the world. The changes that have taken place in students' own families and cultures as a result of or in response to these events should also be considered. Construct timelines and personal family histories in relation to world events.

Culture, Race, and Ethnicity

The terms *culture*, *race*, and *ethnicity* share some common denominators but are also distinct from each other in some ways. The definition of culture used in this chapter emphasizes beliefs, values, and ways of knowing that are represented and passed on to new generations through symbol systems. *Race* is used to specify distinctions among people largely on the basis of skin color and facial features. As anyone knows, however, there is tremendous variability in color and other physical characteristics among any so-called race, and in fact there is no biological basis for the entire concept of race. There are no discrete, genetically identifiable groups that have specific physical characteristics not manifested in other groups. It would be more accurate to think in terms of a continuum of characteristics rather than discrete categories such as "Negro" or "Caucasian." There are no absolute differences between populations from different geographic areas, only differences in the relative frequency of given characteristics (Lewontin, Rose, & Kamin, 1984).

Denying the biological reality of race is counterintuitive to many people, who believe that they can identify race visually. However, race is a *social* category used to define people, more often than not, for purposes of discrimination or privilege. People often respond to each other on the basis of perceived race, and much social conflict and misunderstanding is race based. Because it does have social power and because it has a strong role in identity development (see, e.g., Branch, 1999; Cross, Strauss, & Fhagen-Smith, 1999), race cannot be dismissed.

Ethnicity overlaps with race. In fact, sometimes the two terms are used interchangeably. The term *ethnic group* is often used to refer to a group that shares common ancestry, culture, tradition, language, religion, and history. "Ethnic identity is allegiance to a group with which one has ancestral links" (Crystal, 1997, p. 34).

There may be many ethnic groups within a perceived racial group. For example, Haitian Blacks and African Americans quite likely differ on all of the elements just listed and may consider themselves different ethnic groups. There are differences among African Americans, too, but the differences between the two groups are much greater.

Among groups of people who are perceived as Black by European Americans, significant intergroup distinctions may be made. For example, Dominicans (from the Dominican Republic

---

Teacher Inquiry

Cultural Study Through Authors

As a professional development activity, form a study group and select an author to read whose work has focused on the unique characteristics of a cultural group and the ways in which membership in a cultural group affects learning and teaching. Schedule discussions to talk about implications for instruction.

Suggestions include:

- Shirley Brice Heath, *Ways with words: Language, life, and work in communities and classrooms* (1996).
- Victoria Purcell-Gates, *Other people's words: The cycle of low literacy* (1995).
- Guadalupe Valdés. *Con respeto: Bridging the distances between culturally diverse families and schools—An ethnographic portrait* (1996).

on the island of Hispaniola), who appear Black to outsiders, may consider themselves not Black but Indio (Indian). They may reserve the term *Black* for their
Haitian neighbors on the other side of the island (Navarro, 2003). As Heath (1986)
has noted, "It is important . . . to recognize that patterns reported for one group of
Blacks or one neighborhood of Spanish speakers or one Chinese-American community may not occur in other communities that will, on the surface, seem to be
similar" (p. 154). Many people are of mixed race and do not want to be forcibly
categorized as of one race or another (Wallace, 2001). The term *Latino*, preferred by many whom the government refers to as *Hispanic*, implies mixed race
to many Latinos, whose roots are indigenous, Spanish, and African (Navarro,
2003). Other Latinos have had identities rooted in Italy, Germany, Japan, or elsewhere. The terms Whte and European American, of course, also obscure many
within-group differences.

Why We Focus on Culture

We focus on culture more than race in this book because our emphasis is on
the values, norms, and beliefs underlying people's use of language—in and out
of school. People may share important cultural values yet have different racial
and ethnic identities. Hence, Chinese and Latino immigrants to the United States
may hold common expectations for their children: to respect teachers, to demonstrate modesty, and to help friends save face. Values such as these translate to
ways of using language.

The dominant culture of the United States, which is very individualistic (see
section below on school culture), has been absorbed by people of many different
racial and ethnic backgrounds, although it was associated mainly with European-American sources. Ironically, teachers from the same cultural "minority"
backgrounds as some of their students may not share some of the cultural values
of those students because of the process of assimilation. In the course of moving
through the U.S. educational system, the teachers have been pushed in the direction of adopting dominant culture values (see, e.g., Trumbull, Rothstein-Fisch,
Greenfield, & Quiroz, 2001).

How Language Reflects Culture

The most obvious aspect of language influenced by a culture's experience,
history, and values is vocabulary. For instance, a culture that has strong spiritual
values is likely to have an extended vocabulary for expressing spiritual and religious concepts. It may not even have a separate concept (and thus word) for
religion because religion is so integrated in everyday life (Locke, 1989). A peaceful
culture may have no word for war. This is reportedly the case with the Sami
people indigenous to Norway, Sweden, and Finland (Hoge, 2001). When an en-
deavor is highly refined or extremely important to a culture, vocabulary is likely
to reflect that status. The Agta of the Philippines, for example, are said to have at
least 31 verbs referring to types of fishing; German connoisseurs of beer in Munich
use some 70 terms to describe their beers (Salzmann, 1993).

A culture that values recognition of elders or superiors may have special verbs that reflect distinctions in social status. For example, in Japanese, to thank a peer or person with lower status than oneself, one uses the verb *ageru*. To thank an elder or superior, one uses *sashiageru*. To fail to observe this distinction would no doubt make one sound very inappropriate indeed to a native Japanese speaker. American culture is more egalitarian, yet one would never show the President of the United States one's appreciation by saying, "Hey, baby, thanks a mil' for supporting the environment bill!" Deference would be conveyed not by special verbs but certainly by choice of words: "Mr. President, on behalf of the Sierra Club, I want to express our deepest gratitude for your support of the environmental preservation bill." In fact, it is the pragmatic aspects of language—how language is used—and not the forms of language that often account for the greatest differences between one cultural group and another, and we will discuss shortly how culture-based differences in language use interact with schooling.

> ## Teacher Inquiry
>
> Think about your own cultural background. What values about language did you learn? For example, when should children speak? How should adults and children interact—at home, in the community, in the classroom? Whose ways of speaking were admired? Whose were considered inferior? Discuss your observations with a group of colleagues.

The Relationship Between Language and Identity

"Languages and styles of speech are prominent badges of ethnic and social identity" (Salzmann, 1993, p. 173). In other words, people use language to show their group membership—another aspect of the social meaning of language. In multilingual countries, choosing to use one language over another in different situations conveys a social intent—not just a communicative intent. In India, for example, where English is the common denominator across some 75 language groups, it is also the language of the colonizer. Bengali, Hindi, Gujarati, Tamil, Kashmiri, and other languages native to the region surely carry positive social and historical meaning for their speakers that English does not. Speaking another person's language expresses solidarity with that person, whereas speaking a different language may communicate distance (Salzmann, 1993). The same goes for choice of dialect: Sometimes we choose to speak the formal dialect of those in power, and sometimes we choose the dialect of a peer group in order to express closeness. For instance, an American Indian college student who has fully acquired the ability to speak Standard English might well choose to speak the dialect prevalent in the community she grew up in when she visits her old friends, in order to maintain the intimacy they have had.

When young people have not been able to learn or maintain the language of their heritage, they may experience challenges to their identity from others who are newly acquiring English or have otherwise managed to continue developing their home language. Valenzuela (1999), in her study of a Texas high school, shows how non-Spanish-speaking students from Mexican backgrounds whose families have been in Texas for some time still consider themselves Mexican, but their immigrant peers may regard them as *agringados* or *americanizados*— Whitened or Americanized. Their loss of Spanish alienates them from their own culture—or one of their cultures—to some degree. Puerto-Rican Americans may experience similar alienation. Young people who have lived their whole lives in New York, for example, and who do not speak Spanish may be regarded disparagingly as "neo-Ricans" (or "Nuyoricans") and not "real" Puerto Ricans by Puerto Ricans living in Puerto Rico (Zentella, 1997). These same people may fully identify as Puerto Rican ethnically.

As Trueba (1993) has said:

> Language is one of the most powerful human resources needed to maintain a sense of self-identity and self-fulfillment. Without a full command of one's own language, ethnic identity, the sharing of fundamental cultural values and norms, the social context of interpersonal communication that guides interactional understandings and the feeling of belonging within a group are not possible. (p. 259)

Threats to development of a solid identity are not trivial. Students may become alienated from school and other social institutions and, caught between two sets of cultural expectations, may also lose connections to family. When home language is devalued and underdeveloped, students may lose the ability to communicate with their own families. When parents and children are not proficient in the same language, what suffers is the family's ability to exert influence over its own offspring (Valdés, 1996; Wong Fillmore, 1991). Obviously, there is an intricate web of relations among culture, language, identity, social and academic success, and family integrity.

Unfortunately, many teachers have not been prepared to entertain the notion of "biculturalism"—students' capacities to function in and master the language and other norms of more than one cultural setting. They may be fearful that by promoting continued use of Spanish and a Mexican identity, for example, they will be preventing the acquisition of English and adaptation to American culture. This is an unfortunate misconception; in fact, considerable research shows that maintaining a strong connection to one's native culture and language are beneficial to learning and adaptation to a new culture (see, e.g., McCarty & Schaffer, 1992; Swisher & Deyhle, 1992; Tharp & Gallimore, 1988). Moreover, a healthy identity—one that is not based on the denial of one's roots—is an important component of human development and helps students to feel that they belong. It appears to be a necessary condition for risk taking, which is necessary for learning (Sheets, 1999a).

There is a parallel between the experience of bilingual students or those whose families speak a language other than English in the home and African-American students who have learned Ebonics, or African-American vernacular English, as a first dialect or language. Their language is part of their identity, and they too are capable of mastering more than one language or dialect and still adapting to mainstream culture (Wolfram, Adger, & Christian, 1999). This topic will be discussed later in the chapter.

The Culture of Schooling

Institutions, like groups of people, can be said to have cultures. *School culture* or *the culture of schooling* refers to the usual ways in which formal education is carried out in the United States. Even though each school has individual characteristics, cultural values and practices are remarkably constant from district to district within the United States (Hollins, 1996). Figure 2-1 shows a set of interactional rules posted in an elementary classroom. It would not be surprising to find this list in almost any school in the country, although some schools may be trying to move away from the heavy restrictions on student talk incompatible with the recent goals of increasing students' active participation in their own learning. Few teachers or principals would think of this list as coming from a specific cultural perspective, so intuitively ordinary are these rules to most people from the mainstream culture. However, these rules are by no means reflective of the norms of many cultural groups. In addition, nearly all could easily be misinterpreted by students who do not have the same culture-based knowledge as the teacher's. What does it mean, for example, to "respect others"? In some cultures, this may mean offering to help someone who is having a problem completing a task. In U.S. classrooms, it often means leaving others alone so they can complete tasks independently.

Figure 2-1. Classroom Rules

1.	Enter the room quickly and quietly and take our seats.
2.	Look and listen for instructions.
3.	Begin work on time.
4.	Work carefully and quietly.
5.	Respect others.
6.	Raise our hands and wait if we have a question or contribution.

Wolfram, Adger, & Christian (1999, p. 94)

Notice how many of these rules are related to language in one way or another. Even silence ("work quietly") is a language norm (Hymes, 1972a). Students are to "look and listen for instructions," presumably to avoid initiating any questions themselves. Speaking one at a time (after raising one's hand) is not a universal way of being appropriate in the classroom. Students from peer-oriented cultures, like those in Alaskan Native villages or those in the Pacific, may be used to answering questions as a group. Questioning by the teacher of individual students may be experienced as confrontational.

In most U.S. schools, great importance is placed on each student's mastery of specified standards or learning objectives, and students are routinely and frequently individually tested to determine whether this is taking place. On the whole, students are expected to work on their own. Cooperative learning groups may be used to help students learn how to work with others or recognize the benefits of pooling their expertise (Bransford, Brown, & Cocking, 2000). But within cooperative groups, students have individual responsibilities and usually receive individual grades. When working on independent tasks—particularly tests—if they help each other too much, they would be accused of "cheating" (Rothstein-Fisch, Trumbull, Isaac, Daley, & Pérez, 2003).

This whole picture is predicated on a largely individualistic approach to learning that is not shared by all cultures (Greenfield, 1994; Hofstede, 1983; Triandis, 1989). Students immigrating to the United States from Japan, Latin America, and many African and other Asian countries will be accustomed to a different set of expectations. In their more collectivistic cultures, the emphasis is likely to be on ensuring that the whole class works well together to achieve academic success. Contributing to the success of the group may be valued more highly than individual achievement. Students' helping each other is promoted and expected, and there may be considerably less concern with individual assessment and individual grades than is usual in U.S. schools. When collectivistic students work in groups, they are truly collaborating—producing a joint product without the expectation that each participant be able to account precisely for his or her contribution (Trumbull, Diaz-Meza, & Hasan, in press). These differences in cultural values have implications for how language is used in groups:

> **Excerpt from Observation of a Culturally Harmonious Classroom**
> Seven third-grade students were sitting on the rug, discussing the material they had just read. [Their teacher] noticed that one child seemed to be answering most of the questions. She encouraged him to "whisper the answer to a friend" so that the other child could answer. During a debriefing following the observation, [the teacher] stated that this practice "lets both children feel successful and work cooperatively." (Rothstein-Fisch, Trumbull, Isaac, Daley, & Pérez, 2003, p. 12)

> **Excerpt from Observation of a Non–Culturally-Harmonious Classroom**
> The children are whispering answers among themselves after one student is called on to respond to the teacher. The teacher then announces to the classroom, "I have heard people whispering, and I really don't like it. Why? They need to learn by themselves, and you really aren't helping them learn." (Isaac, 1999, p. 34)

The two teachers represented here have entirely different ideas about children's whispering. Neither teacher is "correct," but each is inculcating very different norms of language use in the classroom related to cultural values about how much helping is appropriate and beliefs about how learning occurs and even what counts as learning. Because most classrooms in the United States are taught by teachers from the so-called mainstream, the values and beliefs of the second teacher are most often honored. Students who come from cultures where children are encouraged to help each other, including in learning situations, may be confused by the norms of U.S. classrooms. In addition, they will be deprived of a culture-based learning strength by having to learn to work strictly independently.

Language Use: A Key to School Success

This section focuses on the cultural values and norms that bear on how language is used for the purpose of learning and how groups differ in the ways they prepare their children to use language. Some cultural groups believe that wise people speak very little and listen a great deal (Philips, 1983). Other groups believe that power and knowledge come through active use of language in social situations (e.g., the teacher's assumptions in Greenfield, Quiroz, & Raeff, 2000). Some groups use language with children primarily to socialize them to expected behaviors, whereas others believe it is valuable to engage small children in talking about what they observe or experience, in ways similar to how language is used in schools (Snow, 1983). Any classroom may have students from cultures that believe the following:

- Children should mostly listen (Heath, 1983; Philips, 1983).
- Children should talk interactively with adults (Snow, 1983).
- Children should speak one at a time, when a question is posed (i.e., common U.S. classroom practice).
- Several children should answer together when a question is posed (Au & Jordan, 1981a; Kleinfeld, 1979).
- Questioning an adult or offering an opinion is a positive sign of cognitive development (Greenleaf, Schoenbach, Cziko, & Mueller, 2001).
- Questioning an adult is a sign of poor upbringing and lack of respect (Eggen & Kauchak, 1997; Greenfield, Quiroz, & Raeff, 2000).
- Self-expression should be emotional, dynamic, and demonstrative (Kochman, 1990).
- Self-expression should be emotionally restrained and modest (Kochman, 1990).
- Talking is a good way to show interest in another person, and silence shows lack of interest (Lustig & Koester, 1999; Wolfram et al., 1999).
- Spoken words are less important than nonverbal communication, and if speaking is necessary, it should entail as few words as possible (Lustig & Koester, 1999).

These beliefs and others about how language should be used are less obvious than a student's mastery of standard phonology, syntax, or vocabulary, but they may be at least as important in the context of schooling. Noted linguist Shirley Brice Heath (1986) has claimed that language use is the most important factor in determining how a child will fare in school. She offers a short list of uses for language that are common in schools, many of which the children may or may not have had experience with at home. Even if they have learned to put language to all of these uses, the rules for doing so at home may differ from those at school.

Differences Between Language Use at Home and at School

Table 2-2 characterizes 10 common uses for language in the classroom. The emphasis is on oral language, but many, if not all, may take written form. Numbers 8 and 9 may be less common in classrooms, but they are at least as important as the others. These language uses are discussed again in chapter 3 in the context of language acquisition.

Differences in language use are associated not only with culture but also with social class and level of formal education of parents. More privileged families tend to engage their children in more verbal interaction (Hart & Risley, 1995), and they tend to use language in ways that schools demand, so in many cases their children will find the language uses of school more familiar (Heath, 1983; Snow, Burns, & Griffin, 1998). In particular, middle class parents often ask their infants and toddlers to label objects in their environment (Gleason, 1977). Slightly older children may be asked to describe or explain experiences they have had and talk about upcoming events. This latter kind of decontextualized language use, in which the immediate topic of conversation is not present or self-explanatory, has been associated with later success in reading (Snow, 1983). After all, to comprehend a text, the child needs to be able to rely on language and prior knowledge alone. There is no immediate, real-life context to clarify the meaning of a sentence.

Other parents may not converse with their children in these ways. They may rely far less on language as a medium for teaching their children (Azuma, 1991). In many traditional cultures, children learn most skills by watching adults or older children perform a task and gradually participating as they are able (Nsamenang & Lamb, 1994; Tharp et al., 1984). To make a fish rack, which will be used to dry the summer's catch of salmon so that there will be food throughout the winter, Yup'ik Eskimo youngsters in Alaska watch their parents and older siblings carefully (Lipka, 1998). They begin to participate by helping at a young age and build skill over time. A parent may correct a child verbally, but more often the child is shown how to improve his or her way of helping. Demonstration is the common means of teaching in many of the world's cultures, and reliance on language to teach and assess children's learning is only one approach.

In reading stories to their children, some parents invite children's comments, encourage them to supply phrases or words, or ask them to guess what might happen next (Dickinson & Tabors, 2001; Flood, 1977; Hammett, Van Kleeck, & Huberty, 2003). These behaviors parallel those that the child will likely be expected to engage in at school. No wonder some students seem to have a head start.

Table 2-2. Common Language Uses in School

School Language Uses	Example
1. Regulating behavior	Teacher tells student(s) to behave in certain ways.
2. Labeling and describing	Teacher names items or asks student(s) for names or attributes of items. ("What...?" "What kind of . . .?")
3. Recounting	Student retells an experience or information known to self and teacher. (Tell about an event, retell a passage read, summarize material, display knowledge in oral and written form.)
4. Following or giving directions	Teacher provides running narrative of events at hand or forecasts events (e.g., teacher tells what day's events will be, what steps to take to complete a task; student may be asked to give directions to a classmate).
5. Obtaining information	Teacher seeks student interpretation or explanations. Student interprets actions or text; answers "why" questions." Student may use language to learn from others orally, such as by asking questions or interviewing someone. Language is heuristic, a tool for learning.
6. Commenting	Student (or teacher) volunteers remarks on an event, on another's performance, or on readings.
7. Narrating	Accounts of true experience or knowledge: Student tells about own experiences to teacher or fellow students or reinterprets known information (e.g., show and tell, reports). Stories: Student gives factual or fictional account that follows format of an animate being moving through a series of events with goal-directed behavior.
8. Arguing or persuading	Student participates in debate or discussion, offering evidence for statements (may use evidence as well as appeal to emotions to persuade).
9. Expressing creativity	Student engages in creative, poetic use of language.
10. Talking about language (metalinguistic function)	Student or teacher talks about features of language (e.g., phonology, word meaning, discourse structure), paraphrases or defines words.
Partially constructed from text by Heath (1986, pp. 166–170) and a chart by Wolfram et al. (1999, pp. 95–96).	

Cross-Cultural Differences in Narrative Structures

One of the ways in which children differ linguistically is in how they have learned to structure narratives (Gee, 1989; Heath, 1983; Michaels, 1981). Children in the United States from the mainstream culture learn to develop rather linear narratives with a clear beginning, a middle, and an end. These narratives, whether accounts of actual events or fictional stories, are characterized by sequentially structured discourse on a single topic ("topic-centered narratives"). So ingrained is the story format in our consciousness that we are likely to judge a story that does not have these elements to be ill formed. The Teacher Note nearby is the beginning of a story produced by a 7-year-old African-American girl from a lower socioeconomic background, recorded by linguist James Gee.

> **Teacher Note**
>
> **Today, it's Friday the 13th—It's Bad Luck Day**
>
> "My grandmother's birthday is on Bad Luck Day. And my mother's baking a cake. And I went up to my grandmother's house while my mother was baking a cake. And my mother was baking a cheesecake. My grandmother was baking whipped cream cupcakes. And we both went over to my mother's house. And then my grandmother had made a chocolate cake. And then we went over my aunt's house. And she had made a cake. And everybody had made a cake for Nana, so we came out with six cakes" (Gee, 1990, p. xvi).

Gee describes how the story went on, with the grandmother sneaking out at night to eat more and more cake and even going to the bakery to get more cakes, becoming covered with strawberries and cream, finally getting sick and "growling like a dog," according to the little girl. Classmates were taken with the story, which had such poetic rhythm and pattern of language, with its repetition of the elements of cakes, baking, and going to people's houses. Nevertheless, would a teacher not familiar with this style see the story as poetic and structured in a particular way, or as simply repetitive and rambling? Would he or she be concerned about the evident mixing of real and imagined events?

A student who follows a "topic-associating" strategy—introducing many linked topics and producing a less linear narrative like the one above—may be viewed as producing no pattern at all. However, for those used to hearing stories of this type, the pattern is in the whole—when the full account comes together. In addition, rhythmic patterns involving repetition of sounds, words, and phrases are often present but may not be appreciated by a listener or reader from a different narrative tradition. In fact, many cultures take this approach to narrative, particularly those that have a longstanding oral tradition.

Written narratives of students influenced by other literary traditions are likely to reflect patterns unfamiliar to teachers. For example, Vietnamese Americans may focus more on setting the scene than developing the plot and be negatively evaluated by a teacher who expects the reverse. Students whose native language is Arabic may produce extended description that appears to a teacher as excessive or digressive. There are parallel issues in expository writing. Korean-American and Chinese-American students may tend to use more inductive logical structures, putting details first and then developing a conclusion, versus beginning with a topic sentence and presenting evidence for an argument (Kaplan, 1988; Leki, 1992; Sö terr 1988). Obviously, the complexity of these possible culture-based differences cannot be fully addressed in this short chapter. Readers should also be cautioned that not all students from these cultures will behave in these ways. However, teachers can bear in mind the possibility that a student's deviation from the expected patterns in both oral and written language may indicate that he or she has simply learned something other than what is taught in U.S. schools. Difference is not equivalent to deficit.

How Do Questioning Strategies Differ Cross-Culturally?

We teachers think nothing of asking a student to provide the answer to a question to which we already know the answer. Of course we know the answer, and now we want to find out if the student does. As simple a matter as this seems to be, it is not self-evidently reasonable to all students. In fact, students from many different backgrounds may not be used to these "known answer" questions (Heath, 1986). In their homes, if someone asks them a question, it is because he or she is actually seeking information—not testing the students' knowledge. Children from such homes will therefore have to acquire a new orientation to questioning if they are to succeed in school. In the meantime, when teachers encounter students (particularly the young or those new to U.S. schooling) who fail to respond to direct "known answer" questions, they may want to consider the possibility that the student just has not been exposed to this kind of questioning.

As noted earlier, the expectation that one student answer at a time is also not universal across cultural groups. Peer-oriented cultures, where children routinely help each other and learn together, may allow—even encourage—more than one student to respond at a time. Another aspect of question use has to do with who may pose a question. In U.S. classrooms, students are often urged to pose questions about things they want to learn. They are expected to ask questions when they don't understand something the teacher has said, and in some instances they may be encouraged to even argue with a proposition the teacher puts forth. These behaviors would be considered extremely disrespectful in many classrooms around the world. Asian-American students, who have learned a different set of communication norms, often find it difficult to volunteer answers or pose questions. "Questions for clarification are rarely asked of the teacher directly; to do so might be regarded as a challenge to the teacher's authority and could threaten her or his face[1] should the answer not be known" (Lustig & Koester, 1999, p. 313).

Direct vs. Indirect Speech

An area of cross-cultural difference that sometimes causes tremendous mis-understanding between people has to do with the degree of directness in inter-personal communication. Some cultures emphasize indirectness and ambiguity, whereas others emphasize directness or confrontation (Lustig & Koester, 1999). In the United States, the norm is to be direct, even if this makes someone else uncomfortable. In fact, many Americans from the dominant culture would think it disingenuous to be any other way. This norm is in distinct contrast to what Mexican Americans or Micronesians, for example, have learned. People from these cultures would be likely to go out of their way to avoid confronting some-one with negative information. They might go to a relative and hope that the message gets around to the target person. From their perspective, everyone could save face by an indirect communication of a complaint. Many a European Ameri-can might be befuddled or annoyed and ask, "Why didn't they tell me directly if they have a problem with something that I have done?" (Lustig & Koester, 1999, p. 93). Of course, there is huge variation in European-American norms of com-munication, partly related to specific origins and location in the United States. However, on the whole they are far more direct then Micronesians or Mexican Americans tend to be (though speech to children in these cultures may be quite direct).

It isn't hard to think of misunderstandings that might arise between students or between teachers and students who have been socialized to two such different norms. When confronted directly with a criticism or correction, especially in front of others, a student from a culture with a norm of indirect communication may feel far more embarrassed than his or her teacher realizes. Parents who expect polite, indirect discourse in a parent-teacher conference may themselves be bewildered by a teacher's direct questions. (See the discussion on parent-teacher conferences below.)

On the other hand, students who are used to direct communication may be confused by indirect language. Teachers often make indirect requests in order to regulate students' behaviors ("Tanya, would you like to take your seat now?"). Students who are used to hearing direct commands ("Sit down now, Tanya.") may interpret the teacher's request as offering a choice when it really isn't (Heath, 1983). Heath's research showed that both Black and White working-class stu-dents had trouble interpreting teachers' indirect requests as commands. Needless to say, when students don't respond as expected, they may be labeled as behav-ior problems and even referred for some kind of counseling or alternative place-ment (Delpit, 1988).

How Language Differences Can Lead to Power Differences

All of these differences add up to a power differential in the classroom that reflects that of the society at large. Students from mainstream groups (groups whose values and behavioral norms are most accepted and who tend to have the most resources and political power) are at an advantage (Cummins, 1993; Delpit,

1988). They know the rules for participation—how to interact in the classroom, how to engage in discussion, how to tell a story, how loudly and how often to speak, how to use the right vocabulary and grammar. Some students from toher backgrounds will simply withdraw from participation in oral language events and perhaps be thought to be shy or tuned out (Dumont, 1979; Philips, 1983).

What's a Teacher to Do?

Learn About Home Cultures

Cultural understanding can go a long way to making teaching easier. Teachers will be in a much better position to get children to participate in classroom talk if they understand how talk takes place in children's homes. This will mean, for example, learning about families' cultural values related to modesty versus self-expression, questioning versus listening to adults, and arguing versus avoiding conflict.

Become Aware of Implicit School Language Expectations

It can be much harder for teachers from the dominant culture to recognize the implicit rules for participation because they simply seem like the natural way of doing things. Teachers need to be conscious of not only how students use language but how they themselves communicate expectations about language use. This chapter maps out many ways in which the language of school may differ from the language of home, and it can be used as a starting point for identifying the expectations in one's own school or classroom.

> ### Teacher Inquiry
>
> How do your own expectations for students' language use harmonize or conflict with what students may be expected to do in their homes and communities? If you're not sure, how could you find out? Discuss these issues and strategies for learning about such cultural differences with your colleagues. Develop a plan for accomplishing the goals of learning about these differences and for integrating culturally responsive strategies in your daily instruction.

Engage in Explicit Instruction

If children have not been expected to use language in "school" ways, they will need time and experience in order to learn them. The power imbalance can be addressed by explicit teaching of the mainstream rules for participation in schooling. Direct explanation of what is expected, rather than soft-pedaling feedback to avoid confronting differences, is recommended by Delpit (1988). This approach can be combined with classroom strategies that incorporate students' own ways of communicating, to foster students' bicultural competence.

Use Strategies to Harmonize Home and School Language

The vignette in the Teacher Note below shows how one teacher bridged the gap between the cultures of her students, who were mostly Latino immigrants, and the culture of school, with its requirements for a very particular kind of discourse.

Teacher Note

The Field Trip

Ms. Altchech's fourth-grade class was preparing to take a field trip to the Ballona Wetlands Park, near its Los Angeles school. The class was lucky enough to have a wildlife docent from the park come to the classroom twice before the trip. When he asked the students what they knew about various animals they would likely see on the trip, they routinely answered with stories about experiences they had had with their families. "One time my grandfather and me we went to Death Valley, and my mom came too. We took my grandfather's truck. We saw a snake behind a rock," offered Armando. Other children told their stories in similar fashion. On the second visit, the docent let a couple of stories go by and then issued the admonition "No more stories!" Ms. Altchech knew that what he wanted was a "scientific discussion," with no "extraneous" commentary. She wasn't surprised, though, when his next question was met with silence. Her students are largely from immigrant Latino families, and their cultures do not always stress the separation of content knowledge from social experience. As in American Indian cultures, scientific knowledge is likely to be considered important in terms of its impact on human beings and not valued for its own sake. Later, Ms. Altchech invited her students to tell their stories that related in some way to the planned field trip. As they talked, she constructed a T-chart on the board, with key elements from the students' stories on the left. Then, she asked them to help her extract the "scientific information" from their stories. For example, she used a student's comment that "the hummingbird's wings moved so fast" to draw out information about the bird's metabolism and feeding habits. The students were participating, and the science lesson was getting taught.

Based on Trumbull et al. (in press)

The following Classroom Extension box shows a reconstruction of the T-chart Ms. Altchech and her students developed. Through her instructional strategy, Ms. Altchech helps students to move from a familiar discourse style to the more academic style expected in the classroom. She uses their own strengths and values (including a strong orientation to family) to shape the instruction. She allows students to relate their stories, which often involve trips or other family activities. The result is a high level of student engagement, ready identification of students' prior knowledge, and a joint construction of the scientific knowledge that is the goal of instruction.

Classroom Extension	
Student Experience	**Scientific Information**
Carolina's Story	*Hummingbird*
I was playing in the garden with grandmother, and I saw a hummingbird near the cherry tree.	Brownish with bright iridescent green and red coloring around head and neck
The bird "stood in the air." I tried to go close to the pretty little bird, but it kept darting away.	Wings beat rapidly
	Bird can hover and fly in any direction
	Has to eat frequently because of using so much energy in its movements

Trumbull et al. (in press, p. 42)

Vary the Ways Students Can Participate

Teachers can improve student engagement in the classroom by varying the ways they structure talk—questioning, discussion, "show and tell," student presentations, and the like. Many students who tend to be quiet in large-group discussions will participate in pairs or small groups. The small-group organizational pattern is also excellent for promoting talk among students learning English as a new language.

The most common form of teacher-student discourse in U.S. classrooms is as follows: (a) The teacher initiates an interaction by asking a question, (b) the student responds, and (c) the teacher comments on (evaluates) what the student has said. This is called the *recitation script*. Students speak one at a time, and all language is mediated through the teacher (Cazden, 1988; Mehan, 1979). A criticism of this kind of discourse is that it gives very little time for each student to talk. Such discussions are often dominated by a few students, who get all the language practice. Even if all students got equal time, that would give only a few minutes a day to each one.

At times, when working with the whole group, a teacher may want to allow more than one student to respond at a time (choral response). The approach isn't as chaotic as it sounds, and it may lead to a great deal more participation. In many classrooms (e.g., in Alaska, Hawaii, and Micronesia) children respond together comfortably (Au & Jordan, 1981a; Kleinfeld, 1979; Nelson-Barber, Trumbull, & Wenn, 2000). The group orientation of the students is mirrored in the instruction and assessment. The teacher may assess students in groups or encourage group presentations rather than individual performances. Direct questioning of students in front of their peers can be experienced as pitting one student against others or forcing students to show off. In some cultures, it is considered rude to address a single person within a group; one should address the whole group (Philips, 1983). The point is to move away from depending on a single approach to classroom discourse. In U.S. cities with great dultural diversity, classrooms will have students from many different cultural backgrounds. One way of fostering student participation is not likely to work for all students. Varying the style in which students may participate verbally is quite likely to result in the participation of more students.

The Instructional Conversation[2]

The *instructional conversation* has been shown to be an effective means for engaging students in classroom discourse (Goldenberg, 1991; Tharp & Gallimore, 1988). Instructional conversations do not follow the turn-taking procedure of the recitation script; rather, "the teacher's interactions with students provide different forms of modeling and feedback, expand utterances, and provide purposeful questioning to guide and support students' learning" (McCollum, 1991, p. 113). There is much more reciprocity in this kind of discourse, with teacher and students learning from each other. Students shape the conversation as much as the teacher does; the teacher does not evaluate every comment a student makes but, instead, helps to move the conversation toward instructional ends by building on what students say. Thus, there are opportunities for students' knowledge and ways of using language to come to the fore.

Teacher Note

Fostering an Instructional Conversation

Mrs. Ortiz, the teacher, began the instructional conversation by opening the floor to all of her students through the use of *wh-* questions, chorus elicitations,* or sentence completion activities. In this way, she did not specifically call on certain students, as teachers commonly do. In addition, Mrs. Ortiz allowed her students to have considerable control over the conversation. In her classroom, students themselves initiated 38% of the conversational interactions, whereas students in a comparison classroom initiated only 9%. Mrs. Ortiz was also more accepting of students' initiations, either commenting on them or incorporating them into the conversation, 77% of the time compared to 46% in the comparison classroom.

Another feature of Mrs. Ortiz's instructional conversation was its sometimes personal nature. Students would "often introduce a personal topic into the lesson and be allowed to expound upon it at great length. Many times, Mrs. Ortiz would introduce information from her personal life or childhood into the lessons as well" (McCollum, 1991, p. 115). The same has been observed in the classrooms of the Bridging Cultures Project (Trumbull et al., 2001). In the case of Mrs. Ortiz's lesson on a story the students had read, *El Cangrejito de Oro* (*The Golden Crab*), about a boy who was learning how to fish, the teacher and students spent a full 9 minutes sharing their experiences about fishing for crabs.

cont.

Mrs. Ortiz's instructional approach, which elevates the role of peers in each other's learning, could be characterized as constructivist. It explicitly engages students in active learning, supports students to connect their prior knowledge and experience to the topics of the classroom, and places the teacher in the role of a facilitator who guides the lesson expertly but does not completely dominate the talking. It is an approach that has been shown effective with immigrant students from group-oriented cultures, such as those in Mexico and Central America, yet it also has all the hallmarks of the kind of instruction identified as exemplary for all students by recent reform agendas.

*allowing students to answer in unison rather than one by one
Based on McCollum (1991)

Incorporate Culturally Appropriate Topics in Daily Instruction

Other strategies for what might be called *linguistic inclusion* have to do with the content of instruction, or what gets talked about. Promoting students' participation in classroom discussion, Bridging Cultures Project teachers choose books related to family when possible from lists of recommended literature (Trumbull et al., in press). Fourth-grade teacher Giancarlo Mercado has found a number of stories from the fourth-grade basal reader that focus on family. "Las Mañanitas" is a story about a small boy from a migrant worker family. The boy always knows when they are about to move because the cardboard boxes show up at their house. Mr. Mercado asked his students how many of them thought the boy should stay with friends if he could, so that he could keep going to the same school and do well, and how many thought the boy should move and help his family. All 28 students raised their hands for the latter alternative. Mr. Mercado says that students were riveted by this story. This example shows how engaged students can be when literature topics coincide with their interests and values. Mr. Mercado is working with colleagues at his school in Venice, California, to select core literature books that are family focused or otherwise reflect students' cultural values.

Cultivate Good Communication with Parents and Community

Cultural differences in styles of expression and communication can affect parent involvement in schooling as well as student behavior. Schools today often expect parents to not only participate in schoolwide events and parent-teacher conferences but also to volunteer in classrooms and serve on committees that set educational policy (Epstein, 1998). The intent behind these expectations is positive: Schools want to foster the engagement and empowerment of parents vis-á-vis their children's schooling—something that has been associated with student achievement (Henderson & Berla, 1994; Henderson & Mapp, 2002). However, because of the special esteem accorded teachers in many other cultures, members of those cultures may believe that decisions about practices and policies should be left to the professionals. Parents holding these cultural values are puzzled when a school tries to involve them in goal setting at parent-teacher conferences and decision making on advisory councils. Teachers, on the other hand, may think that such parents are uncaring or unconcerned about their children. If the parents speak little or no English and the teacher cannot speak the language of the parents, communication problems are compounded. However, it is more often the values and intentions underlying the language that cause misunderstandings between home and school.

Parent-Teacher Conferences

The parent-teacher conference is a mainstay of home-school communication in the United States. Some 85% of schools formally schedule parent-teacher conferences at least once a year. Ideally, the parent-teacher conference provides a chance for parent and teacher to evaluate a child's academic and social progress needs and jointly set goals for the child. However, establishing mutual understanding about a child's development and needs depends on shared views about what is important and how it should be achieved. Not unexpectedly, cultural values come into play as teacher and parent take up these issues. When these two adults are from different cultural backgrounds, the opportunities for misunderstanding multiply. Consider the Teacher Note "Are We on the Same Page?", which is a fictionalized version of a portion of an actual parent-teacher conference that took place in southern California between an immigrant Latino parent and his child's teacher (Greenfield et al., 2000).

Teacher Note

Are We on the Same Page?

Fourth-grade teacher Susan Francis was conducting a conference with the father of 9-year-old Julio Lopez. Julio's family had come to California from Mexico when the boy was 4, and he had recently moved into her class, which was taught mostly in English. Here's how the conversation went:

Mrs. Francis: "I'm happy to say that Julio's performance in math is outstanding."

Mr. Lopez: "How is he behaving?"

Mrs. Francis: "Julio is behaving just fine. (*Quickly moving to another topic*) He did extremely well on the district writing assessment in March."

Mr. Lopez: "Marco, he can write, too" (*indicating his 4-year-old son who had accompanied him to the conference*).

Mrs. Francis (*rather shrilly, conveying some irritation*): "Well, that's wonderful!"

Mr. Lopez: (*Says nothing. Looks down at his lap.*)

Mrs. Francis: "Julio's oral skills are coming along really well. In fact, he contributes a lot to classroom discussions and is learning to express his opinions quite successfully."

During the next several minutes, while Mrs. Francis finishes discussing the report card, Mr. Lopez remains silent. As she is showing him where to sign the report card, Mr. Lopez looks up at her and asks, "He's not talking too much?"

Based on
Greenfield et al. (2000)

What is going on here? Teacher and parent are apparently able to understand each other's words. Julio is, according to his teacher, doing extremely well in fourth grade. He has a parent and a teacher who care about him and who have arranged to meet to spend time talking about his progress. Even from this brief segment of the conference, however, it is evident that communication has somehow gone awry.

Getting below the surface of communication. If we deconstruct the conversation a bit, we can identify points of cultural conflict and the kinds of cues that teachers can look for to determine how communication is going in their own interactions with parents (see the next Teacher Note on page 57, "Diagnosing and Repairing Communication Problems").

Mr. Lopez is a Mexican immigrant who has had the benefit of eight years of schooling in his country of origin. His conversation suggests that he holds strong collectivistic values that are in some conflict with the teacher's and school's expressed values. Using some knowledge of Mr. Lopez's background and analyzing the conversation, we surmise the following:

- Mr. Lopez is concerned that his son be a contributing member of the classroom group; he sees Julio's behavior as an integral part of his son's overall academic development. Mrs. Francis wants to focus on Julio's academic behavior apart from his social development.
- Mr. Lopez sees his family as a whole unit and wants to consider Julio in that context; hence the introduction of a comment about Marco. Mrs. Francis believes the conference should focus on Julio and not his siblings.
- Mrs. Francis sees Julio's self-expression and willingness to express opinions as a positive development. Mr. Lopez is concerned that his son is not showing modesty and consideration for the other students or that he may not be properly respectful of the teacher.

Mr. Lopez's increasing silence and Mrs. Francis's evident impatience are indicators that the communication in the conference is not going well. Yet neither seems to understand why, because cultural conflicts like these tend to remain below conscious awareness. The resulting discomfort is undoubtedly felt by both participants in the conversation, but it cannot be resolved without increased cross-cultural understanding.

Acting to improve communication. Mrs. Francis could begin to improve future communication by taking the following steps:

1. View the parent-teacher conference as an opportunity for real two-way learning: teacher *communicating to* parent about school expectations, norms, and child progress and *learning from* parent about how he or she views the child in the context of schooling.
2. Use discourse analysis as a way to diagnose how the conversation is going.
3. Adjust her own communication to harmonize with parent focus and needs.

We know that teachers do routinely use the conference as an opportunity to learn about what is going on with the child at home and about concerns the parents have. Nevertheless, when talking with a parent from a different cultural background, this process is more complex and may require a more ethnographic approach. That is, the teacher may have to become a student of culture—learning about parents' values, approaches to childrearing and schooling, and how their own educational experiences (perhaps in a different country) affect their views of school.

When a participant in a conversation does not respond to a topic, remains silent for an extended period of time (recognizing that there are cultural differences in the amount of time between conversational turns), or changes the topic, the conversation could be characterized as discordant or uncooperative. Something isn't working.

Teacher Note

Diagnosing and Repairing Communication Problems

A teacher can monitor the success of a conversation with a parent (or other family member) by considering the following questions:

- Does the parent ratify (validate or acknowledge) a topic the teacher has brought up by verbal or nonverbal means?
- Does the parent verbally elaborate on the same topic the teacher has introduced?
- Does the parent confirm a specific comment or observation the teacher has made?

Ratification, elaboration, and confirmation are all signs that the parent agrees (at least to some degree) with the teacher about the importance of what he or she is saying and with the teacher's interpretation of the facts. Parent and teacher are on the same wavelength. Because communication is a reciprocal process, both teacher and parent should be introducing topics and responding to the other's comments. Consequently, a teacher might want to also ask the following:

- Do I ratify a topic the parent has brought up by verbal or nonverbal means?
- Do I elaborate on the same topic the parent has introduced (verbally)?
- Do I confirm a specific comment or observation the parent has made (verbally or nonverbally)?

Based on Trumbull et al. (2001)

Identifying conversational harmony and discord. The next Teacher Note shows excerpts from two actual parent-teacher conferences. The parents were both Mexican immigrants living in southern California, and the teacher was European American. In these conferences, we can see some of the same cross-cultural conflicts exhibited in our fictional vignette with Mr. Lopez and Mrs. Francis. We can see instances of conversational harmony and discord, revealed by whether the parent ratifies, elaborates upon, or confirms the teacher's comments. Conversational turns in each example are numbered sequentially.

Teacher Note

Discourse Samples from Parent-Teacher Conferences
Note: Examples A, B, and C are from one conference. Examples D and E are from another.

A. **Parent ratification of a topic introduced by teacher**
Teacher: Also I hope that she has time to read orally . . .
Mother: (*Nodding and smiling*) Ah-huh.
Teacher: . . . and also silently every night.
Mother: Ah-huh.

B. **Parent elaboration of a topic introduced by teacher**
Teacher: . . . with you orally and with her silently in the bed for a book in which she has an interest.
Mother: Ah-huh. She took out from the library. How many? Seven?

C. **Parents' confirmation of teacher's comment**
Teacher (*pointing to report card*): Takes pride in her work. Most of the time her work is neat, but I'd like her to work a little bit harder on trying to make sure that just—not perfect, but as—
Father: Yeah.
Teacher: —as neat as possible.
Mother: Yeah, a little bit.
Teacher: Yeah, a little neater.
Mother: A little bit neater.
Teacher: Yeah, work on your (child's) handwriting a little bit.
Mother: Yeah, she could improve it.

D. **Lack of parent ratification of a topic introduced by teacher**
Teacher: She's doing great. She's doing beautifully in English and in reading. *And* in writing, *and* in speaking.
Father: (*Looks down at lap.*)

E. **Changing of teacher's topic by parent**
Teacher: It's wonderful.
Father (*turning to point to younger son*): The same, this guy, he—
Teacher (*interrupting, with shrill tone*): Good!!
Father: He can write—
Teacher (*cutting him off*): He can write in English?
Father: —well, his name.

Based on Greenfield et al. (2000)

Harmony. In examples A and B in the Teacher Note box, the teacher and parent appear to agree that reading activities are important for the child. We don't know whether they have the same reasons for believing this, but there is no evident conversational discord. In example C (which comes from the same conference), there is apparent agreement on a goal of handwriting improvement and on the need for the child to be a little neater.

Discord. In examples D and E in the Teacher Note box, parent and teacher are having communication problems. As in the Lopez-Francis vignette, the father does not ratify the topic of the child's academic progress, nor does the teacher seem comfortable talking about the development of a younger sibling. As the researchers explain, "The father shows discomfort when the teacher recognizes his daughter as outstanding; he responds by looking down at his lap. According to our analyses, her recognition may threaten the collectivistic goal of integrating each child as an equal contributing part of the family group. Hence when the teacher symbolically constructs his daughter as an outstanding individual learner, the father implicitly *reconstructs* her as a normative part of the family group by equating her academic skills to those of her younger brother" (Greenfield et al., 2000, p. 101).

Helping parents to connect with school. As mentioned, when parents and teachers feel uncomfortable during a communication session like the parent-teacher conference, they may not be able to figure out why. The kind of monitoring we propose here does not, of course, always reveal why a parent changes the topic or doesn't respond, but it is an important step toward improving communication. An observant teacher can take the parent's cues as to what he or she is interested in, and that will go a long way toward developing mutual understanding. Perhaps, then, the teacher can explain why certain topics are important in the context of U.S. schooling and show parents how they may connect with larger goals that both they and teachers have for students.

Written Communication Between Home and School

Communicating across cultures also takes place through written messages between home and school. In areas where students' families speak a language other than English, schools will often translate notes into home languages, but translation alone (even when parents are fully literate) does not ensure *communication*. All messages entail assumptions based on cultural values. Failure to respond to a message from school does not mean that parents have not read it or do not consider it important. Other factors may come into play, as we can see from the camping-trip vignette in the Teacher Note box below based on an experience of a teacher mentioned earlier—Mr. Mercado.

Differences in values surrounding childrearing and schooling can cause conflict in simple situations like this one. In fact, research from the Bridging Cultures Project suggests that schools and teachers face situations like this one daily when they serve families from nonmainstream cultures. Underlying many such conflicts is a culture-based difference that remains invisible to parties on both sides. Mr. Mercado's experience with getting permission for students to go camping shows how important it can be to get adequate information for interpreting parents' responses to written communication.

Teacher Note

The Camping Trip

Mr. Giancarlo Mercado teaches fourth- and fifth-grade students in Los Angeles. For the past few years, he has been in charge of the fifth-grade camping trip. When he first started supervising the trip, he noticed that some parents returned the permission slips for their children quickly, whereas others didn't respond for several days. He had sent the notices home in the languages of his students' parents, and he knew that students could read them to their parents if necessary. So what was going on? Mr. Mercado began to make some phone calls to those parents, and he discovered that it was not simply a matter of a parent's deciding to let a child go on the trip. In his students' homes, helping the family was an important value. It was common for each child to have a job within the family. If someone was going to be away for 2 or more days, arrangements had to be made to ensure that the responsibilities would be met. In addition, in the cultures of his students, who were mostly from Central America and Mexico, it was unusual for children to be away from home without members of their family. For many students, it would be the first time they would stay overnight in a place with no family member present.

Mr. Mercado came to understand that two important cultural norms related to a strong family orientation were causing the parents of his students to delay signing the permission slips. With this new understanding, he was able to explain to parents about the benefits of the trip, reassure them about their children's safety, and give them the time necessary to make the decision. In time, most parents allowed their children to go on the camping trip. Without the personal contact (also valued above impersonal notes in his students' cultures), he might not have found out what was going on. Real communication between home and school in this case depended on the teacher's acquired cultural understanding, not his ability to speak Spanish.

Adapted from Trumbull et al. (2001, p. 79)

Letters, newsletters, or signs posted on the school grounds that are written to inform parents about school policies may be based on tacit assumptions that are not shared by families. In one instance, a school in Los Angeles wanted to put a stop to the practice of mothers' bringing preschoolers and eating breakfast with their young children enrolled in the school (Raeff, Greenfield, & Quiroz, 2000). Not only did officials believe that their funding would be jeopardized, they also felt that mothers were taking food away from the children for whom it was rightfully designated. A sign was tacked up near the cafeteria reading, "Only students allowed in the eating area." Mothers were outraged and insulted. From the perspective of their (immigrant Latino) culture, having breakfast with their children demonstrated their caring for their children. Bringing younger siblings was a way of sharing and showing their concern for the welfare of the whole family.

An elementary teacher who learned about this unfortunate cross-cultural misunderstanding was able to prevent a potential problem in her own school in Los Angeles. Hearing that administrators were about to undertake a course of action similar to the one described above, she persuaded them to allow her to work with the bilingual director to craft an explanatory letter to families. Once parents understood the reason for the policy, they accepted it (Trumbull, Rothstein-Fisch, & Hernandez, 2003).

Language Variation

All speakers use one or more varieties of the language they speak. Regional dialects have traditionally symbolized allegiance to a region; conveyed positive, shared connotations associated with valued traits; and signaled social bonding within class and ethnic groups (Chaika, 1982). Accents and dialectal variations, however, have also had negative connotations and in many societies are impediments to access to social, educational, and economic opportunities. Attitudes toward language influence our perceptions about other people's social identity, social status, and intellectual ability (Ramirez, 1985). Hence, it is particularly important for teachers to be sensitive to their own responses to different language varieties.

Dialect

A *dialect* is a variety of a language that is distinguished from other varieties of the same language by features of phonology, grammar, and vocabulary. Pace of speech, volume, and other nonlinguistic behaviors—such as how close to stand to a conversational partner—are also likely to vary. Dialects may differ as well in discourse conventions—how stories are structured and told, rules of conversation, and how written language is used. One traditional definition of dialects holds that they are mutually intelligible versions of the same language. For example, despite variations in pronunciation or usage, a speaker of southern U.S. English can generally understand a speaker from the Northwest. However, in the case of Chinese, different varieties, such as Mandarin and Cantonese, are usually considered to be dialects even though they are not mutually intelligible in spoken form. (The fact that they use the same characters means that they *are* mutually intelligible in written form.) On the other hand, Swedish and Norwegian are mutually intelligible, yet for sociopolitical reasons they are treated as separate languages (Linguistics Society of America, 1998).

Dialects are identified by their use by a particular group of speakers who are separated from others geographically or socially (*Webster's Encyclopedic Unabridged Dictionary*, 1989). In the United States, we might distinguish at least the following regional dialects: southern, mid-Atlantic, New England, New York City, midwestern, southwestern, Appalachian, and northwestern. There are other dialects with smaller numbers of speakers within these regions. In Pennsylvania, for example, Pennsylvania Dutch speak a dialect of English influenced by German. Hawaii has its own pidgin (Hawaiian Creole English), and Alaska has many dialects of English among the communities of Alaska Native peoples. An example of a dialect that is based on social group rather than region is African-American Vernacular English (AAVE).

Teachers need a basic understanding of what a dialect is and that it represents a functioning, rule-governed language system. That is to say, all dialects have internally consistent rules of pronunciation and syntax. Differences from what we take to be Standard English are not random errors but systematic patterns. What is grammatical to a person depends on what dialect(s) he or she has learned (Crystal, 1987). Each nonstandard dialect is fully as logical as any so-called standard (socially preferred) dialect. As mentioned in chapter 1, many people who speak the more socially accepted dialects of English believe that use of forms like the double negative ("I don't want no more dessert, thanks") that appear in AAVE are illogical. "Two negatives make a positive," they say—reasoning from their knowledge of math. However, many languages mark the negative with two morphemes. In French we say, "Je *ne* sais *pas*" ("I don't know"). *Ne* and *pas* together signal a negative. Likewise, in Spanish, there are many cases where two morphemes are necessary to communicate the negative: "*No* se *nada*" ("I know nothing"). It is not a matter of logic but of convention to use one or two morphemes to indicate a single negative. We need to be careful about making inferences about the logic or validity of ways of expressing things in other languages or dialects on the basis of our own language or dialect. The use of two negative morphemes in AAVE is no more illogical than such use in French or Spanish.

A nonstandard dialect is by no means substandard language and is certainly not slang. (All dialects of English have their own slang.) There is a tendency for people to confuse the social status attached to a dialect with its linguistic adequacy or value, but this is a mistake that teachers should avoid. Otherwise they may make false judgments about students' language skills or intelligence. In fact, sophisticated language skills are needed to master any dialect (Rickford, 1998), and all dialects can express abstract concepts.

Although teachers do not routinely get the opportunity to learn about language structures and usage the way linguists do, in a sense they need to become linguists of a sort to understand how language comes into the learning process as well as what constitutes a language deficit versus a language difference. "A child doesn't need to know any linguistics in order to use language to learn; but a teacher needs to know some linguistics if he wants to understand how the process takes place—or what is going wrong when it doesn't" (Halliday, 1980, p. 11).

Standard English

So-called Standard American English is simply one dialect among many equally valid and complex dialects of American English. It is the one that "happens to be used by the elite and written down, while the others are not" (McWhorter, 1998, p. 33) and is, as such, the "power code" (Delpit, 1988). In fact, Standard English is actually a hodge-podge of British dialects (McWhorter,

1998). What is accepted as Standard English has changed even within the past 50 years, with a shift from a national preference for an accent associated with the Northeast to a midwestern one such as newscasters use (McWhorter, 1998). On top of all this, what counts as standard varies somewhat from place to place, so it would make more sense to talk about the "local Standard English dialect" rather than a single standard dialect. Nevertheless, what is perceived as standard holds great sway in social institutions like schools, and there are great social pressures to conform to this perceived standard.

In any language community, close-knit social or ethnic groups use a range of language varieties.[3] These varieties come into the work of the school in one way or another. Children may have two or more dialects that they use in their everyday communication, perhaps one dialect used in the home, another in the peer group, and a third in the school. Largely because of the school's influence, this last dialect may come to be very close to the standard variety.[4] At the same time, many children arrive in schools with little or no contact with the dialect that is used as the language of formal education. Often these children are penalized (socially and instructionally) for having a dialect that is different from the one that has high status in the school. Dialects that have routinely been disparaged include Appalachian, southern, and AAVE. Yet there is absolutely no reason to conclude that a nonstandard dialect interferes with academic learning (see, e.g., review in McWhorter, 1998). With greater understanding of the dialect issue, teachers are more likely to respect and value students' language and seek strategies that help students become bidialectal.

Learning a New Dialect

It is fairly obvious to most people that learning a new language presents challenges, but for some children learning a new dialect is the task they face when they go to school. For these children, rarely are there programs or practices in place to help them with this task. In addition, their teachers may not understand that their students' dialects are perfectly systematic and logical. They may hear these dialects as merely deviations from Standard English and strive to override them with corrections.

It appears that in some ways it is more difficult to learn a new dialect than a new language, because most of the time communication takes place despite the differences in pronunciation, vocabulary, or grammar. Therefore, the need to learn the new dialect may not be felt. It is apparently hard to bring the differences to conscious awareness in order to master a new dialect and make choices about when to use which one. Linguist John Baugh (1994) notes, "Dialects differ in subtle ways, and complete mastery of a second dialect is extremely difficult. Meryl Streep is a highly regarded actress because of her ability to manipulate different English dialects, but we demand this type of linguistic dexterity from our minority students as if the task were somehow quite simple" (pp. 199–200).

As they do with languages, many people master more than one dialect; it is not necessary to get rid of one to learn another. Because there is so much focus in our schools on helping English language learners master English, or nondominant dialect speakers master the dominant dialect, we often forget that children have already mastered complex linguistic systems.

African-American Vernacular English

Many African-American children speak what has variously been called African-American English, African-American Vernacular[5] English (AAVE), Negro Nonstandard Dialect, Black English, Black English Vernacular, Black Language, or U.S. Ebonics (Perry & Delpit, 1998). Specific attention is devoted to AAVE, the term used here, because it is spoken by a substantial number of students and because, in our observation, myths about AAVE still abound.

This dialect or language (scholars argue over the designation), like all other natural linguistic systems, has its own rules and is capable of serving all of the intellectual and social needs of its speakers (Labov, 1972). The choice of terms reflects both social and linguistic beliefs. The name *African-American Vernacular English* (AAVE) reflects a general preference among many African Americans (over *Negro* or *Black*) and has been used by African-American linguists. It also implies that it is a dialect of English (Baugh, 1994; Rickford, 1997). However, African-American linguist John McWhorter uses *Black English*, and several prominent African-American educators use the term *Black Language*, on the basis of their belief that this language system is not a dialect of English but a distinct language based on African languages (Smith, 1998).

AAVE is not uniform across all African-American communities. What has been studied most is the spoken language of less educated African Americans, and descriptions of AAVE in the literature are based on the speech of those studied. In truth, "there is a continuum from what we would call a 'deep' Black English through 'light' Black English to Standard English . . . African Americans' use of Black English falls at different points along this continuum" (McWhorter, 1998, p. 147). Rickford (1998) notes that most African Americans speak some variety of AAVE. For our purposes here, we will speak as though there is a common AAVE dialect, keeping in mind that the degree to which any student manifests a deep version of this dialect will vary.

Although AAVE is not accepted by the larger society as standard, it is in no way substandard. It has multiple forms—oral and written, formal and informal, vernacular and literary (Perry, 1998). It has been shaped, in part, by the social circumstances surrounding African Americans' history in the United States. Words and phrases were coined to serve the need to keep some things private from the dominant White culture during the time of slavery. According to Stanford University linguist John Rickford (1997), "the song 'Wade in the Water' meant that the master was sending bloodhounds or something after you, so to be safe, stay in the river" (p. 3). It has also been influenced by the particular dialects of English spoken in the southern United States and in turn has influenced southern White speech.

Roots and Features of AAVE

Some argue that the forms and uses of AAVE can be traced to West African and Niger-Congo languages (O'Neil, 1998; Smith, 1998) and that AAVE more resembles an African language than English. Certainly slaves were often separated from models of English usage and likely developed their own pidgin and then a creole[6] language (Rickford, 1997). In addition, slaves from the same language background were isolated from each other so that they could not communicate easily—a strategy designed to prevent insurrection. As a result, they creatively used a combination of African and English words and grammar (Baugh, 1994). Some students of AAVE point to specific features of AAVE that seem to mirror those of African languages. For example, deletion of the final consonant in a consonant cluster (wes' for west or col' for cold) brings English words more in line with the form of words in some West African languages (Smith, 1998). Nevertheless, an analysis of the syntax and phonology of AAVE reveals that it has much greater similarity to English than to West African languages (McWhorter, 1998). In contrast, the creoles found in the Caribbean bear a much stronger resemblance to African languages than to the French, English, or Dutch spoken in schools. Some teachers may have students who speak Haitian Creole (Kréyol), which is based on French and African languages.

In addition to features of syntax and phonology, the oratorical devices (e.g., rhythm, rhyme, metaphor, repetition) used by African-American preachers are distinctive elements of AAVE (Perry, 1998). In fact, many other discourse conventions distinguish AAVE, including particular structures for oral storytelling or narrative writing (Ball, 1997; Heath, 1983; Michaels & Cazden, 1986). Although teachers cannot be expected to be linguists, they do need to have some basic understanding of their students' dialects so that they can make sense of students' oral and written communication. If a student uses an unfamiliar narrative structure in telling a story, it may be that this is not a defective "mainstream" approach but a completely legitimate strategy associated with a different dialect or language. (Recall the story about Friday the 13th.) As noted, many people speak more than one dialect, choosing the appropriate one depending on the situation or with whom they are speaking.

The Dilemma for Students

Decisions about whether to require students to speak and write in the standard dialect in school are fraught with controversy. Insistence on Standard English may add a layer of demands that make acquisition of other skills more difficult. On the other hand, if students do not learn Standard English, their life opportunities may be limited. If Standard English is to be required, students need to understand the value and purpose of learning it—in terms meaningful to them (Christian, 1987). Nevertheless, students may still be faced with a dilemma. Most educators believe that it is important for speakers of nonstandard dialects to become bidialectal in order to succeed in school and in society. As Chaika (1982) observes, the speech of children and adolescents resembles that of the people with whom they identify. AAVE, for example, is strongly valued by many

African Americans as a symbol of intimacy and solidarity—it represents "inter-group distinctiveness from the white community" (Beebe, 1988, p. 65).

Differences between AAVE and Standard English are constantly socially reinforced and, according to some, apparently increasing, whereas others suggest that AAVE is not changing any more rapidly than any other dialect of English (McWhorter, 1998). Students who do not identify with speakers of Standard English are not likely to emulate their speech patterns. In addition, students who choose to use Standard English must often confront peer pressure; and those who use AAVE may have to accept corrections from teachers that they may interpret as insulting to their own speech patterns and self-identity.

Instructional Strategies for Bridging the Dialect Divide

Successful teachers of students whose primary dialect is AAVE have found many strategies for teaching Standard English to those students who seem to need it without negating the value of AAVE. Sociodrama, for example, is a technique that has been reported to help students develop proficiency in Standard English appropriate to various situations, without relying on excessive use of grammar and pronunciation exercises (Chaika, 1982). In a typical sociodrama exercise, students are asked to assume roles and act out situations in which they would be using standard forms of the language (e.g., interviewing for a job, complaining to someone in authority, and speaking in a style suitable for the assigned role). A similar technique can be applied to writing (e.g., newspaper articles) and used in combination with group work and peer editing.

As with students whose narrative and conversational styles differ from those of the dominant U.S. culture, with speakers of AAVE, teachers need not negate the value of their knowledge and skills in order to introduce new ones. Oakland, California, teacher Ms. Carrie Secret (1998) encourages her elementary students to use Standard English when they are writing, but she also acknowledges the value of their language (which she calls Ebonics):

> We read literature that has Ebonics language patterns in it. For example, last year in fifth grade we read Joyce Hansen's *Yellow Bird and Me*, and in fourth grade we read her book *The Gift Giver*. The language was Ebonic in structure. The language was the bonding agent for students. The book just felt good to them. (p. 81)

Table 2-3 outlines some of the issues surrounding teaching students who speak AAVE and suggested strategies for addressing them. The first one, contrastive analysis, comes from the field of second-language teaching.

Table 2-3. Dialect Issues in Instruction

Possible Dialect Conflicts	Possible Instructional Strategies
Students omit final consonants or consonants in clusters.	*Contrastive Analysis* Draw attention to the contrast between students' pronunciation and spelling and Standard English pronunciation and spelling. Generate a list of words with a similar pattern (e.g., *cold, bold, mold, fold, hold*) and have students note where the difference lies. Note: This does not require correcting pronunciation, simply pointing out the differences and choices. *Word Discrimination* Help students to hear the differences between pronunciation of words in AAVE and Standard English. Generate a list of words in which a consonant is not pronounced in AAVE and is in Standard English (*help* (pronounced *hep* in AAVE), *cost, kept, most, cold*, etc.). The teacher pronounces each word twice—sometimes the same way, sometimes in both dialects. Students have to say whether the two are same or different.*
Students use more complex verb patterns than Standard English employs (e.g., "He be going . . ." to indicate a habitual behavior).	*Selecting for Expressiveness* Have class or small group brainstorm about alternative ways *to get* across the same meaning. ("He often goes . . .", "He usually goes . . .", "He has a habit of going . . ."). Have student choose the best form for his or her intended meaning. Discuss when AAVE or Standard English would be more appropriate or expressive.
Students omit the copula (the verb *to be*) or the *'s* possessive in places Standard English would use it. (e.g., "She thrilled about her brother good luck" vs. "She is thrilled about her brother's good luck.")	*Dialect Substitutions* Again, using Ms. Secret's strategy, help students to make explicit the differences between the two dialects and make conscious choices about when to use either one. Draw on the knowledge of the group to surface alternative forms and record them.

cont.

Students use AAVE style in a situation where Standard English would be more socially effective (e.g., writing a request for information to a public agency, preparing to give a plea to the school board for additional resources for a special program).	*Sociodrama* Use sociodrama to take on different roles, highlighting how one would communicate effectively in different situations. Sometimes Black Language will be more effective, and sometimes Standard English will be; identify which applies where.
Students use rhetorical features in writing that are considered oral strategies from the dominant dialect's point of view (e.g., re petition of phrases or themes).	*Style-Purpose Links* Discuss whether or how this is effective to the student's purpose in writing. The student's strategy could be powerfully effective, depending on his or her intended audience.

* Taken from Perez (1999); adapted from Herrell (2000).

Dialect Discrimination

AAVE transcends regional specificity and is the home language of many students in U.S. schools. However, many teachers will need to learn about the norms of other dialects—the dialects of their students. Appalachian dialect, for example, is spoken by many families; and research suggests that students who speak it can expect to encounter similar misunderstandings and misjudgments about their abilities when they go to school (see, e.g., Heath, 1983).

Dialect discrimination—making and acting on the assumption that someone's language is inferior because it is different—appears to be socially acceptable. Wolfram (1993) has written as follows:

> Public discrimination on the grounds of ethnicity, religion and social class differences is no longer acceptable; yet discrimination on the basis of dialect is still quite tolerable, even though many of the differences that serve as the basis for exclusion correlate with regional, class and ethnic variables. People who speak stigmatized dialects such as African American Vernacular English or Southern vernacular English continue to be rejected on the basis of their speech even when their dialects have nothing to do with their performance of job-related tasks and general competence. (p. 29)

It is a short step from devaluing a person's language to devaluing that person.

Many teachers—particularly new teachers—may not recognize that a child's speech "errors" are due to a difference in dialect. In one case, a student teacher is eliciting rhymes for various words:

> The mood is light-hearted, especially when one child offers the word *kiss* as a rhyme for *miss*. The mood changes abruptly, however, when another child calls out "twis(t)", following the rules for consonant cluster reduction in Ebonics. "Twis/ Twis?" asks the student teacher, clearly at a loss. She wrinkles her face in confusion. "What do you mean, *twis*?" she asks,

the heavy emphasis on *twis* making it sound like something repugnant. The child who called out his word with such enthusiasm and confidence says nothing . . .

As this student teacher's supervisor, I am able to intervene diplomatically and firmly. This is not the case on the day I observe a child answer "50 cent" during a math lesson. The teacher responds to this correct answer not with affirmation, but with a clumsy, and from the child's perspective, totally confusing attempt to teach "Standard English" grammar in a math lesson. "Noooo, not fifty cent . . . ," the teacher says, her voice fading into a pause to which there is no response from the child who seconds before had been so sure that his answer was correct. (Meier, 1999, p. 102).

Teacher Inquiry

Student Dialects

What dialects do your students speak? If some speak nonstandard dialects, what strategies do you or could you use to both support their home dialects and help them succeed with the standard dialect expected in school?

You might want to form a professional study group to research, explore, and discuss strategies for helping students to maintain their home dialects while also learning the standard dialect that is required for success at school and in business.

These examples show that teachers' judgments about student language can be damaging. Who can imagine that those two students will so readily volunteer an answer in the future? What lesson have they learned about the validity of their own language? Either situation could have been an occasion for both accepting the student and his language *and* introducing an alternate form, if that were deemed necessary.

How Attitudes Toward Language Differences Affect Learning

Attitudes and values attached to some facets of language (e.g., regional or national accent) are evident and widely acknowledged. These are often captured in jokes and parodies. However, people are rarely aware of the depth of reactions to divergent language styles and the speakers who use them. "The ideal of linguistic democracy, in which the speech of every citizen is regarded with equal respect by all others, is perhaps the most unrealistic of all social ideals. Speech is one of the most effective instruments in existence for maintaining a given social order" (Christian, 1972, p. 183). The movie and play *My Fair Lady* illustrate some of the language attitudes and the resulting social consequences to which Christian is alluding. In this case, a speaker of the most prestigious British dialect of English (Professor Henry Higgins) takes on the task of teaching his dialect to the speaker of a socially devalued dialect (Eliza Doolittle). In so doing, he intends to help her improve her socioeconomic status. At one point, Professor Higgins is talking with a fellow professor, who, of course, speaks the socially privileged dialect. He says (sings), referring to Eliza Doolittle (who is a street flower vendor), "If you spoke as she does, instead of the way you do, why you, sir, might be selling flowers too!" In U.S. society, those who speak devalued dialects tend to have a lower degree of socioeconomic success (Peñalosa, 1980).

Language attitudes—both positive and negative—also operate within the classroom and can affect the teaching and learning process. Language plays a major role in establishing the social identities and relationships of teachers and students in the classroom. As Ramirez (1985) observed, the initial impressions teachers form about students are often based upon features of their speech. Once established, these views appear to remain relatively fixed and may influence teachers' expectations of students. Moreover, negative teacher attitudes may reinforce similar student attitudes toward their own or others' nonstandard language use. Thus, students may be subjected to teacher and peer prejudice because of the dialect they speak (see Perry, 1998; Piestrup, 1973).

Reflections

If the topic of language, culture, and society were a tree, it would have countless intertwined branches and a complex system of roots. No single person can claim to have a full grasp of this topic, informed by multiple disciplines, including linguistics, sociology, anthropology, psychology, history, and geography. Nevertheless, many teachers must engage in cross-cultural communication daily and make judgments about how to structure their instruction so as to meet the needs of a diverse population of students. Students from different backgrounds can be expected to have learned different rules about how language should be used. It is clear that to ignore these differences or assume that all students can participate equally in typical instructional patterns is inequitable. It is also clear that some students are at an advantage because the ways language is used in their homes are parallel to how language is used in school.

No teacher can have deep knowledge about every single culture, yet increased awareness about culture—one's own and another's—can be a basis for further exploration. Increasing the ability to observe language use and infer the kinds of rules students may be using to participate in the classroom is a good starting point. It is obvious from the examples offered throughout this chapter that common assumptions about appropriate participation and language use may not be shared by all students.

If a teacher understands that the typical discussion pattern in U.S. classrooms (whole-group conversation mediated by the teacher, with students speaking one at a time) is but one possible format and that it may be unproductive for some students, he or she is likely to try new formats. At the same time, to succeed in U.S. schools, students do need to develop some comfort with participation formats that are likely to come up again and again, so teachers have to find the balance between accommodating students' differences and introducing them to new ways of interacting. Some multicultural educators speak of forging hybrid cultures in the classroom—where elements of students' home cultures are maintained alongside typical U.S. classroom features (Banks, 1988; Gutiérrez et al., 1999).

An informed perspective on dialects (and not necessarily a linguist's exhaustive knowledge of all the features of students' dialects) goes a long way toward making the classroom a place where students can both be themselves and acquire new skills. Because language and identity are so bound up with each other, rejection of a student's language can jeopardize that student's sense of belonging in the classroom. No one should have to compromise his or her personal and social identity for the sake of acquiring additional language skills or doing well in school.

Building positive relationships with parents is dependent on good communication. Schools often focus on problems of parents' understanding English or invest energy in getting translators. Of course, when a translator is needed, schools should make that investment. However, often the communication problems go deeper than the actual language code to cultural misunderstandings. That is why a good translator actually interprets, often explaining the rationale for many school practices. Understanding when parents (and their children) may encounter cultural conflicts between home and school is essential to fostering good communication and parent comfort with the school. A basic knowledge of how to monitor conversation with parents is useful for improving home-school communication.

Notes

1. Face has been defined as "the favorable social impression that a person wants others to have of him or her" (Lustig & Koester, 1999, p. 274, citing Goffman, 1967).

2. The instructional conversation is discussed again in chapter 6.

3. The term *language variety* is used to refer to any form of a language, whether a geographical or social dialect, a patois, a creole, or some other code of a language. Most speakers of a language use a variety that differs in recognizable ways from the standard variety; none of these varieties is in any sense inherently inferior to the standard variety in grammar, accent, or phonology (Corson, 1994). At the same time, these sociocultural and geographical variations within a language are signaling matters of great importance to those who use them. Varieties serve valuable group identity functions for their speakers; they express interests that are closely linked to matters of self-respect and other psychological attributes. It follows that all language varieties deserve respect and recognition in education.

4. All this means that there is greater diversity in language varieties than most people realize, and this kind of language knowledge is highly local and context specific. Sometimes it is not easy to make teachers aware of differences that only they themselves are in a position to discover.

5. The term "vernacular" tends to refer to "the current spoken daily language of a people or of a geographical area, as distinguished from the literary language used primarily in schools and in literature" (Pei & Gaynor, 1969, pp. 228–229).

6. A *pidgin* is a simplified code that is based on two languages, (e.g., Hawaiian and English). It does not have a fully developed syntax and is usually used for basic cross-cultural interactions like business dealings. A *creole* is a complete language that may grow out of a pidgin but retains features of its two forebears.

For Further Reading

Adger, C., Christian, D., & Taylor, O. (Eds.). (1999). *Making the connection: Language and academic achievement*. Washington, DC: Center for Applied Linguistics.

Delpit, L. (1995). *Other people's children: Cultural conflict in the classroom*. New York: New Press.

Frank, C. (1999). *Ethnographic eyes: A teacher's guide to classroom observation*. Portsmouth, NH. Heinemann.

Hollins, E. R. (1996). *Culture in school learning: Revealing the deep meaning*. Mahwah, NJ: Erlbaum.

Trumbull, E., Rothstein-Fisch, C., Greenfield, P. M., & Quiroz, B. (2001). *Bridging cultures between home and school: A guide for teachers*. Mahwah, NJ: Erlbaum.

Wolfram, W., Adger, C.T., & Christian, D. (1999). *Dialects in schools and communities*. Mahwah, NJ: Erlbaum.

Chapter 3

Language Acquisition and Development in Young Children

Beverly Farr

In chapter 1, we cited Wong Fillmore and Snow (2000), who present a strong case for making sure that teachers have a solid foundational knowledge of language, specifying what teachers need to know and be able to do to educate children to meet the high standards that have been set by various organizations for all subject areas over the last decade. One important area of understanding is language acquisition. In this chapter we synthesize what linguists have learned about how children learn their first language and discuss the implications for that information for classroom instruction. We provide examples of applications of this knowledge to the design of instruction. Children's language development continues throughout their school years and beyond. Thus, it is very beneficial for teachers to understand the processes the children used to master the elements of language in order to continue supporting their language development in school.

Understanding How Children Learn Language

Teachers may wonder why it is important for them to learn about and understand how very young children learn to use their native language. Although the importance of understanding the language development of school-age children or of second-language learners may seem obvious, it is also very worthwhile for teachers to understand the process of language acquisition as it unfolds in very young and preschool children, because it reveals important information about the ways in which children learn. Such information provides a good basis for designing instructional opportunities for school-age children.

> New research evidence and theories have given us insight into language and language development to use in developing new criteria for building sound, effective instructional programs. Viewing language as social-personal invention puts the teaching and learning of literacy in a new light. It can now be seen as a natural extension of language learning. That makes it possible to think in terms of building on what children already know, working with them rather than at cross purposes to them. (Goodman, 1996, p. 83)

Understanding the normal course of development of a first language also helps teachers to assess the kind and level of linguistic demands imposed by various classroom tasks, vis-à-vis their students' developmental levels. It aids in making judgments about which language skills may need more explicit instruction and when a student needs to be referred for a language evaluation.

Efforts to apply linguistics to pedagogy are not new. Many applied linguists and educators have tried over the years to translate linguistic knowledge—and in particular sociolinguistic theories of language learning—into recommendations for curriculum and instruction. These new works reemphasize and clarify the importance of ensuring that teachers are equipped with this knowledge.

> Teachers need a thorough understanding of how language figures in education, and for that reason, they must receive systematic and intensive preparation in what we will call *educational linguistics.* A thorough grounding in educational linguistics would support teachers' undertakings overall, and in particular their capactiy to teach literacy skills (see Snow, Burns, & Griffin, 1998) and to work with English language learners (see August & Hakuta, 1997). (Adger, Snow, & Christian, 2002, p. 9).

Children as "Little Linguists"

Scholars who have conducted extensive research on the language learning of children often describe their behavior as that of "little linguists" (Bohannon & Warren-Leubecker, 1985, p. 187) because young children demonstrate a great facility for taking in enormous amounts of oral data—analyzing, testing hypotheses, and producing language samples that reveal a gradual and largely predictable development in their understanding of the phonological, morphological, syntactic, and semantic systems of language. Their behavior shows that they are using productive principles rather than imitation to master all of these systems (Berko, 1958; Bowerman, 2000; Pinker, 1984). Children accomplish this feat without any formal lessons and with models that are far from perfect. They learn in the context of communication that is meaningful and of sufficient personal importance to sustain their attention.

The far-from-perfect models referred to above are provided to children by their parents or primary caretakers—family members, siblings, and others who come into their experience. The models are imperfect because they vary in idiosyncratic ways—individuals all express their own dialectal variations and are inconsistent in using syntactic and semantic structures. They respond and interact using a conversational style that reflects incomplete sentences, short phrases and clauses, colloquial expressions, slang, and even invented expressions.

Young children also hear people interact in a variety of registers. That is, family members or acquaintances talk to each other about a wide range of topics, varying the level and vocabulary of interaction depending on the participants in the interchange and the social context within which they are speaking. They change their language in response to situational variables. For example, siblings interact with age-mates in ways that are very different from the ways in which they interact with parents and the ways in which their parents interact with other adults. When any of these children or adults interacts with the language-learning baby or young child, they also adopt a variety of interactional styles. Some adopt styles that have been given specific labels such as "baby-talk" (Ferguson, 1977) or "motherese" (Newport, 1976). Despite all this variety in the input—or perhaps because of it—young children are able, over a very compressed period, to master the fundamentals of a highly complex linguistic system. In cases in which they receive roughly equivalent inputs from more than one language, they are able to master more than one and become bi- or even trilingual. How is such an unbelievable feat accomplished?

Children learn language with such apparent ease that it is common to underestimate the task that they accomplish. Since we do not typically witness children learning thousands of languages around the world, we do not consider how miraculous it is that simply by being immersed in the linguistic pool, they figure out the sounds that are relevant to the particular language (or languages) they hear and induce the complex rules that govern that language. How they accomplish this feat has been studied and theorized about for centuries. Owens (2001) asserts that in the seventh century B.C., Psammetichus I, an Egyptian pharaoh, studied two children who were raised with sheep and heard no human speech. He did so in order to determine the "natural" language of humans, which he undoubtedly expected to be his own. St. Augustine and Charles Darwin also wrote about language development.

What Motivates Children to Learn Language?

It may be useful to consider briefly what theorists have said about *why* the human infant begins to communicate—in the prelinguistic phase. Like other aspects of child language development, this consideration has also been debated. The debate is not over the fact that human beings learn a language because communication achieves a goal, but, rather, over the nature of the goal. Some have put forth the theory that communication is driven by the ability to use tools to obtain desired ends, whereas others make an "intersubjectivity" argument, which portrays communication as being driven by a desire to share thoughts and feelings with others (Reddy, 1999). The former is in keeping with Piaget's theory of development during the sensorimotor period (the first 2 years of life), which he divided into six stages. Piaget saw language as another tool that the child uses and that it emerges as a result of a change in sensorimotor intelligence.

Other theorists have supported a greater independence for language development, but in the Piagetian sense language is a reflection of changes in thought (as discussed in chapter 1). The "tool-use" theory has maintained a high degree of support as the reason that children develop language, but it seems intriguing to consider the possibility of both goals collaboratively serving to drive the development of language. This would also resonate with Halliday's taxonomy of language functions (see "Sociolinguistic Theory" below), which can largely be divided between the use of language to get things done and the use of language to express oneself. In any case, knowing these potential goals for even the earliest communication in infants can be helpful in developing instructional programs that support such goals as they are pursued through children's school careers and lives.

Theories of Language Development

Various theories of language development have competed for acceptance over many years, and none has been found to be fully acceptable for describing an inordinately complex process for learning a language and for learning to communicate in that language. In chapter 1, we described what language is—its various features, elements, and units. This provides a basis for understanding some of what a child learns when he or she learns language. Theorists have also struggled to describe the process of learning language. Teachers will, perhaps, appreciate a similarity to the controversies that have surrounded efforts to understand how children learn to read. In summarizing the competing theories about language learning, Owens (2001) suggests that it may, in fact, be possible that none of the theories proposed to explain language development completely explains the process that children undergo. "In each case, linguists have imposed adult classification models upon child language. Children may be organizing their worlds in very nonadult ways as they play and explore, as they fantasize and create, and as they think and speak" (p. 64). A colossal challenge is understanding how a child goes from an immature linguistic system to a full-fledged adult linguistic system. What are the mechanisms that propel such development? Here we discuss the most important theories that have been offered to explain language development in children.

Different scholars use different terminology to classify the various theories, but regardless of the terms used, they seem to represent an evolution in thought about language development. That is, as a theory was put forth, empirical evidence that was gathered suggested that the theory was inadequate to explain the complexity of the process. Early language research (at the turn of the 20th century) was more or less anecdotal, and data collection was inconsistent. Many of the studies conducted during the 1930s and 1940s are referred to as "count studies" because they measured the frequency of language behaviors.

Behaviorist Theory

The predominant theorists of the mid-20th century proffered a behavioral description of language development; they considered language to be a subset of other learned behaviors. Language was seen as a set of associations that were learned through the process of relating a stimulus and a response. Complex behaviors were considered to be chains of stimulus-response sequences. B. F. Skinner's well-known treatise on language as a learned behavior was *Verbal Behavior* (1957). According to this view of language learning, parents provide modeling and reinforcement and thus establish the child's repertoire of sounds. Language, in this view, is learned through a process of imitation, practice, and selective reinforcement.

Other theorists saw numerous limitations to the behaviorist notions of language development, and the one who became the most prominent advocate for what has been called a nativist, mentalist, or psycholinguistic theory, Noam Chomsky, wrote a review of Skinner's work pointing out the inadequacies of each of the elements in the proposed behavioral process. Parents, Chomsky explained, reinforce only a small percentage of children's utterances. He further observed that they rarely respond to grammatical correctness, only to the accuracy of what children say. Similarly, he noted that children use imitation sparingly beyond age 2 and that adults provide a poor model for imitation.[1]

Nativist Theory

Chomsky's nativist view is that at least some aspects of language are innate and are part of a child's biological makeup, rather than a product of learning. Chomsky referred to the innate or inborn language-acquisition mechanism as the "language acquisition device" or "LAD" (Chomsky, 1965). Theorists who espouse this point of view see evidence of it in all the various aspects of language development—pragmatic, phonological, lexical, and grammatical (Pinker, 1984). Some theorists have argued, for example, that infants are born with the intention to communicate. Others assert that the speed of word learning would be impossible without innate structures to facilitate such lexical development. Indeed, support for this family of theories is found primarily in the fact that the sheer complexity of what a child learns suggests that he or she must be in some way "hardwired" (genetically programmed) with the fundamentals of language learning. Plunkett and Schafer (1999), for example, reviewed studies on the perceptual abilities of infants and found that "Long before they are capable of understanding or producing speech, infants appear capable of making judgments about speech sounds which resemble the judgments made by mature speakers" (Barrett, 1999 p. 51). They further report that although adults have trouble discriminating between pairs of similar sounds that do not form phonetic contrasts in their own language, "infants from the ages of 6 to 10 months have little difficulty making such discriminations." The authors refer to the infant as a sort of "universal phonetician" (p. 52).

Cognitive Theory

Alternative theoretical positions that have been put forward suggest that language is not genetically specified as a separate kind of cognition but that it is secondary to general cognitive development, and language is dependent on that development (Bates, Bretherton, & Snyder, 1988; MacWhinney, 1999; see also chapter 1). Some of the same research findings that are used to support the in-nateness hypothesis are interpreted in a different fashion to support the argument for learning and development. For example, although it is true that infants have strong phoneme discrimination abilities from the outset, these abilities undergo significant developmental changes during the second half of the infant's first year as he or she is exposed to more and more language (Barrett, 1999).

Psycholinguistic Theory

In contrast to the behavioral emphasis on language production, psycho-linguistic theorists of the late 1950s and 1960s emphasized language form and the underlying mental processes that are represented by these forms. Building on the specific, innate capacity for language, these so-called Chomskians and neo-Chomskians believed, humans rely on a set of underlying language rules to de-velop languages that differ only superficially.

> Although the LAD is innate, linguistic input is needed to activate the analysis
> mechanism. Hypotheses are formulated on the basis of the speech the child
> hears. Often ungrammatical, this linguistic input cannot serve as a com-
> plete model for language learning. However, it is regular enough to enable
> the child to extract linguistic rules based on his or her innate knowledge
> (Owens, 2001, p. 44).

Owens (2001) refers to this model put forth by the psycholinguistic theorists as the "syntactic model" because it emphasizes the universal grammatical rules of language that are evidenced in the language that children develop. In this model, each language is composed of a limited set of basic sentence structures and transformations of those structures. Chomsky later updated this model to account for the great diversity in human languages and explain the development of grammars by children who learn language by being presented with very lim-ited input. This model has been criticized on the grounds that it ignores seman-tics, phonetics, and pragmatics. Critics argue that a full description of language must include meanings, or semantics and the purposes to which people put lan-guage. As noted earlier, a theoretical evolution has resulted from efforts to give a full accounting of the complexity of language development.

Semantics-Based Theory

The movement toward a theoretical stance that included a consideration of semantics was signaled with the work of Lois Bloom (1970), who analyzed the language development processes of three children. She found that using a syn-tactic analysis technique such as Chomsky suggested was inadequate to explain the language structures she observed in the children. This change in stance was referred to as the *semantic revolution* and represents an important shift in under-standing language development in children. It was theorized that the semantic basis for language develops prior to syntax. In the semanticist's view, children learn to use language to talk about things they know; that is, thought precedes language.

From the perspective of this theory, the ability of a child to put semantic relationships into language reflects the development of cognitive structures in a child (see "Cognitive Theory" above and chapter 1). Thus, one's ability to understand the concept of object permanence (in the Piagetian sense) is reflected subsequently in one's use of language to describe appearance and disappearance. Some theoreticians have studied what they called the "semantic bootstrapping hypothesis" to examine the development of syntactic-semantic relationships in child language, and it has been supported to some degree by research. Essentially, the hypothesis is that children use semantic notions that they have developed as "evidence for the presence of grammatical entities" (Rondal & Cession, 1990). Thus, although a child may not have exact words for grammatical categories (noun, verb, adjective), he has some notion that some words "name things" and others "indicate actions." He uses this information to further develop his categories and to apply the rules for how they work to produce clauses and to comprehend speech. A child who is learning a second language can use what she knows about semantic categories and relationships in her first language to learn the structures and relationships in the second language (see Teacher Note box nearby).

Bloom observed that a child's language did, in fact, reflect simple word-order rules, but she also found that by doing a semantic analysis and applying what was called a "rich interpretation," two-word utterances typically used around 18 months of age could be interpreted differently within different contexts. Thus a child who says "Mommy book" might be asking to have her mother read, describing whose book it is, or indicating that her mother has the book. Bloom and other semanticists identified the major semantic relationships of early language. This approach cast some doubt on the innateness hypothesis, since the presumption was that semantics was a way of representing mental experience and that all children developed language in similar patterns of cognitive development rather than on the basis of innate structures (Owens, 2001).

Teacher Note

Teaching Second Language Learners
The concept that children learn to use language to talk about what they know and that it parallels their cognitive development has implications for considering an instructional approach for second-language learners. Such learners have a storehouse of meanings, and they have one linguistic system in place to express meaning. They simply have to learn to use the underlying meaning and graft the new language onto it. Teachers need to use what children know about the world and about language to help them learn a new system. That is, they can draw on both on the content of what they know (e.g., common story structures) and the cognitive strategies they have learned to use to figure out the world (e.g., predicting, deducing, making inferences) to develop competence in a second language.

Sociolinguistic Theory

In the evolution of language acquisition theories, the semantic and cognitive theories were limited in that they did not clearly explicate the reasons for language acquisition—the nature and purpose of a child's transactions within a social context (Owens, 2001). Both the syntactic and semantic theories relied on an analysis of structural units. Sociolinguistic theory focuses on the communicative context and the unit required to convey information. The analysis is centered on the functions of language. With such an analysis, it is possible to examine the language produced in terms of what it reveals about the speaker's knowledge of the listener and by the context in which the language takes place—including not only the setting, but also the status and history of the participants. Muma (1978) identifies two broad functions of language—the *intrapersonal* and *interpersonal* (as did Vygotsky, 1962). The first is used for memory, problem solving, concept development, and other ideational functions, whereas the second function is communication.

Michael Halliday (1975a, 1975b) contributed significantly to this sociolinguistic theory knowledge base with studies that began with his analysis of the language development of his son, Nigel. Through this study, he produced a speech-act taxonomy and asserted that a child was able to use adultlike functions around age 2. Halliday's taxonomy is described in Table 3-1, with definitions adapted from Pinnell (1975). (See also the following Teacher Note box for instructional implications.)

Table 3-1. Functions of Language*

Instrumental	Used to get what we want, to satisfy needs or desires. In later stages, takes on forms of persuasion and argument.
Regulatory	Used to control behavior of others, getting them to do what we want them to do.
Interactional	Used to establish and define social relationships (negotiation, encouragement, expressions of friendship). Language used to establish relationships, work cooperatively, and enjoy companionship. Effective use of this function is an important factor contributing to personal success in life.
Personal	Used to express individuality and personality. Expression of strong feelings and opinions. Though often neglected in classrooms, personal language enables children to relate their own lives to subject matter, establish identities, and build self-esteem and confidence.
Imaginative	Used to create a world of one's own, express fantasy through dramatic play, drama, poetry, or stories. Unless fostered, can disappear in later years and hamper children's ability to write with imagination.

cont.

Heuristic	Used to explore the environment, to investigate, to acquire knowledge and understanding. Heuristic language is used for investigation, for wondering, for figuring things out. Though it should enjoy predominent use in classrooms, it is often underused.
Informative	Used to communicate information, to report facts or conclusions from facts—the language of school. Includes recall of acts, synthesis, inference, and conclusions.

*Another function of language, discussed in chapter 1, is the metalinguistic function. Language can be used to talk about language, to reflect upon itself.

Other sociolinguistic research has focused on units beyond the speech act and has examined the development of turn taking, topical structures, and conversations. In all of this, it is clear that the role of a child's various communication partners is critical in facilitating his or her language development. For example, the infant's early reflexive behaviors lead to responses by the primary caregiver that, in turn, allow the infant to learn to communicate his intentions (Snow, 1977; Trevarthen & Aitken, 2001). These skills are then refined through repeated interactions. Although the infant's early utterances may not be easy to interpret, the various caregivers treat them as meaningful social communication.

Teacher Note

Using Language Functions to Plan Instruction

The important role played by a child's communication partners has strong implications for the role that teachers play in the classroom as children continue to develop language in their school years. Gay Su Pinnell (1996) developed a useful list of activities based on Halliday's taxonomy of language functions that teachers can insert in their daily instructional program. The following is adapted from Pinnell's list and is presented according to Halliday's language functions.

Instrumental Language
1. Be accessible and responsive, but teach independence by having children state their requests clearly and effectively.
2. Encourage use by providing help and direction to peers.
3. Analyze advertising and propaganda to see how people use language to get what they want.

Regulatory Language
1. Create situations that let children be in charge of small and large groups.
2. Find instances of inappropriate use of regulatory language in order to teach appropriate use.
3. Attempt to decrease teacher use of regulatory language.

cont.

Interactional Language

1. Create situations that require children to share work areas or materials and talk about how they will do it.
2. Find ways of having small-group discussions on various topics and subject areas.
3. Let students work together to plan field trips, social events, and projects.
4. Whenever possible, mix children of different ages, sexes, races, and language proficiencies in work or discussion groups.
5. Have informal social times and participate yourself in talk that is not "all business."

Personal Language

1. Use personal language to give permission to children to share personal thoughts and opinions (use caution, though, as some parents do not want their children to be encouraged to share personal details of their family's lives).
2. Be willing to listen and talk personally when possible. Converse with children when you have the opportunity.
3. Provide some comfortable, attractive areas in the classroom where children can talk quietly.
4. Encourage parents and family members to visit and participate in the classroom.
5. Read stories or books that prompt a personal response from students.

Imaginative Language

1. Create situations that elicit spontaneous dramatic play.
2. Read stories and books that feed the imagination and are a stimulus for art, drama, and discussion.
3. Provide time for children to talk in groups and/or with partners before they begin their writing on imaginative topics.

Heuristic Language

1. Structure classroom experiences to revolve around interest and curiosity.
2. Create real problems for children to solve.
3. Put children in pairs or work groups for problem-solving activities.
4. Use heuristic language to stimulate such language. Saying things like "I wonder why" can promote such language in children.
5. Try projects that require study by the whole class, including the teacher. Find questions to which no one knows the answer.

Informative Language

1. Plan activities that require children to observe carefully and then to summarize and draw conclusions from their observations.
2. Require children to keep records of events over time and then look back at them and draw conclusions, such as keeping records on classroom pets.
3. Use questioning techniques to elicit more complex forms of describing or reporting.
4. Have children give reports to small groups and encourage feedback and discussion.

Adapted from Pinnell (1996)

Factors That Affect Language Development

Ninio & Snow (1988) point out that it is the social interaction surrounding language input that makes language acquisition possible. Maternal expressions are most often function specific; that is, they serve a single function and are used repeatedly for that function. Thus they become predictable and provide a basis on which a child can figure out semantic and syntactic categories. The consistent set of behaviors on the part of the mother (playing games like "peekaboo" and "this little piggy") enables children to predict outcomes and to anticipate what will come next.

The important observation is that "the degree of parental responsiveness appears to be positively correlated with later language abilities" (Owens, 2001, p. 60). Owens goes on to explain that parents respond by expanding the form or extending the meaning, by replying or commenting, imitating, or giving feedback. They also provide a simplified model of adult speech. "Thus, the language-development process is a reciprocal one involving the language-developing child and a 'socializer-teacher-nurturer' who is a competent language user" (Holzman, 1984; cited in Owens, 2001, p. 61).

There are a number of environmental factors that contribute to a child's acquisition of language, and these, too, have implications for classroom instruction that would promote language development. The most obvious is that young children must hear a language in order to acquire it. It is not enough, however, for a child to listen to a radio or to language as it occurs on television. Sachs, Bard, and Johnson (1981), for example, reported on a case study in which the child of deaf parents was exposed only to television and developed a very abnormal linguistic system. For children to learn language successfully, language must be in the form of interactive, social speech.

There have been numerous studies of the linguistic input or caretaker response—its characteristics and effects. Many researchers have noted the fact that caretakers react to errors of content in children's early utterances much more frequently than to errors in form. The form of the response has also been shown to have differential effects. For example, in an important study by

Teacher Note

Linguistic Input in the Classroom
The findings cited here represent ones that are suggestive of appropriate linguistic input in the classroom. That is, it is most conducive to children's language development if you respond using relevant conversational replies, and the level of the reply should include vocabulary and linguistic structures that are just above their level of functioning. This means that children should hear higher level vocabulary and more complex sentence structures than they typically use, in order to increase their linguistic power. This is particularly true for young children, who are still refining and expanding their syntactic structures as well as building their vocabulary. It is also true for students who are learning a second language and those who use a nonstandard dialect and must be exposed to appropriate models so that they may shift their register when the situation calls for it.

Cazden (1968), replicated by Feldman (1971), it was demonstrated that relevant conversational replies accelerated language development more than expansions. An *expansion response* enlarges or extends the child's expression, such as "The doggie is running" in response to a child's saying, "Doggie running." A conversational response to this expression would be "Yes, and isn't he cute" (Cairns, 1986).

There are clearly some properties of language input that are essential if a child is to succeed in acquiring language.

> If a child heard only discourse about international affairs in sentences with
> structures far beyond her processing ability, she would undoubtedly never
> learn language. On the other hand, if she heard only language at her own
> level, she would never receive sufficient information to make progress.
> (Cairns, 1986, p. 7)

One study revealed a level of speech to which children respond best that is evocative of Vygotsky's *zone of proximal development*;[2] that is, speech that is just a bit above their current level of functioning (Shipley, Smith, & Gleitman, 1969). (See the previous Teacher Note box for suggestions of appropriate response strategies in the classroom.)

The Language Skills of Preschool Children

There is considerable value in understanding how much language children know when they come to school and how they attained that knowledge. This information has direct implications for how their language development continues throughout their school years and how best to support such development. For teachers of primary school children, this understanding will provide guidelines for assessing the status of children's language development as they begin school. For teachers of elementary and secondary school students, it will provide insights into vocabulary development, ways to support reading comprehension, and strategies for supporting the development of writing skills. In addition, for teachers of students from so many parts of the world, such information can help them to understand the use of different dialects and the process of learning a second language.

In describing the complexity of the task faced by a language-learning child, Barrett (1999) goes through the following impressive litany:

> In order to master this [linguistic] system, a child has to: analyse and seg-
> ment the acoustic signal of speech as it is produced by other people, and
> identify within that speech stream the units of the language which is being
> spoken at the multiple levels of phonemes, morphemes, words, and sen-
> tences; master all of the complexities of the intricate articulatory patterns
> necessary for producing individual phonemes and sequences of phonemes;
> master the set of phonological rules which govern how phonemes may be
> combined to form syllables, morphemes, and words; acquire the enormous
> number of individual lexemes which constitute the lexicon of the language

which is being learnt, and map all of these lexemes individually onto their appropriate meanings and word-forms; acquire the complex set of morphological and syntactic rules which dictate how the morphemes and words of the language can be combined, organised, and sequenced into grammatically well-formed sentences that encode particular meanings; master the various communicative functions of language, and how each one of these functions should be linguistically realised in different contexts; master the skills which are necessary for participation in a successful conversation, including turn-taking, topic-continuation, adaptation to the other, etc.; and master the skills which are necessary for producing discourse, including those required for coherence, appropriate sequential organization, adaptation to the listener, etc. (pp. 8–9)

Consider the fact that the basics of this learning process are mastered by the time the child is age 2! It is also important to realize, however, that the process continues into early adolescence and beyond, and this is where the teacher can play a very significant role.

Cognitive Development

Bowerman (1974) identified cognitive factors that need to be present for a child to acquire language:

- Ability to represent objects and events not present
- Development of cognitive structures related to space and time, classifying types of actions, embedding action patterns, object permanence, relationships between objects and actions, and a model of one's own perceptual space
- Ability to derive linguistic-processing strategies from general cognitive structures and processes
- Ability to formulate concepts and strategies to serve as structural components for the linguistic rules

Generally, these cognitive abilities develop during the first year of life. Early development suggests that the child's early sensorimotor interactions help him to develop a process for organizing stimuli from the world, and there is evidence that—contrary to some claims—imitation may be an early foundation for building language. As a child continues to explore the world and learns to represent reality in symbolic ways, he develops the ability to use language to represent referents.

As a child develops the concept of "object permanence," he begins to be able to represent objects that are not present. Apparently, representational capacity depends on the child's being able to conceive of a world outside the here and now, apart from her own moment-to-moment sensations and interactions with the environment. (See also discussion of development during the sensorimotor period in chapter 1.)

Stages of Language Development

Descriptions of language development in the youngest humans are often provided based on a series of stages. Important stages are often characterized as: neonates, 2–3 months, middle of first year, 7–12 months, and 12–24 months. Owens (2001) gives similar periods very descriptive names: 1–6 months: Examiner; 7–12 months: Experimenter; and 12–24 months: Explorer. (In Tables 3-2, 3-3, and 3-4, we have adapted material from Owens to provide indicators of young children's development in cognition and communication.)

Neonates

Understanding communication in neonates serves as an important starting point for understanding the phenomenal accomplishment of human beings in learning language. Findings from research show that human infants are already predisposed at birth to be interested in people, particularly those aspects of people that are relevant to communication—faces and voices. This fact lends some support to the notion of the predisposition toward language as being innate. Infants show preferences for voices over other sounds, for sounds within the human voice range, and for their mother's voice over other female voices (De Casper & Fifer, 1980; Eisenberg, 1975; Friedlander, 1970). They also demonstrate an ability to discriminate variations in sound (e.g., between certain consonant and vowel sounds). The Teacher Note box on page 87 provides some information on how studies are conducted to determine that they are able to do this.

At this stage, the child acts reflexively and does not really engage in active communication. Within the next 4–6 weeks, however, changes can be noticed. The child expands his or her communicative behaviors, and there is more coherence to them. Social smiling begins to appear between 4 and 8 weeks, and by the third month, evidence of coherent responses and initiations sometimes involve the whole body. Babies' responses seem to be within a communicative interaction, and for this reason, they are often referred to as *proto-conversations*. These interactions show coordinated patterns and are done in coordination with the gaze, verbalizations, and gestures of the adult (Reddy, 1999). Table 3-2 summarizes the kind of development that tends to take place in the first 6 months, beginning with the neonate stage.

2–3 Months

Subsequent to the intensive interactions with primary caregivers, at 2 and 3 months, infants start to become more aware of their environment and to look beyond a caregiver who is interacting directly with them. In order to maintain the child's attention, the caregiver often makes rhythmic vocalizations or abrupt changes in sounds—actions that have been found to elicit the most laughter in children. These behaviors often become games or routines that many researchers have indicated are linked to the acquisition of social and syntactic rules (Bruner & Sherwood, 1976; Dore, 1983; Ratner & Bruner, 1978).

Teacher Note

Research on Infant Language

You might wonder how linguists are able to conduct studies that allow them to draw conclusions about a neonate's ability to discriminate speech sounds. They have devised a variety of ways to determine that infants recognize certain features of speech sounds. Eimas, Siqueland, Juscyk, and Vigorito (1971), for example, used a technique called *high amplitude sucking*. Infants are trained to suck an artificial nipple and are rewarded by repeated presentation of a sound. The more they suck, the more they hear the sound. They become bored by this repetition, and their sucking rate decreases, but if they detect a difference in the sound presented, the sucking rate increases. Interestingly enough, during the first six months of life, infants are actually better than adults at tasks that require sensitivity to contrasts in sounds.

Infants can even distinguish between sounds that are phonologically quite distant from their own language (e.g., a click contrast in Zulu). Adults, on the other hand, have difficulty discriminating between similar sounds that are not phonemic contrasts in their own language (For example, /l/ and /r/ are phonemic contrasts in English, but not in Japanese.) At around 1 year of age, the ability to discriminate between pairs of sounds from any of the world's languages disappears in infants, as they apparently hone in on the sounds of the language(s) of their environment.

Other studies use a technique of *conditioned head turns.* In this case, infants are conditioned to look at an interesting toy when they hear a particular sound. Presenting new stimuli, the researchers can determine if the learning transfers or whether the infant treats the new stimulus as equivalent to the training stimulus (Plunkett & Schafer, 1999).

Middle of First Year

Through the middle of the first year, the games and rituals or routines, which are initially a primary source of enjoyment, become opportunities for the young child to take the lead and even to initiate new games or routines. Notable here would be the familiar "towel over the head" game or other versions of "peekaboo." These games or rituals have a defined structure, typically consisting of "initiation, mutual orientation, greeting, a play dialog, and disengagement" (Owens, 2001, p. 166). Although not every exchange will have this exact structure, it is common enough that it is an interesting precursor to conversations using language. Again the child is seen to be taking in linguistic data and then manipulating or playing with it to figure out how the language system works—structurally and socially. Ruth Weir (1962) identified infants' tendencies to play with the sounds of language very early and wrote about it in *Language in the Crib*.

The first speech sounds that children utter are typically those that are the simplest to articulate and are present in the majority of the world's languages. Weir refers to them as the "pure stop consonants (voiced and voiceless, i.e., /b/ and /p/, /d/ and /t/, /g/ and /k/) and vowels." The sounds of /f/ and /s/ are known as "continuants" and come in later, and the last to be pronounced correctly are the "liquids," /r/ and /l/, and the "affricates," /c/ (as in church) and /j/ (as in juice). Various adaptations that involve simplification or assimilation of speech sounds occur as children are learning. Less complex sounds are often substituted for more complex ones. Final sounds may be reduced from voiced to voiceless, such as *bet* for *bed*. Through assimilation, sounds within words often take on characteristics of other sounds in the word based on similar points of articulation, such as *guck* for *duck*. Unstressed syllables may be deleted, such as *nana* for *banana*. Phoneme clusters may be reduced to the least complex sound, such as *pay* for *play*. These variations are typically due to the immaturity of the child's articulatory system rather than to any misperceptions of words, and, in fact, children often believe that their pronunciations are more nearly correct than they are.

Table 3-2. Stages in Young Children's Cognitive and Communication Development (1–6 mos.)

Cognitive Development	Cries from distress Prefers visual patterns Remembers an object that reappears within 2½ seconds	Visually prefers face to objects, regards own hands, and follows in a circle Repeats own actions Gets excited in anticipation of objects Increased awareness of environmental stimuli	Attains full focus; can glance smoothly between objects Visually searches for sounds Begins exploratory play; explores own body Stops sucking to attend to parent's voice	Localizes to sound Stares at place from which object is dropped Remembers visually for 5–7 seconds Recognizes mother in group; senses strange places and people	Begins to play Visually follows a vanishing object; recognizes familiar objects; anticipates whole object after seeing a part, is capable of 3–hour visual memory Explores objects by mouthing and touching Remembers own actions in immediate past	Looks and reaches smoothly and quickly Inspects objects Reaches to grab dropped objects
Communication	Responds to human voice, which usually has quieting effect Cries for assistance Makes pleasure sounds	Distinguishes different (speech) sounds Makes more guttural or throaty cooing	Coos single syllable (consonant-vowel) Turns head when hears a voice Responds vocally to speech of others Makes predominantly vowel sounds	Babbles strings of consonants Varies pitch Imitates tones Smiles at person speaking to him or her	Vocalizes to toys Discriminates angry and friendly voices Experiments with sound Imitates some sounds Responds to name Smiles and vocalizes to image in mirror	Varies volume, pitch, and rate Vocalizes pleasure and displeasure; squeals with excitement, intones displeasure
Age in Months	1	2	3	4	5	6
Piaget's Sensorimotor Stages	1 – Reflexive	2 – Coordination of sensory schema	2 – Coordination of sensory schema	2 – Coordination of sensory schema 3 – Repetition of actions of others	3 – Repetition of actions of others	

Adapted from Owens (2001)

7–12 Months

According to Piaget, a child is in the fourth stage of the sensorimotor period from 8 to 12 months and exhibits the first evidence of thought. The child can identify a goal and think about how to attain it before pursuing it. In this period, the child also becomes interested in exchanging objects with others. This leads to the development of new games and routines—opportunities to expand and extend language. She now starts to deliberately produce actions that will get attention. She will demonstrate a developing sense of mischief by violations of routines, noncompliance, offer-and-withdrawal of objects, and disruption of others' actions (Reddy, 1999). Such behaviors show that a child is able to understand the attentional and emotional reactions of others. She also begins to cooperate with commands and prohibitions.

It is during the second 6 months of life that an infant begins, then, to assert more control (see Table 3-3). With each success in communicating intentions, she is motivated to communicate more and better. The primary modes at this point are gestural and vocal. As caregivers recognize the infant's increasing ability to follow conversational cues, they make more references to objects, people, and events, and the infant demonstrates more selective listening (Owens, 2001). The infant is more compliant with simple requests, responding and imitating simple behaviors, such as waving bye-bye (What American baby *hasn't* been taught to do that?). At about 8–9 months, the infant begins to show *intentionality*, exhibited when he encodes a message for someone else—considering the audience. She may touch her mother to get her attention and make signals or gestures toward objects. Functions such as requesting, interacting, and attracting attention are fulfilled first prelinguistically and later through language (Bialystok & Hakuta, 1994; Owens, 2001).

Table 3-3. Stages in Young Children's Cognitive and Communication Development (7–12 mos.)

Cognitive Development	Visually searches briefly for toy that disappears Imitates a physical act in response Sorts by size Remembers that jack pops up at the end of jack-in-the-box song	Can store color and form separately; recognizes object dimensions Prefers novel and relatively complex toys Explores shape, weight, texture, function, and properties (e.g., in/out)	Recognizes object dimensions Uncovers object if observes act of hiding first Anticipates outcome of events and return of persons	Points to body parts Attains a goal with trial-and-error approach Searches for hidden object but usually in a familiar place	Imitates increasingly Associates properties with objects	Can reach while looking away Uses common objects appropriately Searches in location where an object was last seen Imitates an absent model
Communication	Plays vocally Produces several sounds in one breath Listens to vocalization of others Recognizes different tones and inflections	Listens selectively Recognizes some words Repeats some words Repeats emphasized vocabulary Imitates gestures and tonal quality of adult speech	Produces distinct intonational patterns Imitates coughs, hisses, tongue clicks, "raspberries," etc. Uses social gestures Uses jargon May respond to name and "no" Attends to conversation	Imitates adult speech if sounds in repertoire Obeys some commands	Imitates inflections, rhythms, facial expressions, etc.	Recognizes own name Follows simple motor instructions, especially if accompanied by a visual cue ("bye-bye"); reacts to "no" intonation Speaks one or more words Practices words he knows and inflection; mixes word and jargon
Age in Months	7	8	9	10	11	12
Piaget's Sensorimotor Stages	3 – Repetition of actions of others	4 – Known means applied to new problems				

Adapted from Owens (2001)

Linguistic Input

Maternal (or caretaker) input is very important for the infant's communicative development. The language used is often systematically modified and has been called *baby talk* or *motherese*, characterized by short utterance length and simple syntax. In the interest of supporting comprehension, mothers (and others) often paraphrase or repeat. Their speech often reflects high rates of redundancy. They also restrict their content to the here and now.[3] *Responsivity* is also crucial in early development. The consistent recognition by the adult of the infant's attempts to communicate and the tendency to provide an appropriate response contribute significantly to the emergence of early communication (Hanzlik & Stevenson, 1986; Siegel-Causey & Ernst, 1989).

Mothers also use common patterns of *paralinguistic variations* in terms of pitch and loudness, rhythm and timing. Interesting is that "there are many similarities in intonation across parents from languages as different as Comanche, English, French, Italian, German, Japanese, Latvian, Mandarin Chinese, Sinhala, and Xhosa, a South African language" (Owens, 2001, p. 179). There are identifiable interactional patterns evident in infant-caregiver communication as well, but there are variations that reflect cultural differences. In mainstream American culture, mothers are the primary communication partners, and their interactions are identified through gaze, facial expression, facial presentation and head movement, and *proxemics*, the use of interpersonal space. In many other cultures, the occurrence of extended families offers multiple caregivers and different types of linguistic input.

Mothers in some other cultures tend to speak less often to their children, but they engage in other communication activities found less frequently in American culture. Mothers in the United States are more information oriented. Japanese mothers may use language as much as American mothers, but they use it less for teaching and more for engaging their children (Lebra, 1994). They, as well as mothers from Mexican-American and American Indian communities, tend to expect children to learn through observation of adults and older siblings (Delgado-Gaitan, 1994a; Lebra, 1994; Suina & Smolkin, 1994; Valdés, 1996).

Mothers from different cultures respond to different types of utterances. It is also important to note that within a culture, race, education, and socioeconomic class influence maternal behaviors as well. In some cases, children are expected to learn more through observation than interaction. Shirley Brice Heath documented language behavior in African American communities in South Carolina and found that children's cries and vocalizations often went unheeded because they were not seen as being capable of intentional behavior (Heath, 1983).

Syntactic Development: Words and Early Linguistic Structures

Children typically begin producing words around the end of the first year. What follows is a relatively slow period of word acquisition (around 50 words) up to about 18 months, when they experience a *word spurt*. Subsequent development focuses on the grammatical system and refinement of the phonological system. The first 50 words have a simple syllable structure. After the word spurt, development involves elaboration of all of the speech sounds, with a period of systematic errors. Their receptive vocabulary is much larger than their expressive one. A child who uses 50 words might understand 250, for example. During the one-word stage that continues through the second year, children build productive vocabularies of several hundred words. Not surprisingly, children initially acquire terms that label objects and actions commonly encountered in their immediate environment, and this is remarkably similar for children acquiring the same language or different languages (Dromi, 1999; Slobin, 1970). Their early vocabularies consist of a combination of nominals (largest percentage; general and specific nouns), action words (*give*, *do*, *up*), modifiers (*mine*, *no*, *funny*), personal-social words (*no*, *please*), and functional words (*this*, *for*). Table 3-4 maps out the typical course of development from 15–24 months.

Overextensions and Underextensions

One aspect of lexical development in children that has been well documented is *overextension*, the use of a word for a class of referents, some of which may be outside the adult category (Clark, 1993). For example, the child may learn the word *doggie* and then extend that to all four-legged animals. Children also exhibit *underextension* in which their use of the word *doggie* might apply only to a stuffed brown dog they own. Use of the terms *up* and *down* may be restricted only to situations involving motion and not appropriately extended to description of locations of objects (e.g., Smiley & Huttenlocher, 1995). These instances reflect the child's hypothesized meanings; the child regularly receives feedback about them and, with increasing experience, uses fewer and fewer overextensions or underextensions (Clark, 1979).

Combining Words

Children begin to combine words into longer utterances at about 18 months of age, and they do so in predictable patterns that appear to be universal. This development coincides with increasing memory and processing skills. During the second half of the second year, the child produces longer utterances by recombining earlier patterns. Prior to the actual appearance of two-word utterances that express apparent semantic or syntactic relationships, he typically produces sequences of words, sounds, and gestures in a variety of combinations and forms. When a child begins to produce two-word utterances, he does so apparently by applying rules constructed for the particular words. Small words such as prepositions are left out. At this level, the meaning given to the utterance may be difficult to interpret. Word order provides some cues to meaning, but the utterance can easily be ambiguous. For example, a child who says "Mommy bed" may be attributing ownership, suggesting that it's time for bed, or requesting to be put to bed. Intonation and gestures or movements also provide clues to meaning. When about half of the child's utterances consist of two words, he then begins to use three-word utterances, most commonly in the form *agent + action*

+ *object*, such as, "Daddy throw ball," and *agent* + *action* + *location,* such as "Mommy sleep chair" (Owens, 2001).

Table 3-4. Stages in Young Children's Cognitive and Communication Development (15–24 mos.)*

Cognitive Development	Imitates small motor acts	Recognizes pictures Recognizes self in mirror Remembers places where objects are usually located Uses a stick as a tool Imitates adult object use	Knows shapes Sits alone for short periods with book Notices little objects and small sounds Matching objects with owners Recalls absent objects of persons	Matches familiar objects Comprehends *one* and *many* Recognized when picture in book is upside down
Communication	Points to clothes, persons, toys, and animals named Uses jargon and words in conversation Has four- to s-x-word vocabulary	Begins to use two-word utterances Has approximately 20-word vocabulary Identifies some body parts Refers to self by name "Sings" and hums spontaneously Plays question-answer with adults	Likes rhyming games Pulls person to show something Tries to "tell" experiences Understands some personal pronouns Uses *I* and *mine*	Has 200-300-word expressive vocabulary; names most common everyday objects Uses short, incomplete sentences Uses some prepositions (*in, on*) and pronouns (*I, me, you*) but not always correctly Uses some regular verb endings (*-s, -ed, -ing*) and plural *s*
Age in Months	15	18	21	24
Piaget's Sensorimotor Stages	5 – Experimentation			

Adapted from Owens (2001)

*Owens does not specifically address 12–14 months.

Social psychologist Roger Brown (1973), who conducted a seminal study of children's early language, described the period when evidence of children's syntactic development emerges in this way:

> I think that the first sentences express the construction of reality which is the terminal achievement of sensorimotor intelligence. What has been acquired on the plane of motor intelligence (the permanence of form and substance of immediate objects) and the structure of immediate space and time does not need to be formed all over again on the plane of representation. Representation starts with just those meanings that are most available to it, propositions about action schemas involving agents and objects, assertions of nonexistence, recurrence, location, and so on. But representa-

tion carries intelligence beyond the sensorimotor. Representation is a new level of operation which quickly moves to meanings that move beyond immediate space and practical action. (p. 200)

In describing children's syntactic development, Tomasello and Brooks (1999) adopt a constructivist perspective through which they specify that children learn gradually, "beginning with more concrete linguistic structures based on particular words and morphemes, and then building up to more abstract and productive structures based on various types of linguistic categories, schemas, and constructions" (Barrett, 1999, p. 161). They ground their description in an understanding of the scenes that make up children's lives—someone pushing, pulling, or breaking an object; objects moving up, down, or into a container (Slobin, 1985). Children respond to such scenes, in these theorists' view, by partitioning them into components using different linguistic elements for each of the components, and using syntactic symbols such as word order and case marking to identify the role of the components in the scene. They further describe how children have different communicative goals with respect to the same basic scene—they may ask a question about it, request that someone make it happen, report on it, or mark its occurrence with a movement or gesture. So for example, "Ball roll" may fulfill any of the goals noted above and constitute a scene in the child's life.

In contrast to other researchers who have described children's syntactic development in terms of lexical or phrasal elements—nouns, verbs, subjects, objects—Tomasello and Brooks (1999) focus on linguistic constructions. This seems to be a useful approach because it describes more accurately what children do with language in the early stages. The authors identify four stages in children's acquisition of these linguistic constructions: (a) holophrases (12 months)—use of a single linguistic symbol to communicate their intentions about an entire scene; (b) word combinations (18 months)—use of multiple words to express their communicative intentions, usually dividing the expression into two component parts; (c) verb island constructions (24 months)—use of syntactic marking such as word order to specify participant roles in a scene; and (d) adultlike constructions (36 months and older)—expression of communicative intentions by filling in relatively abstract linguistic constructions. Table 3-5 provides a summary adapted from explanations presented by Tomasello and Brooks.

Summary

To this point, we have discussed children's acquisition of some basic linguistic structures. Some key milestones are as follows: The ability to distinguish sound categories is determined in the first year or two, and the ability to produce all sounds of the language and their appropriate combinations is acquired by the time a child enters first grade—and often much earlier. Children also know the rules for forming words and governing syntax by 5 years of age.

Table 3-5. Major Steps in Syntactic Development in Young Children

Form	Purpose/Use	Examples
Holophrases (12 months)	Request or indicate existence of objects	*Doggie; naming*
	Request or describe recurrence of objects or events	*More, Again, Another*
	Request or describe dynamic events involving objects	*Up, Down, On, Open*
	Request or describe the actions of people	*Eat, Kick, Ride, Draw*
	Comment on the location of objects and people	*Here, Outside*
	Ask basic questions	*What's that?; Where go?*
	Attribute a property to an object	*Pretty, Bad*
	Use performatives to mark specific social events and situations	*Hi, Bye, Thank you, No*
Word Combinations (18 months)	Used to talk about same basic scenes as holophrases	*Lemme see*
	Different words used to indicate different components of the scene	*More apple*
	One event-word used with a wide variety of object labels	*Allgone sticky*
	Consistent ordering of pattern of event-word and participant-word	*Gone juice*
Verb Island Constructions (24 months)	Verbs serve as organizational focus	*Draw apple on paper.*
	Word order or grammatical morphology to indicate participant roles in a scene	
Adult-like Constructions (36+ months)	Relatively abstract marked for whole classes of scenes	*He falled me down.*
		She's gonna pinch it on my foot.
		I'll brush him his hair.
		I'll capture his whole head off.
		He got dunked.

Adapted from Tomasello & Brooks (1999)

Semantic Development: Vocabulary

Although aspects of all systems of language continue to be developed and refined after 5 years of age, the child's command of the language is largely complete by the time he or she enters school. Word-meaning acquisition is the one exception, however, because it continues throughout one's lifetime.4 The typical 2-year-old uses between 50 and 600 words and adds an average of 10 words per day, reaching a vocabulary of approximately 14,000 words by the age of 6. Once they enter school, children are exposed to 10,000 or more new words each year and add 3,000 or so to their vocabulary. An adolescent who graduates from high school, is likely to know more than 50,000 words. An adult may easily have a vocabulary in excess of 100,000 words. The development of word knowledge is a key aspect of a child's semantic development, the aspect that develops most significantly throughout one's lifetime. The word meanings developed by children are inferred without direct teaching by adults. Only part of a word's overall meaning is stored in a child's memory, but researchers speculate that a child uses a "fast-mapping" strategy that allows the child to make a connection between a word and its referent after only one exposure.

Teacher Note

Carol Chomsky's Research on Classroom Exposure to Books

Children of school age are still actively engaged in acquiring their native language. "Language development is much slower than during the preschool years and not as noticeable as in the earlier years, but studies show that it continues in much the same manner as with younger children." Chomsky made this statement in a discussion of some research on language development she conducted with children between the ages of 6 and 10. She found that children progressed at very different rates and that "(A)ge was not the whole story. What was different about the children in the study. who progressed quickly. . . . compared to those who moved along more slowly? Chomsky found that children's independent reading was related to their linguistic stage. "Apparently it doesn't matter whether children listen to a book read aloud or read it themselves. What is important is the exposure to the language of books. Written language tends to be more complex than speech, and children who read benefit from a range of linguistic inputs that are unavailable to the child who has no access to books." Chomsky also states: "It would be useful to teachers to read aloud to children regularly, and to encourage them to read widely on their own, for pleasure. Books as complicated as children are willing to tackle are a good idea. For other suggestions, see *Reading Is Only the Tiger's Tail*, where ways to encourage classroom reading are engagingly described."

Cited in Pinnell (1980, pp. 56–57)

In addition to learning words from the context of everyday conversation as well as sources such as radio and television, children expand their vocabularies significantly through storybook reading with their parents or other caretakers. "Especially helpful for children are the contextual discussions that accompany the narrative" (Senechal, 1997). This has implications for activities in which we should have children engage during school to advance their language development (see Teacher Note box on page 95).

One of the interesting features of a child's vocabulary development is the tendency to invent words when gaps exist because he or she has forgotten or never known a word. So, for example, a child may say, "I'm spooning [stirring] my coffee," or "You sugared [sweetened] your coffee." "The pond is icellated [having heard *isolated*]." Often these invented words reflect adult practices; a child hears *fisherman* and *policeman* and subsequently coins *cookerman* and *pianoman*, or overgeneralizes from *house* and *houses* to construct *mouse* and *mouses*. This observation of common linguistic structures created by children also reflects what was mentioned at the beginning of this chapter as a child's tendency to operate as a "little linguist," or to play with language. The teacher should take advantage of this inclination and give children many opportunities to play with, have fun with, and manipulate language.

Pragmatic Development

Pragmatic development along with the development of imaginative language discussed in the following section are two aspects that are not as commonly thought about when we consider how well a child knows a language. Pragmatic development is the process of learning to use a language for practical purposes (discussed in chapter 1). During the preschool years, the child learns some conversational skills, typically beginning with a focus on the here and now. Gradually, as he or she learns conversational formats and routines, they serve as a scaffolding, which, in combination with developing cognitive abilities, allows the child to talk about nonpresent referents—usually around 18–24 months. In these situations, the primary communication partner—the mother or primary caretaker—relies on shared knowledge of known or routinized events (or scenes) to engage in conversation. "Remember when we went to the zoo yesterday?" "In a few minutes, we'll do your bath." The child also engages in monologues or self-conversations that again promote development through practice. In general, the young child is good at introducing new topics but doesn't sustain them beyond one or two turns. In contrast, a 5-year-old can often sustain certain topics through about a dozen turns. There is an increase in overall talkativeness around 36 months of age (Owens, 2001).

Development of Imaginative Language

The 2-year-old can also use language in imaginative ways and to express feelings. These affective responses typically double between the ages of 3 and 4. The child also begins to gain an understanding of shared assumptions. Thus she knows that she doesn't have to say all the words to communicate. In response to a question such as "What are you doing?", she knows she can communicate accurately by saying, "Playing" (Owens, 2001).

By age 4, children can adopt different registers, or assume various roles, with language. Typically, they will use pitch and loudness to convey the role of a parent, nurse, teacher, or store clerk. The child's ability to vary register depends on age and experience, and there are some notable gender differences: Girls tend to do it more.

Using Language to Get Information

Children use language to ask questions or to get clarification. Many of these uses are nonverbal, as, for example, a confused expression. They often seek general information using expressions like "What?" and "Huh?" Often they are unable to state the question more clearly because they have trouble determining what is misunderstood.

Maintaining a Topic

By age 2, a child can maintain a topic for consecutive utterances, but it is not until between the ages of 2 and 3 that he or she is able to maintain the coherence of a topic more, typically through enacting scenarios or engaging in sociodramatic play. The preschool child thus becomes increasingly adept at knowing what information to include (developing background assumptions about a listener's knowledge), how to arrange it, and which lexical items and forms to use (Owens, 2001).

Making Requests

Everyone is familiar with the preschool child's use of language to give directives and make requests. By age 2, the child can use some attention-getting words with gestures and increasing volume or rising intonation, but she is often unsuccessful (and adults often ignore the commonly used "Hey!", although they frequently emphasize the importance of using "please"). By age 3, a child begins to use modal auxiliary verbs by asking, "*Could* you give me . . .?", "*Can/may* I have . . .?", or "*Do* you have . . .?", but he is still generally ineffectual in making requests by the time he enters school. This is an example of an area where a primary school teacher could provide opportunities for young children to learn effective ways to (a) gain someone's attention, (b) state the goal, (c) be aware of social roles, and (d) be more persuasive and creative.

Engaging in Oral Narratives

Oral narratives differ from conversations in that they contain different organizational patterns and are decontextualized—that is, they do not focus on an experience within the immediate physical context. Children have a basic understanding of familiar events and the positions of actions at the beginning, middle, and end of sequences even before the occurrence of their first words (DeLemos, 1981). Although 2-year-olds have some basic patterns for familiar events, referred to as *scripts*, they are not able to describe sequences of events accurately

Teacher Note

Oral Narrative Types Used by Young Children
- Recount: Tells about past experiences in which the child participated or observed or about which the child read.
- Eventcast: Explanation of some current or anticipated event. Children may use it to direct others in imaginative play sequences (e.g., "You be the teacher. You tell the children to go outside").
- Account: Spontaneous narrative in which children share their experiences, but the listener usually does not share the accounted experience.
- Fictionalized story: Story with endless content variation created with a known and anticipated pattern or structure. Usual pattern is one in which main character must overcome some problem or challenge.

until about age 4 (Kemper & Edwards, 1986). Nevertheless, children younger than 4 can talk about things that have happened to them, and their accounts are typically characterized by a high degree of evaluative information ("It was yucky," "I hate that kind," "I cried").

It is important to note (and this applies to the foregoing discussions on the development of other language components as well) that the preponderance of language development research has been done on White, middle-class children—sometimes the children of linguists! (This is not as true for some of the socio-linguistic research and cross-cultural studies.) We mention this here because some interesting research on the development of children's narratives has delineated differences based on the language communities within which children are raised. Emerging narratives reflect different cultures (Heath, 1986). Although children from all cultures hear and produce at least four basic narrative types, the distribution, frequency, and degree of elaboration of each of them varies greatly. Stein (1982) has identified the three factual genres as *recounts, eventcasts,* and *accounts;* the fourth is *fictionalized stories* (see Teacher Note box on Oral Narrative Types).

Stories created by 2- and 3-year-olds typically center on highlights of their lives and may have a vague plot. Themes are often about some disquieting event or something disruptive or extraordinary. Early stories often lack identifiable beginnings, middles, and ends.[5] A sense of a time frame is usually vague or nonexistent. By the time a child is 4, however, there is significant evidence of an understanding of *story*, and this has significance for a teacher's approach to story as soon as the child comes through the schoolhouse door. (See Teacher Note box on Story Grammar[6]).

Teacher Note

Story Grammar Lessons[6]
The use of a story grammar framework (setting, characters, plot, structure, attempts at problem resolution, and resolution) is one of the most commonly researched instructional techniques. The goal of story grammar lessons is helping students to develop adequate summaries of narrative texts. *Adequate* is defined largely as a recitation of the key elements of the story—the story grammar elements listed above (Allington, 2001b, p. 99).

The elements of event knowledge are seen in the narratives of four-year-olds. Underlying every story is an *event chain*. Events include actions, physical states such as possession and attribution, and mental states such as emotions, dispositions, thoughts, and intentions that are causally linked as motivations, enablements, initiations, and resultants in the chain. Causal explanations contain many of these same features. (Owens, 2001, p. 290)

By the time most children enter school, they are familiar with all four types of narration, and they are expected to use these forms. For children from nonmainstream cultures, this can present a challenge. Chinese-American children, for example, are encouraged to give accounts within their families but not outside the household (Owens, 2001). Heath (1983) reports that in some White working-class southern communities, recounts are controlled by the questioner and are the predominant form during the preschool years. Accounts do not come into being until children attend school, and children and young adults seldom tell stories. Southern African-American working-class children, however, produce mostly accounts or eventcasts and rarely give recounts. School expectations are usually those of the majority culture. The differences in linguistic development in the area of narratives may place students from minority or bidialectal children at a disadvantage (see chapter 5).

Teacher Note

Phonemic Awareness in Children
Preschool children's awareness of phonemes, the speech sounds that correspond roughly to individual letters, has been shown to be highly predictive of their ability to learn to read. A child's level of phonemic awareness upon entering school is the strongest single determinant of the success he or she will experience in learning to read. Research indicates that "without direct instructional support, phonemic awareness eludes roughly 25 percent of middle-class first graders and substantially more of those who come from less literacy-rich backgrounds" (Adams, Foorman, Lundberg, & Beeler, 1998). Using this research as a basis, a number of approaches and programs have been developed (including one by the authors just cited) that can be incorporated in the primary instructional program. The program, *Phonemic Awareness in Young Children: A Classroom Curriculum,* can be ordered from the publisher by visiting its Web site (www.pbrookes. com). Other programs (as well as assessments of phonemic awareness) are available, or teachers can incorporate strategies that support such development in their own programs once they have gained an understanding of the aspects of awareness that need to be developed.

Language Learning in School-Age Children
What Children Know About Language?[7]

Adults are able to do more with language than use it. They are able to think about it as an object, to be aware of it and make judgments about it. Very young, preschool children are not able to make judgments that require them to separate the form of language from its content. Around early school age, however, there seems to be an explosion of what are referred to as *metalinguistic abilities*, and these abilities appear to be related to the development of other cognitive abilities. Children's ability to think about language as an object includes the ability to recognize ambiguous sentences, judge whether sentences are well formed, identify sentence pairs that are paraphrases of one another, and indicate awareness of the phonological structures of words (see Teacher Note box on Phonemic Awareness). These metalinguistic abilities have been demonstrated to be related to reading ability that is, children with good metalinguistic abilities are also good readers. These skills also seem to be related to aspects of humor that flourish during this early-school period. In this regard, language becomes a source of pleasure as well as a vehicle for communication (Cairns, 1986). Children go through stages in developing their abilities to judge whether sentences are well formed, synonymous, or ambiguous. In the preschool years, children seem unable to judge the form of a sentence apart from its comprehensibility (deVilliers & deVilliers, 1972; Gleitman, Gleitman & Shipley, 1972). Thus, they would judge "Drink the chair" to be anomalous, but "Teeth the brush" would seem correct.

Around kindergarten age, they are able to discriminate ill-formed sentences, but it is not until around 5 to 7 years of age that they can provide an explanation (Hakes, 1980; Scholl & Ryan, 1980). Their ability to judge pairs of sentences as meaning the same thing develops around age 6, but it is not until about second grade that children can report on the ambiguity of sentences that depend on words with multiple meanings for their ambiguity (Cairns, 1986, p. 37). The ability to discriminate syllables in a word is possible for a child of 4, but it is not until about age 6 that children can segment a word into phonemes. The ability to read is based on the ability to perceive the relationship between letters and phonemes. The metalinguistic skill of phoneme segmentation is a necessary precursor to the ability to learn to read (Liberman, Shankweiler, Liberman, Fowler, & Fischer, 1977).

Aspects of Language That Continue to Develop Through School

The demands of the classroom require major changes in the way a child uses language. The child must learn to negotiate when he can have a turn to speak, for example, and he must respond in very specific ways to questions that are raised in the classroom. Language related to textbooks and the language of ideas become much more important than social, interpersonal language. The child is held much more accountable for the language she uses and must be more precise in his use of words. In addition to vocabulary—the most obvious area of development during their years in school—children develop more sophisticated understanding and use of certain linguistic forms. At the earlier stages, they continue to develop their phonological system as well as the morphological (word structures) and syntactic aspects of language. Through these and the next stages, they expand their semantic or meaning systems, their metalinguistic abilities, and their pragmatic uses of language (see chapter 5 for more detailed discussion).

Phonological Development During School-Age Years

By age 6, a child can identify syllables and recognize that language is composed of units identified in linguistic terms as phonemes, this is evident from his rhyming ability. From about age 7, a child can manipulate sounds in a word, such as by removing one sound from a word and identifying the word that remains: (*s*)*and*. By about age 8, a child can produce all English speech sounds competently, and many children are proficient well before that.

There are some other regular changes in English, referred to as *morphophonemic* changes, that a child learns gradually through elementary school. These occur when two morphemes (word parts) are placed together. So, for example, a word ending in /*k*/ becomes /*s*/ as in *electric* and *electricity*. The 5-year-old knows the rule for the regular plural /*s*/, as in *ants,* and its partner, /*z*/, as in *bugs*, but it takes longer for her to master the /*ez*/ as in *roaches*. There are also vowel shifts that are learned only gradually, continuing to about age 17 (e.g., *divine* and *divinity; explain* and *explanation; sane* and *sanity*).

Finally, stress or emphasis is also learned during the school years, with the period from age 3 to 5 seeming particularly important for several languages. In English, the relationship between two words and whether a word is a noun or a verb is signaled by stress: black *board* versus *black*board; high *chair* versus *high* chair; *pres*ent versus *pres*ent; *con*duct versus con*duct* (Owens, 2001). These patterns occur regularly in English (and other languages), and it is good practice to allow children to become aware of these patterns by playing with words and raising their consciousness of the regularity. This helps them to learn that English is more rule-governed than it otherwise appears (see the Teacher Note box below).

Teacher Note

Raising Children's Metalinguistic Awareness of Language

Carol Chomsky has done extensive work on children's language development. She encourages many experiences in the classroom that enable children to explore their language and become more aware of its forms, rules, and idiosyncrasies. "Language facility can be developed also through a more direct approach," she says. "I think that, starting in the upper elementary grades, it is effective to heighten children's awareness of language and their sensitivity to sentence structure and word meaning. Rather than teaching facts of grammar, I suggest providing ways for children to become aware of features of language that they know implicitly and use but have never had reasons to examine directly. What I recommend are linguistic consciousness-raising sessions." Chomsky goes on to suggest the following sample activities:

* **Sentence composition**. Children construct sentences under a variety of conditions. The result must be a grammatical sentence. Children must exercise judgment about grammar and acceptability in language and consider the form of the language. (Noam Chomsky's famous sentence, "Colorless green ideas sleep furiously" comes to mind.)

cont.

- **Alphabeteasers**. Children start with any letter of the alphabet and compose a sentence in which each word in succession begins with the next letter of the alphabet. (*Baby cougars don't eat fireflies.*)

- **Word grid.** Develop a grid with a single word in each box. Children form sentences by starting in one box and moving to a neighboring box, continuing until they form a plausible sentence.

- **Riddle language.** Children analyze riddles (the source of humor is often linguistic) to find out why they are funny. Chomsky offers this humorous example:
  Milkman: Are you sure you want twelve gallons of milk?
  Buyer: Yes, my doctor said that I have to take a bath in milk.
  Milkman: Do you want it pasteurized?
  Buyer: No, only up to my nose.

Chomsky reports that after a sixth grader had gone through a variety of such "consciousness-raising" activities, he was asked to compare the work to that of his language arts textbook. He answered that in his book, he learned new things like nouns and verbs. "Where do you feel you learned more?" he was asked. "Here," he replied, "because all this stuff makes you *think!*" This bears out the findings of numerous studies that the direct teaching of grammar does not have much benefit on children's language and writing.

Morphological and Syntactic Development During School-Age Years

During the school years, children continue to form rules as a result of exposure to oral language and text. Morphological rules that they refine include *inflectional suffixes*, although the main development is in the addition of prefixes (*un-*, *dis-*, *non-*, and *ir-*). The development of the latter is a very long, drawn-out process and continues into adulthood.

Derivational suffixes are those that change the class to which a word belongs (e.g., adding *-ment* to establish). They are first learned orally, although reading strengthens learning (Carlisle, 1987), and they are a very large set of word parts and have many irregularities. A general order of acquisition is *er* (*big*, *bigger*), *-y* (used to form adjectives, as in *fluffy*), noun compounds, and *-ly*. Mastery of these forms continues into adolescence. Some of these word definitions are taught directly, but in general, children use their knowledge of morphology and make generalizations to figure out new words. This is critically important, as less frequently used words are encountered more as they move through the grades and increase their reading grade level (Owens, 2001).

Comprehension of linguistic relationships increases throughout the school years. Children learn to differentiate between subject (*he* or *she*) and object (*him* or *her*) pronouns and manipulate adjective ordering within a noun phrase (*large, green creature*). The distinction between mass (*water*, *sand*, *sugar*) and discrete (*pencil*, *cup*, *house*) nouns is acquired slowly throughout the school years. Verb phrases are more difficult for school-age children than are nouns and noun phrases (most likely because of the difficulty of stating the underlying relationships), the use of particles (e.g., pull *off*, put *on*), auxiliary verbs, and the like.

Sentence production continues to expand during the school-age years and through adulthood. Sentences become longer, and embedded phrases and clauses are used. For instance, whereas a younger child may have difficulty with "the boy whom the girl invited to the party," an older one will likely process such a phrase with ease. Again, teachers can provide opportunities for children to play with the addition of words and with combining and embedding phrases and clauses to expand their sentences. Passive-voice sentences provide some difficulty for children, although they comprehend them by the time they are about $5\frac{1}{2}$. Production of them begins in the late preschool years. Owens (2001) provides the summary shown in Table 3-6, which highlights some of the developing linguistic forms with an identification of the ages by which children appear to master them.

Table 3-6. Summary of School-Age Child's Development of Language Form

Age in Years	Syntax/Morphology
5	• Produces short passives with *lost, left* and *broken**
6	• Comprehends parallel embedding, imperative commands, *-man* and *-er* suffix • Uses many plural nouns
7	• Comprehends *because* • Follows adult ordering of adjectives
8	• Uses full passives (80% of children) • Uses *-er* suffix to mark initiator of an action (*teacher*) • Is able to judge grammatical correctness separate from semantics
9	• Comprehends and uses *tell* and *promise*
10	• Comprehends and uses *ask* • Comprehends *because* consistently • Uses pronouns to refer to elements outside immediate sentence • Understands difference among *definitely, probably,* and *possibly*
11	• Comprehends *if* and *though* • Creates much with mass nouns • Uses *-er* for instrument (*eraser*)
13–15	• Comprehends *unless* • Comprehends all types of embedding

*These are equivalent to adjectives. A full passive such as "Carolyn was read a story by Mimi" is more challenging.

Metalinguistic Development During School-age Years

As described earlier, metalinguistic abilities appear during the preschool years, but children do not develop full awareness until age 7 or 8. There is wide variability in the mastery of metalinguistic abilities, with some children failing to acquire them without explicit instruction (Trumbull, 1984). This means that the child is able to judge grammatical correctness without being influenced by semantics.

> By kindergarten, the child is just beginning to separate what is said from
> how it is said, to separate referents from words, and to notice structure.
> Even so, school-age children may still judge correctness more on semantic
> intent or meaning than on grammatical form (de Villiers & de Villiers, 1972;
> Gleitman & Gleitman, 1979; Sutter & Johnson, 1990).

Some of these abilities are conscious, and some are not. A child of school age is able to judge if utterances are appropriate for a specific listener or setting. He is able to correct sentences that have been identified as being wrong (Gleitman, Gleitman, & Shipley, 1972; Menyuk, 1977). She can identify linguistic units and provide definitions of words, and she can construct puns, riddles, and other forms of humor (Cazden, 1974; Geller, 1981; Owens, 2001). However, these skills, such as tapping tacit knowledge about words (e.g., noting grammatical or semantic features); or defining words, continue to develop well into middle childhood and adolescence (Carroll, 1974; Snow, 1990a; Sulzby, 1980).

Instructional Implications for Vocabulary Development in Children

The question of how children acquire vocabulary (and knowledge of grammar) during the school-age years has been the subject of numerous research studies and considerable debate. What are the conditions under which optimal language learning takes place? The debate, as explicated by Elley (1997) in a report on his own research on the role of incidental learning, is framed by the following set of questions, all with practical implications:

- Do pupils learn new vocabulary best by direct instruction, word by word, or incidentally, by frequent immersion in meaningful language?
- Do children learn the grammar of a language best by deliberate classification of parts of speech and analysis of model sentences, or do they acquire it naturally by inference from authentic language input?
- Do young children learn to read best by systematic study of sound-symbol correspondences and regular word study, or by regular exposure to a rich diet of meaningful, interesting text?
- Do students learn to spell best by frequent rehearsal of words in lists, or by wide reading and regular writing?

Suggestions for how children learn new vocabulary include silent reading, regularly listening to stories read aloud, frequent conversation with mature language users, watching television, and deliberate study of word lists and dictionaries. Since television programs directed to children provide such a limited range of vocabulary, it has been ruled out as a significant resource. During the preschool years, conversation is a major factor, but typical oral interchanges do not extend children's word knowledge after they have learned to read. Deliberate study generally results in the acquisition of about 3,000 words per year. Elley (1997) concludes that the primary means for developing vocabulary are by reading silently and listening to others read, and he cites several studies in support of this premise. The studies on silent reading were conducted with students at various grade levels, by several different researchers, and on both first- and second-language learners. They provide a substantial body of evidence that there are significant gains in vocabulary as a result of wide reading of natural text, versus direct teaching of lexical items. Elley speculates that when exposed to unfamiliar words, the typical reader makes tentative hypotheses about meaning based on the context and retains this hypothesis until subsequent encounters allow for confirmation or revision.

Elley (1997) also reports on studies of reading aloud to children. His own research with ESL pupils in the South Pacific revealed substantial increases in word knowledge after the reading of just a single story. The increases became somewhat greater in subsequent presentations in which brief explanations were given of target words as the teacher read the story. "These studies were promising, as they supported the hypothesis that young children learning English as a second language can acquire much new vocabulary from stories read aloud to them, with and without some help from the teacher" (p. 9).

The findings of these studies were later confirmed in a larger study of students learning in their native language. The gains were greatest when the words occurred often in the story, were illustrated with pictures, and were surrounded by a helpful verbal context. In addition, the results were most pronounced with stories that were of high interest and engaging to the children. The gains were as great for the weakest readers as for the strongest ones, and a follow-up test showed a high level of retention. The treatment that included brief explanations produced the highest results. The good news here is that children can learn new words from stories, but the bad news is that this form of vocabulary building may be considerably less effective without the support of adult input.

In addition to the studies on vocabulary, Elley (1997) reports on studies of incidental learning of grammar. Citing research investigations that have shown that deliberate teaching produces no measurable benefits in students' writing or editing of English, Elley again reports on the aforementioned studies (the Fiji Book Flood project), which showed that elementary school students who were "exposed to a large supply of illustrated story books learned their English grammar structures more effectively than the control groups, whose lessons focused on the systematic study of the specific structures that were tested in the project" (p. 14). Furthermore, the enriched reading groups wrote much better and made fewer mechanical or grammatical errors. These studies illustrate the importance of children engaging in "meaningful conversations"—in this case with texts—to continue their language development.

Language Problems That Children Might Have When They Enter School?[8]

It is, of course, important to know when children evidence a linguistic variation that is, in fact, due to a specific disorder or impairment. There is sometimes a tendency to overdiagnose such problems, when the problem may be part of a child's (or family's) dialect, a linguistic feature of a child's non-English native language, or a physical problem. Communication disorders have traditionally been classified as organic (with some physical origin), nonorganic, or combined. Nonorganic causes would include such things as faulty learning or environmental deprivation (Owens, 2001).

Distinguishing Difference from Deficit

It is important for a teacher to know enough about such disorders to recognize them and to refer children when it is appropriate. She should also know enough about the features of the native languages (or nonstandard dialects) of children in her classroom so that she does not refer a student for speech therapy because of such features. For example, Spanish speakers may leave off endings or put an /e/ sound before words beginning with /sp/ or /st/ because it exists in common Spanish words such as *estudiante* and *español*. Speakers of African American Vernacular English (Black Language) may substitute *f* or *v* for /th/ sounds: *birfday* for *birthday*, *muvver* for *mother*. Students who speak a nonstandard dialect may be referred because their syntax includes verb forms that are considered ungrammatical. In such cases, students need to be immersed in language and to hear a model of Standard English on a regular basis. Teachers may explicitly cue students to the ways in which the dialects differ, but such students do not need to be treated for communication disorders.

Language Delay

Some children may be language delayed for a variety of reasons. Such children often show some form of impairment in all forms of language. These deficits often become milder as the child matures, and by 5 years of age, many children will have overcome any earlier delays. For children with some form of communication disorder, many speech-language pathologists use a developmental intervention strategy. Using this strategy, the clinician begins treatment at the lowest level of functioning and continues at that level until the child demonstrates competence with all aspects of language at that level. Language learning is not always so direct or linear, however, so such an approach can easily be done incorrectly or use such a fixed set of sequences that the approach is less than maximally effective (Owens, 2001). Nonetheless, it is not the classroom teacher's job to treat children with significant language delays or disorders. If there is doubt about a child's language ability, it is wise to consult a speech-language pathologist, but it is also important not to make premature judgments about a child's language development based on sketchy information.

Assessing Children's Proficiency with Language

In their book for teachers on language development, Power and Hubbard (1996) report on a kindergarten teacher, Vivian Gussin Paley, who "describes turning on her tape recorder in the classroom as a turning point in her teaching" (p. 71). She explained how the tape recorder helped her really hear her children. Paley, who is featured in the book, *Classroom Crusaders* (Wolk & Rodman, 1994), describes the "philosophical discussions about God, fairies, and robbers as well as speculative discussions about whether stones melt when they are boiled" that she heard after she began taping. Taping classroom interactions also gave her the opportunity to examine how she responded to children. Although the tape recorder can be an extraordinarily useful tool, it is nevertheless important to plan how to use it so that it will not become overwhelming or add too much to your teaching load. It is neither possible nor advisable to tape everything, but some well-timed snippets of classroom exchanges will provide a wealth of information.

Although some teachers actually transcribe the exchanges that they tape in the classroom, it is also possible for a teacher to listen to the tape and develop some anecdotal records of the quality and quantity of the language that one hears from individual children. The various pieces can be analyzed in terms of the following evaluation factors for determining the child's communication facility (Lilja, 1980).

Awareness. Is the child aware of language as a method of communication, serving specific purposes?

Spontaneous use. Is the child secure in the use of language, showing spontaneity in using it?

Use of nonverbal signals or body language. Does the child tend to respond to questions using signals—pointing, walking toward an object, head movements, hand symbols—rather than words to communicate?

Baby talk. Does the child have speech patterns that seem immature in word choice, pronunciation, or sentence structure? There will be developmental differences, but a second grader should be beyond this stage.

Dialect or regional language usage. Does the child use words or syntactical structures that occasionally prevent her from communicating effectively? Although adults may search for alternatives, a child may be unable to do so. It is the teacher's job to help a child learn how to *code switch*—to learn the forms and structures of the mainstream dialect so that she can switch into it when the situation calls for it or when effective communication is at stake.

Use of time-, place-, and thought-holders. How often does a child say "ya know" or "hm-hm" or "uh-uh" to hold a discussion position while thinking about what to say next? Although some of this is normal and common, some children may need to be guided to find words to communicate more effectively.

Word choice. Does the child seem to possess an ample basic vocabulary to enable smooth, comprehensive expression? Does he know the names of most objects, activities, and emotions encountered every day? Is there any attempt to use word variety in everyday speech? How often are baby talk and unusual words used instead of familiar, easily understood ones? Is there evidence of curiosity to know words and their meanings? Are there questions about or evidence of experimenting with words and sounds?

Sentence patterns. Is the child able to orally present a total thought, and in a complete sentence structure, when appropriate? Can the child use a variety of sentence structures, including questions and exclamations, with variations in word order?

Thought structure. Is the child able to structure ideas into clear communication units?

To collect information, Lilja (1980) suggests tape-recording or having an aide listen for specific language patterns. She also suggests that the teacher pay attention to the kinds of concepts or topics a child wishes to discuss and to listen to or record playground language. Finally, she proposes that the teacher plan and structure discussions with various thought-provoking questions serving as a stimulus. These should focus on questions requiring nonfactual answers to encourage spontaneous, free language usage.

"Discovering what children know about language, especially how well they understand the language forms used by teachers and in books, is an essential prerequisite to planning learning experiences for them," says Muriel Saville-Troike (1980). She adds that "testing what children know about language can be accomplished as an integral component of the ongoing interaction in the classroom, rather than an isolated, unrealistic activity" (p. 109). Saville-Troike makes the following suggestions for assessing various aspects of a child's competence with language.

Meaning. The most commonly tested area of language is vocabulary. A range of commercial assessments is available to assess vocabulary, and the most common format is to ask children to identify a picture or an object that is named. Abstract concepts or relationships are not so easily assessed, but one way is to check on a child's physical response to demonstrate the meaning of an action or of spatial and temporal relationships.

Phonology and grammar. It is relevant to test children who do not pronounce plural or past-tense endings for their understanding of the grammatical concepts of number and tense. One way to assess this understanding is through the use of nonsense words: one *wug*; two *wugs*.

Receptive knowledge about number, tense, and other points of grammar can be tested by asking children to identify which of a pair of spoken sentences correctly describes a picture or situation: "John is walking" or "John walked"; "Mary is cold" or "Mary has a cold"; "We have a hamster" or "We have hamsters"; "Bill is taller than Tom" or "John is taller than Bill."

The understanding of direct and indirect objects can be tested by placing objects on a table and asking children to follow directions such as "Give a horse to the doll" or "Draw a circle on the paper."

Intent (pragmatic competence). Children's understanding can be tested by asking them to paraphrase or provide a translation: "When I say 'Johnny, would you like to sit down now?', what do I mean?"

Social use. Both the testing and teaching of socially appropriate language can be accomplished by constructing role-playing situations with children taking different roles in different suggested settings (in the classroom, on the playground, at the dinner table). In such hypothetical situations, a purpose for the communication should always be specified, such as comforting someone who is hurt, requesting a toy or second cookie, or apologizing for breaking something. Teachers may also participate, making calculated mistakes in sociolinguistic behavior for children to identify.

Finally, the model for identifying functions of language developed by Halliday and described earlier in this chapter can be used as a basis for observing language use in the classroom (Pinnell, 1996). Two questions would frame the assessment: (a) To what extent is a child using the various functions of language and how effectively? (b) Which functions occur in the classroom—where, when, and under what circumstances? Which are being neglected? Pinnell suggests that the teacher observe the same child in several different settings in the classroom and in formal and informal activities in other areas of the school. The teacher should be familiar with Halliday's list of functions and record the variety of functions used by a child on a regular basis. A simple form might be developed for this purpose. By examining observational records, a teacher can determine which functions are being used and which are not and plan accordingly. For example, if little or no heuristic language is used by the children, the teacher might need to introduce materials or plan situations that stimulate curiosity and inquiry.

Reflections

Many, if not most, of the activities that are commonly part of the instruction in our schools are supportive of one or another aspect of language development. These situations can be optimized if the teacher is aware of language development processes and is more intentional and strategic when planning instruction—that is, if he deliberately designs activities that will promote specific aspects of both oral and written language development. Here we present three general guidelines to direct this approach.

1. Integrate listening, speaking, reading, and writing. In our daily experiences, oral and written language experiences most often co-occur and are not separated—that is, they occur together, integrated in specific communication events. When one person in a household reads the newspaper, for example, she will often comment about something that she has read to someone else. When bills arrive in the mail, discussion about the contents often occurs between members of a household. Many instructional activities in school also involve two or more of the language arts: A primary-grade teacher reads a picture book aloud, allowing children to make predictions along the way. He then asks the children to write a response to the story and to read it aloud with a partner when it is finished. "In school, you enrich each school day when you give children opportunities to interweave oral and written language for functional, meaningful learning purposes" (Peregoy & Boyle, 2001, p. 107).

2.   When focusing on language development, take into account grammatical forms, communicative functions, and social contexts. The teacher should consider phonology, morphology, and syntax and how they work together with semantics to create meaning. Students need to learn to use standard language forms and to adapt their register (or dialect) for different social contexts. Teachers should also develop specific activities to expand students' ability to use language to carry out a variety of communicative functions (review material on Halliday's functions of language). Establishing cooperative learning groups, for example, supports the interactional function, as identified by Halliday.

3.   Vary classroom activities as much as possible to enable flexible integration of language skills and the development of the various aspects of language (identified in no. 2). A characteristic of classrooms is that they often reflect a narrow range of instructional activities that lead to the same type of language use. While establishing routines in classrooms is important, too much sameness will not allow students to explore the richness of language and to practice using it for a variety of purposes, in a variety of contexts, and with a variety of styles.

Notes

1.   Some research suggests, however, that imitation takes on a larger role in autistic children and those with Down syndrome (Tager-Flusberg & Calkins, 1990).

2.   "Russian psychologist Lev Vygotsky (1896–1934) introduced a useful concept about learning and development when he pointed out that what the learner can do with assistance today, he or she can do alone tomorrow" (Peregoy & Boyle, 2001). He referred to this teaching opportunity as the *zone of proximal development*.

3.   Some have observed that mothers' modifications are not as systematic as claimed (Newport, Gleitman, & Gleitman, 1977).

4.   Of course, all aspects of language continue to develop; vocabulary growth is, however, the most dramatic area of change. Academic language and familiarity with a range of discourse patterns are other areas strongly influenced by schooling (see chapter 5).

5.   Not all storytelling traditions require that a narrative have a beginning, middle, and end.

6.   A story grammar in English consists of the characters, setting, and the episode structure of a narrative (Mandler & Johnson, 1977). There appears to be a sequence of stages in the development of children's understanding of English story grammars (Glenn & Stein, 1980). In addition, it has been shown that children who are sensitive to this underlying structure (or who become sensitive to it through instruction) exhibit better reading comprehension (Meyer, Brandt, & Bluth, 1978; Pearson & Camperell, 1981).

7.   This topic is addressed further in chapter 5 in the context of how literacy learning takes place.

8. This topic is taken up again, in the context of instruction, in chapter 6.

For Further Reading

Fromkin, V., Rodman, R., & Hyams, N. (2003). *An introduction to language.* Boston, MA: Heinle.

Power, B. M., & Hubbard, R. S. (1996). *Language development: A reader for teachers.* Englewood Cliffs, NJ: Prentice-Hall.

Tomasello, M. (2003). *Constructing a language: A usage-based theory of language acquisition.* Cambridge, MA: Harvard University Press.

Chapter 4

Second-Language Acquisition and Development

Beverly Farr and Katherine Richardson Bruna

Research on first-language acquisition has a long and developed history. The research base for second-language acquisition has been accumulating over a much shorter period, and much of it has relied on what we know about first-language acquisition. However, there are documented differences between first- and second-language acquisition, and what we know about those differences can help us to design instruction that meets the needs of second-language learners. In addition, knowledge of second-language acquisition processes can be useful to teachers in supporting the continued elaboration of their skills in all aspects of language. Perhaps most important is understanding the linguistic knowledge base that second-language learners bring to the task of learning a new language. They do not start from scratch but can use their existing knowledge of language (both its forms and functions) as a basis for new learning.

Alicia is a preservice teacher who attended a public elementary school in the United States as a young child. Recalling her school experience, she comments as follows:

> For me it was a culture shock to go into a school and realize that people spoke a language other than Spanish because in my community no one spoke English. When I first went to school, I kept waiting for someone to speak like I speak, but no one spoke like I spoke. I went home crying to my mom saying I didn't want to go back because I didn't understand what was being said. I felt lost.

Alicia had the experience that allows her to understand that teaching second-language learners requires more than a one-size-fits-all approach to instruction. She continues:

> I always see how they're culturally and linguistically different, and I think
> it's really important that you keep that in mind when you're teaching . . . If
> I were to go in there and teach, not appreciating who they truly are, I would
> not be doing my job.

Her "job" as a teacher is to give her students what she missed: an appreciation of the ability to speak two languages and to move between two cultures and
two worlds (Richardson Bruna, 2002, p.5).

All teachers need to appreciate the knowledge and skills that children bring
to school with them. Preservice programs often do not include adequate
coursework or information about language—the knowledge and skills that children have acquired through learning their first and second (or third) languages,
cultural influences on language, and how best to utilize this information to plan
effective instruction and assessment procedures.

This chapter will present information about theories of second-language acquisition, about how learning a second language is similar to and different from
learning a first, and the implications of the process of second-language learning
for classroom instructional practices. It is important to acknowledge that *all* teachers need such information. Although Alicia's personal experience as a second-
language learner certainly helps her to relate to her students, it does not necessarily
provide her with specific knowledge about the complicated nature of second-
language development or the insight for applying that knowledge to her instructional practice. Along with other teachers engaged in preservice preparation, she
will need to build up a repertoire of professional knowledge and skills to become
an effective teacher of English-learning students (Richardson Bruna, 2002).

Theoretical Perspectives on
Second-Language Acquisition

What It Means to "Know" a Language

This issue can be addressed for either an individual's first or additional
language(s), but it is addressed here in relation to second-language learning because there are a number of differences from learning one's first language, and
these differences are especially critical when a child is in a classroom where a
language other than his or her first is the language of instruction and learning. A
major question about children learning two languages is whether the learning of
either language resembles the process and path experienced by a monolingual
child. Very often it does not. Children learn second languages in many different
ways. If they learn their first and second languages simultaneously, their process
and path are arguably not the same as those of children learning (and being exposed to) one language. Among children learning more than one language simultaneously, there are also differences in the degree of exposure and the extent
of use of one or both languages (e.g., Who in the household speaks which language to the child—parents, a nanny, siblings, a grandmother? What opportunities does a child have to speak one or the other language? Which language is he
or she encouraged to use under what circumstances?).

Although we present a review of alternative models or perspectives on second-language learning, accumulating research demonstrates that it is far more complex than such models imply. "Learning a second language," in fact, "may challenge the very foundations of thought" is the way that Bialystok and Hakuta (1994, p. 110) put it. They point out that we learn much more than a set of words and rules, that we "adopt a set of values and a range of behaviors that are part of using that language" and that we may also modify our conceptual structures. They and other researchers have argued that the mind of a bilingual speaker actually has a different structure from the mind of a monolingual (see Albert & Obler, 1978). Keep this in mind as we explore the various theories that have been put forth to describe what it means to know a language and to explain second-language acquisition.

Views of Second-Language Learning

Theories of second-language acquisition tend to be divided between those considered to be formalist and those considered to be functionalist. The *formalist* views hold, in general, that there is a singular mechanism and a set of parameters—that is, an underlying abstract structure of language—that children must acquire, whereas *functionalist* views are concerned with understanding language in the contexts in which it is used. A formalist theory (such as the theories of Chomsky discussed in chapter 3) would predict greater similarity in the processes of learning a first and second language than would be predicted by a functionalist theory. According to formalist theory, whether second-language acquisition is simultaneous or sequential does not make much of a difference, because in both cases the process is guided by the mechanism of the language acquisition device and the constraints of universal grammar (both Chomskian notions).

Functionalist assumptions differentiate the sequence and timing of simultaneous and sequential second-language acquisition, because social interaction and previous knowledge are seen to play a major role. Resolving questions about these assumptions is not simple and defies empirical investigation. Studies of vocabulary acquisition, for example, have demonstrated a high degree of variability among children. To study the effects of bilingualism on vocabulary acquisition, one would need to compare the vocabulary of bilingual children in terms of its size, conceptual breadth, and sophistication to the vocabulary they would have had in each language if they had been learning only one (Bialystok, 2001). In the absence of such studies, comparisons are made among groups. Since the variability among individuals is so great, these comparisons do not provide a very sound basis for making judgments. Comparisons of the acquisition of other aspects of language (e.g., syntax, phonology) are somewhat easier to make. Based on what *is* known, "the predominant view regarding the way that children learn the *structure* of the two languages is that it is parallel to that found in monolingual children in each language" (Bialystok, 2001, p. 67; emphasis added).

Critical Period of Language Learning

Another concept that has had a strong influence on studies of language acquisition is the notion of a *critical period*—an age range within which it is possible for children to master a language quite easily. The theoretician most often associated with this concept is Eric Lenneberg (1967). Lenneberg's studies of individuals with brain injury revealed that if an injury resulting in loss of language function occurred after puberty, language recovery was virtually impossible. Some have extended this concept to second-language acquisition, but Lenneberg himself was more cautious when discussing second-language acquisition and noted that some adults learn a foreign language perfectly well "since natural languages tend to resemble one another in many fundamental aspects" (p. 176). It has long been held that children are generally more successful than older learners in learning a second language, and that a younger start usually yields a higher level of proficiency. More recent research, however, has demonstrated that other factors—social, input, and cognitive—play strong roles and can facilitate second-language learning for older learners.

> ## Teacher Inquiry
>
> **Student Study**
> For your own professional development or in collaboration with colleagues, choose a student on whom to conduct an action research project. What do you know about his or her second-language learning timeline? What kind of special services has he or she received and for how long? What do you know about his or her first-language proficiency? At what level is he or she literate in the home language? How might you discover this information? What could you learn from such information? Why might it be useful in your instruction of this student?

What is useful for a teacher to know from all this research, which is still struggling for definitive answers? The research does carry some implications for how teachers should approach instruction for English learners. Without landing conclusively on the side of either the formalist or the functionalist divide, one can reliably assume that there is, in fact, an underlying abstract structure of all languages and that teachers can help learners to discover this structure by doing things like making structural comparisons and identifying patterns across languages. Since we also know that children learn languages in different ways through social interaction and building on prior knowledge, teachers should be sure to construct a variety of situations and tasks and to use a variety of materials to help children engage with the language in diverse ways (see chapters 5 and 6 for examples.)

Theories of Second-Language Acquisition

Much of the research on second-language acquisition has drawn heavily on the research on first-language acquisition.[1] Thus, it has focused primarily on the development of linguistic structures—the morphological and syntactic features that are largely in place when a language learner reaches 5 or 6 years of age. Similar to the descriptions of the process of child language development discussed in chapter 3, the various theories fall along three lines: those considered *formalistic* (also referred to as *innatist*)—defining the process as one of deriving abstract linguistic knowledge from limited linguistic input; *cognitive*—those that have been propounded by cognitive psychologists, who include considerations of vocabulary and of pragmatic and communicative skills; and *sociolinguistic*— those that emphasize the social and interpersonal aspects of language acquisition. Views of communicative competence are essentially combinations of the latter two theoretical strands. Such theories are often also referred to as "interactionist."

Bialystok and Hakuta (1994) devised a useful and accessible organizational structure for discussing second-language acquisition theory, which they discuss in their informative book, *In Other Words: The Science and Psychology of Second-Language Acquisition*. They note that language learning takes

Teacher Inquiry

As you read the various theories presented here, as well as the section on factors affecting second-language acquisition, try to identify the channel (as outlined by Bialystok and Hakuta) that is the central focus of the theory.

place in a "complex ecology"[2]: "The full repertoire of our human nature, ranging from our cognitive machinery to our social and communicative needs, is engaged in the activity" (p. viii). Although Bialystok and Hakuta examine the process through five channels—brain, language, mind, self, and culture—they note that studies of language learning have most often approached the problem through only one of these channels.

We will now discuss second-language acquisition theories more specifically. Once again, it should be noted that the theories that have been put forth are less than totally explanatory and that the necessary research is difficult to conduct. Nonetheless, there are concepts from the research and other development work that has been done that are useful to teachers as they help students to meet the challenge of mastering a second language while also mastering a wide range of academic content.

Many labels that are given to second-language acquisition (SLA) theories are essentially variations on the three strands described above. As was noted in chapter 3 and in earlier sections of this chapter, the influence of the linguist Noam Chomsky has been far-reaching. He inspired a paradigm shift away from behaviorism, with its emphasis on language as observable behavior, toward mentalism, with its emphasis on language as abstract knowledge. For Chomsky, the work of linguists was to look for universal principles that govern a human being's innate talent for language learning. Because of his universalist focus, he overlooked the role that culture could play in language learning. Others have attempted to address this oversight. The theories discussed below are summarized in Table 4-1.

Table 4-1. Second-Language Acquisition Theories

SLA Theory	Theorist	Main Idea and Limitations
Acculturation	Schumann	Language—as one element of culture—forms a tie between the learner's community and the target language community. Second-language acquisition occurs as one acculturates to the target culture. Lack of a cognitive dimension.
Nativization	Anderson	Stresses internal processing mechanisms—assimilation and accommodation (similar to Piaget's notions). Learners simplify the learning task by forming hypotheses based on innate, language-specific knowledge. Adjusts internalized system to fit the input (McLaughlin, 1987). Little attention given to changes in individual motivation and attitude.
Accommodation	Giles et al.	Takes into account the manner in which social and psychological factors are subject to constant negotiation. How the in-group defines itself relative to the out-group may change constantly in accordance with shifting views of identity and the boundaries of group membership.
Discourse	Hatch	In adjusting their speech to negotiate speech with nonnative speakers, native speakers provide a type of input that shapes the rate and route of acquisition. It is through language use and interaction that second-language acquisition occurs. Through a variety of discourse opportunities, learners sort out how language is used.
Variable Competence	Ellis	Product of language is a continuum that spans from spontaneous communication (unplanned discourse) to lectures or reports (planned discourse). As a process, language use includes both linguistic competence and linguistic capacity.
Neurofunctional	Lamendella	There is a connection between language function and neural anatomy. Some parts of the brain contribute more to language function than others.
Monitor Model	Krashen	Five major hypotheses: • Acquisition and learning • Natural order • Monitor • Input • Affective filter

Acculturation Theory

One theory that has drawn attention to the important role of culture is Schumann's (1978) acculturation theory. An SLA view of acculturation recognizes that language, as a key element of culture, forms a tie between the learner's community and the target language community. The central hypothesis of this model is that "the degree to which a learner acculturates to the target language group will control the degree to which he acquires the second language" (Schumann, cited in Ellis, 1986, p. 251). What is missing from Schumann's model is a cognitive dimension. He says that social and psychological distance decrease input, but he does not try to explain what this means in terms of internal processing.

Nativization Model

Anderson's (1983) nativization model attempts to compensate for the lack of a cognitive dimension. The two general forces that guide SLA are, according to Anderson, the processes of nativization and denativization. "Nativization consists of assimilation; the learner makes the input conform to his own internalized view of what constitutes the L2 [second language] system . . . Denativization involves accommodation; the learner adjusts his internalized system to make it fit the input" (Ellis, 1986, pp. 253, 354). Nativization entails making the new language conform to an internal norm. Denativization, on the other hand, entails making use of inference strategies to orient one's approach to the new language around an external norm. Successful SLA is thus described as a developmental sequence in which the learner moves away from an internal and toward an external norm. Social and psychological distance, as described in the acculturation theory, may cut the learner off from input, and the effect is to impede the learner's development toward a denativized, or external, linguistic norm.

Limitations of Acculturation Theory and the Nativization Model

The acculturation theory and the nativization model do not attend to the ways in which input is influenced by contextual variables related to a particular communicative situation between the learner and the speaker of the target (new) language. Schumann talked about the relationship between the learner's social group and the target language community, but he did not acknowledge the dynamic and complex nature of this relationship. In contrast, Giles, Bourhis & Taylor (1977) recast these intergroup relationships as relative and dynamic, "subject to constant negotiation during the course of each interaction" (Ellis, 1986, p. 256). This negotiation results from the different perceptions of identity and social distance held by one group member toward another at any given moment. Giles et al. write that "people are continually modifying their speech with others to reduce or accentuate the linguistic (and hence) social differences between them depending on their perceptions of the interactive situation" (cited in Ellis, 1986, p. 257). (This identity dimension of language is discussed in chapter 1.) These modifications, according to Giles et al., are seen in their use of *ethnic speech markers*.

Accommodation Theory

Accommodation theory holds that a learner who is positively motivated toward the target community will deemphasize the use of these speech markers. This is called *upward convergence*. On the other hand, someone who is negatively motivated toward the target community will emphasize their use. This is called *downward divergence*. In any communicative interaction, the speaker may fluctuate between downward divergence and upward convergence in response to her ongoing perception of herself (as a member of her in-group) in relationship to the out-group community and her desire to mark the ethnolinguistic boundaries that exist between them. Giles et al. suggest that progress in SLA occurs when the overall pattern of the learner favors upward convergence; an overall pattern of downward divergence will result in fossilization, or lack of progress.

Discourse Theory

The interest in language use that we see in accommodation theory is also present in discourse theory. Just as Giles et al. suggest that speakers manipulate their linguistic repertoire to perform an action in the world (to strengthen or weaken their in-group membership during the course of a communicative interaction) and that patterns of such use may result in positive or negative SLA outcomes, Hatch (1978) suggests that it is through language use and interaction that SLA proceeds. The main principle of discourse theory is that native speakers, in adjusting their speech to negotiate meaning with nonnative speakers, feed to these learners a type of input that shapes the rate and route of acquisition. This input contains frequencies of various grammatical features that influence the order in which the L2 grammar is learned. "Thus," as Ellis (1986) explains, the natural route, accounted for by discourse theory, "is the result of learning to hold conversations" (p. 258). Or, as Hatch says, "social interaction may give the learner the 'best' data to work with" (cited in Ellis, 1986, p. 261).

Variable Competence Model

Like discourse theory, the variable competence model (Ellis, 1984) proposes that "the way a language is learnt is a reflection of the way it is used." The product of language use can be thought of as a continuum that spans from "entirely unplanned to entirely planned" discourse (Ellis, 1986, p. 266). Unplanned discourse is spontaneous communication, like everyday conversation. Planned discourse, like lectures or reports, is, in contrast, the result of advanced thought and preparation. Ellis draws a distinction between the ideas of language use as a product and language use as a process. As a process, language use includes both linguistic competence (knowledge of the rules of language) and linguistic capacity (knowledge of how to use the rules in discourse).

Neurofunctional Theory

Neurofunctional theory attempts to describe SLA by positing a connection between neural anatomy and language function. In general, it examines the roles played by two areas of the brain, the right and left hemispheres, shown to be closely involved in the comprehension and production of language. The right hemisphere is thought to be responsible for processing the routines and patterns of formulaic speech, and, because of this, is said to play a major role in the early stages of SLA and in the acquisition that takes place in informal settings. The left hemisphere, on the other hand, is associated with syntactic and semantic processing, with the motor operations involved in speaking and writing, and with creative language use. It is suggested that the neural circuitry in some of these areas develops (and fossilizes) earlier or later than others and that the differences in neural circuitry account for the different kinds of language processing (e.g., pronunciation or syntax). The fact that older learners have a much more difficult time attaining nativelike pronunciation in a second language than they do syntax is regarded as evidence for this claim (Ellis, 1986, p. 272).

Monitor Model

Several of the ideas included in some of the previously mentioned theories—the influence of affective factors, the importance of input, and the existence of a natural path for acquisition, for instance—were incorporated by Krashen (1981) into what became his well-known monitor model. It is by far the SLA theory that has enjoyed the most attention by language educators, but like all SLA theories, it has its share of weaknesses. Although it has been widely criticized, it provided a theoretical base for the "natural approach," which has largely changed second-language instruction in the United States (Díaz-Rico & Weed, 1995).

It may be apparent by this point that the theories discussed thus far do a better job of describing the situations in which, or processes through which, language learning is likely to take place than they do of describing the actual internal mechanisms by which L2 knowledge is internalized and used. In this sense, language learning—what goes on in the learner's head—is still relegated to a "black box." Krashen's monitor model, as we will see, gets us no further in this regard. What it does do, however—which is why it has achieved such prominence—is attempt to account for a relationship between the internalization of new knowledge, the storage of this knowledge, and its use.

Krashen's SLA theory has five major hypotheses. His model has been widely criticized, largely because several of the hypotheses have not been proven through empirical research (examples are given under each hypothesis). However, because the ideas behind these hypotheses have gained widespread acceptance within second-language teaching circles and have had such a profound impact on second-language instruction, they are described below. (Some information about instructional implications is presented in the Teacher Note box following these descriptions.)

The Acquisition-Learning Hypothesis. The acquisition-learning hypothesis is central to Krashen's theory. It attempts to explain how second-language knowledge is processed, how it is stored, and how it is used. Krashen uses the term *acquisition* to refer to the unconscious process of internalizing a second language. This unconscious internalization results from participation in natural communication, in which the focus is on meaning. Once knowledge of the second language is acquired, it is stored in the language areas of the left hemisphere of the brain and is available for automatic processing. Krashen believes that acquired knowledge serves as the major source of comprehension and production.

Krashen uses the term *learning* to refer to conscious study of the rules of language. This conscious learning results from formal (classroom-based, non-natural) language education, in which the focus is on form. What is significant about the acquisition-learning distinction for language educators is that acquired and learned knowledge are processed, stored, and used differently. Krashen's theory maintains that in order for knowledge to be available for automatic processing in tasks requiring comprehension and production, it must be acquired through communicative activities in which the focus is on meaning. The acquisition-learning hypothesis has had a tremendous influence on language instruction today as educators have turned to more communicative, proficiency-oriented tasks in their teaching.

Krashen's distinction of unconscious versus conscious knowledge is interesting and seems to make sense with respect to our own experiences with foreign and second languages, but Krashen cannot prove that the distinction exists in terms of separate cognitive processes. What exactly the learner does with input to make it available for controlled or automatic processing is a question Krashen does not answer. Another related critique is that acquisition and learning may not be entirely separate processes after all. Several researchers (Gregg, 1984; McLaughlin, 1978; Rivera, 1980; Stevick 1980; Sharwood-Smith, 1981) believe that learned knowledge can become automatized through practice so that it can, in effect, transform itself into acquired knowledge.

The Natural Order Hypothesis. SLA research shows that acquisition of grammatical features proceeds in a more or less predictable, natural order. Several studies of the use of linguistic structures across different languages, for example, led Dulay and Burt (1974) to conclude that the natural order is independent of language background; that is, it is not only natural but also universal. The natural order hypothesis speaks to the overall uniformity of morphological development from one learner to the next. For example, simple terms of negation (*no* and *not*, in English) will be among the earliest morphemes a child masters.

With this hypothesis, Krashen asserts that the natural order will manifest itself in SLA, but only when the student is engaged in communicative, meaning-focused (as opposed to form-focused) tasks. Studying grammar, Krashen believes, will not affect the natural order. The implication of this for language educators is, therefore, that proficiency-oriented activities stand a better chance of tapping into the natural order. Krashen is careful to note, however, that he does not support the idea of trying to organize a language curriculum around the natural order. Each learner will go through the natural order in his or her learning of the second language, but the rate at which a learner moves through the natural order will vary from individual to individual, depending on a number of factors, several of which are discussed in a later section of this chapter. Thus, Krashen believes it is impossible to plan instruction based on the natural order; rather, the best thing is to develop lessons rich in input and output opportunities for the student and assume that in fulfilling the meaningful tasks these lessons require, the student's progression through the natural order will be encouraged.

The Monitor Hypothesis. Krashen's "monitor" is the language-processing device that learners use to edit their performance. The ability to use the monitor is what differentiates older from younger learners; older users are better able to use the monitor because they are more cognitively mature. According to Krashen, the optimal use of the monitor is when students use it to take learned (form-focused) knowledge and adjust the language they produce as a result of acquired knowledge. He notes that this optimal use can occur only under specific conditions, however. First, the student must have enough time to use the monitor. Second, he must be focused on form, not meaning. Third, he must know the rule. What teachers should be doing in their classrooms is modeling appropriate monitor use and designing activities that make possible that appropriate use.

McLaughlin (1978) and Rivera (1980) point out that in foreign- and second-language learning, one can feel, in an intuitive way, the need to modify an utterance without necessarily being conscious of the need to apply a rule or, for that matter, of which rule to apply. They note that in addition to not taking into account how the monitor mechanism may work with acquired knowledge, Krashen's idea of the monitor does not account for how monitoring can result from a collaborative negotiation of meaning (again in the context of acquired knowledge) instead of just an individualistic, form-focused language exercise. Finally, they argue that Krashen's model does not speak to stylistic differences in SLA. They believe that it is based on the faulty assumption that all acquired knowledge will appear the same. What SLA theory needs, they say, is a model that explains the variability of competencies that we see in language learners.

The Input Hypothesis. The input hypothesis accounts for the variation in acquisition that can be seen from one language learner to the next. This variation in acquisition is due to variation in the nature of input that learners receive. According to Krashen, in order for input to encourage acquisition, it must be comprehensible. Krashen defines *comprehensible input* as input that is a little beyond the learner's current level of competence. Many factors can produce variation in input and, as a result, in acquisition. Krashen believes, for example, that in the case of first-language acquisition, younger learners receive more comprehensible input than older learners because their parents, caregivers, and teachers go to great efforts to modify their speech so that it is understood. (Recall the term *motherese*, discussed in chapter 3). A similar type of comprehensible input is "foreigner talk"—an effort by those interacting with a new learner of a foreign or second language to adapt their speech to his or her level.

The idea of comprehensible input, like the acquisition-learning distinction, has had a great impact on language instruction in recent decades. Nevertheless, some are quick to point out that input is not the whole story of SLA. According to Swain (1985), the catalyst for acquisition is not input but output. The opportunities that learners have to generate output, and how much they take advantage of these opportunities, lie at the heart of their language development potential.

Swain's reasoning is that output is important because, as language use, it indicates how much input is being understood, it generates more comprehensible input, and it allows the learner to test his or her hypotheses about the language.

The implication of the input-output debate for teachers is straightforward. Language learners need to be put in situations where they have access to rich and meaningful input and where they are motivated to produce output. The relationship between input and output defines the communicative purposes for which language is used to negotiate a multitude of tasks and a multitude of interactions within the contexts of our daily lives.

The Affective Filter Hypothesis. The affective filter hypothesis is based on the proposal by Dulay and Burt (cited in Ellis, 1986, p. 263) that a mechanism, or "filter," controls how much input is actually converted into intake. Intake is the language information that is taken in by the learner's developing linguistic system and the information that is, as a result, able to feed the process of SLA. The working of this mechanism is influenced by affective factors like motivation, self-confidence, and anxiety. If these affective factors are low, there is a greater possibility that comprehensible input will be converted into intake. If these affective factors are high, there is a lesser possibility that the comprehensible input will be converted into intake.

As has already been noted, Krashen's hypotheses—though to a large extent unproven—have been found useful in getting teachers to recognize that language learning and acquisition have complex cognitive and emotional components. For that reason, they have influenced classroom practices to a significant extent. It seems that Krashen's theory simply makes sense to teachers and appears to explain their own observations. Aspects of the model that have been translated into effective classroom practices are presented in the Teacher Note box below.

Teacher Note

Krashen's Monitor Model and Instructional Strategies

Many second-language educators have written about suggestions for instructional practice based on Krashen's monitor model. Díaz-Rico and Weed (1995) summarize his model and present one such set of recommendations.

Krashen's (1981) theory is that people acquire second-language structures in a predictable order only if they obtain comprehensible input, and if their affective filters are low enough to allow input into the system. A monitor edits language usage. An incorporation of these hypotheses into teaching practices would be as follows:

- *Acquisition versus learning.* The most important facet of acquisition is that language is used to communicate. Conveying meaning is more important than drill and practice. An important part of acquisition is that children be given time to internalize language before they are expected to respond. Partial comprehension and incomplete utterances are acceptable.

- *Natural order.* Teachers need to recognize that the mind does not assemble from simple sentences to more complex sentences in any struc-

cont.

tured way. Rather, language learners seem to find order by seeking patterns from the input they see and hear. Therefore, the curriculum need not be organized around grammatical structures. Language generated in inquiry and problem-solving situations will naturally contain structures from which students can acquire rules.

- *Monitor.* Additional mediation can be provided for students in the form of specific suggestions or explicit grammatical hints. On the whole, however, rich input is the appropriate means by which students develop and internalize a sense of structural and communicative models. Students will monitor themselves. The teacher's explicit correction rarely changes students' writing or speaking behavior.

- *Comprehensible input.* Simplified language, such as caretaker speech, probably works better with some students than others. Factors such as the learner's needs, age, socioeconomic status, gender, and first-language characteristics need to be considered (Larsen-Freeman, 1985). Teachers can provide comprehensible input in a number of ways: by making instruction relevant and meaningful; by using shorter and less complex sentences with a subject-verb-object word order, fewer contractions and pronouns, frequent comprehension checks, and variety in intonation, volume, and pitch.

  (It should be noted that some second-language educators object to the notion of comprehensible input, arguing that much of the language that young children are exposed to as they learn their first language is rich in context and often quite complex. It is from this "rich soup" of language that children deduce the rules of language and develop ever more sophisticated forms. The input that a teacher provides a second-language learner clearly needs to be determined from a quick review of the situation and responding to what the child is trying to do with language.)

- *Affective filter.* Teachers can lower the affective filter by fostering a spirit of mutual respect, high expectations, and cooperative learning. Moskowitz's (1978) *Caring and Sharing in the Foreign Language Class* offers techniques designed to relax students, increase the enjoyment of learning, raise self-esteem, and blend self-awareness with an increase in proficiency in the target language.

Adapted from Díaz-Rico and Weed (1995)

What do these theories contribute to our understanding of second-language acquisition? Each of these theories draws our attention to important facets of it. Taken in the aggregate, they give us an appreciation for the complex interactions among many factors—cultural, social, cognitive, and emotional—in language learning. They also point to the complex nature of language itself. Each one contributes something to our understanding, though we need to be careful to remember that they are theories and not reality. What are the limitations of existing second-language acquisition theories? Researchers interested in bilingualism point out that current models of SLA do not account for the bilingual experience. Valdés and Figueroa (1994) argue that the assumption behind SLA theories to date has been that the learner, moving through a series of stages, will arrive at a full or nativelike stage in the target language. They believe this assumption is based on the idea of a monolingual population learning in a foreign-language context. They assert that failure to account for the uniqueness of language acquisition in bilingual settings is a fundamental problem in the current discussions about how best to teach English to bilingual children.

In the 50 years since Skinner's behaviorist description of stimulus-response chains (see chapter 3), we have learned a great deal about what it takes to learn language. We now know, as Valdés and Figueroa (1994) write:

Teacher Inquiry

Are there any particular incidents from your work with English-learning students that these theories help to explain? Where do their explanations fall short? Can you think of a student whose progress (or lack of progress) these theories fail to adequately describe? Consider what kind of action research project might help you to answer your question. What kind of data could you collect? What would you hope to learn?

> Communicative language ability is a multifaceted, complex phenomenon that involves not only intuitions and innate knowledge about the structure of the language, but also the ability to select appropriately from among an enormously large set of options, the linguistic form(s) that will most effectively enable the speaker to realize her momentarily changing goals. (pp. 33–34)

How best to develop these communicative language abilities in students is another complicated question that theorists and educators are trying to answer.

How Children Learn a Second Language

The Relationship Between First-Language and Second-Language Learning

There are many ways in which first- and second-language learning are two different processes. Whether they realize it or not, second-language learners bring a considerable store of knowledge about the social and linguistic system of their first-language to their learning of the second. This knowledge can be both a help and a hindrance. "The English speaker's problems are evidence of the pervasive truth that learning a new language rarely allows you to set aside all that you have come to know about your first-language" (Bialystok & Hakuta, 1994, p. 11). If the social and linguistic systems of the first and second languages are alike, this knowledge will facilitate learning, a process referred to as *transfer*. (Spanish-speakers, for example, would be expected not to have any difficulty producing the statement "It is *a* book" because Spanish also uses articles—"*Es un libro.*") But if the social and linguistic systems are not alike, this knowledge may impede learning, a process referred to as *interference*. (Japanese-speakers would be expected to produce "It is book" instead of "It is *a* book" because marking nouns for definiteness or indefiniteness does not occur in Japanese: "*Hon-wa desu*" consists of *book* as the subject and the particle *it is*.) It seems reasonable to believe that a teacher who is familiar with a student's first language may be better able to understand the source of her difficulties and help the student to use knowledge of the first language to help learn the second.

The process of predicting the difficulties a learner will have in mastering a new language by documenting similarities and differences between the two is known as *contrastive analysis* (Kaplan, 1988; Stockwell, Bowen, & Martin, 1965). Bialystok and Hakuta (1994) report that although research using contrastive analysis ultimately yielded disappointing results, the attention that was given to errors during the popularity of that approach led to an important discovery: Learners approach the task of learning a second language in much the same way as they do their first (Corder, 1967, Dulay & Burt, 1974). After studying the errors made by groups of second-language learners, Dulay & Burt (1974), for example, concluded that only 4 percent could be clearly linked to a source in the first language.

> **Teacher Inquiry**
>
> **Contrastive Analysis**
> Do your own contrastive analysis research. Keep a record of your students' first languages and their persistent errors. Then obtain a copy of Swan & Smith's *Learner English: A Teacher's Guide to Interference and Other Problems* (1987) and see if the authors' accounting of likely difficulties faced by English-learning speakers of languages ranging all the way to Arabic and West African languages, accurately depicts what you see in your classroom.

This finding led theorists to view second-language learning as a process of "creative construction" equally influenced by both the first- *and* second-language systems. Thus, the language of second-language learners came to be understood as a complex intermediate, or interlanguage, linguistic system, influenced by a host of natural developmental factors, only one of which is the relationship of the first language to the second (Schachter, 1992; Selinker, 1972). Chomsky's publication of his linguistic theory (discussed in chapter 3), which posited a biologically innate language acquisition device and universal grammar, had already begun to put forth new ideas about what these developmental processes looked like, so the idea of "creative construction" readily gained disciplinary acceptance and, ultimately, substantially displaced the behaviorist model (see discussion below on second-language acquisition theory).

What was most radical about Chomsky's ideas for first-language learning was also what was most radical for second-language learning. That is, individuals learn language not through the process of memorizing a finite number of utterances (in the case of the first language) or of overcoming a finite number of points of interference (in the case of the second language), but by exercising what they know about their first (and second) language to discover the essential formulas through which an infinite number of correct and novel utterances can be generated.

Brown and Hanlon's (1970) research on first-language development in children showed that this was precisely the case. The errors that Brown and his colleagues found children making were not haphazard but rather illustrated how they were sharp formulators and testers of grammatical rules. For example, a child who said *foots* instead of *feet* was showing that he or she had inferred a rule about plural formation. It also showed that children learned certain grammatical forms in a more or less regular sequence and, in addition, did so without the benefit of formal correction. Soon the research on second-language development uncovered similar findings. As Bialystok & Hakuta (1994) write:

> The data were quite clear in indicating that commonalities in second-language learning were due to factors beyond native language characteristics. Second-language learning was not a process of modifying what you already knew to arrive at the second language. Instead, it was, quite simply, "language learning," a process of constructing a new system from all our available resources (p. 31).

Differences Among Second-Language Learners

From reading the discussion above about the distinction between foreign- and second-language learning, the reader may have developed the impression that, in general, the second-language learning population is homogeneous in terms of its experiences in learning a second language; this is very far from the truth. In reality, second-language learners in the United States are a heterogeneous group and have very different language-learning experiences. Some members of second-language communities are more disadvantaged by their English-learning status than others.

In California, where Hispanics and Asians are the fastest growing ethnic groups (Hispanics increased from 12% of the population in 1970 to 30% in 1998, and Asians increased from 3% of the population in 1970 to 11% in 1998), there is a striking Hispanic-Asian educational attainment gap. About 70% of Asians have some college education—a figure comparable to that of Whites. Nearly half of Hispanics, on the other hand, fail to complete high school (Reyes, 2001). Understanding why this gap exists requires a deeper grasp of majority-minority relations than may be immediately visible in the foreign- versus second-language distinction. It requires, as Ogbu (1992) writes, recognizing

> the nature of the relationship between minority cultures/languages and the culture and language of the dominant White Americans and the public schools they control. The relationship between the minority cultures/languages and the mainstream culture and language is different for different minorities. And it is this difference in the relationship that is problematic in the ability of the minorities to cross cultural and language boundaries and that calls for understanding to enhance the success of intervention and other efforts. (p. 7)

Thus, not all second-language learners are alike. To theorize about the process of second-language development as if it stood apart from the larger realm of intergroup relations is to ignore the myriad ways in which the context of the individual learner can be affected by the context of his or her group.

Young children growing up in monolingual English-speaking homes in the United States will learn their first language without being influenced by an explicit or implicit understanding of the differences in social status between two language systems. Young children growing up in Spanish-speaking homes in the United States, for example, will at some point begin to perceive that there is a difference in social status between the language used at home and the language used outside the home, in school and in the larger society. Negotiating the social as well as linguistic demands made by becoming a speaker of two languages of disparate status makes second-language learning a very different psychological process from what is typically involved in first-language learning.

Factors That Affect Second-Language Acquisition

As noted in the section above on SLA theories, learning a language is now commonly seen as a process of hypothesis testing and retesting in which the individual learner, as an active creative, agent, plays a central role. This means that teachers will encounter challenges in instruction due to a multitude of individual learner characteristics—things like aptitude, motivation, attitude, personality, cognitive style, and age—over which they may have little or no control. Since the learner comes to the classroom with a disposition that is already influenced by these factors, the effective teacher's job is to respond to each one as it presents itself in the course of learning. The teacher therefore needs to understand general factors, such as the disparity between the status of the home language and the status of English and the degree of similarity between the first and second languages, as well as the factors that manifest themselves differently in each individual.

Language Aptitude

One of these individual factors is language aptitude. Carroll (1981) defines *aptitude* in terms of a cluster of abilities: phonetic coding ability, grammatical sensitivity, rote learning ability, and inductive learning ability. *Phonetic coding ability* is the ability to identify distinct sounds, to form associations between those sounds and the symbols representing them, and to retain these associations. *Grammatical sensitivity* refers to the skill with which one recognizes grammatical functions of words in sentence structures. *Rote learning ability* refers to the skill that enables one to learn associations between sounds and meanings rapidly and to retain these associations. *Inductive language ability* is the ability to infer or induce language rules (Larsen-Freeman & Long, 1991, p. 167).

In making the distinction between rote learning and inductive language ability, Carroll (1981) is referring to the kinds of language learning tasks that students encounter in the classroom. They may be asked, for example, to memorize a chart of the letters of the alphabet with their accompanying sounds (rote learning), or they may be presented with text in the second language and asked to look for patterns in word formation (inductive learning). Students will vary in their ability to perform rote or inductive learning, just as they will vary in their ability to perform phonetic and grammatical recognition. Aptitude tests[3] are designed to capture such variation precisely because they are based on an understanding of language proficiency that has this formal type of learning (learning about language inside the classroom) at its center.

The language-learning aptitude of bilingual or English-learning students has not received psychometric attention equal to that of the monolingual English speaker. In the absence of information about the English-learning students' aptitude, what is important for the second-language teacher to know is that the students will undoubtedly display variation in skills when performing certain language tasks. Some of this variation is due to innate differences in ability, but some of the variation is also due to differences in type of exposure to English (nonclassroom vs. classroom settings); no standardized test can account for this. Thus it is best for the teacher not to mistake perceived differences in aptitude for wholesale differences in cognitive capability; that is, just because a learner shows less aptitude than his peers for learning English in the classroom does not mean that he is any less able, with time, to become a successful speaker.

Other Cognitive Factors

It is thought that general cognitive factors having to do with modes of information processing also play a part in second-language success. One distinction made in cognitive style is with regard to field independence or field dependence; that is, it concerns the ability of individuals to break up a whole into its constituent parts. *Field independence* refers to the ability to isolate one element from the context in which it was presented. A field-independent style is said to be better for formal classroom learning, in which a language system is reduced to its parts of speech. *Field dependence*, on the other hand, relies more heavily on context in the learning process. For this reason, it is said that field-dependent learners are more suited to informal (out-of-classroom) learning (Witkin, Dyk, Faterson, Goodenough, & Karp, 1962; Witkin & Goodenough, 1981).

Although some studies have tried to link cognitive styles to particular cultural groups and assert, for example, that Mexican-American children tend to be more field dependent than their European-American peers (Ramírez & Castañeda, 1974), such findings have been criticized (Irvine & York, 1995). The critics point out that linking cognitive style to culture is dangerous because it presumes that all members of a particular cultural group will behave in the same way, for example, that all Mexican-American students come from strongly group-oriented families (which is said to cause field dependence) and that all European-American students come from strongly individualistic families (which is said to cause field independence). Since no studies exist that demonstrate a clear association, the critics of cognitive styles suggest great caution in interpreting individual student behavior by cultural membership.[4] An effective teacher will provide instruction that satisfies the activity-type and grouping-type preferences of both field-independent and field-dependent learners, helping students to find something in the instruction that suits his or her particular cognitive style in learning a second language.

Motivation

Motivation, which is considered an affective factor along with personality and attitude, also affects second-language learning. A student's aptitude for language learning may influence his motivation. If he finds the tasks of language learning to be especially difficult, he is more likely to experience a decrease in his motivation to perform those tasks. Social psychological factors may counter his drop in motivation, however, because of the promise of what learning the second language will allow him to do in life. In their series of studies on English-speaking Canadian students studying French in school, Gardner and Lambert (1972) described what they termed integrative versus instrumental orientations toward language learning.

One experiences *integrative* motivation in language learning when one wishes to identify with another cultural and linguistic group. *Instrumental* motivation, on the other hand, is an indication that the student's learning is fueled by an idea of what she will be able to do (obtain a job) or get (receive course credit) by studying the language. A student who wants to learn English for a future career or to meet an educational requirement is exhibiting instrumental motivation. A student whose learning of English is fueled by the desire to be more like her English-speaking peers experiences integrative motivation. English learners undoubtedly experience both orientations, and these orientations will, to varying degrees in each individual, influence motivation and, thus, achievement.

It is unlikely that the students in Gardner and Lambert's studies—English speakers learning French—experienced the kind of draw toward French as a vehicle of upward mobility and social acceptance that Spanish speakers experience toward English in the United States. An effective teacher of English learners will tap into the students' sources of motivation for learning the language but will also reinforce the importance of their first languages as a connection to family, community, and culture.

Personality

Personality factors also seem to have intuitive importance for second-language learning. That is, it seems to make sense that a student's self-esteem, degree of extroversion, level of anxiety, disposition toward risk taking, sensitivity to rejection, capacity for empathy, inhibition, and tolerance for ambiguity will determine, to some extent, how successful he or she will be in second-language learning. The body of research on the correlation between these (and other) personality characteristics and achievement, however, comes to no firm conclusions (Chastain, 1975; Naiman, Frohlich, Stern, & Tedesco, 1978; Suter, 1976; Swain & Burnaby, 1976; Taylor, Catford, Guiora, & Lane, 1971). What can be said with certainty is that these personality factors are linked not to cognitive capabilities but to affective behaviors that can limit the opportunities the student has for practice (the input received and the output produced) in the second language. Effective teachers of English learners will design meaningful and varied classroom contexts for communicative interaction so that, personality factors aside, every student has an equal opportunity for learning. How a student's personality propels him or her to take (or not take) advantage of such opportunity is something, like attitude, over which the instructor has little actual control.

Attitude Toward Language Learning

Closely related to aptitude, motivation, and personality is the factor of attitude. *Attitude* is how one thinks and feels about learning the second language. Although the definition of attitude may be simple, the source and influence of attitude are quite complex. A student may think that he has a natural talent for learning a second language (aptitude), may not have a strong reason for learning a second language (motivation), or may not feel comfortable doing the tasks required of him in learning a second language (personality). All of these factors affect a student's attitude toward learning. Attitude (and the reasons for it) may also be linked to the attitudes (perceived or real) of one's parents, siblings, community, friends, peers, and teachers. Deciphering a student's attitude toward language learning may be quite difficult; in fact, it may be impossible. As was the case with personality, effective teachers will do what they can in their classrooms to nurture positive attitudes in their students.

Age

Research on the influence of age on second-language learning has concluded that there are three important differences between the process of learning a second language as a child and learning a second language as an adult. These differences point to the conclusion that older second-language learners, due to their cognitive maturity, may more quickly learn some aspects of the second language than younger second-language learners, but in the long run it will be the younger learners who are most able to attain nativelike proficiency. For example, Krashen, Long, and Scarcella (1979) report that adults more quickly move through the earliest phonological, syntactical, and morphological stages of learning a second language; that older children move more quickly through the syntactical and morphological development stages than younger children; but that younger children learning a second language reach higher levels of oral proficiency in accent and syntax than do adults. Effective teachers will understand that older students bring a cognitive advantage to second-language learning and build on this to encourage grammatical and vocabulary development. They will also understand that their older students are less likely than younger students to achieve nativelike pronunciation.

In considering the role that factors such as aptitude, motivation, attitude, personality, cognitive style, and age are thought to have on second-language learning, it is important to note that most of the research that has been done in these areas has taken the native English speaker as the norm. Some scholars have made arguments that suggest that the bilingual learner may be substantially different cognitively from this "norm" population and that the bilingual difference warrants reconsideration, not only of past findings but also of the future research agenda for second-language learning. During the 1970s, many studies were conducted that explored differences among individuals that could be demonstrated to contribute to success in second-language learning. The only conclusion that could be drawn was that the factors were so confounded with the context for learning that it was not possible to delineate the profile of a "good language learner" (Bialystok & Hakuta, 1994).

The Complexity and Difficulty of Second-Language Learning

The reader will have noted that the theories reviewed above touched on one or more channels (brain, language, mind, self, culture) through which a second language is learned (or, in the case of Krashen's theory, various aspects of the process), yet none really captures fully the difficulty and complexity of the process. Understanding the process of learning a second language is much more of a challenge than understanding the process of learning a first or native language, but it also has the potential of giving us a great deal of useful information about how human beings learn.

> If observing first-language acquisition is like studying the forces of gravity at work by dropping feathers in a vacuum, perhaps taking a look at second-language acquisition is more like watching a feather drop from an airplane, buffeted by winds, weighted by moisture, and slowed by pressure. Just as observing the feather in a real and changing atmosphere teaches us about winds and other environmental factors, studying how one acquires a second language holds out the promise of helping us to understand the role of the diverse conditions under which human learning occurs. (Bialystok & Hakuta, 1994, p. 4)

Although we have research that shows quite clearly how, for example, learners begin by perceiving second-language features according to native-language categories and then shift their perceptual boundaries as they learn more (e.g., Williams, 1980), the process is still much more complex than such explanations imply. For example, infants up to 1 year of age can detect phonetic distinctions from a nonnative language that are not present in their native language. However, after that time, they perform much like adults in detecting such distinctions (Werker & Tees, 1984), despite the fact that children up to the age of at least 7 or 8 are capable of learning to pronounce words in a new language without a detectable accent.

As we consider how the channel referred to in Bialystok and Hakuta's (1994) structure as the "mind" makes meaning and connects it to a second language, we begin to get a sense of just how complex the process is. For centuries, philosophers have been debating how mental categories relate to linguistic categories. According to Bialystok and Hakuta, it is *meaning* that unites the knowledge of the world and the knowledge of the mind. Researchers have been successful in creating artificial language and developing machines to which they can teach certain aspects of linguistic structure, but these machines do not understand the meaning of the grammatical sentences they produce; do not appreciate nuance in words and phrases, puns and jokes; and cannot intuit the intent behind indirect speech.

As discussed in chapter 3, children learning a first language face two challenges: They must develop a conceptual system for understanding their world, and they must learn the linguistic system for expressing those concepts. What happens, however, when someone strives to learn a second language? She already has the meanings and categories for her world concepts. Does she simply attach new labels to existing meanings? What happens when the labels don't seem to quite match one's existing meanings and concepts? Benjamin Whorf (1956) hypothesized years ago that the language we learn to speak shapes the concepts and categories we develop: Language determines thought. Does someone thus alter his meaning concepts as he learns a second language? In exploring these questions, Bialystok and Hakuta (1994) point out that "the two languages cannot be strictly coincident with each other, but neither can they be completely autonomous" (p. 118). They conclude that some of what is learned in the second language is directly attached to the first language and that other aspects result in new ways of thinking and organizing information; thus the mind of a bilingual speaker has a different structure from that of a monolingual. However, Whorf's theory, that one's cognition is severely constrained by one's language, is largely discredited by more recent research. Despite the limitations of translation, people can learn new ways of categorizing and talking about experiences and ideas.

The Effects of Bilingualism

Since "language use is central to many kinds of intellectual operations," (Carroll, 1971, p. 97), it seems possible that the brain of a monolingual and the brain of a bilingual would work in different ways. Scholars first presumed that bilingualism had a negative effect on cognitive development and later presumed that it had a positive one. Uncovering clear evidence to support either hypothesis has been difficult. Today, the generally accepted position is that bilinguals *are* significantly different from monolinguals; however, questions remain about the precise nature of that difference and, specifically, in what ways bilingualism may be cognitively advantageous.

Peal and Lambert (1962) were among the first to examine the assumption that bilingualism is a damaging experience for a child, posing hurdles to his or her intellectual development and later emotional adjustment. They showed that some bilingual children scored higher than monolingual children on tests of verbal and nonverbal ability, using this evidence to claim that bilinguals had better concept formation and mental flexibility than monolinguals. This attribution of superiority, however, was extended only to what they called "true" bilinguals, or individuals who master both of their languages at an early age.

A Reasonable Timeline for Second-Language Acquisition

Whereas some researchers have taken the position that it is impossible to establish norms for second-language acquisition because there are too many variables to consider (Dulay, Hernandez-Chavez, & Burt, 1978), other researchers have attempted to describe a timeline for second-language acquisition. In her review of 20 years of research comparing the French immersion programs in Canada, monolingual English programs in Canada, and French programs in France, Swain (1985) found that immersion students perform as well as native French speakers in reading and mathematics after 5–6 years, but their skills in speaking and writing are not nativelike even after the completion of high school.

In studying Canadian students with limited English proficiency from kindergarten through ninth grade, Cummins (1981a) found that they could master basic interpersonal communication skills in approximately 2 years, but it took them 5–7 years to reach the level of native speakers in reading tasks that required them to understand less contextualized sources. Krashen and Biber (1988) found that it took students 3–6 years to perform at the 50th percentile in academic areas taught and assessed in English. Collier (1987) similarly found 8- to 11-year-olds performing at grade level in their native language upon entry to U.S. schools 2–5 years to reach the 50th percentile national norm in all academic areas.

What all these studies indicate is that language learners can quickly acquire some degree of fluency in the target language when they are exposed to it in the school environment. Nevertheless, despite this rapid growth in conversational fluency, it generally takes a minimum of 5 years for them to catch up to native speakers in academic aspects of the language (Cummins, 1980a, 1981b, 1984). Another study found that early-grade students were still very far from grade norms even after 4 years of structured English immersion (Ramírez, Yuen, Ramey, Pasta, & Billings, 1991). SLA theorists, educators, and other English-learner advocates believe that we should be looking for interventions that will substantially improve bilingual students' long-term academic progress rather than expecting any short-term quick-fix solution to their underachievement in English.

Cummins (1991a, 1991b) and Williams & Snipper (1990) suggest that one substantial step would be to recognize that the first-language and second-language systems are interdependent and, consequently, that a strong native-language foundation acts as a support, not an obstacle, in the learning of English. Cummins argues that, due to what he calls a "common underlying proficiency," the learning that goes on in the first language will readily transfer to the second language. For example, once the basic principles of reading are mastered in the first language, a student does not have to relearn those reading skills; they are part of a common underlying proficiency that can be tapped in learning the second language. Other skills that constitute common underlying proficiency can be seen in the Teacher Note on page 36. Thus, for Cummins, it stands to reason that students should be taught academic content in their first, more developed, language so that academic knowledge can be mastered and transferred to the second language.

Teacher Note

Aspects of a Common Underlying Academic Discourse Proficiency

- Literacy-related skills directly related to decoding, print awareness (letters and words represent language in a systematic way), directionality, etc.

- Comprehension strategies: readers' and listeners' ability to follow extended texts (or orally presented lectures), link one idea with another, and mentally keep the important components together and form a coherent understanding of the message

- Analytical abilities that allow the student to examine different aspects of a text (e.g., an argument), one text against another, one in relation to another, and if necessary, to integrate the ideas and concepts in accord with the intentions of the author or in a new way

- Ability to apply logical operations to texts and discourses

- Knowledge of different text types and genres: how content or information is organized in each type, and the patterns one can expect when reading or listening

- Critical thinking and evaluation

Francis & Reyhner (2002, p. 93)

Studies examining language-minority students' long-term academic achievement in the United States generally confirm that students who have been in late-exit bilingual programs, where they have had more opportunity to learn academics in their first languages, perform better than those who exited bilingual programs early (and have had less opportunity to learn in their first languages) (Collier, 1992; Ramírez, 1991). The idea of the interdependency of the first and second languages therefore supports bilingual programs that develop proficiency in English while also maintaining and developing a child's first language. In order for the principle of interdependency to function effectively as a mechanism for language and academic development in English, however, children must be given the chance to attain a certain minimum threshold level of proficiency in their first language.

The Stages of Second-Language Development

We have noted elsewhere that second-language learners vary substantially in the process, sequence, and timing with which they learn. Nevertheless, there are generally accepted stages of development through which they seem to progress. Terrell (1983), for example, suggested that there are three stages: comprehension, early production, and extending production.[5]

The *comprehension stage* is also referred to as the *silent period* or *preproduction stage*, as it is the time during which learners absorb vast amounts of data about the new language, and they exhibit great anxiety if they are expected to produce speech. Responses during *the early production stage* generally consist of single words, two- or three-word combinations and phrases (in a manner that is similar to the language development stages of young children learning their first language). In the *extending production stage*, second-language acquisition speeds up considerably, and learners begin to use longer and more complex utterances, correct their own errors, and become more comfortable initiating and sustaining conversations.

The American Council for Teachers of Foreign Languages (ACTFL) has developed an oral proficiency scale that depicts the progression of language from novice to nativelike proficiency (Díaz-Rico & Weed, 1995). Since there is now general agreement that learners do progress through a predictable set of stages, albeit at their own pace, the teacher can benefit from reviewing such discussions and materials related to acquisition stages. (Because there are many parallels between first- and second-language acquisition, readers may benefit from reviewing Tables 3-2, 3-3, 3-4, and 3-5.)

Second-Language Learning Versus Foreign-Language Learning

Before we continue, a distinction between the use of the terms *second language* and *foreign language* may be useful. The distinction is important because of its social and psychological implications for the learner.

Additive and Subtractive Approaches to Bilingualism

In most U.S. high schools and colleges, many English speakers study Spanish, French, or German as part of their graduation requirements. These courses are referred to as *foreign* language courses, reflecting the idea that the languages taught have "no status as a routine medium of communication" in the United States (Crystal, 1987, p. 368). For native English speakers, foreign-language learning is *additive*: It is favorably viewed as adding new language skills to those already possessed in English (Lambert, 1975). The process of learning to speak a foreign language has also been called elective bilingualism to emphasize the fact that the movement toward bilingualism is primarily under the individual learner's control (Valdés & Figueroa, 1994, p. 11). For new immigrants to the United States or for students who come from communities and households in which non-English languages are spoken, studying English in school is not the same as studying a foreign language. As the main medium of communication in the United States, English is not "foreign." It is a second language that they will need in order to succeed in school and society. These children don't "elect" to learn a second language as individuals; rather, it is essential for them to learn a second language due to circumstances pertaining to their group membership that are outside their control (e.g., movement of peoples, conquest, colonization, immigration); they are referred to as circumstantial bilinguals (Valdés & Figueroa, 1994, p. 11). Because English is the main medium of communication in this country, it carries more economic and social status than the circumstantial bilingual's primary, or home, language.

Teacher Note

Culturally Sensitive Teaching

Effective teachers of second-language learners understand that attending American schools puts students' languages and cultures at risk. They want to help their students develop English language skills, but not in the subtractive sense, in a way that requires that children lose their primary languages and cultures to do so. They want to help students participate in the standard English-language practices of school and society so that they can attain academic, social, and economic success, but they do not want to cut them off from the rich "funds of knowledge" (Moll, 1992) that their non-English speaking homes and communities offer. They don't want to see their students lose the ability to communicate with and learn from their elders.

Second-language teaching, then, requires the teacher to be sensitive to issues regarding the status of the first language and its speakers in U.S. society because these issues may reflect a history of oppression resulting from the contact of majority and minority languages and cultures. This is not a concern in the foreign-language environment, where there is no pressure on the learner to assimilate to the target culture for the purpose of social and economic survival.

Instead of seeing English as a language developed *in addition* to the native language, American schools often try to develop English *in place of* the native language. For many second-language learners in U.S. schools, learning English is *subtractive* (Lambert, 1975; Valenzuela, 1999). Students may acquire new language skills in English, but often at the expense of losing skills in their native language (Wong Fillmore, 1991). It has long been the case that the fourth generation of an immigrant family is monolingual in English, having adopted completely the language of the majority society (Fishman, 1964). Recent studies suggest that this trend of language loss is happening even more quickly among some groups, by the second or third generation (Tse, 2001).

Supporting a Positive Process of Acculturation

Many of the English-learning students in U.S. classrooms are first- or second-generation immigrants, and thus they and their families are still in the process of acculturating to American society. Because they are newly arrived or have limited exposure to English, these students are most at risk of becoming educationally disadvantaged. Even though research shows that development of the primary language can play an important role in the development of the second language as well as in academic achievement (Cummins, 1983; Cummins, Harley. Swain, & Allen, 1990), the policy of English-learner education in the United States strongly favors English-only approaches to schooling.

Planning Instruction for Second-Language Learners

Here we spell out more specifically what language proficiency instruction requires and must, in many ways, promote. We emphasize a communicative competence approach to language proficiency. In particular, we focus on the nature of the academic language that students will need to develop and the different perspectives that educators have found useful in understanding it.

Communicative Competence

As a result of his research, Brown (1987) described *communicative competence* (a concept first introduced by Hymes, 1972b) as the aspect of language users' abilities that enables them to convey and interpret messages and to negotiate meanings interpersonally within specific contexts).[6] A competent speaker is recognized as one who knows when, where, and how to use language appropriately. Language is seen as a form of communication that occurs in social interactions; it is used to persuade, to command, and to establish social relationships. This concept can be very useful to teachers of English language learners. Canale (1983) identified four components of communicative competence:

- **Grammatical competence**. Knowing the language code: vocabulary, word formation and meaning, sentence formation, pronunciation, and spelling.
- **Sociolinguistic competence**. Knowing how to produce and understand language in different sociolinguistic contexts, taking into consideration such factors as the status of participants, the purposes of the interaction, and the norms or conventions of interaction.
- **Discourse competence**. The ability to combine and connect utterances (spoken) and sentences (written) into a meaningful whole. Discourse ranges from a simple spoken conversation to long written texts.
- **Strategic competence**. The manipulation of language in order to meet communicative goals. The use of specific strategies to compensate for breakdowns in communication (e.g., paraphrase or gesture) or to enhance the effectiveness of communication (e.g., raise or lower voice for effect) (Díaz-Rico & Weed, 1995).

Bachman (1990b) expanded Canale's model even further, to propose that language competence involves *textual competence* (cohesion and rhetorical organization) and *illocutionary competence* (ability to carry out functions by means of language—i.e., ideational functions, manipulative functions, heuristic functions, and imaginative functions). This fuller understanding of what it means to "know" a language is presented in Figure 4-1. The hierarchical organization of the figure depicts Bachman's understanding of the relationships between the different competencies, which, he emphasizes, are not separate and static but interactive and dynamic in response to the communicative context.

Figure 4-1. Components of Language Competence

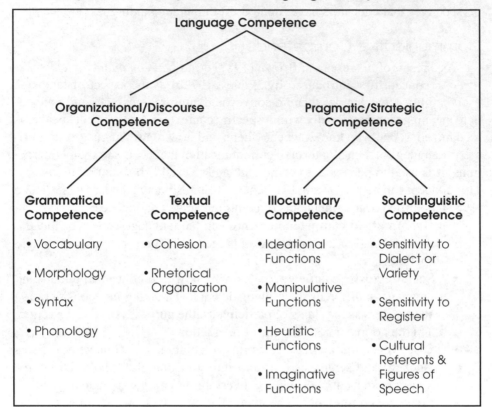

Teachers can increase students' skills in discourse, sociolinguistic, and strategic competence by building experiences into the curriculum that involve students in solving problems, exploring areas of interest, and designing projects. Students are then able to participate by carrying over knowledge of how to communicate from experiences they have had in their first language. They tap this knowledge as they develop specific forms and usage in English (Díaz-Rico & Weed, 1995) (see the next Teacher Note box for general suggestions for instruction.)

Proficiency Levels

There are many factors that have made it very difficult to document the process of second-language acquisition. In the material above, for example, we discussed the variability in how individuals learn second languages, the difficulty of determining the role that a first language plays, and the effect brought about by the circumstances in which individuals acquire a second language.

Teacher Note

Strategies Used in Second-Language Development

Chesterfield and Chesterfield (1985) found a natural order of strategies in students' development of a second language. These incorporate sociolinguistic, discourse, and strategic factors. Teachers who are aware of this order can recognize the strategies and use them to build on students' developing competence. These strategies are presented below in their order of development.

- *Repetition:* Imitating a word or structure used by another.
- *Memorization:* Recalling by rote songs, rhymes, or sequences.
- *Formulaic expressions:* Using words or phrases that function as units, such as greetings ("Hi! How are you?").
- *Verbal attention getters:* Using language to initiate interaction ("Hey!" "I think . . .").
- *Answering in unison:* Responding with others.
- *Talking to oneself:* Engaging in subvocal or internal monologue.
- *Elaboration:* Providing information beyond that which is necessary .
- *Anticipatory answers:* Responding to an anticipated question, or completing another's phrase or statement.
- *Monitoring:* Correcting one's own errors in vocabulary, style, or grammar.
- *Appeal for assistance:* Asking another for help.
- *Request for clarification:* Asking the speaker to explain or repeat.
- *Role play:* Interacting with another by taking on roles.

One of the concepts that has been useful for a variety of purposes is the advancement of English Language Development (ELD) standards or proficiency levels to describe, in general, the developmental sequence that second-language learners follow. Although such information is particularly useful for understanding a learner's progress in language development, it must be emphasized that such a continuum has to be viewed and used flexibly—that is, with an understanding that the process is idiosyncratic to the learner. Thus, the descriptions of various stages or levels of proficiency should be taken as general guidelines when assessing the progress of an individual learner or planning instruction for groups of students at various proficiency levels.

ELD standards emerged along with the development of standards in other content areas over the last decade. Some have questioned the need for a set of standards separate from general language arts standards, which include descriptors for oral language development. The difference is that the ELD standards are more fine-grained and provide much more specific and useful information about the development of English proficiency for second-language learners (see additional information about the use of standards in chapter 6).

An important contribution to the understanding of proficiency levels for second-language learners was made by James Cummins (1979), who specified a distinction between two dimensions of proficiency that indicate how people use language for thinking. He referred to these as *basic interpersonal communication skills* (BICS) and *cognitive academic language proficiency* (CALP). Cummins was concerned that superficial considerations of fluency based on conversational ability gave teachers inappropriate "readings" of their students' ability to use English for academic learning tasks. In fact, a child's first language may be surpassed by English, but not at a level that is fully developed enough for her to express herself fluently at the increasingly more abstract levels required by school. It is in the development of a student's academic English that an effective teacher can make a substantial contribution to his students' education and success. Cummins encouraged teachers to examine the cognitive demands of the tasks they present to students to determine how well students of different language proficiencies will be able to handle the tasks.

Academic Language

Effective teachers of second-language learners should set a goal of developing their students' ability to participate in academic situations at a level equal to that of their native-speaking peers. As noted above, the language required to succeed in higher order, literacy-related tasks of the classroom is what Cummins (1979), and later, Cummins and Swain (1986), called CALP. Without CALP, students, particularly at the higher grades in subjects requiring a great deal of specialized language, like math and science, will not have the ability to comprehend the language of instruction.

Unfortunately, the teacher may respond to a student's lack of comprehension by attempting to provide him with more accessible readings than those provided to his native-speaking peers. This well-intended gesture actually does the student more harm because it withholds access to the primary sources of academic discourse. Similarly, a student's lack of oral participation in the class, which may result from the tension and conflict the student feels over losing the native language but not yet speaking English well, deprives her of verbal interaction with her peers. As Francis & Reyhner (2002) write:

> When children are ashamed of, or are overly self-conscious about, how they sound when they speak in their second language, they tend to prefer passive interactions with teachers and other students. Inhibited from speaking and using their second language for other purposes (especially academic), the opportunities for developing higher-order language skills through the second language become more and more limited. (pp. 71–72)

The provision of academic English instruction must be planned. Left to chance, instruction is likely not to help the student develop the particular academic competencies required for each content area. Although academic language has been broadly defined by Chamot and O'Malley (1994) as "the language that is used by teachers and students for the purpose of acquiring new knowledge and skills . . . imparting new information, describing abstract ideas, and developing students' conceptual understanding" (p. 40), more linguistically oriented definitions of academic language revolve around the idea that it involves mastering the registers of several academic contexts. This means that each academic context has its own constellation of lexical and grammatical features that sets it apart from other academic contexts (Halliday & Hasan, 1989; Martin, 1992). These signature registers distinguish different genres. Just as the genres of fiction and nonfiction can be distinguished by features of their text, Schleppegrell (2001) writes, the following is true as well:

> In academic contexts, too, there are clearly recognized text types that are characteristic, and these text types are instantiated through grammatical features that are common to school-based uses of language and that reflect the purposes for which language is typically used in schooling. Researchers have explored several genres expected in school settings, including sharing time narratives (Michaels and Collins 1984; Christie, 1985); recounts (Heath, 1983), descriptions (Schleppegrell 1998b), definitions (Snow, 1990), expository essays (Martin, 1989), research papers (Swales, 1990) and others. Each genre has its own register features, but . . . school-based genres exhibit many common register features. This is due to the similar purposes of academic genres. Certain lexical and grammatical features are functional for "doing schooling." (pp. 3–4).

Children who acquire the genres of academic English are more likely to have interactions with the teacher that further develop their language skills, whereas students who are unable to approximate the genre are considered disorganized by their teachers and thus are not as likely to be supported toward further language development (Michaels, 1981). For example, Snow, Cancini, Gonzalez, and Shriberg (1989) found that kindergarten children from different socioeconomic backgrounds handled formal definitions differently and that these differences resulted in differential teacher treatment and academic success. They wrote as follows:

> Some treated a request for a definition as the initiation of a decontextualized school-based task, giving autonomous, well-planned, lexically specific information about the word meaning without incorporating either conversational devices or personal information. Other children tended, in contrast, to treat the request for a definition as the introduction of a new conversational topic, and to provide information, but no definition in response. While, from a communicative point of view, the adequacy of the more formal definitions of the middle class children was not significantly greater than those of working class children in the same classrooms who defined words using less formal language, the students who responded to the task more formally did better academically. (p. 239)

Their work suggests quite straightforwardly that understanding and meeting the school's expectations for use of academic language is an important element of school success.

In a recent study of professional development institutes for teachers of English learners (Richardson Bruna, Eaton, & Smith, 2003), researchers found that teachers, as well as institute providers, expounded a wide range of definitions of academic language. In the guidelines for the statewide network of institutes, academic language was explained as being the "language demands of each subject area and how the subject area relies on language to scaffold the content" (p. 25). This is by no means a simple concept, and thus documenting the ways in which institute providers and participants construed academic language became an interesting outcome of the study. Drawing on the scholarly literature as well as their observations of the professional development institutes, the researchers proposed the following typology of orientations toward academic language development. It is important to bear in mind that (a) the classification scheme reflects the various understandings that the researchers encountered during their study of the institutes—that is, it is not a complete synthesis of all work on the subject, and (b) the classifications should not be viewed as mutually incompatible; the researchers note it was not uncommon for institute providers and teachers to understand academic language in a number of overlapping ways.

Epistemological orientation. This approach to academic language development has to do with cognitive processes. Academic language is regarded as the result of epistemological differences (or differences in "ways of knowing") between the disciplines. For example, the cognitive process involved in understanding long division is different from what is involved in understanding the principle of acceleration or in understanding a historical account (August & Hakuta, 1997). To date, limited research has been devoted to discovering the precise manner in which language (or different languages) interacts with these cognitive processes.

Linguistic orientation. This approach is closely related to the epistemological orientation in that differences in cognition (meaning) are accompanied by differences in language use (form). In this approach, academic language is understood as the style, or register, of a particular type of discourse, or genre. It is "the constellation of lexical and grammatical features that characterizes particular uses of language" in particular academic disciplines (Schleppegrell, 2001, p. 25). This orientation is informed by a body of work generally referred to as Systemic Functional Linguistics.

Functional orientation. Whereas the linguistic orientation emphasizes an understanding of specific linguistic features associated with language use in particular disciplines, the functional orientation focuses more generally on the idea that language is used to perform certain functions in school. Within this framework, academic language is regarded as the language necessary to accomplish certain purposes common to the educational environment, like "seek/relate information, compare/contrast, cause and effect, conduct research, persuade" (Dutro, 2001).

Vocabulary and grammar orientation. In this approach, academic language is thought to be (a) *specialized* (discipline-specific) vocabulary and grammar—the key words and structures of a particular content area, or (b) *nonspecialized* vocabulary and grammar that is featured in a lesson. The first understanding resembles the linguistic orientation in focusing on discipline-specific aspects of language, but it differs in that it is not informed by a comprehensive linguistic perspective on the relationship among text, meaning, and form. The second understanding is primarily setting driven (as opposed to language driven)—that is, any classroom language is construed as "academic" by virtue of its occurrence within the classroom.

Study-skills orientation: Academic language here is defined in reference to developing students' awareness of text presentation and comprehension strategies. It includes metacognitive goals such as helping students to understand the importance of titles and subtitles, picture captions, and graphic text; using dictionaries; and monitoring their own understanding.

Testing orientation: This conception of academic language attends to the language of the educational environment as it is reflected in standardized tests. It involves the "broad knowledge of words, phraseology, grammar, and pragmatic conventions for expression, understanding, and interpretation" that is commonly assessed by test items, such as summarizing texts, evaluating evidence, composing an extended and reasoned text, and interpreting word problems (Wong Fillmore & Snow, 2000; see also Butler & Bailey, 2002).

Table 4-2 summarizes these approaches to academic language and gives the researchers' examples of their presence in the institute materials.

Table 4-2. Approaches to Academic Language

Approach to Academic Language	Focus	Example of Focus from Institute Materials
Epistemological	subject-specific cognitive processing	"While it is clear that at some level of abstraction, generalities across subject areas do exist (i.e., general ability to read English, to construct meaning, and to understand and follow spoken discussions), these generalities are not enough to address the differentiated knowledge demands of the academic subjects. "To understand long-division problems, the student must grasp an underlying principle that includes fundamental multiplicative relationships . . . One aspect of the study of science that can be especially difficult for students is the deceptive simplicity of many of the theories . . . What might start out as a simple "plug the number into the formula" problem turns into a multi-layered, means-end solution path, misleading students with its false impression of simplicity . . .

cont.

		"In the study of history, students must construct a coherent narrative or expository historical account that carries both multiple perspectives and a sense of layering—of event as it occurred, of event as it was recorded, and event as it was interpreted" (UCOP Request for Proposals, cited in August & Hakuta, 1997).
Linguistic	subject-specific discourse	"Teaching history to ELLs means helping them gain control of the language needed to talk and write about complex events and concepts. When students have not yet developed the language proficiency to needed to read grade-level texts, teachers can provide scaffolding through guided grammatical analysis that gives students access to significant content . . . Academic language is more than just vocabulary, it is the patterns of grammar though which meanings are made . . . We want to show students how textbook authors make particular choices in writing history textbooks, and that those choices enable the author to present events as well as points of view about events. Analyzing these choices helps students become critical thinkers about history . . . "Analyzing the language of a particular text from this point of view can help students understand what they read" (Schleppegrell & Achugar, 2002).
Functional	non-subject-specific classroom language	"Functions are the purposes and uses of language—(to) make statements, joke, inquire, compare—in formal and informal settings, and for social or academic functions purposes . . . Functions are the building blocks for connecting thinking and language . . . Language functions are used in a continuum from simple to complex, orally (express opinion, participate in a discussion) and in writing (persuasion, description). They are determined by the situation and the content concept. The language function determines the form or structure needed" (Dutro, 2001).
Vocabulary and Grammar	subject-specific or non-subject-specific words and structures	"A rich and varied vocabulary is needed to be a fully proficient English speaker and writer . . . One way to look at vocabulary is to consider three types of words or phrases: basic, general utility, and low-utility or content-specific words. These can be described as 'mortar' or 'brick.'

cont.

		• Mortar words: These are the basic and general utility words that are required when using certain sentence structures. Some examples Include: connecting words required to construct complex sentences (*because, then, but*), prepositions and prepositional phrases (*on, in, under*), basic regular and irregular verbs (*leave, live, eat*), general academic vocabulary (*notice, think, analyze*) • Brick words: This is the vocabulary specific to the content and concepts being taught (*government, symbols, arid, revolt*) • Forms, or structures, refer to grammatical structures and word usage. They are the building blocks for discourse, reading and writing, complex language, and cognitive processes . . . • Grammar: parts of speech, verb tenses, noun-verb agreement • Sentence structure: conjunctions, compound sentences • Syntax: word order "Mastery of forms ensures perception as a proficient speaker, allows students' full participation in academics, and use of voice to advocate for personal rights" (Dutro, 2001; see also Scarcella, 1996)
Study Skills	meta-cognition	"Students with limited comprehension skills need help organizing information in ways that will be easy for them to recall and useful for them to study. SDAIE teachers cannot assume that their students have the organization and study skills necessary for them to successfully study on their own. SDAIE teachers . . . show their students how to scan for key information and access resources provided in their textbook" (Nickolaisen, n.d.).
Testing	test language	"A recent study of prototype test items for a high school graduation examination for one of the 26 states that require an exam for graduation revealed that whatever else was being assessed, competence in the register that we refer to as academic English is necessary to pass . . . The language used in this test was the language ordinarily used in textbooks and discussions about science, mathematics, literature, or social studies. To pass this test, students have to be able to do the following: summarize texts, analyze texts, extract meaning from texts" (Wong Fillmore & Snow, 2000; see also Butler & Bailey, 2002).

The researchers found that the vocabulary and grammar orientation and the functional orientation were the most commonly held approaches to academic language. They noted the need to develop the linguistic (and, by extension, the epistemological) orientation among teachers, stating that English learners need to have knowledge not only of the semantic and syntactic *content* of the discipline but also of the appropriate *representation* of that knowledge in accordance with the genre of the discipline. This statement was made in response to data suggesting that instead of making sure that English learners receive exposure to sophisticated, academic text in a discipline, teachers often withhold from them the very input they need to master such text. The following excerpt from a focus group exemplifies the tendency to give English learners simplified text:

> Researcher: What difficulties do you encounter in teaching your English-learner students?
>
> Teacher 1: The most frustrating thing is that they can't read the textbook. They say we can't buy special textbooks for them, but what then?
>
> Researcher: So what do you do?
>
> Teacher 2: You use handouts or articles written at a lower level that they can understand.
>
> Teacher 3: You bend the rules. You buy the special textbooks and say they will be used as a supplement to the text. You get out the required text and you say, "Look at the pictures" and then you go back to the special book and say, "Now we're going to read this book." That's the only way you're going to get it done.

Unfortunately, these teachers' frustration over their students' difficulties in reading the textbook has resulted in the removal of the textbook. The "special textbook" that the teachers use, with its semantic and syntactic modifications, may be more immediately comprehensible to their English learners, but because of the modifications, it is likely to no longer retain its authenticity to the disciplinary genre and to provide them with the input they need to acquire the appropriate stylistic register.

Rather than thinking of the academic language orientations in a hierarchical fashion—that is, that one orientation is "better" than another—it is undoubtedly more productive and more realistic to acknowledge that they are all aspects of a multidimensional understanding of academic language. To succeed in school requires attainment of each form of academic language, as each is essential to the different kinds of tasks that schooling demands. However, given the finding that teachers may prefer to use simplified text with English learners to avoid their own frustration (rather than thinking of alternative ways of engaging them with the more challenging text), it is important not to understate the need for a more linguistically inspired orientation to academic language. As García (2002) says, "Simplifying and reducing their [English learners'] language and literacy context in school may result in better scores on standardized tests in the early grades, but it will not get them to develop the advanced literacy needed for professional status as adults" (p. 245).

Implications of Second-Language Acquisition Theory for Instruction

Although we do not have a perfect theory to guide us in planning instruction for second-language learners, we do know a great deal about their processes of learning, the factors that affect those processes, and the kind of language proficiency they will need to succeed in U.S. schools.

Making Instructional Decisions for English Learners

To make sound instructional decisions for students, it is good practice for teachers to base them on the best knowledge available—that gained, in this case, from research on second-language acquisition and the needs of second-language learners. Teachers are often caught, however, between recommendations or suggestions based on such research and the mandated policies or practices of their school, district, or state. There is an abundance of SLA theory and research that, though still more indicative than conclusive, depicts the second-language learner as innately equipped to make sense of the language instruction environment, as long as the environment contains elements appropriate to the learner's level of development and is otherwise well-suited to the learner's social and psychological needs. In this view, the student's first language is seen as a resource for the second, which can take up to 7 years or more to develop fully. An effective teacher will not be trapped by conflicting theories or practices. With a solid base of understanding of the abilities, experiences, and needs of their students, teachers can design a language-learning environment that will allow their students to meet the same achievement goals as monolingual students.

Children with nonstandard language practices (from non-monolingual English-speaking backgrounds) are at a disadvantage in school, so the teacher's job must include instruction that standardizes their use of language at school, thus ensuring them access to the same kinds of teacher expectations and socioeconomic opportunities as their monolingual and standard dialect–speaking peers (Delpit, 1988). The teacher may also need to question the standards that shape current thinking about second-language learning and teaching and to inform and enrich their practice and their professional community with the many challenges—and insights—that their day-to-day work with bilingual students will undoubtedly bring. Understanding the bilingual learner as a bilingual means recognizing "the unique organizational, structural, and processing characteristics of bilingual and mixed-language competencies, as well as the unique environmental and contextual linguistic demands for L1, L2, and L1/L2 hearing and speaking" (Grosjean, 1989, cited in Valdés & Figueroa, 1994, p. 84).

Effective Instructional Practice for Second-Language Learners

The need to provide effective instruction for second-language learners is growing steadily in the United States as the student populations in our schools become increasingly multilingual. Hamayan (1990) pointed out that in 1980, more than half of the teachers in the United States either had English language learners in their current classrooms or had taught them previously, while only 1 in 17 had any coursework in teaching English as a second language. Over the last decade, the number of English language learners has increased dramatically. Statistics from 1997 to 1998 showed that there were almost 3.5 million limited English proficient students in K–12 schools across the country (Macías, 2000). Chapter 6 in this book provides a more in-depth discussion of effective instructional strategies for English language learners and other students with language difference, with many specific examples. Our purpose here is to provide some general guidelines and suggestions that are based on what has been learned about second-language acquisition.

The differences among the second-language acquisition theories discussed earlier in this chapter are reflected in a general division between two groups of instructional theorists who have made recommendations for teaching second-language learners. On one side are those who embrace the theory that a second language is learned in much the same way as a first language and therefore suggest that the classroom should be structured to allow "natural" language acquisition. Instructional suggestions supported by this theory would include such approaches as cooperative learning, in which the need for interaction is great and students learn from one another. On the other side are those who believe that the diversity in capacities, attitudes, experiential backgrounds, and learning sequences of a classroom of learners suggests that much can be missed if only a natural approach is used; they recommend that language be "systematically and explicitly taught" (McLaughlin, 1985). Schmida (1996) provided evidence that students who were in classrooms where natural language learning was the adopted approach did not develop sufficient language skills for academic success. Our suggestion is that a combination of formal and informal approaches can optimize the learning environment for students who have an urgent need to learn English. Thus, allowing them plenty of opportunity for informal interaction and purposeful conversation along with focused instruction on linguistic elements will give students the best chance to learn English as rapidly as they need to in order to succeed academically. Certainly older students who have learned more about language formally can benefit from formal learning approaches as well as natural ones.

Guidelines for Providing Effective Support for English Language Learners

Although research support for effective approaches remains somewhat inconclusive, there is enough support from some of the research and from reports of effective classroom practices that prompts us to provide the following guidelines.

Be aware of sociocultural factors. The important role of sociocultural factors in learning language has been introduced in this and the previous chapter and is explored in much greater depth in chapter 2, but we don't think it can be emphasized enough.

> As one masters a language, one is also becoming a member of the community that uses this language to interact, learn, conduct business, love and hate, and participate in a myriad of other social activities. A part of the sense of mastery and enjoyment in a language is acting appropriately and understanding cultural norms. (Díaz-Rico & Weed, 1995, p.40)

Many students fail to achieve proficiency in English even after prolonged exposure and even when their well-meaning teachers use the most up-to-date pedagogy. Many believe that this is because they fail to become socially and culturally comfortable with the second language. As was noted in the discussion of Schumann's (1978) acculturation model in the section on theories above, "the degree to which a learner acculturates to the target language group will control the degree to which he acquires the second language" (p. 34).

The first challenge for teachers is to understand the cultural norms of their students. Although they will not be able to learn every nuance of every language, there are general patterns of behavior that will help teachers to understand the worlds of their students and thus, in turn, to help students understand the cultural norms of school life (Díaz-Rico & Weed, 1995). Since any learning is based on previous learning, students need to feel sure that what they bring to the classroom is important and respected. Teachers need to learn as much as possible about the values, beliefs, practices, social customs, mores, childrearing practices, and learning styles of the cultures of the families of their students (see chapter 2).

To learn about their students, teachers should use techniques that are akin to ethnographic methodology, through which one gathers data about a situation or culture by observing and participating in the life of the community (Fetterman, 1989; Trumbull et al., 2001). Observations should be carried out in structured ways, "with the perspective that one is seeing the culture for the first time from the point of view of a complete outsider" (Díaz-Rico & Weed, 1995, p. 250). Nunan (1993) calls this the use of an "estrangement device." Observers should strive to be descriptive and objective and recognize when their own attitudes and values are hidden sources of bias. Other data collection methods would include interviews, home visits, and classroom presentations or involvement by members of the community.

Using instructional approaches that are sensitive to the cultures of the students in a classroom is variously referred to as *culturally responsive pedagogy* or *culturally compatible teaching*. Much useful information has appeared in the literature over recent years that includes suggestions for providing such instruction. Teachers should consider sociocultural factors that apply to teacher-student interactions, to classroom organization, and to curricular content and learning activities. Examples of things to keep in mind are provided in the Teacher Note box below.

Teacher Note

Culturally Responsive Classrooms

Fischer and Fischer (1979) identified teaching styles that teachers should vary to accommodate the cultures of different students in their classrooms:

1. The practice of establishing a child-centered classroom or curriculum through which children pursue their own interests may not be comfortable for some students. Some children come from cultures that center around adults and their needs, and children may find a child-centered approach mystifying.

2. Some students do not respond well to the idea of planning cooperatively because they are not comfortable taking this kind of responsibility for their learning.

3. Teachers who are subject-centered focus on covering the curriculum and may not give careful consideration to the relevance or appropriateness for children in their classrooms who come from nondominant cultures.

4. Some teachers use an approach that may be considered emotionally exciting rather than more subdued. Students from some cultures may find such an approach overstimulating and may be unable to complete tasks.

Adopt a communicative approach to second-language learning. A communicative approach to language learning was supported by the research of Hymes (1971), who focused on practical uses of language in the real world, and Halliday (1970) (see references to Halliday's functions of language in chapter 3) who criticized the use of grammar lessons and provided a map of the purposes for which people use language. The focus of such an approach is on knowing how to use a second language to creatively produce questions or responses for real purposes and in a variety of settings. The content of the lesson is based on the language needs of the students and the contexts in which language will be used, not on language skills that lack situational or motivational contexts (Cuevas, 1996).

Using such an approach, a teacher would introduce students to situations that promote creative use of language. Rather than serving merely as a grammar teacher, the teacher serves as a facilitator for projects requiring use of the language. Materials used for instruction are real world or authentic—job applications, literature, informational materials.

Tune in to students' individual learning needs. One of the most powerful suggestions that Frank Smith (1973), a scholar who wrote extensively on the acquisition of reading skills, gave to teachers was "Respond to what the child is trying to do." As noted earlier, students who are learning English as a second language have had a wide variety of experiences with their first and second languages, vary in their abilities and attitudes toward learning language, and have had a range of experiences with school (often in both their native and their adopted country). A teacher's challenge (and it is by no means a minor one) is to learn about the individual learning needs of her students so that she can, in fact, understand and respond to what a child is trying to do to learn and use his second language in ways that will allow him to succeed in school.

Adjust your input to the situation. Krashen's model of language acquisition generated the recommendation that teachers should use language that is just beyond students' current abilities by embedding language within a meaningful context, modifying the language presented to the student, using paraphrase and repetition, and involving students in multimodal learning activities—what he referred to as *comprehensible input*. Other researchers have objected to the use of comprehensible input on the basis that it may result in language that is artificial, stilted, or without the rich vocabulary and syntactic variation of language as it occurs naturally. Once again, adopting an approach that embraces the advantages of each of these techniques seems wise. Thus, a teacher must assess the learning situation and the capacities of his students and determine whether a language adjustment or modification is called for or whether the exposure to more sophisticated language will provide the challenge that second-language learners need to advance their language development.

Respect the learner and his or her language and culture. The language and culture that students bring from home is the foundation for their learning. In some ways, they *are* their language because language presents their face to the world. Language is their means for presenting their personality, conveying their needs, expressing their emotions, describing their life, and reporting their learning. When students whose first language is not English arrive at schools in the United States, they learn soon enough that it will be essential for them to master the language of school; they will suffer through countless instances of confusion, frustration, and demoralization as they strive to understand, follow directions, engage in learning activities, convey their questions, and demonstrate what they have learned. What they most need is for the teacher to convey to them a sense of respect for the language and culture they bring with them, for what they have learned to do with language, and for the vast amounts of knowledge they have already gained.

In order to convey this sense of respect, a teacher needs to be aware of cultural and linguistic differences so that she does not appear to be mystified, dismayed, or disdainful of the behaviors or language use of her students from other cultures. As we noted above, it may not be possible for a teacher to understand every aspect of every culture, but he can learn a lot by listening to, watching, and asking them about their lives, interests, and cultural practices. Respect for learners helps them to develop the self-esteem that is vital to their learning.

Adopt systematic questioning strategies. The most common instructional practice in U.S. classrooms is the use of questioning. Through their questions, teachers lead discussions and determine students' comprehension. Standard questioning strategies can be fraught with peril in working with language-minority students, however (Díaz-Rico & Weed, 1995; Schieffelin & Ochs, 1986). Two general areas are considered here. The first concerns the way questions are framed relative to students' proficiency levels; the second has to do with sociocultural aspects of displaying knowledge (Díaz-Rico & Weed, 1995, p. 78).

As we discussed in the section above on the timeline of second-language acquisition, some students may be in what has sometimes been called the silent period, and questions requiring a nonverbal response—head nod, pointing, manipulating materials—should be used to obtain a satisfactory response. Once students are beginning to speak, questions such as those that pose either-or scenarios, such as, "In the story, were the children learning to cook or trying an experiment?" will help students because they have the appropriate terms embedded in them. When students are more comfortable with language, interjecting *wh-* questions will be more appropriate. This is not to say that the teacher should never use higher order questions or questions that require more language when students are at lower proficiency levels with English, because the context of the situation may allow students to respond, even if haltingly, and with imperfect language, and the modeling of more sophisticated language is important.

Check often for comprehension or clarification. Regular clarification checks are a good way to maintain a two-way interaction centered on instruction. Teachers should establish routines through which students can express their need for clarification, recognizing that even this behavior is influenced by cultural norms. Thus, giving students different options for requesting help when they are not comprehending either what is being said or what a task or activity demands is an important consideration. Teachers should use a variety of strategies to check on students' understanding—asking them to show how they will do something, to restate or paraphrase what they heard, or to otherwise verbalize their understanding.

Develop effective error correction strategies. There are several principles that are useful for determining how and when to correct students who are learning content at the same time that they are learning a second language. First, the research shows that the input given to young children learning a language focuses much more on errors of meaning or factual accuracy than on errors of structure. This is important to keep in mind when children are learning a second language as well. (See Teacher Note box on page 55.)

Use both direct and indirect strategies. Oxford (1990) developed a useful taxonomy of learning strategies categorized as direct and indirect. *Direct strategies* are those that require mental processing and are further divided into three groups: memory, cognitive, and compensation. Teachers can help students to aquire *memory strategies* by using such tools as applying images and sounds, creating mental linkages, reviewing, and employing some physical response, such as writing. *Cognitive strategies* include practicing sounds, patterns, or natural verbal interchanges; sending and receiving messages; analyzing and reasoning; and creating structure for input and output such as taking notes, highlighting, and summarizing. *Comprehension strategies* include guessing, the use of gesture, or coining new words; these will help students to communicate when their language fails. *Indirect strategies* are ones that make learning easier but are not language based. These include affective strategies that "regulate emotions, motivations, and attitudes by lowering anxiety, using means of self-encouragement, and learning to gauge one's own feelings to remove learning blocks" (Oxford,

1990, p. 80). When students request clarification or correction, when they cooperate with others, and when they empathize because they share cultural backgrounds, they are using social strategies to help them learn. Finally, relying on metacognitive strategies is another way that students support their own learning. These strategies allow learners to control their thinking and to connect new learning with material that is already known. Other metacognitive strategies include selecting strategies, setting goals, organizing conditions for learning, and seeking opportunities to practice.

Teacher Note

Error Correction Strategies

Principle 1: In the early stages of language learning, fluency is more important than accuracy. A teacher who expects near-perfect speech and is constantly monitoring and correcting can add unnecessary anxiety to the student who is developing proficiency in his second language.

Principle 2: The most important strategy is to converse and model appropriate language. A teacher should generally respond to student utterances that may include errors of vocabulary or syntax with an appropriate response to the intended meaning of the utterance. When possible, the response can incorporate the correct form. For example, when a student says, "Pencil broken," the teacher might respond by saying, "If your pencil is broken, you can go sharpen it."

Principle 3: Focus on the student's message and provide judicious correction when the meaning is not clear. Teachers should be aware of the types of errors their students are making, and when they observe systematic errors in the class, they can discuss them with the class, with small groups showing the same errors, or with individuals.

Principle 4: Older students may profit from specific lessons or feedback on recurring errors. Older students are more aware of school practices and are able to apply rules they have learned and, therefore, can more readily profit from specific and direct feedback, but this depends on their level of proficiency.

Adapted from Díaz-Rico & Weed (1995)

Assess progress in language development using formal and informal measures. It is common for teachers to assume that the responsibility for assessing students' progress in language development or proficiency lies with a specialist who will test students at specified times—when they arrive as newcomers, when they are considered for placement in special classes, or when they seem ready for redesignation to mainstream classes given in English only. It is always good practice not to rely on a single measure to determine proficiency or academic achievement. This is even more the case when a student is striving to master a second language and will use it well or not so well depending on the situation and the demands of that situation. The purpose of informal classroom assessments is to ensure that students are properly placed and instructed. Teachers should make certain that cultural factors are not influencing a student's performance or their interpretation of that performance.

Teachers can use checklists, observation (including audiotaping), interviews, and performance tasks to determine students' proficiency in English. These should be as much as possible to be systematic and consistent across students and points in time. Teachers should strive to assess not only what linguistic structures students are able to use, but also what they are able to do with language (recall Halliday's functions of language, for example). Chapter 7 provides much more extensive information on language assessment.

Reflections

In this chapter, we have presented information to help teachers understand how the acquisition of a second language differs from acquiring one's native language and what it means to "know" a language. We have presented details about some theories of second-language acquisition, which, though not yet fully explanatory, provide a good basis for making some important instructional decisions. One of the most important ideas that will shape the instruction for English language learners is the nature and level of the input provided. According to Krashen's theories, the teacher should provide comprehensible input, and others have supported other simplifying strategies for enabling English learners to have access to information provided in English. To some extent, this has resulted in an oversimplified curriculum for English learners, in effect a "dumbing down" of instruction that has prevented English learners from achieving at high levels.

Knowledge of how children acquire their first and second languages reveals that, for the most part, they are provided with very rich input from which they extract the rules and structures they need to know in order to learn language and to use it effectively. Aída Walqui (2002), a researcher at WestEd in San Francisco, exhorts teachers, using the phrase "Amplify, don't simplify," when she makes suggestions about educating adolescent English learners. Although her work has focused largely on adolescent learners, much of what she propounds has applicability to all English learners.

> Rather than simplifying the tasks or the language, teaching subject matter content to English learners requires amplifying and enriching the linguistic and extra-linguistic context, so that students do not get just one opportunity to come to terms with the concepts involved, but in fact may construct their understanding on the basis of multiple clues and perspectives encountered in a variety of class activities. As Gibbons (2003) puts it, the teacher provides message "abundancy," also referred to as message "redundancy." (Walqui & Galguera, 2002, p. 7)

Rich context and redundancy are but two characteristics of first- (and often second-) language learning environments that have significant implications for instructional design for English (or any second-language) learners. Others features include behaviors such as the "gradual release of responsibility" that parents or caretakers afford as children advance in their language, support for the development of metacognitive awareness, interaction as the primary process by which learning takes place, positive feedback and support for the learner, and modeling. These and other features that facilitate second-language learning are discussed in detail in chapter 6.

Notes

1. Neither first- nor second-language acquisition is completely understood yet. Much research still needs to be done. However, current knowledge has important implications for providing effective instruction based on what we know to this point.

2. *Ecology* refers to the environment (or, more properly, the study of the environment), including the physical, social, and historical context in which development takes place.

3. Standardized tests designed to assess aptitude include the *Modern Language Aptitude Test* (MLAT), developed in 1959 by Carroll and Sapon and modified later (1967) as the EMLAT (*Elementary Modern Language Aptitude Test*) for younger children, and the *Language Aptitude Battery by Pimsleur* (1966) (PLAB). What these tests have in common is their recognition that aptitude for language learning cannot be characterized as a single ability, but only by reference to the interaction of a number of abilities, like a skill for phonetic coding and grammatical sensitivity, as described by Bialystok and Hakuta (1994, p. 130).

4. Although the learning-style literature is fraught with pitfalls, this is not to say that cultural values that influence language norms are not worth learning about (see, e.g., Philips, 1983; Rogoff, 2003; Trumbull et al., 2001). The risks of overgeneralizing need to be balanced with the usefulness of learning about tendencies within groups that can point to areas teachers need to investigate in order to make instruction responsive.

5. A classification system for assigning proficiency levels to students in the classroom may use categories such as Beginning, Early Intermediate, Intermediate, Early Advanced, and Advanced.

6. One of the first sociocultural challenges made to Chomsky's idea of language as grammatical competence was by Hymes (1972b). Hymes's idea of communicative competence was that it takes more to know a language than just understanding what are and are not correct sentences; it also takes knowledge about when, where, and with whom to use which sentences in a given situation. Hymes's questioning of the relevance of Chomsky's ideas with regard to a speaker's knowledge and decisions about language use prompted others to account for a richer description of what it means to "know" a language.

For Further Reading

Bialystok, E. (2001). *Bilingualism in development: Language, literacy, and cognition*. New York: Cambridge University Press.

Cummins, J. (2000). *Language, power, and pedagogy: Bilingual children in the crossfire*. Toronto: Multilingual Matters.

Genesee, F. (1994). *Educating second-language children: The whole child, the whole curriculum, the whole community*. Cambridge, UK: Cambridge University Press.

Pérez, B., & Torres-Guzmán, M. (1996). *Learning in two worlds: An integrated Spanish/English biliteracy approach*. White Plains, NY: Longman.

Chapter 5

Language and Literacy

Elise Trumbull

Proficiency with reading and writing is the foundation of academic proficiency. Literacy is required for success in all subject areas, and despite the computer revolution, "well-read" is still a synonym for "educated." Literacy depends upon well-developed oral language skills, but it also requires other skills not likely to be acquired without instruction. As with oral language, literacy is steeped in sociocultural values and takes on different meanings for different individuals and groups. Teachers at all grade levels play a strong role in supporting students to establish their own purposes for reading and writing, along with the skills necessary to become truly empowered as individuals and members of society.

A major educational goal of the United States, espoused by most citizens, is that all students graduate from high school with well-developed oral and written language skills (Kaestle, Damon-Moore, Stedman, Tinsley, & Trollinger, 1991; Resnick & Resnick, 1988). These skills are necessary for academic success, for effective participation in a democratic society, and for economic security. British researcher Gordon Wells (1986), who followed 32 children from age 15 months through the end of their elementary education, observes the following:

> What has emerged . . . as the major determinant of educational achievement is the extent of a child's mastery of literacy. As children progress through the primary years, the content of the curriculum comes increasingly to be presented symbolically through uses of language that are more characteristic of writing than of conversation. Without the ability to cope with this literate form of language, therefore—that is to say with the linguistic representation of ideas that are disembedded from a context of spe-

cific personal experience—children become progressively less able to meet
the demands of an academic curriculum. (p. 193)

This chapter begins with a broad perspective, examining the construct of
literacy. It then focuses largely on reading, describing the components of reading
proficiency and summarizing the course of their development in the learner. The
major pedagogical controversy in the field of reading is addressed, and suggestions for sound instructional practices are offered. Because reading and writing
are reciprocal processes, ideally developed in tandem, the chapter deals with
writing to some degree. However, for a fuller understanding of the development
of writing and implications for instruction, readers will want to look into additional resources.

What Is Literacy?

The term *literacy* commonly refers to the ability to read and write. Current
definitions focus heavily on the ability to make meaning from print and to put
one's own thoughts into print. In the Information Age, "print" extends to new
types of graphics associated with information and multimedia technologies that
require particular interpretive skills (Cope & Kalantzis, 2000; Rafferty, 1999).
Hence, written language is "an important medium through which we interact
with the human environment" in uncounted ways (Ferdman, 1990, p. 181).

A broader definition of literacy includes what might be called the "literate
uses of oral language," such as the ability to use the domain-specific language
associated with academic subjects and the ability to use evidence and rhetorical
strategies to argue a point or to give an effective public presentation. Some have
used the term *critical literacy* to mean the ability to use language in all of its
forms as a tool for thinking and communicating (Calfee & Nelson-Barber, 1991).
The term *critical* is also used to refer to the practice of reading with an eye to
identifying hidden meanings and biases in written texts and other media (Freebody
& Luke, 1990; Gillet & Temple, 1994).

Although at times this chapter focuses more on print literacy (using the term
literacy in that narrow sense), in fact it is not possible to talk about development
of literacy or literacy instruction without also talking about oral language. Furthermore, though the chapter highlights differences between oral and written
language for purposes of illustrating certain points, an oral-written dichotomy is
sometimes false, as the broader definition above suggests.

Literacy as a Sociocultural Phenomenon

Like any language process, literacy involves communication with other people
and is, hence, social. It also takes place in cultural contexts. "Literacy can be
viewed . . . as the ability to think and reason like a literate person, *within a
particular society*" (Langer, 1991, p. 11). A society's or culture's approach to
literacy will color how an individual learns to read and write and use literate
language. It will help to determine what the meaningful purposes of literacy are

for that person. Literacy is not just a set of technical skills. In reality, it can be characterized in quite different ways, depending on what counts as important among the members of each cultural group (Bowman, 2000; DeCastell & Luke, 1983; Gee, 1999; Gutiérrez, 1993; Reder & Green, 1983). Cultures differ even in "what they consider to be their texts and in the values they attach to [them]" (Ferdman, 1990, p. 186). In addition, any culture's notion of literacy is likely to change over time, in response to differing social and cultural needs (Luke & Freebody, 1999).

Cross-cultural literacy researcher Stephen Reder (1994) speaks of literacy as "a set of social or cultural *practices* and its participants as a *community of practitioners*." He goes on to say, "As a set of socially patterned activities, literacy develops and spreads through a process of *socialization*, the means of which may include but are not necessarily limited to formal instruction" (pp. 33–34). Linguist James Gee (1990) suggests that it is artificial to think of literacy practices apart from the social institutions or groups in which they occur. He says:

> Literacy practices are almost always fully integrated with, interwoven into, constitute part of, the very texture of wider practices that involve talk, interaction, values and beliefs. You can no more cut the literacy out of the overall social practice, or cut away the non-literacy parts from the literacy parts of the overall practice, than you can subtract the white squares from a chess board and still have a chess board. (p. 43)

> **Teacher Inquiry**
>
> To what degree and in what ways has your personal experience in developing literacy reflected harmony between your home culture and school culture? What were your parents' literacy practices (including types of oral discourse you heard at home)? Invite a colleague to discuss his or her own response to these questions, or write your own reflections and share with each other.

Gee's statement notwithstanding, this chapter *will* be analyzing some literacy processes and practices as such, yet the reader should bear in mind that these can be understood best in the social context in which they occur—whether that of the classroom or the wider community.

"Literacy, then, in large part, involves facility in manipulating the symbols that codify and represent the values, beliefs, and norms of [a given] culture" (Ferdman, 1990, p. 187). A person may be considered highly literate in one society and not in another. Ferdman offers the example of an immigrant to the United States from Malaysia who reads his home language, teaches his sons to read the Qur'an, and maintains a complex accounting system for his business. Yet because he is unable to read or write in English, and perhaps unable to use oral forms of discourse preferred in the United States, he is likely to be regarded at his workplace as functionally illiterate.

Literacy as a Personal Phenomenon

Literacy is also personal. Although people are members of groups—social, cultural, professional—they have individual preferences, abilities, and needs that influence their learning processes (Anderson, Greeno, Reder, & Simon, 2000; Ferdman, 1990; Mahiri & Godley, 1998). Students have individual profiles of skills and their own identities as readers (Schoenbach, Greenleaf, Cziko, & Hurwitz, 1999). It is clear that students' classroom experiences interact with background factors to influence their development of skills and how they think of themselves relative to literacy. These background factors relate to both group membership and individual characteristics.

Historically, the research and literature on reading has emphasized individual psychological processes. To understand a student's orientation to literacy, however, one needs to understand both the student's cultural background and his or her personal goals and dispositions. Consider the example in the following Teacher Note box, which shows how instructional practice can meet the needs of students when it responds to them both as cultural beings and as individuals.

Teacher Note

High School Research Groups

Dr. Rosa Hernández Sheets taught an experimental 2-hour language arts–social studies block ("Block") for a multicultural group of 27 "at risk" high school freshmen in an urban school district in the Pacific Northwest. She hypothesized that allowing students to display aspects of their ethnic identity would support their engagement in schooling and positively affect their achievement.

Sheets asked her students to choose topics for research that interested them and to work independently or in small groups, as they wished. She also brought them together for whole-group discussions regularly. By choice, the students formed four groups of six to eight. Groups were quite homogeneous in terms of ethnic identity, with African-American and White-Black biracial students forming two groups, Asian and Asian-White biracial students another, and European Americans and a single White-Black biracial female the fourth group.

Students' research topics were close to their daily lives: 1) None of Ya Business: African-American Student Perception of Gossip, 2) Student Perception of Interracial Relationships: Can Love Cross Colors?, 3) The Impact of Peer Pressure on Sex Life, Drug Use, and Conformity to Social Group Standards, and 4) Student Perception of High School Truancy. Groups 1 and 2 and 1 and 3 collaborated to meet various research needs with the skills of individual students (e.g., tallying frequency counts on surveys and generating percentages, mediating group disagreements, organizing daily tasks).

All four groups shared knowledge such as how to fill out forms and represent data in their reports. Sheets accepted different styles of working, and groups "generally completed assignments," according to her. Groups 1, 2, and 3 worked collaboratively and communally, whereas Group 4 members tended to work independently to complete assigned pieces of the project. Within at

cont.

least three of the groups, members chose roles and activities through which they could contribute the most.

At the end of the term, most students In the Block received As as final grades, and nine earned honors credit for the portfolios they had kept for the class. All four groups' studies were accepted for presentation at the annual conference of the National Association for Multicultural Education (NAME) in 1996.

Unfortunately, most of these same students continued to do poorly in their other classes, exhibiting high degrees of absenteeism, low grades, and disciplinary problems.

Based on Sheets (1999b)

The elements of Rosa Sheets's approach that were responsive to students' group and individual differences included the following:

- Sheets built a climate of support for students' display of their ethnic and racial identities in the classroom, partly by allowing them to group themselves as they wished. This nurturing environment allowed students to reveal themselves and to see each other as sources of learning and support.[1]
- Students were allowed to choose their own research topics, and the teacher did not screen topics against a predetermined set of expectations.
- Different styles of participation and learning were permitted.
- A high level of expectation was communicated.

Allowing students—even encouraging them—to deal with topics like race, ethnic identity, and social inequity may seem too risky to many teachers. Yet adolescents, particularly those from nondominant groups, must have a lot of energy around these issues. Tapping this energy to promote high-level literacy activities and empower students as authentic participants in their own education and development would seem to be a very positive thing. Perhaps collaborating with other teachers, especially teachers from a range of cultural, racial, and ethnic backgrounds, would be a way to support moving beyond the curriculum of the textbook.[2] In addition, Sheets's project outcomes suggest that without collaboration with other teachers, the effects of such a powerful intervention may stay within the four walls in which it takes place.

Literacy as a Political Phenomenon

Different ways of using language—oral and written— have different status in U.S. society, and one's ability to use language in the ways accepted by the dominant cultural group has a positive impact on one's status in the larger society. This has been talked about to some extent under the topic of dialect in chapter 2. The Brazilian educator Paolo Freire has written at length about the potential for literacy to empower groups of people who have not had political influence (Freire, 1970; Freire & Macedo, 1987).[3] In fact, we don't need to move beyond the history of the United States for an example of how the opportunity to learn to read and write was purposely denied to large numbers of people precisely to prevent their empowerment: the case of slaves during the era prior to the Civil War. Inequities in access may be somewhat less intentional or extreme today, yet they remain.

Teachers recognize that students need to acquire the kind of literacy valued by the dominant culture—what Delpit (1995) calls the "power codes"—in order to progress through the educational system and successfully into adult life. Some have a conscious agenda of social justice, of working toward equality for all of their students. What they may not always be aware of is that home-culture forms of literacy need not be devalued or supplanted in the process of acquiring school forms. In fact, it is far more likely that students will be successful if their home culture practices are valued and regarded as resources in the classroom (Au & Jordan, 1981a; Barnhardt, 1982; McCarty, 2002; Tharp & Gallimore, 1988, Trumbull et al., 2001). Students who do not actively participate in classroom literacy practices may, in fact, be resisting rejecting their own community-based norms and practices (Malcolm, 1982).

Is Print Literacy an Unmitigated Good?

As long ago as the time of Plato and Socrates, scholars argued about the advantages and disadvantages of literacy. Socrates was concerned that reliance on the written word would mean that people would fail to develop their memory capacity. Plato distrusted reliance on the oral tradition of education, believing the oral mode to be the "enemy of logic" (Scribner & Cole, 1978/2001, p. 187). Print literacy does not necessarily bring unmitigated good into people's lives. Consider the potential effects of misleading advertising and political or ideological tracts that distort facts to promote extreme, antisocial acts. People may be harmed by both kinds of texts. On the other hand, writing has allowed people to not only maintain historical records but, more immediately, to spin out their ideas without having to rely on memory to the same degree as they would in the oral medium. Complex arguments that depend on lengthy chains of evidence can be developed and reviewed by the writer and reader, by looking back at what has been written (Chafe, 1985). Some argue that much of scientific development would not have been possible without print literacy (Smith, 1985).

Because print literacy is usually associated with formal schooling, it is often presumed to be the foundation for higher level cognitive activity. However, research shows that not all people who read and write engage in "school-like" thinking, and people who do not learn to read and write still develop abstract thought and can perform all the necessary cognitive operations important in their daily lives (Scribner & Cole, 1978/2001).

Indigenous groups of the Americas and elsewhere have been faced with a difficult decision because, despite what they see as negative aspects of literacy, they may have a better chance of preserving their languages if they develop writing systems for them (see Teacher Note box below). Of the approximately 300 languages spoken by American Indian tribes, only about 50 have more than 1,000 speakers; very few have more than 10,000 (Crystal, 1997). When languages are lost, entire ways of thinking are lost because groups use language both to construct social worlds and to make sense of their physical worlds (Hinton, 1994).

Teacher Note

The Oral Tradition

Throughout history, most languages have not been written (Hinton, 1994). Print literacy, something so valued in U.S. dominant culture, is not uniformly meaningful across cultures. Some societies have chosen to maintain an oral tradition and not put their languages into print. Such societies have sophisticated oral genres that serve many of the same purposes as written language: maintaining and passing on scientific knowledge, narrating morally instructive or entertaining stories, and preserving knowledge of their groups' histories. Many American Indian and Alaska Native groups have struggled with the question of whether they should keep their ancestral languages unwritten. Even when the decision has been made to develop written language, groups may continue to question what the role of written language is in the education of their children or the continuation of their culture (Leap, 1991; Linguistic Institute for Native Americans, n.d.).

Within groups that have developed writing systems since contact with European cultures, some members continue to choose nonliteracy—a term that is used rather than *illiteracy*, which implies lack of ability or opportunity to learn (Kwachka, 1994). Those societies and individuals who choose nonliteracy—something almost unimaginable to many Americans—are aware of the social costs of literacy. Among these are the erosion of traditional roles of elders (because one can always go look something up in a book rather than ask an elder) and the loss of oral traditions and skills.

Groups with oral traditions typically have highly sophisticated oral strategies for organizing lengthy narratives and social strategies that ensure group memory. One strategy is to designate individuals who are responsible for understanding and remembering certain knowledge and passing it on to other appropriate individuals. When literacy is introduced, it can disturb this whole system. Moreover, oral strategies that develop memory (such as use of rhyme and special ways of organizing stories) may atrophy when a culture moves to the use of written language.

Some consider the pressures upon nonliterate peoples to become literate to be nothing short of linguistic imperialism. They suggest that the "historical transformation that has accompanied the spread of literacy in the modern world . . . [has done] enormous damage to most of the ancestral and primarily oral languages of the world, as well as their cultures" (Cope & Kalantzis, 2000, p. 217, citing Phillipson, 1992). Others believe that if these endangered languages are written and language samples audiotaped, there will be historical records of them. In theory, posterity will then have access to the worldviews they represent. Teachers who understand these tensions may be more successful in working with families from communities struggling with such issues.

The Relation Between Oral and Written Language

"Written language is not a brand-new kind of language, but a kind that was founded on the resources of spoken language and that has in the meantime developed certain expanded possibilities" (Chafe, 1985, p. 107). It is a relatively new historical development, not much more than 5,000 years old. It is "historically secondary" to oral language in that very few people in human history have been literate, and even today human beings spend much more time using spoken language than reading or writing (Chafe, 1985). Written language uses the same vocabulary, phonology, and—with some exceptions—syntax as oral language. For this reason, when children (or adults) are learning to read and write, they already have a vast, applicable knowledge base from which to draw.

Print, whether alphabetic like English or logographic like Chinese, represents spoken words. Reading involves matching written strings of letters, words (or logograms), and sentences to oral language forms and meanings. It is not surprising that nearly all aspects of oral language proficiency in young children—ranging from verbal memory to vocabulary, grammatical skills, and sensitivity to sounds in words—are positively correlated with later reading success (Snow et al., 1998).

Contrasts Between Oral and Written Language

Oral and written language are different in several ways, and additional skills beyond those necessary for oral language will be necessary for success with reading and writing. The bulk of preschool children's language experience is conversational, and learning to read text introduces a new set of linguistic demands (Greenfield, 1972; Mattingly, 1972; Menyuk, 1976, 1995; Olson, 1985; Rubin, 1980). Students will have to learn how to become conscious of aspects of language that have largely remained automatic or unconscious.

An important cognitive difference between oral and written language is the fact that written language is doubly symbolic. Oral language is a *primary symbol system*; it directly symbolizes thought (Mattingly, 1972). Written language is a symbolic representation of oral language—a symbol system that represents another symbol system. Thus, linguists call written language *second order symbolism*. In order to process written language, a reader or writer has to become at least somewhat conscious of his or her knowledge of oral language—something that isn't necessary in speaking most of the time (Flood & Menyuk, 1983; Liberman & Shankweiler, 1985).[4] For instance, the ambiguity of a word like *sanction*, which can mean both to approve and to disapprove, may be quite clear in conversation but require conscious analysis in a complex written sentence. Pronoun references need not be so specific in conversation. If a speaker says, "She told me to help him," a listener may well be able to infer that *she* is the teacher and *him* is Henry, the student sitting nearby. Information about what is being said and what is meant by a message can also be gleaned from looking at the speaker's lips, from facial expressions, and from intonation and pauses or pacing of speech.

Table 5-1 lists the principal contrasts between the oral and written forms of language. It illustrates the fact that although written language is based on oral language, there are significant differences between the two other than simply modality. Beyond the need to learn the code, or how oral language is represented in written form, readers and writers need to learn how to process language out of context—how to construct meaning in the absence of the usual cues associated with face-to-face communication. Perhaps for these reasons reading and writing are not universally acquired skills like oral language.

Table 5-1. Contrasts Between Oral and Written Language

Oral Language	Written Language
Uses auditory-vocal channel (ears and mouth)*	Uses visual and manual channel (eyes and hand)
Signal is temporal (time-linked) and fades rapidly (sound waves disappear)	Has spatial form and produces a permanent record of what is "said." (Message can be reviewed without request for repetition and processed at varying speeds)
Generally takes place face-to-face, allowing for processing of facial expression, stress, intonation, and speed as well as body language (Notable exceptions are telephone and other electronic means—which lack several of the features of face-to-face communication)	Takes place without a direct inter-locutor—i.e., the author is not present—and no facial clues to meaning are available; has a one-way quality, even though there are presumed receivers of the message
Offers opportunities for eliciting clarifications from one's interlocutor	Offers no opportunity for clarifica-tions between writer and reader
Takes place in a physical and social context. There may be environmental information that helps disambiguate unclear meanings (e.g., words with multiple meanings may be clearer)	Takes place out of any immediate context; the reader supplies the context
Topics tend to be familiar or clear in context	Topics are not necessarily familiar
Tends to have shorter and less complex sentences	Is likely to be more complex grammatically
Is acquired without explicit instruction and mastered adequately by all except the most handicapped people or those with specific language disorders	Is learned almost always through direct instruction, and from 4% to 17.5% of students in the U.S. are considered reading disabled, depending on the stringency of the criteria used (Snow et al., 1998)
Is estimated to be a human capacity dating back some 150,000 years	Originated about 5,000 years ago
	Adapted from Rubin (1980)

*Note that the primary language of the deaf is visual and manual, and it is equivalent in function and complexity to spoken language.

Many of the contrasts listed in Table 5-1 are between conversational speech and written language. Oral language may take on many of the characteristics on the written side of the ledger when it is more formal. Written language may also have characteristics of speech when it is used for informal purposes, as in a personal letter or journal. In addition, the vocabulary and syntax of the formal oral language used in lectures or much of classroom instruction may be more comparable to what one would encounter in a text than to what is common in conversation.

Continuities Between Oral and Written Language

Although contrasts between oral and written language are highlighted, it must be understood that beginning readers do not come to the task of learning to read and write without considerable linguistic knowledge that can immediately be applied. For example, young children already have familiarity with at least some narrative structures; they have plenty of vocabulary and a working knowledge of a wide range of syntactic forms. They also most likely have been exposed to rhymes or rhyming games in which they are implicitly beginning to explore the phonological structure of words, something that will be key to their learning to read in an alphabetic writing system (Menyuk, 1995).

Some linguists believe that contrasting conversation with expository writing (the usual comparison between oral and written) leads us to overlook a possible way of understanding language differences that do not fall along strictly oral and written lines (Chafe, 1985; Tannen, 1985). They suggest it is more useful to examine differences in the degree of involvement of a piece of language, whether it is oral or written. In general, oral language entails more personal involvement with a speaker and, quite likely, with one's topic of conversation than written language does (Chafe, 1985). Often, conversation is more about connecting with another person than about conveying information. Writing, especially literature, however, may also incorporate features of oral language that make it personal and involving. In addition, it is not hard to think of examples of oral language that display low personal involvement—lectures, presentations, and perhaps even the common conversation of professors—where the emphasis is on the information rather than on human connections. Cultures differ in the degree of personal involvement expected in school discourse.

Language Skills Involved in Reading

All areas of language proficiency contribute to proficiency with reading (and writing). These include verbal memory, phonological skills, semantic (vocabulary) skills, grammatical skills, pragmatic skills, and discourse skills. In addition to utilizing these primary language skills, readers and writers depend on metalinguistic skills. That is, they need to make their implicit knowledge of language more explicit, or at least more accessible. For instance, when a third grader writes a story, she needs to be able to make decisions about spelling, word choice, sentence construction, and organization of the story. To do so, she has to step back from the automatic use of language and think about language in a more objective way. Activities that both draw on children's natural language and build awareness of language patterns are useful for emergent readers (see Teacher Note box).

An important set of linguistic skills not universally developed by school age has to do with children's experiences with so-called decontextualized or reduced-context language—opportunities to use language in unfamiliar situations that call for explicit descriptions and explanations (Snow, 1983; Snow & Tabors, 1993). For instance, a child who lives in an urban environment, where he has the chance to observe his mother negotiating transactions at the bank, the post office, and the grocery store, will have a different base of linguistic experience from the child who lives in a close-knit rural community with few opportunities to hear conversation with strangers. The effect of such experience on reading development is not surprising, because (as discussed above) the text itself presents readers with the need to decipher meaning out of any immediate social or real-world context, unlike ordinary conversation, in which the situation itself supports understanding of the language and there are opportunities for clarification if necessary. In essence, the reader needs to supply a good deal of the context on the basis of his or her own knowledge and experience. Linguist Deborah Tannen (1985) calls this process *recontextualizing*.

Teacher Note

Tapping and Extending Language Skills

There are ways to make texts for young readers more accessible. Some early-reading textbooks use conversational language familiar to young children ("Look! It's a spider. She's got eight legs!").

Another widely used way to make text links to children's ways of expressing themselves is through the "language experience" method of having children dictate their own stories or accounts of events and read them back, with the teacher's assistance if necessary (see chapter 6). When children are supplying their own meaningful context and their own natural language, the distance between a text and the reader is reduced.

Some have argued that memorizing familiar patterns without being able to identify individual words is "false" reading (Grossen, 1997). However, many others see this kind of reading as an important developmental step in understanding how books work. Such low-risk activities not only engage children but also give them a direct feeling for how oral and written language are related (Cambourne, 1988; Gillet & Temple, 1994; Neuman, Copple, & Bredecamp, 2000).

The Nature of the Reading Process

The vast majority of reading theorists agree that reading is a constructive process (see, e.g., Bartlett, 1932; Beck & McKeown, 1991; Goodman, 1992; Halliday & Hasan, 1976; Kintsch, 1988, Rosenblatt, 1938/1976; Rumelhart, 1980; Shu, Anderson, & Zhang, 1995). That is, the sense a reader makes of a text depends at least in part on his or her purpose for reading, knowledge about the topic, interest and beliefs, and knowledge of how texts work (structures and literary conventions). "Meaning is constructed each time a reader and text come together" (Freeman & Freeman, 2000, p. 24); it is not something that simply resides in the text. "What readers do is compose a text of their own . . . This composition, this new text, is what becomes meaningful" (Smagorinsky, 2001, p. 149). This is fairly evident to any teacher who has asked students for their personal responses to a story or to any adult who has been a member of a book club. People inevitably use their own personal experience and knowledge to understand new ideas or other people's experiences.

The phenomenon does not apply only to literature; students understand new science content they read, for example, in light of what they already know or think they know (see, e.g., Driver, Asoko, & Leach, 1994; Tiberghien, Jossem, & Barojas, 1997). The process of comprehension entails making inferences—that is, integrating what one already knows with what one is encountering on the page (Gagné, 1985; McCormick, 1992; Tierney & Pearson, 1981). Good readers make use of prior knowledge to help them understand what they read; less successful readers do not draw on what they know to the same extent, perhaps not realizing the importance of activating their related knowledge (Tierney & Cunningham, 1984).

New learning is built on what is already known; that is, children and adults actively construct understanding and knowledge in any domain. They do not just absorb what is presented by a parent or teacher in some direct fashion (Bransford et al., 2000; Cobb, 1994; Piaget, 1928; Vygotsky, 1978). A knowledgeable teacher can mediate[5] a student's learning; that is, he or she can interact with the student in ways that move students into what Vygotsky called the zone of proximal development—the place where a student can perform at his or her highest level with some outside support (which could come from a knowledgeable peer as well) (McCollum, 1991; see also chapter 6).

Although it is clear that the teaching-learning process needs to be interactive, it does not follow that teachers should never engage in direct instruction or direct transmission of information. Drill and practice have their place as well. Practice is certainly essential to attaining fluency and automaticity with skills. The trick is to find a balance of direct instruction and student-constructed learning, to support learning both within context and across contexts (make generalizations), and to find tasks that allow students to practice without becoming bored (Anderson, Reder, & Simon, n.d.).

Researchers like Jerome Bruner, Michael Cole, Sylvia Scribner, Patricia Greenfield, Barbara Rogoff, Jean Lave, Geoffrey Saxe, and Lev Vygotsky have shown how cultural values and practices also shape learning, from infancy through adulthood.[6] Children are naturally oriented to what their culture deems important. This applies to literacy as well as any other domain. A constructivist and a sociocultural approach to literacy teaching and learning go hand in hand. The experiences and prior knowledge on the basis of which students construct new understanding and knowledge are rooted in sociocultural contexts. Not only what they know but also how they know it and how they go about learning new things or interpreting text are influenced by culture (see chapter 2 for an extended discussion of this point.)

Components of Literacy Proficiency

Table 5-2 summarizes seven major components of literacy proficiency.[7] These are the key elements in learning to read and becoming a fully empowered reader—one who makes meaning of a broad range of texts (from oral, visual, and print media) and can use literacy skills critically for one's own purposes. Comprehension, or making meaning of text, is not treated as a component of literacy proficiency in this schema: It is, rather, the most important goal or outcome of the interaction of the multiple processes involved in reading. Likewise, communication of meaning through successful use of a range of skills is the foremost goal of writing. Interwoven with discussion of each component are implications for instruction. Here the term *literacy* is used to refer to reading and writing, although the focus is on reading. In fact, all of these elements come into the process of writing in one way or another. Writing, however, is arguably more demanding in some ways. For instance, students may need explicit instruction on sentence writing (Routman 1996) or special lessons on how to write within various genres (Calkins, 1994), even though they have successfully read sentences and different kinds of texts.[8]

Table 5-2. Components of Literacy Proficiency

Purposes for Reading & Writing	Students need to read and write for many purposes and come to establish their own purposes for doing so; they need to vary strategies depending on purpose.
Vocabulary & Prior Knowledge	Students draw on oral vocabulary and past experience to make sense of text and to compose text. They must continue to build new vocabulary and develop new knowledge bases.
Metalinguistic Awareness	Students tap implicit phonological knowledge about sound patterns of words and acquire phonemic awareness; come to distinguish the units of language and how they may be combined; tap grammatical knowledge to monitor reading comprehension and effectiveness of their writing.
Code Knowledge and Skills	For decoding and spelling, students need to know how the alphabet represents spoken sounds and how letters are combined to capture English morpheme patterns.
Metacognitive Knowledge and Skills	Students need to self-regulate when reading—anticipating, monitoring comprehension, and interpreting as they move through a text.
Discourse Knowledge and Skills	Students need to recognize how sentences are grouped into larger text patterns to suit different purposes, both for reading and composing.
Critical Skills	Students need to be critical, analytical consumers of print and other media, recognizing a writer's purpose(s), biases, and values.

How Variation in Purpose Affects Reading and Writing

"Reading (and for that matter, speaking) always and only occurs within specific practices and within specific genres in the service of specific purposes or content" (Gee, 1999, p. 3). Students don't just read, they read *something* and for a reason. The range of purposes for reading or writing varies from person to person, depending on experience, starting with the family. In some homes, reading may primarily serve religious purposes—reading the Bible, for example. Other purposes of literacy are to keep up with the news, make lists for shopping or planning, seek out information, keep and review records, gain pleasure or escape, communicate with distant relatives, or complete tasks for one's job (Teale & Sulzby, 1991).

A student's orientation to the purposes of literacy may influence his or her expectations on entering school. However, it is dangerous to assume that because a student has limited exposure to texts of various sorts in the home, he or she will not be a good reader—or will not be open to new ways of relating to print. Many believe that real engagement in the reading task is a key to learning to read, and that "children must be motivated to want to read for authentic purposes, connected to their own lives in meaningful ways" (Braunger & Lewis, 1998, p. 33). Engaged learners are most likely to develop the full range of oral and written language skills associated with schooling (Wilkinson & Silliman, 2000).

Of course, writers have purposes, too. They may intend to entertain, to inform, to provoke thought, or to persuade the reader to adopt a particular point of view or purchase a certain product. This topic is discussed further below.

> ### Teacher Note
>
> **Setting Purpose in Reading**
> Teachers can help students to expand their purposes for reading through instruction and exposure to a range of opportunities to engage with books. Students can learn to vary their reading strategies according to their purpose for reading (Schoenbach et al., 1999), whether to skim and scan, read for specific content, or immerse themselves in a text for the sheer pleasure of it. A tantalizing array of books in the classroom—both literature and expository text—and extended opportunities to explore them are two conditions that support students' expanding their purposes for reading.

The Roles of Vocabulary and Prior Knowledge in Literacy

Vocabulary and prior knowledge are crucial to comprehension. Vocabulary knowledge is so important to reading comprehension that it can reasonably be used as a measure of proficiency in written English (Pearson & Hernandez, 1994). Vocabulary knowledge and prior knowledge are obviously intertwined: Words represent concepts, and students' vocabularies are greatly dependent on their experiences gained through daily life, as well as through reading and instruction. Students must be able to understand the words they decode. In fact, because decoding yields only an approximate phonological representation of a word, the reader has to make a bit of a mental leap to determine what the real word on the page is. If it's a familiar word, the leap is shorter.

As students develop, their vocabulary knowledge not only expands in terms of the numbers of words students understand and use, it expands in terms of the degree of elaborated understanding that students have for the existing words in their vocabulary (Pease & Gleason, 1985). For instance, a word like *butterfly* may evoke an image of an insect with large wings. Greater experience with butterflies, or more exposure in school, will likely lead to a more elaborated sense of the word's meaning: stages of development of the butterfly, habitats, geographical distribution, types of butterflies, differences between butterflies and moths, and the like. In addition, as they develop their semantic system, students will learn to attach metaphorical meanings to the word: "float like a butterfly"; "His metamorphosis was like that of a caterpillar becoming a butterfly."

The knowledge base upon which students construct meaning in interaction with the text is equally critical to comprehension (Anderson & Pearson, 1984). Vocabulary is a component of prior knowledge, in effect; but students also have experiential knowledge for which they may not have elaborate vocabularies. A student who has helped his family plant crops in a terraced fashion along a hillside brings a great deal of conceptual knowledge to a story about growing grapes in Greece, even though he may not know a number of words in such a passage.

The Impact of Unknown Words on Comprehension

Because students are largely focused on comprehending what they read, they may skip over new words. Sometimes they can comprehend a passage quite well even if they don't know a considerable number of words, but once the proportion of unknown words exceeds 5% of the words in a text, comprehension will suffer noticeably (Hirsh & Nation, 1992; Hsueh-chao & Nation, 2000). Research has strongly implicated low vocabulary knowledge in the comprehension problems of students beyond the third grade (Cunningham & Stanovich, 1997), particularly for students from less privileged families (Hart & Risley, 1995) and English Language Learners (ELLs) (Garcia, 2000). The current public focus on early code skills and attaining fluency by third grade does not address the discrepancies in opportunities to develop a large vocabulary associated with social class differences. It is quite possible for students to master all of the early code skills, only to exhibit serious comprehension problems later on (Cunningham & Stanovich, 1997).

The Complexity of Vocabulary Knowledge

Long ago, Kenneth Goodman pointed out that "What we commonly call a vocabulary problem is never simply a matter of putting a verbal label on an object. In reality, it may represent a variety of different problems" (Goodman, 1976, p. 487). He outlined the components of the problem as follows:

1. The word is part of the student's oral vocabulary but is not recognized in print (the simplest problem, because the reader has prior knowledge from

which to draw).

2. The word itself is unknown to the reader, but he or she knows the concept it refers to (so now it's just a problem of getting new language to express something one knows).

3. The word is unfamiliar, and the reader has no prior knowledge of the concept it represents (a double whammy).

4. The reader understands the written word but doesn't mentally encode a pronunciation for it, so it doesn't become part of his or her oral vocabulary.

In fact, to say that a student "knows" a word or not is a vast oversimplification of the issue. There are many aspects to word knowledge, and students may have some and not others (see Teacher Note box below).

Teacher Note

Five Components of Word Knowledge

Incrementality: There are various degrees of knowing a word. It is not an all-or-nothing proposition. A student may know only that the word *clarinet* refers to some kind of musical instrument and not know more than that, or may know not only what a clarinet is but that it is a woodwind instrument that comes in different registers and was played by a famous jazz musician, Benny Goodman.

Multidimensionality: There are many aspects to the knowledge a person has (the pronunciation, the meaning, the grammatical category, what other words it is related to and what words it can be combined with. For instance, a student may know that *sweep* can be a verb but not know that it can be a noun, as in "clean sweep."

Polysemy: Words have multiple meanings. The student may know one or two meanings of a word like *light* (a noun meaning "something that illuminates," or a verb meaning "to illuminate," but not an adjective meaning "weighing little" or a verb meaning "land").

Interrelatedness: Words are not known in isolation but in relation to other words. Consider a family of words like *big, small, huge, medium-sized, tiny*. Most theorists who study vocabulary knowledge believe that our vocabularies are organized like vast networks, with words that are closely related or used together commonly more closely linked in memory.

Heterogeneity: Word knowlege also entails recognition that there are different kinds of words. For instance, a word like *is* or *the* entails different kinds of knowledge from a mathematical word like *tangent*.

Based on Nagy & Scott (2000)

The Role of Context in Word Identification

Students learn word meanings incidentally through reading, and reading is believed to be a major source of new vocabulary (Jenkins, Stein, & Wysocki, 1984; Nagy, Herman, & Anderson, 1985). Context is often cited as a source of meaning identification that students need to use consciously (Clay, 1989;

Freeman & Freeman, 2000; Gillet & Temple, 1994). However, research suggests that the probability that a reader will actually learn an unfamiliar word encountered in a text is about 1 in 10 (Nagy et al., 1985; Shu et al., 1995). Whether a reader figures out the meaning of an unknown word depends not only on the amount of contextual support but also on the conceptual difficulty of the word. When an unknown word is "surrounded by rich contextual information" (Shu et al., 1995, p. 89), it is more likely to be learned. Learning from context, however, is apparently based on prior knowledge, and if a reader has to build a whole new concept, the task is all the more difficult (Goodman, 1976; Shu et al., 1995).

Context is a good source of information for confirming or disconfirming one's accuracy in word identification, but a skilled reader recognizes words so rapidly that context is not a factor until after the fact (Gough, 1983; Stanovich, 1984; Stanovich & Stanovich, 1995). That is, the reader may use context to confirm that he or she has correctly identified a word and to infer its meaning in that context. Tunmer and Chapman (1993) state, "We believe that when confronted with an unfamiliar word, the child should be encouraged to look for familiar spelling patterns first and to use context as a backup support to confirm hypotheses about what the word might be" (pp. 3–4).

In fact, as texts become more difficult, important content words are not reliably easy to predict from context (Gough, 1983; Perfetti, Goldman, & Hogaboam, 1979), and certainly not with any speed or efficiency. Consider the following sentence from a text written by Jack London: "He had never seen dogs fight as these w___ish c___s f___t, and his first ex_____t t___t him an unf_____able l____n" (Grossen, 1997, p. 13). Without reference to the original text, we might guess most of the words (e.g., "wolfish curs fought"), but what does "ex____t" stand for? Even missing a single content word in this sentence will hamper comprehension.

Of course, when readers confront less common words or words that are not securely established in their spoken vocabulary, they may very well use context to help them identify them (Frederiksen, 1981). Furthermore, despite the repeated finding that good readers use orthographic information more than poor readers do, researchers continue to find that good readers do not use this information exclusively. Both good and poor readers also use semantic and contextual information (Kim & Goetz, 1994).

Vocabulary Instruction

Many researchers argue that development of the rich vocabulary required for success in school cannot be left to chance or the usual current practice. They believe that more frequent and more intensive vocabulary instruction is called for (Biemiller, 2001; Blachowitz & Fisher, 2004; Juel & Deffes, 2004; Nagy & Scott, 2000). Instructional strategies that focus on building and drawing on students' background knowledge before reading are likely to be more effective than vocabulary exercises like looking up a word in the dictionary and putting it in a sentence (Coady & Huckin, 1997; Marzano, 2003; Smith, 1997). According to

Stahl & Fairbanks (1986) who conducted a meta-analysis of studies on vocabulary instruction, three principles should be observed in vocabulary instruction:

1. Provide definitions as well as contextual information about words.
2. Encourage learners to process information about words at a deep level (see semantic mapping, below).
3. Provide learners with multiple exposures to a new word.

An experimental program. Recent research conducted with English-only (EO) speakers and Spanish-speaking ELLs showed that a vocabulary program incorporating several elements could benefit both groups. Students read fiction and non-fiction on the topic of immigration, and teachers organized vocabulary instruction around those texts. Researchers conclude, "We found that a challenging curriculum that focused on teaching academic words, awareness of polysemy [multiple meanings], strategies for inferring word meaning from context, and tools for analyzing morphological and cross-linguistic aspects of word meanings did improve the performance of both ELL and EO fifth graders, to equal degrees" (Carlo et al. 2004, p. 203). Students not only improved their vocabularies and learned strategies for approaching new words, they also improved in reading comprehension.

Analytic vocabulary instruction. One method that has successfully been used to promote vocabulary development is called *analytic vocabulary instruction* (based on Beck, McKeown, & Kucan, 2002). It addresses the three principles identified by Stahl and Fairbanks. Teachers engage in the following strategies (summarized in Juel & Deffes, 2004):

1. Focus on words contextualized in literature.
2. Provide clear explanations and examples of word meanings in different contexts and have students discuss, analyze, and use words.
3. Give students repeated opportunities to hear the words in different contexts and relate them to their own experiences.
4. Encourage students to use the words in new contexts and to discover other interesting words.

Elucidating semantic relationships. Semantic mapping is a specific strategy that has long been used in both literacy and content area instruction (Beck, Perfetti, & McKeown, 1982). Figure 5-1 shows a semantic map, which is a graphic way of representing the relationships among words. Semantic mapping can be used to tap and build background knowledge on any topic. Because it deals with words in relation to each other, one can argue that it reaches deeper levels of meaning.

Dealing with multiple meanings (polysemy). Learning multiple meanings of a single word has been characterized as a task of oral language but it is most certainly necessary for successful reading as well as promoted by students' reading. Many of the most common words in any language have multiple meanings; consider a simple word like *top*, which can be a noun, a verb, or an adjective and can mean "the highest or loftiest point or part of anything," "a lid," "the best card of a suit in a player's hand," "the first half of an inning in baseball," "a child's spinning toy," "to rise above," and about 45 other things, according to *Webster's*

Encyclopedic Unabridged Dictionary of the English Language (1984). There is an underlying semantic core, or kernel of meaning, that is reflected in each specific meaning. A teacher can help students to learn to home in on core meanings and use context to infer more about the specific meaning (Coady & Huckin, 1997).

Figure 5-1. Vocabulary Development Through Semantic Mapping

One technique for developing vocabulary and preparing to read a text of any kind is *semantic mapping* (Johnson & Pearson, 1984). In the simplest version, students brainstorm, as a group, all of their associations to a central concept. That concept (often represented by a single word) is written inside a bubble, and radiating lines are drawn to a new bubble for each association. So, for example, if students are going to read an informational book about bears, they may prepare by creating a map like the one below. The map may be elaborated by having subcategories within a branch (as the "habitats" bubble is elaborated).

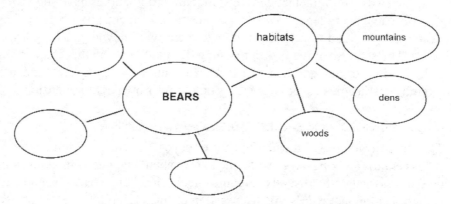

The idea is to build comprehension by linking the known and the unknown. The process of creating the map evokes the knowledge of the group, making a much broader knowledge base explicit than would be possible child by child. The technique is one example of a tool for conceptually driven vocabulary development.

Based on Pearson (2003)

Using prior knowledge. Readers do not rely on *word* knowledge alone to comprehend what they read; their *world* knowledge (prior knowledge) is also an important factor in comprehension. World knowledge is not just a random collection of memories but is organized. One's store of knowledge can be thought of as a collection of schemata, or mental frameworks that organize related information (Piaget, 1954). For example, children are quite likely have schemata for experiences like *recess, dinner time, birthday party,* and *bedtime*. When they read a story about a boy going to a birthday party, the appropriate schema should support text comprehension.

As readers move through a text of any kind, they combine their own knowledge with what is on the page to make inferences about text meaning (McCormick, 1992). Thus, they need both reader-based and text-based information to comprehend (Tierney & Pearson, 1981). Comprehension depends heavily on making good inferences, and to do so, readers need to be able to active the appropriate prior knowledge—tapping the right schemata (Anderson & Pearson, 1984). A reader who cannot summon the right schema or who does not have a schema for a relevant experience will have to rely on the text, and there may not be enough contextual information to make sense of what is going on—an issue that looms larger when the child is crossing from a different home culture to the school setting. Different aspects of reading proficiency interact with each other, however. Good comprehension skills apparently can compensate for lack of prior knowledge to some degree; likewise, good background knowledge can help a less proficient reader (Adams, Bell, & Perfetti, 1995).

Students can benefit from explicit instruction on how to make their own world knowledge conscious and relate it to what they are reading—something they often do not do automatically (Pressley, n.d.). Making use of prior knowledge requires a degree of metacognitive skill. Numerous studies have shown the benefits of teaching students how to pose questions to themselves before, during, and after they read to help them engage their own knowledge (Pressley et al., 1992). The strategy of reciprocal teaching discussed later in this chapter, for example, is one formalized effort to teach students how to develop and use metacognitive strategies successfully to promote their own comprehension.

The Role of Metalinguistic Knowledge and Skills

The term *metalinguistic* means "outside or beyond language." Metalinguistic awareness entails *thinking about* what one knows about language—making conscious the knowledge that usually remains unconscious, such as the sound patterns that form English words. As discussed in chapter 1, children are expected to use language to talk about language almost as soon as they get to school. The teacher may ask kindergarteners, "Think of a word that begins with *T*" or "Dictate a sentence about your birthday." To respond to such questions requires becoming conscious of the units of language—words, syllables, phonemes, sentences, and, later, word endings (grammatical morphemes, such as *-s* for plural or *-ed* for past tense). In reality, there are degrees of metalinguistic skill, ranging from awareness to the ability to use that awareness to solve decoding or comprehension challenges. For shorthand, the term *awareness* is often used that is the term used in much of the literature on metalinguistics. Nevertheless, it should be understood that awareness must be applied to be useful. Making linguistic knowledge explicit is critical in the writing process (Beers & Henderson, 1977; Rowe & Harste, 1986). At the same time, both reading and writing help students to become more metalinguistically aware (Morais et al., 1979; Vernon & Ferreiro, 1999).

Knowing What a Word Is

Learning about what counts as a word, a syllable, or an individual sound within a word is a developmental process (Sulzby, 1986; Tunmer & Bowey, 1984). A 5-year-old may judge "Happy Birthday" to be a word. As mentioned in chapter 1, if asked to count the number of words in a sentence, many 6- and 7-year-olds count only the important content words. "My dad is a bus driver" will be judged to have three words: "My-dad is a-bus driver" (Papandropoulou & Sinclair, 1974). Even some 8-year-olds have difficulty reliably distinguishing among word, syllable, and phrase (Downing & Oliver, 1974). The Teacher Note box describes some simple activities that promote word awareness.

Teacher Note

Teaching Word Awareness

Awareness of "words" can be taught through games and other activities. For example, students can build sentences with word cards, counting the number of words they use, or cut sentence strips into words and put them back together again. To demonstrate that a word's length has nothing to do with the size of what it refers to, teachers can have children give one-word labels for picture cards (asking the group to judge whether the label offered *is* a single word) and write the words on a list on the board. Discussion can center around the length of words, how a short word can stand for a big thing (Estrin & Chaney, 1989; Trumbull, 1984). A snake is a long creature, but the word *snake* is not.

Phonological Awareness

Great attention has been paid, increasingly in the last decade, to the development of phonological awareness as a basis for learning to read and write. This section will explore the research on the topic and attempt to sort out the conflicting claims in the literature. Phonological awareness (such as identifying the number of syllables in a word or recognizing rhymes) is rarely necessary in oral communication, but it is important for learning to read. It is "the ability to attend explicitly to the phonological structure of spoken words, rather than just to their meanings and syntactic roles" (Snow et al., 1998, p. 111). Small children show beginning phonological awareness when they play with language sounds by making up silly rhymes—*baby, waby, maby, laby, taby*—or giving playful labels to items or people in their environment like "Sammy wammy" or "Judy ludy."

To be phonologically aware is to be able to break words into syllables orally, to detect patterns like rhymes (*lake, cake, bake, break, steak*), to separate the initial consonant from the rest of a word (*l-ake*), or (at a more abstract level) to learn to hear the individual sounds (phonemes) in a word (*l-a-ke*). Phonological awareness is particularly important in learning to read an alphabetic script, like that of English. However, aspects of phonological awareness have been shown to be a factor in successful reading by Chinese students as well, whose written language is in the form of logograms, or whole-word symbols (Chen & Allport,

1995; Ho & Bryant, 1997). In fact, many logograms contain both a meaning component and a pronunciation (phonological) component (Crystal, 1997).

Morphophonological Awareness

At another level, phonological awareness means being able to recognize the relationship between words like *intervene* and *intervention* or *integrate*, *integral*, and *integrity*. Linguists speak of *morphophonological awareness* when they refer to this kind of skill. This almost unpronounceable word is itself a potential illustration of an important concept: Words are often composed of more than one meaningful chunk (e.g., words with two or more morphemes, such as *beauti-ful*, *dis-comfort*, or *understand-able*). The task for the developing reader is not only to hear words as composed of sounds but to perceive their underlying structure—their morphophonological structure.

The word *morphophonological* can be easily understood when a reader knows the meaning of each of its chunks. *Morpho* refers to morphemes, which can be words (*beauty*, *comfort*) or the small pieces combined with words (*-ful*, *dis-*) to add particular meaning; *phon*, refers to *sound*, and *ologi* (*ology*) to the study of something (in this case sounds). The remainder of the word is an ending (*-cal*) that turns the word into an adjective.

To be morphophonologically aware, children have to learn about how not only sounds but also morphemes may be combined in English and the relations between the pronunciation and spelling of multi-morphemic words. For instance, a five-syllable word like *undeniable* is pronounced with the stress on the third syllable, as are a great many other five-syllable words of the same pattern (e.g., *indescribable*, *conversational*, *inconceivable*, *disambiguate*).[9]

Phonemic Awareness

Phonemic awareness—one aspect of phonological awareness—is an essential element in learning to read (Adams, 1990; Ehri et al., 2001; Ehri & Wilce, 1985; Grossen, 1997; Juel & Minden-Cupp, 2000; Liberman & Shankweiler, 1985; Stanovich, 1984). This skill—being able to hear and manipulate the individual sounds (phonemes) in spoken words—is fundamental to grasping the alphabetic principle, that letters represent speech sounds. Considerable research evidence going back several decades suggests that a large number of early reading difficulties are attributable to problems with phonemic awareness (Adams, 1990; Bruck, 1985; Hogaboam & Perfetti, 1978; Liberman et al., 1974).[10] Yet as important as this skill is, it is not altogether natural. Human brains seem to be wired to perceive syllables rather easily (Liberman et al., 1974), but people do not automatically perceive phonemes independently of the syllables in which they occur (Morais et al., 1979).

Teacher Note

Building Phonemic Awareness.
(Activities move from easier to more difficult.)

Phoneme matching	Do *pen* and *pipe* begin with the same sound?
Phoneme isolation	What is the first sound in *rose*?
Odd word out	What word starts with a different sound? *bag, nine, beach, bike*?
Sound to word matching	Is there a /k/ in *bike*?
Phoneme deletion	What word would be left if the /k/ sound were taken away from *cat*? What sound do you hear in *meat* that is missing in *eat*?
Phoneme counting	How many sounds do you hear in the word *cake*?
Blending phonemes	What word would we have if you put these sounds together: /s/ /a/ /t/?

Adapted from Grossen (1997), p. 10, based on Stanovich (1994)

Children do not naturally hear dog as *d-o-g* but as a single unit of sound; however, they can come to hear those phonemes with direct instruction. The process is really one of analysis and synthesis: the reader has to be able to analyze a word into component sounds and then synthesize (blend) them to hear them as a word. Spelling requires similar skills, and some research suggests that the process of writing itself helps young children to get a grip on the sound structure of a language (Juel & Minden-Cupp, 2000; Vernon & Ferreiro, 1999). The activities described in the Teacher Note box above are simple and probably familiar to most teachers. They can be used to teach phonemic awareness as well as assess where a child is in the process of developing this awareness. It should be noted that many students who are low in phonological awareness when they enter school go on to acquire the necessary skills and become successful readers. Most children *will* be able to learn how to hear the individual sounds (phonemes) in words and how letters map onto the sounds in spoken words with appropriate instruction.[11]

In addition, phonological skills appear to be necessary elements of reading proficiency, but they are certainly not sufficient. Other kinds of skills and dispositions are also necessary for development of reading proficiency. Phonological skills are perhaps the most critical in terms of rapid word recognition (Laberge & Samuels, 1974; Perfetti & Lesgold, 1977). When readers read very slowly, they risk forgetting the beginning of a sentence by the time they get to the end, so automaticity in word identification is critical to gaining adequate speed for comprehension. Of course, rapid word identification does not ensure comprehension, so teachers need to be careful not to rely on word identification as the only index of reading skill.

Teachers may assume that writing, except for practicing the alphabet and copying words, is a premature activity for children who cannot yet read and who have not mastered phonemic awareness or full sound-letter knowledge. However, the act of attempting to put speech into writing seems to be an excellent way to increase children's phonological knowledge about words (Vernon & Ferreiro, 1999). Reading researcher P. David Pearson (2002) says, "Phonics is so much more transparent in spelling than it is in reading that I think it's easier for kids to deal with" (p. 2). In addition, it is a fine diagnostic tool, in the sense that the teacher can get information about how a child understands the mapping of oral onto written forms that may not be evident in an oral task. "When we ask children to write something (i.e., a word or phrase) that they have not yet been taught to write, we can witness a real process of construction" (Vernon & Ferreiro, 1999, p. 398).

Grammatical Awareness[12]

Grammatical awareness entails accessing tacit knowledge about how sentences may be formed in English. Grammatical awareness has been associated with both comprehension and word identification (Bowey, 1986). It is likely that sensitivity to the grammatical aspects of a sentence (in combination with phonological knowledge) helps readers to identify words (Chaney, 1994). Consider the following sentence from a Japanese folktale translated into English: "That evening, the greedy neighbor trudged out into the woods and found the same tree" (Uchida, 1986, p. 44). A reader may sense that *greedy* has to be an adjective and *trudged* a verb[13] for the sentence to be grammatical and will use that knowledge to help identify the words—or at least to develop some comprehension on the basis of that intuitive knowledge.

Students who are able to judge whether a sentence is grammatical or not while they are reading are more likely to self-correct errors, and good readers are more sensitive to their own errors than are average or poor readers (Flood & Menyuk, 1979, 1983). One activity that has been shown to promote grammatical awareness is *altered stories* (Trumbull, 1984). The teacher takes a story familiar to the children and introduces a grammatical error into about every other sentence (see Teacher Note nearby). He or she reads the story to the class or a

---

Teacher Note

The Country Mouse and the City Mouse

Once upon a time there was a country little mouse. She lived in the corner of a farmer's field. She was a very mouse happy. She had a nice place to live and enough to eat. One day, the little country mouse speaked to her cousin the city mouse and asked him to come visit.

Soon, the city mouse comed to visit. The country mouse brought out peas and seeds to eat. The city mouse am very upset. "Is this all you have to eat?" he asked. "You must coming to the city with me and see how I live."

So, the country mouse what to the city to see how her cousin lived. The city mouse lived in a house big. He often ate food from the table, after the people finished their meals. The two mouses ate all they wanted.

But just as they got to dessert, a huge cat did ran into the room. The two mice barely escaped with their lives. Later, when the cat disappeared, the city mouse said, "Now can eat some more we." "No, thank you," said the mouse country. "I'm going back home!" And she did.

small group. The children have to decide whether each sentence is okay. If they judge that a sentence is not okay, they are asked to fix it. It is important to avoid grammatical discrepancies based on common dialect differences exhibited by children in the class, unless a goal of instruction is to illustrate dialect differences.

This game of error detection and correction was very successful with second graders who had shown little grammatical awareness and were having reading problems. They enjoyed it, and their grammatical awareness (and reading skill) increased significantly after a series of sessions with this activity as well as others designed to promote metalinguistic awareness.

Another aspect of grammatical awareness is the ability to detect and resolve ambiguity, as in the sentence "The turkey is ready to eat." Who is going to be doing the eating? Failure to recognize that there is more than one possible reading of a sentence can result in failure to comprehend. The ability to recognize paraphrase has also been shown to play a role in comprehension. A reader needs to recognize that "Prohibition was associated with a huge increase in crime" is a rough paraphrase of "A significant increase in crime was observed not long after Prohibition became the law." Paraphrase, of course, can be applied to longer stretches of discourse, such as whole paragraphs or sections of text. Paraphrasing is one of the skills developed through *reciprocal teaching*, discussed later as a technique for enhancing comprehension.

The Role of Code Knowledge and Skills

A code is the system by which oral language is mapped onto written language through use of letters and patterns of letters (the orthography). Code knowledge and skills require developing readers and writers to make explicit many aspects of their implicit linguistic knowledge. To successfully use an alphabetic code such as the code for English, the reader needs to learn how individual sounds and groups of sounds are represented by letters and to hear words as being composed of individual sounds (phonemic awareness). The term *phonics* is frequently used for sound-letter knowledge and skills. Readers who are not able to use code knowledge rapidly and efficiently are seriously hampered in word identification and, hence, comprehension.

The Relation Between Alphabet Knowledge and Phonemic Awareness

Knowledge of the alphabet has been shown to be a strong predictor of early reading success. In fact, taken alone, it is the strongest predictor. As Snow et al. (1998) say, "Just measuring how many letters a kindergartner is able to name when shown letters in a random order appears to be nearly as successful at predicting future reading as is an entire readiness test" (p. 113).[14] Why might this be? Researchers have speculated that perhaps alphabet knowledge is associated with particular home experiences or with advanced cognitive development, but these hypotheses have not been borne out by research (Adams, 1990).

Letter-name knowledge alone is not enough to give a child an advantage in learning to read; hence, simply teaching the alphabet doesn't provide the benefit. For prereaders, researchers believe that the key is for children to be extremely fluent with their knowledge of the letters and able to name them accurately and quickly (Stanovich, Cunningham, & Cramer, 1984).[15] In other words, with beginning readers, speed and accuracy in reading are associated with effortlessness in letter recognition (Biemiller, 1977–78). In addition, the secure knowledge of letter names seems to speed up children's learning of the sounds associated with the letters. The names of many letters contain information about the sounds they represent, which helps children to remember and perhaps even figure out their sounds (Adams, 1990).

A child who spells *man* "mn" may be using cues from the letter names, even without explicitly being taught those two sound-letter associations. Adams (1990, p. 84) gives the example of a child's spelling *people* as "ppl." What a wonderful inference on the part of a beginning reader and writer! Here the child is showing awareness of the syllabic structure of the word (*peo-ple*) and knowledge of sound-letter relationships as well. It may be easier for a child to invent spelling for a two-syllable or three-syllable word than a one-syllable word (Vernon & Ferreiro, 1999) because the syllabic structure of words is easier to perceive than the phonemic structure. As mentioned, the process of writing supports development of phonological and phonemic awareness. Research on invented spelling shows how some young children have creative and logical notions of letter-to-sound mapping with little or no instruction (Clay, 1975; Read, 1971). Consider the title of educator Glenda Bissex's book, *GNYS AT WRK: A Child Learns to Read and Write* (1980). It is based on a note her 4-year-old son tacked on his door: DO NAT DTRB GNYS AT WRK (Do not disturb. Genius at work.) This young boy's spelling shows considerable awareness of the alphabetic code of English.

The Role of Code Knowledge in Word Identification

Many reading theorists emphasize teaching the beginning reader to attend to several types of clues in order to identify unknown words: visual (Do I recognize a familiar pattern?), orthographic[16] (Can I make use of spelling-to-sound relationships?), meaning based on context (Does the word make sense?), and grammaticality (Is the sentence acceptable with the word you have identified?) (Clay, 1989; Freeman & Freeman, 2000). However, numerous studies have shown that good readers are skilled at identifying words on the basis of orthographic information, whereas poor readers rely more on context (e.g., Briggs, Austin, & Underwood, 1984; Perfetti et al., 1998). The same appears to be true for younger readers in comparison to older readers (e.g., Stanovich, West, & Freeman, 1981).

Frequent exposure to a word facilitates its rapid recognition (Share & Stanovich, 1995), but because so many important content words are not encountered frequently, readers must have efficient mechanisms for identifying words in the absence of automatic visual memory for them. Research suggests that once readers have mastered the skill of phonemic analysis and synthesis, they begin to deal with chunks of words—patterns they will see over and over when they read (Juel & Minden-Cupp, 2000). Some examples are:

- *back-pack-sack-tack-lack*
- *day-pay-say-way-may-bay*
- *pat-sat-rat-cat-fat-hat-bat*
- *fish-dish-wish*
- *quickly-slowly-badly*

When word identification becomes more automatic, readers spend only milliseconds on word components, moving efficiently to recognition of the whole word. (The Teacher Note box below explains one way of highlighting patterns for students.)

Instruction in breaking down one-syllable words into *onset* (initial sound) and *rime* (the rest of the syllable), as in *l-ake*, and decoding a set of words based on that pattern (*c-ake*, *f-ake*, *s-ake*, *t-ake*, *w-ake*) may be helpful (Goswami, 1995), once students have learned phonemic analysis (Bruck & Treiman, 1992; Vandervelden & Siegel, 1995). Reviewing the literature on phonics instruction, Juel & Minden-Cupp (2000) conclude, "A structured phonics curriculum that included both onsets/rimes *and* the sound blending of phonemes within the rimes seemed very effective" (p. 485).

The Role of Metacognitive Knowledge and Skills

The term *metacognitive* refers to purposeful uses of cognitive resources, moving away from the automatic part of reading to somewhat consciously engage with the text in a strategic way. Good readers use these resources, whereas poor readers tend not to (Palincsar & David, 1991). To comprehend a text, a reader needs to read strategically, not simply proceed word by word, or even sentence by sentence. Michael Pressley (1999) notes:

> Self-regulated reading is much more about getting the meaning from whole texts than about processing of individual words . . . Fully-self regulated comprehenders consciously attempt to get the most out of reading, particularly doing what they can to abstract information that serves their goal in reading a text (pp. 90–91).

Teacher Note

Teaching Word Patterns

Cunningham (1999) and her colleagues have had success with an *analogic* approach to phonics instruction. In this approach, rather than learning phonics rules, children are taught to recognize patterns in words and to figure out new words on the basis of patterns in the words they can already read. If a student has learned the word *like*, the teacher could have him generate a list of rhyming words such as *hike*, *bike*, *dike*, *Mike*, *pike*, and *trike* – reading those words by analogy to *like*. However, it is important to stress that their approach uses many other instructional strategies, which may combine for a positive effect. In addition, children do not appear to use this analogical strategy successfully unless they have also mastered phonemic analysis skills.

Based on Ehri & Robbins (1992)

According to Pressley, successful readers do the following:

- Look back and forth in a text to clarify a confusing point
- Read more slowly when they come to a section relevant to their goal for reading
- Anticipate what might come next
- Monitor whether their predictions come true and how well they are comprehending
- React to text (e.g., checking against their prior knowledge)
- Interpret what they read
- Think about the text after they have read it

The section below on older students addresses how teachers have had success modeling and cuing these kinds of strategies for students. However, it is not only older students who can benefit: Studies have shown that students from second grade on up can learn to monitor themselves while they read (Anderson, 1992; Brown, Pressley, Van Meter, & Schuder, 1996; Collins, 1991). One procedure that has been shown to promote metacognitive skills in young students is *reciprocal teaching* (Palincsar & David, 1991) (See Teacher Note box).

The Role of Knowledge of Discourse Structures and Conventions

Another component of literacy proficiency has to do with students' knowledge of different kinds of oral and written discourse structures. Reading and writing entail producing and comprehending extended stretches of oral and written text organized in different ways, depending on their purposes. Ability to make use of text structure has been associated with success in reading (Mandler & Johnson, 1977; Meyer, 1975; Pearson &

> ### Teacher Note
>
> **Reciprocal Teaching**
>
> The purpose of reciprocal teaching is to help students "construct the meaning of the text and to monitor the success with which comprehension occurs" (Palincsar & David, 1991, p. 129). It has been shown to be effective with students as early as first grade. Teachers model for students how to (1) ask questions about text, (2) summarize what they have read, (3) clarify meanings while reading, and (4) make predictions about upcoming content. The approach is based on the idea that through dialogue with others (and modeling by a more competent other—the teacher), students gradually internalize the ability to engage in these strategies by themselves.
>
> To teach students how to use the strategies, teachers model by thinking aloud about their own reading processes—how they generate a summary, what cues they use to make predictions. In group discussions, the teacher provides only so much support as is necessary to keep students on track with raising questions or discussing difficulties in the text. Teachers also talk with students about *why* these strategies are important. For example, if a reader cannot paraphrase a section of text, he probably hasn't understood it adequately. If a reader doesn't monitor comprehension as she reads, identifying points at which she doesn't understand a word or concept, her comprehension will suffer.

Fielding, 1991; Stein & Glenn, 1979). A first grader who has heard many stories, whether read or told, will have internalized knowledge of text structure—what some call *story grammar*. Most stories or narratives begin with the presentation of a problem that is resolved through a series of episodes that often involve a lead character with whom the listener or reader can identify. There may be a moral to the story. Such stories are usually written in a sequential format, so that a clear beginning, middle, and end are evident. A typical story of European-American origin will have three such episodes.[17]

Not only narratives but also expository forms—such as argumentation and persuasion, description, and explanation—have predictable sets of patterns that readers become familiar with and come to expect when reading in the content areas (Calfee & Curley, 1984). For instance, a science passage about metals as elements may be organized as a topical net, with paragraphs on the different characteristics (e.g., crystalline structure when in solid state, salt-forming capacity). Figure 5-2 shows samples of common narrative and expository patterns. These patterns vary culturally (Gee, 1989; Kaplan, 1988; Kochman, 1989; Montaño-Harmon, 1991; Soter, 1988). The particular structures common in the United States

Figure 5-2. Examples of Graphic Organizers for Text

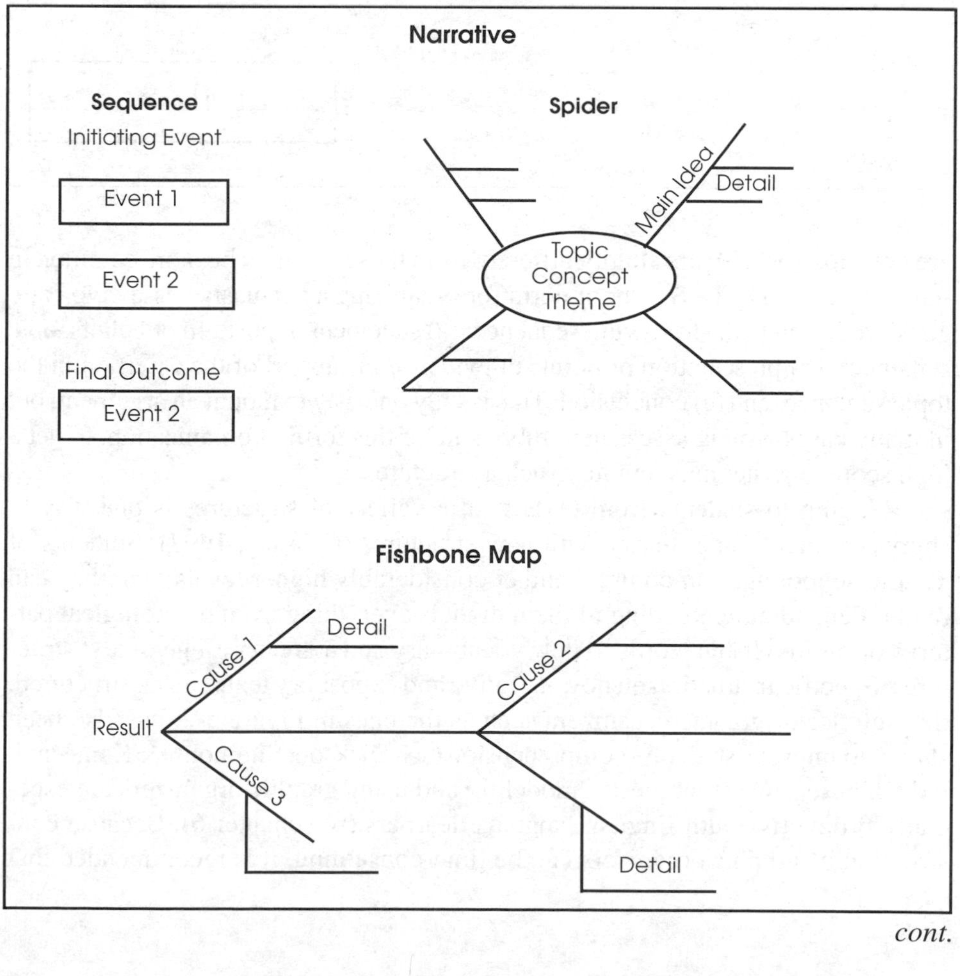

cont.

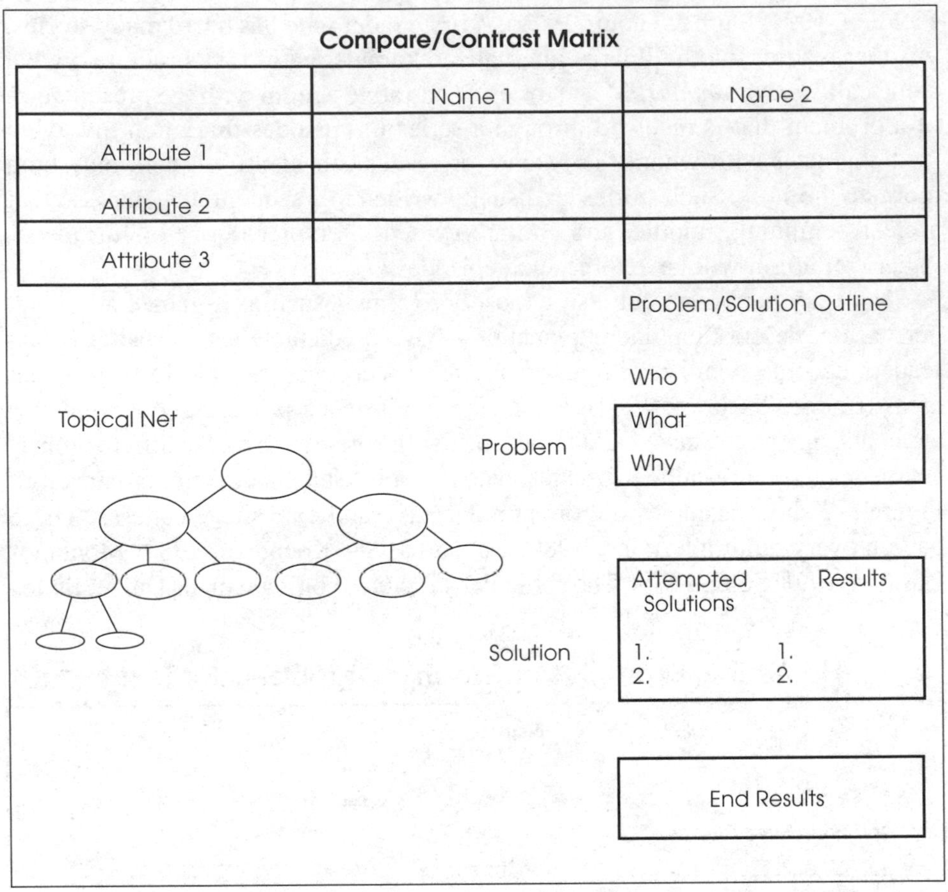

Compare/Contrast Matrix

	Name 1	Name 2
Attribute 1		
Attribute 2		
Attribute 3		

Problem/Solution Outline

Topical Net

Who

What
Problem
Why

Attempted   Results
Solutions

1.   1.
Solution   2.   2.

End Results

are not superior; they are simply different from those that may be more common in other cultures. The U. S. school norm for organizing a persuasive essay typically goes according to the following sequence: (a) statement of position or belief (topic sentence), (b) presentation of points of evidence in support of the assertion in the topic sentence, and (c) conclusion. This is only one way to mount an argument, but in many cases writing assessment rubrics favor this form of organization; to get a high score, a writer must employ such a structure.

Reading to students from texts with a variety of structures is one way to support students' familiarity with new structures (Grossen, 1997). Students of middle school age can comprehend at considerably higher levels than they can read independently. Reading to them models everything from phonological patterns of multisyllabic words to new vocabulary and a greater range of text structures. Specific instruction on how narrative and expository texts can be structured, through use of graphic organizers such as the ones in Figure 5-2, has also been shown to improve students' comprehension (see Dickson, Simmons, & Kameenui, n.d.). These same strategies of modeling and using graphic organizers are especially productive with English language learners (see chapter 6). Because construction of graphic organizers can be time-consuming, it is recommended that teachers collaborate on developing them and share them with each other (Dickson et al., n.d.).

The Role of the Ability to Approach Texts Critically

Becoming a critical reader means recognizing that "texts are not neutral, that they represent particular views and silence other points of view, influence people's ideas; and that [they] can be critiqued" (Luke & Freebody, 1999, p. 3). Students need to be able to recognize points of view and how writers use persuasion to influence readers (Ludwig, 2003). Ultimately, they can agree or disagree with the premises of a text on the basis of their own experience and the evidence they bring to bear. In recent years, the concept of *media literacy* has been introduced (Tyner, 1998). This term is often used to refer to familiarity with the techniques used to influence listeners' or viewers' thinking and behaviors (e.g., to purchase something, to endorse a political candidate, to espouse certain social values). More broadly, media literacy relates to all of the visual and expressive arts (painting, photography, film, music, and dance, in addition to forms of oral and written language) and interactive technologies (Hobbs & Frost, 2003). All of these media can be used to represent ideas and points of view, and savvy consumers interpret their messages critically. High school students can readily learn to critically analyze the messages of television news, for example, with some instruction in media literacy (Hobbs & Frost, 1999, 2003).

Many reading theorists argue that to become successful readers children need to see themselves as text analysts even in the early grades (e.g., Freebody & Luke, 1990). In her book *Social Worlds of Children Learning to Write in an Urban Primary School*, Ann Haas Dyson (1993) cites examples of early primary school children's adopting "a reflective, sometimes critical stance toward the content of [the discourse of] pop culture." She observes that they discussed whether Michael Jackson was real or not real, dead or alive, old or young. "In their playful talk, they revealed their knowledge about the talk of TV announcers, cartoon characters, and pop culture figures" (p. 225). Thus even very young children have the capacity to critically examine what they are reading, hearing, and viewing.

A critical stance toward literature and other texts (including spoken) and the opportunity to bring in one's own perspective are key ingredients in keeping students from different backgrounds engaged in high-level literacy practices (Sheets, 1999b). Texts will be experienced and interpreted in different ways, depending on students' backgrounds; particularly in classrooms composed of students from more than one cultural group, opportunities for elucidating more than one reading of a text will be rich. Of concern to all students should be questions of how various ethnic and racial groups are portrayed in all forms of media—their roles, their status, their language, their presence or absence. Students are likely to be more aware of these issues than a teacher may expect. For example, Dyson (1993) reports that as early as third grade, students are sensitive to how linguistic variation (e.g., dialect) is connected to racial and cultural identity.

A Continuum of Literacy Development

Students develop proficiency in each of these seven realms over many years—beginning long before they enter school. Some aspects of literacy knowledge and skill continue to develop throughout life, particularly for avid readers who explore new domains through reading and writing. Table 5-3 (see pages 192–193) shows one way of characterizing the stages readers move through as they mature (Gillet & Temple, 1994).[18] Stages are not entirely discrete; for example, although critical reading in its most developed form is a rather adult capacity, it can begin to develop early. Children may read for pleasure long before they have built fluency. The term *continuum* is used to convey the fluidity and overlap of growth in each of the seven skills or knowledge areas across time. Nevertheless, it is probably useful to label broad points of development as Gillet and Temple have done. The descriptions in each cell of Table 5-3 are generalizations that do not, of course, apply to every student, but they do give a sense of the course that development tends to take. In addition, a single student may be very well developed in one component and not another. Once again, although the focus is on reading, many observations apply to writing as well.

Emergent Literacy

Emergent literacy (Neuman & Roskos, 1992; Strickland & Morrow, 1991; Teale & Sulzby, 1991; Yaden, Rowe, & MacGillivray, 2000) is a useful concept for understanding literacy-related development in young children, much of which occurs before children enter school. "Emergent literacy refers to the reading and writing behaviors and concepts of young children that precede and develop into conventional literacy" (Kaderavek & Justice, 2000, p. 82). In past decades, it was thought that children were not ready to learn to read until they began school, and readiness to learn to read was often assessed by tasks like matching visual forms and detecting visual patterns. Sometimes even motor skills were evaluated, in the misguided belief that they predicted reading success or failure.

Now literacy experts recognize not only that language development is a far better indicator of readiness but also that for most children in the United States, learning to read and write begins in infancy, with exposure to literacy activities and materials. By age 3, many children know what a story is and how picture books work (front to back, right side up, with pictures elucidating the story). Some are beginning to grasp the fact that the print tells the story and perhaps to recognize a letter or two in their own name—or even that letters are written on the page from left to right. They have implicit knowledge of a range of purposes for reading and writing from having seen their parents writing lists, reading the newspaper, doing a crossword puzzle, writing a check, or using *TV Guide* (Teale & Sulzby, 1986).

Children from lower socioeconomic status (SES) homes tend to have fewer and different early literacy experiences compared to those from more advantaged homes (Purcell-Gates, 1996; Purcell-Gates & Dahl, 1991; Teale, 1986). It must be quickly said that despite this tendency, there is great variability in the preschool literacy experiences of such children, according to these researchers. In a study of 24 low-SES children from 20 families, Purcell-Gates (1996) found that their families did indeed engage in a variety of reading and writing activities. The 4- to 6-year-olds in Purcell-Gates's study had what she calls "the big picture" about reading and writing, the basic functions of print. However, many of them scored poorly on tests of emergent literacy, showing problems with more fine-grained concepts of print such as how letters encode sound patterns.

Teacher Note

Family Literacy

Family literacy is often associated with emergent literacy because it refers, in part, to home literacy practices that shape early emergent literacy development. There are family literacy programs to nurture adult literacy development and particular ways of interacting with children to promote their literacy development. These programs often target families with lower educational and economic resources, some of whom may speak English as a second or third language. Despite their good intentions, however, family literacy programs may actually inflict harm by promoting the "deficit model"—when they act on the implicit belief that low-income or "minority" parents need improvement, rather than seek to support children's emergent literacy through family strengths. Another concern is that the research supporting the value of family literacy approaches over separate child and adult literacy programs has yet to be done (Caspe, 2003).

Rather than a prescriptive approach, a social constructivist approach to family literacy would involve families in defining what they want from such programs as opposed to what educators prescribe for them (Neuman, 1995).

Here are some recommendations offered by the Family Involvement Network in Education (Caspe, 2003) for ensuring that family literacy programs meet the needs of the people they are designed to serve:

1. Learn about families' literacy strengths and literacy histories.

2. Provide opportunities for families to reflect on their uses of literacy and its meaning in their daily lives.

3. Respond to the interests of families (adults and children).

4. Work with families to empower them in ways that are meaningful to them and that engage them actively in their own learning.

Based on Caspe (2003)

Two factors appear to be associated with greater emergent literacy skills: *frequency* and *type* of literacy experiences. Purcell-Gates (1996) found that children apparently needed experiences in which they didn't just observe literacy activities but with which they were personally involved (see also Wilkinson & Silliman, 2000). In addition, they benefited from involvement with text at "more complex levels of written discourse"—that is, story reading rather than reading labels or identifying single words. A review of 34 studies on emergent literacy

Table 5-3. Continuum of Literacy Development

Key Points on the Continuum					
Components of Proficiency	**Emergent Literacy**	**Beginning Reading**	**Building Fluency**	**Reading for Pleasure, Reading to Learn**	**Mature Reading**
Purposes for Reading and Writing	Having some sense of literacy purposes, related to home experiences; possibly "writing" for different purposes (story, letter, birthday card)	Observing new purposes modeled by teacher; becoming aware of a wider range reasons to read and write	Beginning to choose own independent reading material; expanding notions of reasons to read and write	Continuing to establish own purposes (may make more explicit with aid of teacher) for reading and writing	Expanding purposes for reading and writing
Vocabulary and Prior Knowledge	Knowing several thousand words (likely), related to home experiences and language exposure	Expanding both through formal instruction; increasing awareness of what a word is	Continuing to build both through home and school experiences (including reading); increasing accuracy and speed of word identification	Continuing to build both; developing specific vocabulary and knowledge based on one's interests and instruction	Continuing to build both; developing more sophisticated vocabulary and knowledge commensurate with cognitive development
Metalinguistic Awareness	Recognizing and producing rhymes, perhaps playing with some sound patterns in words and hearing syllables in words; making up nonsense rhymes; detecting errors that result in distortion of meaning (quite variable on entry to school)	Expanding through play and formal instructional activities; beginning to distinguish linguistic units from each other (word, syllable, sound); developing phonemic awareness; beginning to detect grammatical errors	Refining knowledge of units of language; developing morphophonemic awareness, e.g., developing morphophonemic awareness, especially related to multisyllabic words; developing ability to detect and correct grammatical errors and use grammatical knowledge to monitor comprehension	Continuing to build morphophonemic awareness, e.g., recognizing patterns for pronouncing multisyllabic words; developing awareness of paraphrase and ambiguity; correcting own errors in reading and writing	Continuing to build awareness through reading and writing; editing writing with more success

cont.

Components of Proficiency	Emergent Literacy	Beginning Reading	Building Fluency	Reading for Pleasure, Reading to Learn	Mature Reading
Code Knowledge and Skills	Possessing some letter knowledge; using invented spelling (likely by kindergarten age)	Developing sound-letter knowledge; using mastering some sight words (some code knowledge helps)	Mastering decoding skills; reading and spelling more complex words	Building knowledge of morphemic and derivational structures (prefixes, suffixes, compounding, etc.) and how mapped onto spelling system	Continuing to develop more sophisticated knowledge of oral-written (spelling) relationships among words (e.g., words from same root)
Metacognitive Knowledge and Skills	Responding to questions about storybooks (depends on family- or preschool-based experiences in book-reading); some children may make predictions, pose own questions	Beginning to incorporate self-questioning strategy modeled by adults—a first step to monitoring comprehension	Continuing to develop ability to read strategically—posing questions before, during, after reading; monitoring comprehension	Continuing to build strategic reading skills with increasingly complex texts in different domains	Using strategic skills with near automaticity and selectively, depending on nature of text
Discourse Knowledge and Skills	Recognizing and telling stories; recounting experiences; describing past events; participating in a conversation	Expanding knowledge of stories and expository forms (teacher reads); learning to participate in orchestrated conversation or discussion	Continuing to build knowledge of oral and written discourse structures, through listening, reading, and writing	Continuing to build knowledge of oral and written discourse structures through discussions and reading texts in different domains	Efficiently using knowledge of wide range of oral and written discourse structures as appropriate to text and situation
Critical Skills	Possibly developing some awareness of critiquing texts through parents' or older siblings' comments and questions about books and other media	Possibly addressing media issues during discussions at rug time or circle time	Developing awareness of point of view, author's purpose and media messages	Increasing ability to critique author's (or other media's) purposes and techniques	Expanding critical skills to include active response—letters to editor, public critique, social action

also supported the notion that reading storybooks to preschoolers is an important way to usher them into the world of reading and writing (Bus, van IJzendoorn, & Pellegrini, 1995). A number of parents in Purcell-Gates's study began story reading with their children once they entered school, perhaps not realizing the value of this activity with preschoolers. So-called family literacy programs have been directed to low-SES families in the belief that such programs can avert reading problems in children (see Teacher Note box on page 191).

Fluency

Fluency is the ability to read a text quickly and accurately and with appropriate expression (National Reading Panel, 2000). Like comprehension, it is really an outcome of many processes coming together. Fluent readers recognize words and comprehend them simultaneously. When readers are not yet automatic in identifying most words in a passage, they will have difficulty reading orally with an expression that reflects the processing of sentence structure and punctuation. Reading fluency is a critical factor necessary for reading comprehension. If children read out loud with speed, accuracy, and proper expression, they are more likely to comprehend and remember the material than if they read with difficulty and in an inefficient way (Laberge & Samuels, 1974; Osborn & Lehr, n.d.; Rasinski, 2004). This makes sense: When a reader has to slow down and read word by word, he or she may have problems keeping in mind what came at the beginning of a sentence and chunking words in meaningful units (Laberge & Samuels, 1974).

> **Teacher Inquiry**
>
> How can you ensure that your teaching reflects the differential needs of your students? What can you do to determine their literacy levels and group them so that they acquire the skills they need but do not plateau in development? How would you maintain enough flexibility to regroup students and change the emphasis of instruction as they demonstrate different needs? For inspiration and ideas, see Juel & Minden-Cupp (2000).

Literacy as a Lifelong Process

The last column in Table 5-3 (Mature Reading) should perhaps be open-ended, to indicate that literacy skills can continue to mature throughout one's life. This potential may not come to fruition for every individual; yet with the changes in society as well as changes in the lives of individuals (e.g., moving from one job or career to another), it is reasonable to expect that most of the students in school now will need to continue to build literacy proficiency over the course of their lifetimes. The literacy demands of daily life over the past few decades have increased and changed (Cope & Kalantzis, 2000). For people whose vocations and avocations entail reading and/or writing, facility with new forms and functions of literacy will be the norm. In reality, literacy demands are linked to specific contexts, such as particular job demands and different purposes for reading (Imel & Grieve, 1985).

Reading Disability

Reading problems are nearly always based on oral language problems and quite rarely on visual deficits, as is commonly thought (Elbro, Borstrom, & Peterson, 1998; Catts & Kamhi, 1999). A gap in phonological skills appears to be the most common source of the problem. The term *dyslexia* has been widely used to describe severe reading disability, which is typically manifested early in a child's process of learning to read. Dyslexia is associated with a medical model for understanding difficulty in learning to read; a dyslexic child is believed to have brain-based problems in processing language (Denckla & Rudel, 1976; Geschwind, 1972; Shaywitz et al., 1998).

A cluster of differences in language processing defines dyslexia: difficulties with rapid word identification; phonemic segmentation; and rapid naming of colors, letters, numbers, and common objects (Blachman, 1983; Bowers, 1995; Denckla & Rudel, 1976; Elbro, Borstrom, & Petersen, 1998; Jansky & de Hirsch, 1972). The difficulty with rapid naming is specific and is not associated with a general vocabulary deficit. It is the automaticity that is the issue. Researchers believe that the problem is a phonological one; that is, dyslexic students have trouble encoding and retrieving words as clear patterns of sounds (Rubin & Liberman, 1983). This interpretation shows the relationship of the naming problem to phoneme segmentation (phonemic awareness) skills and rapid word identification in reading.

Differences between a *disabled* reader and a *poor* reader may be only a matter of degree, something that suggests caution in labeling. In fact, most students who are slow to become readers have difficulty acquiring phonological awareness (e.g., Snow et al., 1998), but one would hesitate to call them all disabled or dyslexic. Moreover, because phonological awareness is not essential to oral language proficiency, it may not properly be considered a language deficit *except in the context of learning to read and write*. Even students who have been diagnosed as dyslexic usually have normal oral language proficiency. Nevertheless, the inability to acquire phonological awareness can become a problem in a society that demands written literacy and has an alphabetic writing system.

Teachers should be slow to conclude that a reading problem resides in the child alone. Reading problems can also be the result of ineffective teaching methods. An *interactionist* new of reading problems is that environmental factors interact with instructional approaches and the child's own biology (Lipson & Wixson, 1986; McCormick, 1994). If a student is not responding to instruction that is effective with other students, different methods can be tried; and the child can be referred for evaluation simultaneously.[19] If there is any single message in the literature on addressing reading disability, it is that one should never give up on trying to find an approach that works for a student who is struggling to become a reader. The consequences of failing to do so can be devastating and lifelong. The next Teacher Note box describes the case of a severely disabled reader and the incredible lengths to which reading clinic staff went over a period of $3^{1}/_{2}$ years to get him successfully on the path of literacy development.

Teacher Note

Peter Learns to Read

Researcher Sandra McCormick documented the course of literacy development of "Peter" for more than 3 years and worked with his tutors to find an appropriate instructional approach for him. This is a long story, but each episode is important for understanding Peter's journey from nonreader to successful reader.

Summer After Second Grade

The summer after second grade, at the age of 8½, Peter began to get tutoring at a university reading clinic. After 2 years of school, he was able to identify only four words, *I, a, and,* and *but*. Peter's oral language skills were above average, so tutors began instruction with the language experience method; Peter would dictate stories and read them back. But because his oral language was so far ahead of his reading skills, he could not reread his stories (although he could retell them). After 20 hours of tutoring, Peter had added only 11 words to his reading vocabulary.

Third Grade

Peter continued to come for tutoring during third grade. Since the language experience approach hadn't succeeded, tutors began to try direct instruction on decoding (which wasn't taught consistently in his classroom). However, Peter had very poor phonological skills and became extremely frustrated—beginning to exhibit behavior problems and low motivation. At this point, the tutors and a researcher decided to try to help Peter build a sight vocabulary so that he could have at least some success with reading. Perhaps when he realized that he could master some aspect of literacy, they could come back to the phonological skills and introduce phonics.

With the support of researcher McCormick, the tutors went into high gear with what came to be known as the *multiple exposure/multiple context* (ME/MC) strategy. Rather than being subjected to word drill, Peter would engage in a wide range of activities that gave many opportunities for repeated response to the same individual words. The process was as follows:

- A book series of high-interest, easy-to-read stories was selected.
- The first chapter of the first book was used as a pretest.
- Practice with unknown words was provided.
- The tutor visually demonstrated progress (counting the words and recording results on a chart).
- Peter reread the first chapter.
- Peter finished the first book.
- Peter reread the first book.

Throughout the process, a wide range of games and activities was used to keep Peter interested. For the first time in a while, tutors used some games focusing on the internal features of words (filling in missing letters, hangman, tracing words, using a magic slate).

Peter could now automatically recognize 65 of 71 new words in the book. Once he had some success, he became much more cooperative and even looked forward to sessions.

cont.

Summer After Third Grade Through Fourth Grade

Despite a 12-week period in which no clinic services were available prior to the summer between third and fourth grade—which resulted in some regression—Peter quickly recouped and moved ahead developmentally once tutoring was recommenced. After a total of 56 hours of the ME/MC strategy, Peter had progressed from nonreader status to second-grade reading level, as he entered fourth grade. Only at this point did tutors begin a more balanced instructional program—including work on grapheme-phoneme correspondences, comprehension, using context for word identification, and word structure. Peter now showed a desire to read. After some time, he demonstrated willingness to persevere through many attempts to identify unknown words—using a range of strategies. Phonics skills were still low, but he was beginning to acquire some.

Fifth Grade

By fifth grade, Peter was reading at about fourth-grade level. His mother then withdrew him from tutoring, only to reenroll him 16 weeks later when the school decided it would retain him in fifth grade. When he was tested at this time, he scored only at beginning third-grade level! With tutoring support, he was able to read fourth-grade books. After 10 such books, Peter had a burst of development. His fluency increased dramatically, and he was soon reading fifth-grade stories successfully and in great numbers.

Fifth Grade (Repeated)

Once again, his mother took him out of the program, this time for a summer break. When he returned to the clinic in the fall, he scored only at second-grade level on a standardized reading test and at third-grade level on a word recognition test. Suspecting test burnout, Peter's tutors tried him out on fifth-grade materials and discovered he was fine at that level. Further evaluation suggested that he could handle sixth-grade texts; he had actually continued to develop as a reader on his own over the summer, without help. During the following weeks, the tutor read to him daily from high-quality adolescent literature and Peter read a large number of books (silently and orally) and kept a daily journal. He enjoyed sharing his journal with his tutor, reading with "great gusto."

During the final period of intervention, in the middle of fifth grade, Peter was proficient with prefixes and suffixes, worked on dictionary skills, read widely in various genres, continued to build an excellent oral vocabulary, and demonstrated new interests (science) and greater confidence. He now moved up to seventh-grade material successfully. One cannot help but wonder whether retention at fifth grade was necessary or advisable.

Based on McCormick (1994)

Contrasting Approaches to Reading Instruction

Any educator who hasn't been in a Rip Van Winkle–like sleep for the past 20 years has likely heard something about the reading wars—the face-off between those who advocate a strong code-based approach in early reading instruction and those who advocate a whole-language approach. The conflict, at its extremes, is based on different views of students and of learning.

Code-Based Instruction

Code-based approaches focus on how the alphabet represents speech sounds and how to analyze and synthesize speech sounds to identify and spell words. Those who want to emphasize a code-based approach, at least at the beginning of reading instruction (e.g., Adams, 1990; Ehri et al., 2001), believe that students need the basics before they can deal with big ideas and that learning is componential and sequential: Start with the small pieces (e.g., word analysis skills), and present them in an orderly fashion so that students have a foundation of basics first. A code-based approach tends to be associated quite naturally with direct, systematic teaching of skills, but it does not preclude attention to meaning or necessitate a total focus on low-level learning. However, when this approach leads to overlooking what students already know about reading and writing and the world—not to mention their interests—it moves away from a constructivist view of learning.

Meaning-Based or Whole-Language Instruction

The whole-language approach emphasizes reading as a meaning-making process. Those who favor a whole-language approach believe that learning goes from whole to part (Freeman & Freeman, 1998), that reading should not be taught as a series of skills but engaged in as an integrated whole that is meaningful to the learner. Skills should be taught as needed in the context of reading and writing and not independently. Kenneth Goodman (1994), who is perhaps the father of the whole-language movement, stresses that literacy learning and inquiry should be integrated—reflecting a view of learners as active and able to take part in constructing their own learning.

From the whole-language perspective, learning to read is a natural process, parallel to learning to speak (K. Goodman, 1986). Learning to speak does not require explicit instruction, just exposure to a language and the opportunity to interact with a competent speaker. Exposure to books that interest the students and writing activities that serve students' own purposes allow them to draw on their own experience, with timely assistance from the teacher or peers in a meaningful context. Of course, young readers will have to learn the specialized language used in literature works, but it is believed that this learning is readily supported by reading to them (Goodman, 1976).

Striking a Balance

The role of the teacher, the role of the student, presumptions about how children learn, and conceptions of what constitute reading all diverge in the extreme versions of these two positions. First of all, it is a terrible misconception that learning proceeds from lower level skills to higher level, that is, that students cannot grapple with big ideas (or understand the meaning of texts) before they master basic skills (Bransford, Brown, & Cocking, 2000; Knapp, Shields, & Turnbull, 1995). Children appear to be programmed to seek meaning. Yet many students do need explicit instruction in code-related skills (e.g., Snow et al., 1998), so that reliance on "learning to read by reading" (a mantra of some whole-language advocates) can hamper their literacy development.

Skilled teachers appear to blend code-based instruction with literature-based instruction and language experience activities (e.g., Juel & Minden-Cupp, 2000). The research literature suggests that the following elements should be included in a literacy program:

- *Selective* systematic, direct instruction in particular skills targeted to students who need it for short periods each day
- Instruction based on literature at students' comprehension level that exposes them to models of good texts
- Opportunities to develop metacognitive and metalinguistic skills
- Oral and written activities that draw upon students' existing knowledge and engage them actively in meaning-making as well as experimentation with the alphabetic code
- Oral and written activities that allow for students' personal choice, reflecting their interests and opportunities to draw upon prior knowledge

Many reading researchers are concerned that reports emphasizing the importance of phonological skills[20] are leading to policies that produce one-sided instructional programs that ignore the value of literature and language experience in early reading instruction (Allington & Woodside-Jiron, 1999; Garan, 2001). In addition, calls for systematic phonics instruction for all students must take into account the research that shows considerable variability in what it takes to get students phonologically and phonemically aware.

Teacher Note

What Works? Combining Strategies

The research of Juel and Minden-Cupp (2000) supports the belief that strategic teaching of phonological and code-based skills in combination with literature-based language arts instruction makes sense.

Juel and Minden-Cupp followed four first-grade classrooms in two schools in the same city for a year. Classrooms had a similar ethnic mix (about 60% African American and 40% Caucasian) and similar levels of student achievement. These small classrooms (about 18 students each) were organized into three reading groups according to performance level, and each spent about 90 minutes a day on language arts. All four teachers were Caucasian females with more than 10 years of teaching experience and were considered "very good" by their principals.

These groups, which had looked virtually the same in September, looked quite different in May. Classroom 4 was the most successful. At the end of the year, children were reading on average at a late-second-grade level. Even children in the lowest reading group were reading near grade level.

At the end of the year, in classroom 1 students were reading on average at primer level; in classroom 2, at end-of-first-grade level (including those who had started off as low readers); in classroom 3, students with "middle-range early literacy skills" at the beginning of the year did exceptionally well.

cont.

However, those who entered with low skills remained relatively poor readers at the end of the year.

What distinguished the instruction in classroom 4 was that the teacher emphasized both phonemic awareness/phonics instruction and literature and tailored instruction to children's developmental levels. She systematically taught phonics to the lowest reading group and emphasized phonics skills over text reading *early in the year*. For those who had already developed considerable phonemic awareness and sound-letter knowledge, she focused instruction through little books, the basal reader, and magazines. By February, this teacher was engaging low, middle, and high groups in activities on vocabulary development, reading text, and discussing text. In other words, *she did not teach all children the same way to begin with*, and *she did not teach the same students the same way all year*. As a result, she was able to bring all of her students up to an acceptable reading level or beyond by year's end.

In classrooms 1,2, and 3, teachers used "little books," teacher-made books and other materials, but they did not systematically teach the phonological and code skills needed by some children. In classroom 3, the teacher taught exclusively through literature. Phonemic awareness and phonics were taught only incidentally in the context of reading—a strategy that was fine for those who already had those skills or who could develop them without much explicit instruction, but not for several students.

Based on Juel & Minden-Cupp (2000)

"Oversimplification [of these issues] actually masks crucial areas literacy educators must balance to effectively teach literacy as a lifelong process" (Pearson & Raphael, 1999, p. 25). As Escamilla (1999) observes, the characterization of code-based and whole language approaches as dichotomous is misleading. Code-based approaches have always had as their goal the comprehension of text, and whole-language approaches have sought to ensure that students acquire skills. "Thus, while the points of departure for beginning literacy instruction may be widely divergent, the end goal is the same for all orientations" (p. 7). Truly balanced programs combine code-based skills instruction "with language and literature rich activities" (p. 8). The Teacher Note box above summarizes some very interesting research that shows how successful balanced instruction can be. Moreover, it cannot be said too strongly that not all children respond in the same ways to the same instruction. Best practices involve a "custom fit," and teachers must learn about their students' cultural communities as well as their individual needs (Gambrell & Mazzoni, 1999, p. 11).

Integrating Reading and Writing Instruction

One potential casualty in the reading wars is an integrated instructional approach to reading and writing. Some teachers may believe that students cannot write until they master a substantial number of code skills. Yet the research on invented spelling (mentioned earlier) clearly shows that with a little alphabet knowledge, many children will plunge right into writing—building code knowledge from that very experience. Notions of story structure and other emergent literacy skills are also quite likely fostered by early forays into writing (Neuman et al., 2000); Vernon & Feneiro, 1999.

As we have said, reading and writing are complementary, reciprocal processes that are best taught in tandem. Combined instruction enhances development in both areas (Graves, 1991; Pearson, 2002; Tierney & Shanahan, 1991; Wells, 1986). Oral language development is also part and parcel of literacy instruction, as students learn academic terms and structures (Wilkinson & Silliman, 2000). For some students, writing is more difficult than reading, yet this may be partly because of the ways it is taught. Whereas proficient reading may be faster than speech, writing takes more time than speaking—even with the benefit of the best computers (Chafe, 1985). It also requires a physical coordination that may develop more slowly in some children than others. However, even at the earliest stages of literacy development, sustained opportunities to write should be cultivated in the classroom.

Reading Instruction for Older Students

Teaching reading has generally been presumed to be the purview of elementary school teachers. Even the dichotomy between "learning to read" and "reading to learn" (Chall, 1983) is misleading. It makes some sense: Until one learns to read, one cannot use reading as a tool for learning. Yet when students are learning to read, they are quite likely learning some new concepts and vocabulary in addition to reading-related skills, such as the ways the spelling system encodes the spoken language or the ways texts can be organized. Moreover, it is not as though the process of learning to read is complete in elementary school. Even very successful readers continue to build skills with different genres[21] of written language, improve their facility with processing complex texts in

> ### Teacher Note
>
> **Reading Apprenticeship**
>
> One approach to boosting the literacy development of secondary students is a reading apprenticeship program in which the teacher serves as an expert reader, a model of successful reading practices. The teacher makes his or her reading strategies explicit to the student, as in reciprocal teaching. Because texts in different disciplines are organized differently, strategies for reading them will differ. Reading apprenticeship involves teachers in orchestrating and integrating four interacting dimensions of classroom life that support reading development—social, personal, cognitive, and background knowledge.
>
> At the heart of the apprenticeship model is an emphasis on building students' metacognition, or awareness of their thinking as they read. Teachers promote metacognitive conversations about the thinking processes that they and students engage in as they read. Eventually, students can learn to persevere through challenging text, to rely less on the teacher, and to develop a sense of competence as readers.
>
> cont.

new subject areas, expand their range of purposes for reading, and develop metacognitive and metalinguistic skills.

Academic texts present particular difficulty for many middle and high school students who have mastered the basics of reading (Donahue, Voelkl, Campbell, & Mazzeo, 1999). Many students need strategies for coping with demanding texts so that they can learn independently from them. However, the problem is not just with poorly written textbooks: Students often have problems with interesting, well-written material as well.

A key to the success of this approach is regarding the student as having powerful resources that can be tapped. Schoenbach and her colleagues in the Strategic Literacy Initiative, who have worked successfully with teachers and students to implement the apprenticeship model, stress that success depends on building a "learning environment that is safe, respectful, and collaborative (p. 13)."

The expert-apprentice relationship emphasizes mutual inquiry, with the teacher learning about the student and the student learning about his or her own, other students', and the teacher's strategies. This approach, which has resulted in significant gains in reading skill for struggling secondary students, is quite a contrast to remedial approaches that focus on isolated skills.

Based on Schoenbach et al. (1999)

Sometimes such students can decode quite well, but they have not learned how to process larger language units quickly to build up a sense of the gist of the text as they go along. Their teachers may attempt to ease the burden for them by reducing the amount of reading assigned, but such a step can lead to a self-defeating cycle in which students fail to build the skills they need (Schoenbach et al., 1999). The Teacher Note box above on Reading Apprenticeship describes a highly successful method for helping adolescent poor readers read more strategically and skillfully.

Teacher Inquiry

What different traditions of literacy and oral discourse are represented by your students' home cultures? Find out more about them by talking with students and parents. How do they parallel or differ from school traditions? One way to expand your school's knowledge base about students' home cultures is to form an inquiry team and have each member choose a culture and/or language to investigate. You can invite experts from the community to become key informants.

Often, paraprofessionals in the school come from the communities of the students, and they may be used to mediate between the school culture and home culture. Your inquiry group can agree on a few central questions to ask each informant to prepare for these interviews. Share what you learn not only with each other but with the rest of the school faculty and personnel.

Recognizing the Literacy Resources of Students

This section focuses on recognizing the culture-based resources of various cultural and linguistic communities.[23] One cultural resource that may be overlooked is a student's home language. The term *subtractive schooling* has been used to describe how the U.S. educational system devalues and fails to continue development of students' home languages and build on their culture-based knowledge (Valenzuela, 1999). Students who are fluent in a language other than English when they enter school rarely have opportunities to acquire academic language in that tongue—meaning that their first-language literacy is attenuated (see, e.g., Garcia, 2000). Even when students have access to bilingual programs, they are typically transitioned to English-only instruction by fourth or fifth grade, and sometimes even earlier, so many students do not reach their potential of full biliteracy. Nevertheless, the home language of an English language learner is a resource to that student and should be recognized as such (Bialystok, 1997; Solano-Flores & Trumbull, 2003; Valenzuela, 1999). Simply speaking, what such a student knows is distributed across two languages and cultures, and to ignore one of them is to ignore an important part of his or her cognitive resources. Other resources are students' culture-based strengths, such as knowledge of how to help each other, a disposition to share, or personal experiences particular to their own culture.

Meeting the Needs of Immigrant Latino Students: An Example of Recognizing Literacy Resources

Teachers in the Bridging Cultures Project (mentioned earlier and in chapter 2) have identified many culturally harmonious literacy practices that they find to be successful with their immigrant Latino students in grades K–5 (Trumbull et al., in press). These practices are designed specifically for their students, whose families tend to be very collectivistic in their orientation to child rearing and schooling.

The Teacher Note "Class Books" shows how third-grade teacher Amada Pérez designed a writing activity that connects well with her students from Mexican and Central American cultures. In their homes, her students tend to learn to focus on shared success rather than individual success; cooperating to accomplish almost any kind of task is the norm. Most teachers would probably agree that the sharing activities described—two instances of making a class book—would be beneficial to any group of students, but they are particularly meaningful in Mrs. Pérez's class.

When Mrs. Pérez has her students make individual books and create an "author's page," they inevitably depict themselves in the context of their whole family. Often, it is impossible to tell which person in the illustration is the child author. In their text, they tell about all of the family members as well. Should Mrs. Pérez instruct the children to focus on themselves? If she did not understand the cultural origin of their behavior, she might. Table 5-4 summarizes several other practices used by Bridging Cultures teachers and indicates which home values each one taps.

Teacher Note

Class Books

Amada Pérez, a third-grade teacher in Oxnard, California, had her students create posters about themselves on 11 x 17 paper as a homework assignment. She explained, "When they brought them back, I interviewed each child. They learned about each other. The collectivistic part is putting them together as a class book." She laminated the pages so that they would stand up to ongoing use by more than 20 students, who took great pride in their joint product.

On another occasion, she paired her third graders with first graders (they have a buddy system) to collaborate on a single book based on a story they had heard called "If." Mrs. Pérez described what happened: "They drew on paper and cut out their drawings. They wrote a sentence on the computer—some in English, some in Spanish. Some of their pages illustrated things like 'If people could smell wind . . . ,' 'If tables could have faces . . . ,' 'If grass could be eyebrows . . . ,' 'If my heart were a butterfly . . . .,' 'If a whale could run in the park . . . ,' 'If apples could eat trees . . . ' Reading the whole finished product as a group, they were in awe of each other's work."

Adapted from Trumbull et al., (in press)

In many cultures, human relationships are more highly valued than the material world of objects, personal achievement, or acquisition of knowledge. For students from such backgrounds, literacy will be meaningful to the degree that these values are recognized. It is easy to see how the values listed in Table 5-4 are interrelated and how the same activity may reflect several or all of them. These activities illustrate how simple it can be to support students to participate in schooling in ways that are compatible with those values. It is also evident from this table that oral and written language are integrated, and activities that support development of one are likely to support development of the other.

Table 5-4. Sample Literacy Practices from the Bridging Cultures Project

Home Value	Classroom Practice
Helping and sharing	1. **Assisted Homework Prep**: Students work in small groups to preview homework assignments and discuss strategies for completing them. Students less proficient in English are grouped with those who are more proficient who can help interpret directions and model responses.
	2. **Assisted Homework Completion**: Volunteers help other students who have not been able to complete their homework. (This practice is in contrast to punishing students for not doing their homework and in recognition of the fact that some may not be able to do so for legitimate reasons.)
	3. **Collaborative Test Practice**: Students work together in small groups on items from practice tests in preparation for the yearly standardized tests. One student reads each item to the group. The group discusses which answer or answers can be eliminated and then tries to decide what the correct answer is and why. Groups report to the whole class on how they answered and why.

cont.

	4. **Collaborative Writing**: Teams of students write stories together. They jointly select a topic, and each has to contribute to the writing. Students whose skills are just developing can have the satisfaction of seeing a complete piece of writing and learn from peers at the same time. (Teachers note that this practice should be alternated with individual writing.)
Focus on the group vs. the individual	1. **Class Books** (See Teacher Note box on this subject)
	2. **Choral Reading**: Students read aloud together as a whole group or as a small group. English learners can practice the rhythm and sound of English without being spotlighted. The group scaffolds everyone's performance. (The parallel, answering an oral question in chorus, is also practiced.)
	3. **Literature Circles**: Students select a piece of literature, and everyone reads it. Each student has responsibility for some aspect of understanding the text. These circles help to develop vocabulary, reading fluency, comprehension, oral language, and critical interpretation. The group prepares and gives a presentation to the class afterward.*
	4. **Unleveled Drama Activities**: Drama is used as a way to get young students at different levels of English literacy proficiency involved in literacy activities. Students get together with a partner, read together, decide who will take what roles, and learn their parts. Teacher and other students assist those who have difficulty reading, but by the time of performance, it is impossible to tell who is a good or poor reader. All students participate in the little plays. (Teachers say this activity builds skill and confidence.)
Importance of family	1. **Literature with Family as Topic**: Teachers select, or have students select, literature that focuses on family. Such books are likely to be highly engaging to students from many immigrant cultures as well as many others where family is highly valued and at the heart of life.
	2. **Family-Oriented Writing Prompts**: When possible, in a schoolwide writing prompt (where it is important to get an extended sample of student writing), teachers use *family* as a focal point of the prompt. In one school the prompt "Write about an experience that you had with your family" elicited much more writing from third graders than the prompt "Write about what it's like to be a good friend."
	3. **Personal Books**: Students write about themselves (always in the context of their families, as would many young children). The Author's Page is to be a drawing of the author with some biographical information. Teachers understand that students will probably want to draw themselves as members of a family and not individually.
Integration of cognitive and social knowledge	1. **Conversational Lesson Structure**: New instructional topics are introduced in the context of an open conversation, where the teacher may toss out an open-ended question that invites all to participate. For example, a second-grade teacher asks her students, "What does anyone know about Mexico?" Students are likely to respond with personal anecdotes about family in

cont.

Mexico or what they like about Mexico. She does not immediately channel their conversation into topics like geography, climate, history, or relations between Spanish colonial governors and the indigenous peoples of Mexico. She encourages all students to participate and welcomes all contributions. She may write a word or two from each student's comment on the blackboard. Her behavior represents a conscious effort to support students in connecting with the topic and to generate interest in further pursuing a more academic approach to the topic.

2. **T-Charts for Expanded Discourse**: Classroom discourse conventions tend to reflect the value of separating academic knowledge from personal experience, whereas many children will naturally want to integrate the personal and social with the academic. Teachers can bridge this discourse divide with a simple strategy. In California, asked about what lives in the desert, many a student will offer a story about a family trip to the desert. The teacher can make a T-chart, putting an abbreviated version of the student's story on the left and recording the scientific information on the right, as he or she elicits it through explicit questions. (see example in chapter 2)

* See also description of literature circles in Freeman & Freeman, 2000
Adapted from Trumbull et al. (in press)

One of the Bridging Cultures strategies is to select student literature with meaningful topics. Using literature related to students' lives can support the learning of not only students (Applebee, 1991; Harris, 1993; Lee, 1993, 1995, 2000; Malik, 1990) but also their teachers. Nathensen-Mejía and Escamilla (2003) used Latino children's literature in a teacher education course to help 75 teacher candidates learn about Latino culture. Three-quarters of these teacher candidates were White, and most would be teaching in schools where the students were predominantly Latino. Nathensen-Mejía and Escamilla chose to use not only folktales but also contemporary literature based on people's lives because these books often illustrate the kinds of challenges children must face when they "live in two cultural worlds" (p. 107). These researchers found that the teacher candidates did indeed learn about Latino culture and began to use their knowledge to make connections with their students during their student teaching experience. Moreover, they developed more positive attitudes toward the children and their communities and began to see parallels in their own life experiences.

Using African-American Students' Culture-Based Knowledge

Researcher Carol Lee (1993, 1995, 2000)[23] at Northwestern University has for some years been investigating how to improve secondary literacy instruction—for African-American students. Her approach is to link instruction to oral and written traditions in African-American culture. In one project, she helped students to develop inferential and interpretive skills by having them read and discuss several dialogues involving *signifying*, a form of talk associated with African-American culture that "may involve ritual insult and almost always involves the use of figurative language" (Lee, 1995, p. 614). Students were able to get below the surface meanings of the dialogues relatively easily, according to Lee, and to interpret irony. Next, Lee had the students read a short story, *My Man Bovanne* by Toni Cade Bambara, and respond to some difficult questions. A similar process followed with the reading of *Their Eyes Were Watching God* by Zora Neale Hurston. Through her questions, Lee modeled the kind of deeper reading students might engage in. Some complained that they weren't used to thinking so much in school!

Although some students were at first less than enthusiastic about these texts—questioning whether signifying was a form worthy of school inquiry and objecting to the African-American dialect in Hurston's book—they changed their attitudes over the course of the instruction. Achievement levels in literacy were affected as well: The students in this experimental group progressed at more than twice the rate of those in a control group. Lee was able to support students in making explicit their tacit knowledge of patterns of oral discourse that African-American authors have incorporated into their writings and use that knowledge to understand some very complex texts. Elements of irony, word play, double entendre, image, and figurative language that students understood in oral discourse could be consciously identified in these writings. Lee suggests that once students develop such strategies for interpreting literature that reflects aspects of their own discourse community, they can more easily move on to writings from a wide range of authors.

Lee's work shows that literature selection for what she calls "disfavored ethnic and racial groups" (1995, p. 626) is not just about providing opportunities for students to identify with characters or see themselves in books, it is also about drawing on and making explicit the tacit knowledge they have that is based in their own discourse communities. This knowledge can help students to develop as readers. She points out that it is not only African-American authors who use oral discourse patterns for literary effect. She cites Mark Twain, Chaim Potok, and Sandra Cisneros, among many, who have done the same.

A Goal of Biliteracy

In the case of students who have a home language other than English, it would be ideal for them to develop a broad range of oral and written proficiencies in both languages (Dworin, 2003; Gutiérrez, 1993). According to Pérez & Torres-Guzmán (1996), biliteracy is really *proficiency with two linguistic and cultural systems* and *the ability to communicate the messages and intentions meaningful in both of those systems.*

Becoming biliterate entails learning not only the two language codes but also how to participate in the discourse communities of home and school.

> From this perspective, effective instruction for language-minority children requires an understanding of the acquisition of biliteracy as a process of language socialization that takes place in the culturally and socially organized activities in which children participate, interact, receive assistance,

and experiment and play with both oral and written forms of their home language. (Gutiérrez, 1993, p. 95)

Students need to learn the rules for participating in the classroom, but as suggested in many of the examples above, these rules can be expanded to include forms of talk parallel to those in students' home cultures and languages. Biliteracy is an ideal that cannot be fully met without teachers who are biliterate, and most bilingual teachers in the United States have not had adequate opportunities to develop both languages to a high level (Guerrero, 1997). Yet schools can promote aspects of biliteracy. When teachers provide opportunities for students to participate in classroom talk in multiple ways—giving positive regard to students' different ways of communicating, telling stories, sharing, asking questions, and the like—they are supporting the development of more than one form of literacy. All students stand to gain cognitively from instruction that acknowledges and promotes linguistic pluralism, including "mainstream" students. Students who learn more than one language or more than one way to be literate are likely to "gain substantively in metacognitive and metalinguistic abilities" (Cope & Kalantzis, 2000, p.15; see also Bialystok, 1991, 1997).

> ## Teacher Inquiry
>
>
> ### Promoting Biliteracy
> If you have students whose home language or dialect is different from that of the school, how can you promote biliteracy? Find out what resources your school has, in terms of people and materials. Investigate how parents would like to be involved to share their own stories, bring in literacy materials, and participate in small-group discussions with students of like backgrounds.

Biliteracy and Second-Dialect Learners

There are parallels between the needs of second-language and second dialect learners. Speakers of African-American Vernacular English can also benefit from teachers like Lee (above) who know their dialect and all of the discourse conventions associated with African-American culture (granting that there is great variation within this community). LeMoine (2001) notes that from 75% to 80% of African-American children entering school at kindergarten or first grade are speakers of African-American language (her term) and generally have limited facility with the language of school.

LeMoine (2001), who is director of the Academic English Mastery Program for the Los Angeles Unified School District, characterizes effective teachers of African-American students who are learning a new dialect and with it new language and literacy norms as follows:

1. They develop their knowledge of their students' nonstandard languages.
2. They use this knowledge in instruction.
3. They use second-language acquisition methods to help their students acquire school forms of language and literacy.

4. They use a balanced approach to literacy instruction—incorporating literature, phonics, and language experience.
5. They infuse the history and culture of their students into the curriculum.
6. They consider their students' learning styles when they design instruction.

Any child who comes from a nondominant speech community could benefit from a teacher's having the same level of consciousness about language, as Gutiérrez (1993) and LeMoine (2001) urge. Teachers' understanding is one crucial component of equity in access to literacy.

Equal Access to Literacy

A sometimes hidden dimension in all of the literature on how best to teach children to read and write is *equity*, equal access to educational opportunities. The fact is that opportunities to learn to read, write, and develop a range of discourse skills are influenced by the economic resources of a child's family and community. It is unfair to students to make judgments about their ability to learn to read at high levels when they have not had equal access to print and particular print experiences early on—factors that reading theorists believe are important to get children on the road to reading (e.g., K. Goodman, 1986; Neuman & Roskos, 1997; Purcell-Gates, 1996; Teale, 1986). Too often the assumption is that families are not preparing their children adequately for school, and blame is consciously or unconsciously laid at their feet. One problem with existing systems of curriculum, instruction, and assessment is that they provide a single perspective on what counts as valuable experience and knowledge (a monocultural view). For that reason, many things children know and can do are overlooked not only by teachers but also by students, like Carol Lee's, who at first did not regard their own rather sophisticated language knowledge as an appropriate basis for school inquiry.

It is important to challenge the assumption that if children are not prepared for schooling in the expected ways they are less intelligent or less capable of learning—or past their critical early learning period. Bruer (1999) painstakingly debunks the myth that the first 3 years of a child's life determine his or her later learning potential, showing how flexibility in learning persists long past early childhood. Furthermore, how can we know which children can learn school content and school discourse if we have not made informed efforts to teach them? Gee (1999) contends that we have a "pervasive *culture of inequality* that deskills poor and minority children" (p. 5). As strong as Gee's language is, it is hard to argue with it. At the very least, it should be possible for the educational establishment to hold the expectation that any student can learn the curriculum of the school, given appropriate support—something that would entail connecting with that student's experience and preferred ways of learning.

It is important to recognize inequities and not leap to categorizing all differences in children's orientations to and experiences with literacy as deficits. Even as we understand that some children have not had access to certain resources, we cannot allow this fact to lead to blanket assumptions about ability or blind us to the knowledge and skills that children do have. For example, some children who do not have access to many books at home may actually be exposed to considerable writing. Teale (1986) found that low-income Latino parents did not read to their children regularly, but they did devote attention to children's writing skills. On the other hand, access to books *is* important (Bus et al., 1995), and as the account in the Teacher Note box below shows, it is clearly associated, at least in some communities, with socioeconomic level.

Teacher Note

Unequal Access to Books

A recent study of four neighborhoods in Philadelphia poignantly illustrates the kinds of inequalities related to income level that can affect opportunities to learn about print. Just consider the following statistics: In Chestnut Hill, a middle-income community studied, there were seven bookstores with special sections for children; in Roxborough, an up-and-coming community (but with less "old money" than Chestnut Hill), there were three bookstores, one with a special children's section. In the two low-income communities, Kingsessing and Kensington (which had a far greater number of children), there were *no* bookstores. Children's books were available in drugstores or corner stores in these two communities, although none had chapter books or magazines for older children. *In the richest community, there were 13 book titles for every child; in the poorest community, there was one book title for every 300 children, and the only books available for them were coloring books!*

In the same study, researchers found that school libraries in the low-income communities had fewer books (12.9 and 10.6 per child) than the middle-income ones (18.9 and 25.7 per child). There were no trained librarians in Kingsessing and Kensington, but school librarians in Chestnut Hill and Roxborough had master's degrees and an average of 12 years' experience. We offer these details simply to point out how lack of resources translates directly into inequities—real-life factors outside homes over which parents and families have little control. Neumann and Celano suggest that it is time to look beyond family characteristics such as book reading habits to understand how some students are advantaged over others vis-à-vis literacy and school success and how whole systems are influenced by the distribution of resources.

Based on Neuman & Celano (2001)

All children are sense-making beings, actively interpreting what they observe and experience, and all come to school with the ability to learn. "All children, from the most to the least socially advantaged family circumstances, come to school knowing and doing various kinds of literacy. Thus, schools start with every child a full child" (Erickson, 1991, p. ix).

Reflections

Literacy is a complex sociocultural, personal, and political phenomenon. It is best understood as making meaning from texts—both oral and written—with the reader, writer, or speaker either interpreting or composing text on the basis of what he or she already knows. This depiction of literacy arises from a sociocultural constructivist view of learners. Teachers have the task of building upon what students know and what interests them and also extending students' purposes for reading and skill with a great variety of texts and topics.

The full range of oral language skills forms the basis for learning to read and write. Metalinguistic skills, such as phonemic and grammatical awareness, often do not develop naturally, but they can be taught through classroom activities. Students' knowledge of discourse conventions and structures can be enhanced, particularly in the early years of schooling, by teachers' reading from a variety of narrative and expository texts as well as by showing students models of text structures. Teachers can support students' comprehension of texts through explicit modeling, discussion, and practice with vocabulary instruction as well as metacognitive strategies. Parents, too, can support emergent literacy, particularly by reading or telling stories to their toddlers and preschoolers—in whatever language they speak.

Successful literacy instruction entails understanding students' culture-based strengths and tailoring curriculum and pedagogical strategies to their needs and interests. Several instructional activities from different cultural settings have been offered in the chapter. These examples come from teachers who have developed extensive knowledge of their students and communities, but the activities are not especially unusual or difficult. It is the understanding of how they may be meaningful in particular contexts that is important. They illustrate how easy it can be to create literacy instruction that meets the needs of students. Perhaps they will inspire readers to explore their own creativity.

Notes

1. Sheets' strategies are similar to some of the strategies promoted by the Strategic Literacy Initiative in its reading apprentice program (Schoenbach et al., 1999).

2. See also Freedman, Simons, Kalnin, Casareno, & the M-Class Teams (1999). Teacher-researchers used ethnographic techniques to learn about their students' backgrounds and consequently made their instruction more effective.

3. Delgado-Gaitan (1994b) writes about working with immigrant parents to support their empowerment. She notes, "Outcomes of the empowerment process manifest themselves through access to resources. Power is the capacity to influence foreseen and unforeseen effects for oneself and others, and the increased ability to create desired change as the individual, parents, family, teacher, and school deem appropriate" (p. 146).

4. This capacity is known as *metalinguistic awareness*, and it can be increased by activities that draw attention to language forms and meanings (Bradley & Bryant, 1985; Stanovich, 1994; Trumbull, 1984).

5. To *mediate* is to bring about a result through some kind of intervention. In the case of teaching, a teacher can serve as a facilitator of learning; this role is in contrast to that of purveyor of information and is compatible with the view of the student or child as an equal actor in the teaching and learning process. It requires sensitivity to the student's level of development and knowledge and a sense of how to help the student move to the next level of understanding or skill.

6. See, e.g., Cole & Scribner, 1974; Greenfield, Brazelton, & Childs, 1989; Greenfield & Bruner, 1969; Greenfield & Lave, 1982; Rogoff & Lave, 1984; Saxe, 1990; Vygotsky, 1978.

7. The National Reading Panel (2000) identified three key areas of reading instruction: alphabetics (phonemic awareness and phonics instruction), fluency, and comprehension (vocabulary and text comprehension instruction). All of the major instructional strategies recommended by the Panel are presented in the chapter.

8. The term *text* refers to any organized network of meanings written down for oneself or others and can include books and magazines as well as notes, lists, and letters (see Wade & Moje, 2000, whose definition extends to oral discourse).

9. Another five-syllable pattern has the stress on the second syllable—*considerable, reconstituted, imperatively.*

10. The research on phonemic awareness has been based largely on monolingual English speakers. When it has included speakers of other languages, data on those students have not been separately analyzed. This is one criticism leveled by Garan (2001), who, as an educator in California, is concerned about appropriateness of conclusions drawn about English learners based on this body of research. Some differences between Spanish and English literacy acquisition are addressed later in this chapter under the topic of biliteracy.

11. What is "appropriate" will not be the same for all students. Some need much more explicit instruction than others.

12. The term *grammatical awareness* as it is used here incorporates morphological and syntactic awareness, which often interact. For example, adding *-s* (a bound morpheme) to the end of a word requires using the plural form of the verb with which it is associated. Hence, a reader or speaker needs to coordinate those elements of a sentence—reflecting attention to both morphology (word structure) and syntax (relations among words). Accepted irregular plurals (*mice*) and verb forms (*went* vs. *goed*) are part of the morphological grammaticality of a sentence. Correct word order (*went to school* vs. *school to went*) is a key part of syntactic grammaticality.

13. The reader need not know the terms *adjective* and *verb* or their definitions to draw upon intuitive grammatical knowledge.

14. Even so, one cannot assume that any predictor is foolproof. For example, in a study of 1,000 students at the end of first grade, Vellutino and Scanlon (1996) showed that more than a third of the students who would be identified as most at risk on the basis of letter naming did fine in first grade, and 14.5% of students predicted to do well actually developed reading problems.

15. In fact, rapid automatized naming of anything—for instance, a series of pictures—is associated with the development of normal literacy skills, whereas slowness in naming is associated with reading problems (see summary of research in Snow et al., 1998).

16. Also called "graphophonic"

17. A narrative from certain American Indian groups will have four episodes; and the beginning, middle, and end may not be evident to an outsider (cf., Heredia & Francis, 1997).

18. The stages are Gillet & Temple's. The components and their developmental characterizations are based on the many sources cited.

19. A useful tool for evaluating phonological awareness is Torgesen and Bryant's (1994) *Test of Phonological Awareness*.

20. Chief among these documents is the report prepared by Ehri and colleagues and summarized in Ehri et al., (2001).

21. *Genre* typically refers to a type of literature such as realistic fiction, fantasy, mystery, or historical fiction (Robb, 2000).

22. Linking home learning with school learning pertains equally to "mainstream" students. Neuman and Roskos (1997) say, "The concept of moving everyday life into schools to reflect more authentic situations has become regarded as essential in the process of enculturating literacy learning" (p. 13). The distance between home literacy practices of students from nondominant cultures and the literacy practices of school may be larger than the distance dominant-culture children have to travel, but there may still be an unfortunate disconnect between in-school and out-of-school ways of knowing.

23. Lee acknowledges that African-American culture is by no means monolithic, but she believes that there is a continuum of African-American culture that is distinct from other cultures. Class, gender, and other factors may influence the degree to which any individual identifies with particular features of a culture.

For Further Reading

Beck, S., &. Oláh, L. N. (Eds.). (2001). *Perspectives on language and literacy: Beyond the here and now*. Cambridge, MA: Harvard Educational Review.

Braunger, J., & Lewis, J. (1998). *Building a knowledge base in reading*. Newark, DE: International Reading Association. (A new edition is due in 2005.)

Cunningham, P. M. (2000). *Phonics they use* (3rd ed.). New York: Longman.

Gambrell, L. B., Morrow, L. M., Neuman, S. B., & Pressley, M. (Eds.). (1999). *Best practices in literacy instruction*. New York: Guilford Press.

Harris, S. L., Kamhi, A. G., & Pollock, K. E. (Eds.). (2001). *Literacy in African American communities*. Mahwah, NJ: Erlbaum.

Hiebert, E. H. (Ed.). *Literacy for a diverse society: Perspectives, practices, and policies*. New York: Teachers College Press.

Osborn, J., & Lehr, F. (n.d.). *A focus on fluency* (With E. H. Hiebert). Honolulu: Pacific Resources for Education and Learning.

Schoenbach, R., Greenleaf, C., Cziko, C., & Hurwitz, L. (1999). *Reading for understanding: A guide to improving reading in middle and high school classrooms*. San Francisco: Jossey-Bass.

Stahl, S. A. (1999). *From reading research to practice:* Vol. 2.*Vocabulary development*. Newton Upper Falls, MA: Brookline Books.

Chapter 6

Effective Instructional Strategies for Students Learning a Second Language or with Other Language Differences

Beverly Farr and Rosalinda Quintanar-Sarellana

When one thinks about students who attend schools in the United States whose language may be different from that of typically developing monolingual speakers of the standard dialect of English, certainly the first students who come to mind are those who have learned a language other than English as their first. The number of these students in American schools is rapidly increasing. The fact that they have to learn English while they meet grade-level standards adds an almost immeasurable challenge. Nevertheless, it is not only English language learners whose language difference must be understood. As discussed earlier, educational practices need to address how instruction can respond constructively to differences in dialect and cultural orientation to language use, as well as to language-based learning differences and language disorders. Difference, of course, is not equivalent to deficit. It is the rare student who actually has a language disorder; nevertheless, teachers need to know when to refer a student for language evaluation. We hope this chapter provides both useful guidelines and meaningful specific instructional activities for students with language differences.

The Demographic Context of U.S. Schooling in the 21st Century

As the 21st century gets underway, the U.S. educational system is facing a student population more culturally and linguistically diverse than ever before (U.S. Bureau of the Census, 2000). To glimpse the future, one need only look at the state of California, where a majority of students are members of a minority group[1] (Olson, 2000a). Thirty-five percent of students across the United States are members of minority groups, and that is expected to rise to 50% by 2040. Although the minority population will remain concentrated in a few states, demographers project that all but two states—Mississippi and Arkansas—will see an increase in their minority enrollments between now and 2015. The largest growth will occur among Hispanics—expected to account for 43% of the U.S. population growth between 1999 and 2010. The Asian and Pacific Islander population will also increase by about 64% over the next 20 years. "The spilling out of immigrants and new ethnic groups across the landscape will be pervasive enough that many districts will have student enrollments that are noticeably different from those in the past" (Olson, 2000b).

"If you look at the Latino population of the United States, historically it's been hyperconcentrated in five states: California, Texas, Illinois, New York, and Florida," says Marcelo Suarez-Orozco of Harvard University. "Yet if you turn to other parts of the country, you really see the beginnings of a transformation that is simply unprecedented in U.S. history" (Olsen, 2000b). Suarez-Orozco points out that from 1990 to 1997 the number of students with limited English proficiency has grown by 429%; in Kansas, by 205%; in North Carolina, by 440%, and in Kentucky, by 208%. Forces driving migration include jobs and quality of life. A breadbasket town like Omaha, Nebraska, has seen its public school population of limited-English-proficient students grow from 500 in 1992 to 3,000 in the year 2000. This number includes not only Hispanics but also a sizable population of Nuer immigrants from southern Sudan, fleeing their country's civil war.

There has been another important shift in the demographics of immigrants: They're getting younger. In 1960, 10% of the immigrant population was under age 25, but in 1997, this figure had risen to 22%. These changes are reflected in the realities of schools today. As an example, Broward County, Florida—the fifth largest district in the nation—has young people from at least 52 different countries who speak 52 different languages, ranging from Spanish and Haitian Creole to Tagalog. The number of children in that district identified as having limited fluency in English has nearly doubled since 1993–1994, from 12,039 to 23,459. Certainly, this offers children a rich melting-pot experience, but it also poses monumental challenges for schools and the teachers in them (Olson, 2000a).

One of the misconceptions that some Americans often propagate in response to programs designed to meet the needs of English learners is that immigrants who settled in the United States many years ago learned English despite the odds and without special programs designed to meet their special needs. This misconception does not reflect an awareness of the reality that in the early 1800s the job market did not require the academic skills that are vital today. Students did not need to achieve the level of literacy, computer knowledge, and critical thinking required in today's job market or to be successful in today's society. Also, in 1870, 61% of children between 5 and 18 years of age attended school. Typically, 95% of that group were in elementary school, 4% in secondary school and 1% in post-secondary school (Tyack, 1974). Attending school for a total of 5 years was considered a tremendous academic achievement. Even in the 1950s, only 50% of the students enrolled graduated from high school.

Schools today are too often not able to meet the needs of students who are learning English as a second language because of a lack of understanding of their needs or a lack of human and financial resources. Not only do schools need personnel who understand students' cultures and languages, they also need appropriate materials to support academic and linguistic development. Furthermore, schools need to be able to provide ongoing professional development to teachers, both those who are specialized in teaching English language learners and those who teach students who have been placed in regular education programs.

Applying Knowledge About Language Development to Instruction

In this chapter we address, in particular, the needs of nonspecialist teachers who, nevertheless, are likely to find themselves teaching students from many cultural and linguistic backgrounds in the increasingly diverse schools of the present day. Most teachers in the United States are currently facing a classroom with students who are learning English as a second language (ESL). Some of the questions they ask are the following: What do we know about first- and second-language development in children that is applicable to teaching English language learners (ELLs)? How should I differentiate instruction to meet the needs of students who speak nonmainstream dialects? What are the cultural factors that must be considered to support second-language development? What are some effective approaches and strategies for supporting English language development? How do I use the English Language Development (ELD) standards effectively in my instruction? This chapter will discuss these and other questions that have an important impact on instructional planning and delivery.

In addition to the specific language needs of ELLs, it is important to consider students with other language differences—those, for example, who speak a dialect such as Ebonics or who may exhibit language disorders or difficulties. Teachers who have these students in their mainstream classrooms also have questions about how to address their learning needs. They may ask: "How do I make sure that the students in my class who use Ebonics [African American Vernacular English—AAVE] learn the form of Standard English that will ensure their academic and vocational success and still respect the dialect that they use most in their daily lives?" "How do I know if a student's idiosyncratic behaviors with language are due to a language disorder, and how do I accommodate his or her needs?" Space in this book allows us to consider these issues only briefly, but they are ones that many teachers need to be aware of and address.

Knowledge Teachers Can Apply

In chapter 3 we described the language acquisition process in very young and in school-age children, and in chapter 4 we discussed the process of learning a second language and distinguished it from first-language acquisition. Although there are some commonalities between learning a first and a second language, there are also ways in which the process is quite distinct. This should be obvious when you think about the difference in the base of knowledge as well as the motivation for learning a second language. Some processes involved in first- and second-language acquisition are important to consider when planning instruction in second-language acquisition. They are discussed only briefly below, since they are discussed more fully in the earlier chapters. Teachers with students who speak dialects or have language differences or disorders should consider these issues for their students because much of this information is applicable to them as well.

Discovering Rules and Generalizations

Young children are constantly hearing other people speak, read aloud, and sing. They analyze the language around them and develop their own linguistic structure. It seems that they are intuitively aware that language has many rules. In fact, research shows that children experiment with linguistic rules and apply them in their speech production. Fantini (1985) reported on a 2-year old bilingual Spanish-English child, for example, who used the feminine article regardless of gender. Children are aware of the need to use an article and often generalize one gender form over another—in this case, the feminine form. These are referred to as overgeneralizations and reflect the child's attempt to apply a rule that she has not yet fully internalized or for which she has not deduced the exceptions.

During the process of acquiring language, a child is also exposed to regular and irregular forms. Often a child applies the regular form to the irregular verb or noun, which results in an error called *regularization* (Dulay, Burt, & Krashen, 1981). For example, a child learns the word *foot*, and when he intends to describe two or more of these body parts, he might say *foots* instead of *feet*. A child might also apply the same rule when converting the singular noun *man* to *mans*. This child is applying the rule of adding an *s* to change an object from the singular to the plural form (Ervin-Tripp & Miller, 1964).

Similarly, in Spanish, a child learns the verb *comer* ("to eat") and that the first-person singular form of that verb is *Yo como* ("I eat"). She may apply the same rule to *saber* (know) and say *Yo sabo* instead of the correct irregular form *Yo sé* ("I know"). Such an error reflects implementation of a rule for regular verbs, and it is a common error for 3- to 4-year-olds. At this developmental phase, they are not familiar with irregular verbs. The mistakes generated by children are consistent with the internal grammar structure that is accessible to them at a particular stage of language development.

Hypothesis Testing

From a very young age, children test their hypotheses about the structure of language. Adults are usually understanding of the child's mistakes and while they may strive to model the correct grammatical form in their response, the main focus is on ensuring successful communication of meaning (Pinker, 1994).

Piper (2003) provides examples of parents asking questions to clarify the child's imperfect speech. For example, a child may say "more tato" and parents negotiate meaning by pointing to potatoes or some object that they think is what the child wants. Golinkoff (1993) calls these episodes *conversational bouts*, in which the parent is trying to derive meaning from a linguistic interaction with the child.

Interlanguage. The circumstances of second-language learners in the school setting are certainly more complex. The impact of students' second-language errors is measured in the ways teachers react to these errors. Corder (1967) posited that learners develop *approximate systems* of the second language that represent a transitional stage in their development. The term *approximate system* was later labeled *interlanguage* (Selinker, 1972). When teachers recognize this transitional stage, they are more accepting of students' errors. Besides understanding that this stage is natural and not a sign of flawed development, teachers should also recognize that drills alone will not help the student through the transition. Strategies such as providing conversational input and eliciting student output, focusing on content over form, and providing techniques to take the student to the next language stage are more constructive.

Although interlanguage theory has been criticized as simplistic, its contribution to pedagogy is that teachers can view errors as the result of learners' testing hypotheses instead of mistakes that need to be corrected in an overt manner. In addition, teaching is slanted toward comprehension and conversation rather than a grammatical and drill approach. There is disagreement among researchers about whether to correct a student or simply provide a model of correctness. Some educators believe that students should be corrected when learning a second language (Birdsong, 1989; Bley-Vroman, 1989; Gass, 1988). Other educators (Krashen, 1981; Pinker, 1984, 1989) believe that correct modeling will suffice to promote language learning. Both sides of the controversy may have valid points, but if we focus on the learner, the question to ask is: How can a teacher give a student feedback without dampening his

> ### Teacher Note
>
> Jayme was reading a story that involved a character, Alice, who was standing at the front of a store and then went to the side of the store to peek through a window. Carlos raised his hand and said: "*Front* and *side* are antonyms."
>
> Jayme: "Interesting observation—why do you think they are antonyms?"
>
> Carlos: "Front is on the outside of the store—and inside, ah inside . . . *side* is not the same as *inside*?
>
> Jayme: "Well, let's see." (She starts to draw a store on the chart paper at her side.) "Carlos, come and point to the front of the store. Now point to the side of the store."
>
> Carlos: "But the inside also has sides—right? I see, *side* and *inside* are different."
>
> Jayme: "Yes, they are different. I guess you were thinking of *inside* and *outside*? I like the way you are thinking about these words."
>
> Carlos: "Does everybody understand the difference between *side* and *inside*? If I am at the side of the store, that is different from being inside the store.

comfort with risking errors and thus his language-learning progress? In the Teacher Note in box above, Jayme, a third-grade ELD teacher, provides a good example. In this case, rather than simply correcting Carlos, the teacher made a public effort to understand his thinking, to make the lexical distinctions he needed, and to model correct forms. Errors can provide a springboard to explain language structures in context. The issue is how to provide feedback and correction, transforming the error into a teaching event.

Selective Teacher Intervention. Varonis and Gass (1985) emphasize the importance of negotiation of meaning. They refer to pauses in conversation where participants ask for clarification or repetition. Such clarification allows them to keep up with the flow of the topic without falling behind. When we translate this into pedagogical practice, we can clearly see the weight that should be given to checking for understanding and guided practice during lesson implementation. *Checking for understanding* should be used in instruction in much the same way it is used in oral interactions—pausing to ask if someone understood; to indicate what is unclear; to paraphrase or summarize what was said. *Guided practice* involves giving students a task and activating the background knowledge needed for accomplishing the task; checking for understanding as they move along; providing clues or cues when they seem stuck; posing questions at various stages; and asking them to explain what they did and how they did it when they complete the task.

Gass & Selinker (1994) have delineated the concept of negotiation of interaction, which focuses on (a) comprehension, (b) production, (c) adjustments (which occur after understanding an error), and (d) the acquisition of language. In this process, two persons engaged in oral discourse produce speech and look to the other to determine if it has been comprehended. If there are indications that something was not comprehended, one may provide feedback to the other to indicate that it was or was not understood and, if appropriate, provide information about adjustments that could be made to make the utterance more comprehensible. Thus, it is a negotiation—an exchange of ideas, a give-and-take of infor-

> ### Teacher Note
>
> Mr. Rodriguez, the teacher, is reading a story to his kindergarten class. When the story ends, he faces the students and explains: "Now we have free time. You can read more books," pointing to the basket full of picture books. "You can also play in the kitchen area," he says, pointing to a corner of the room with a simulated kitchen area. "There is also the option of playing with the computers," he adds, gesturing to the computer section.
>
> Mai, a student recently arrived from Vietnam, stands up, and looking at the teacher, said: "Play," pointing at the computers.
>
> Mr. Rodriguez: "Yes, Mai, you can play with the computers."
>
> Mai, pointing at herself: "You can play."
>
> Mr. Rodriguez, pointing to himself: "I . . . will read a book." He pretends he is reading. Then he gestures again, "I", pointing at himself, and "you" pointing at Mai.
>
> Mai, pointing at herself: "I play."

mation until both parties are satisfied that they have gotten what they needed. This concept of negotiation is vital for classroom teaching when we are trying to help ELLs. It is empowering for the student to know that he can venture forth and take risks and that he will be given appropriate feedback on his performance. The emphasis is on feedback, not critiquing students' errors. The Teacher Note box above contains an example of the negotiation process. In the same manner as illustrated by this simple vignette, parents and teachers are constantly negotiating meaning with children and thus helping them to acquire language.

Discovering Patterns in Language

Oral production, or *output*, enables learners to use their language knowledge in real-life situations. Output provides students with the opportunity to test hypotheses of the target language and to develop language patterns (Gass & Selinker, 1994). Once a pattern of input and output has been established, the language use becomes somewhat automatic, as in the case of greetings. When an individual becomes comfortable with the target language, he can respond in an automatic way, without having to deliberate on the correct form. McLaughlin (1990) referred to this language phenomenon as *automaticity*.

How is this knowledge relevant to teaching? Teachers would probably respond by saying that it is important for the learner to have many opportunities for input and output. The richer the opportunities, the more possibility there is for a language learner to discover the patterns of a target language—something the language learner is always seeking to do. Once again, it is important for learners to have access to correct modeling and to receive feedback on their output. The more comfortable the learner feels about using her target language, the more she will use it and participate in conversations (Krashen, 1982).

Hakuta (1974) studied how children learn language patterns through memorization. Children used some memorized patterns to launch their communication in the target language. For example, children used the speech segment "What is that?" and then attached different nouns, such as *toy* or *food*, in order to compose different sentences.

Similarly, Wong Fillmore (1976) analyzed children learning a second language. One of the initial strategies she observed was children's learning formulaic expressions and the use of them in the appropriate conversational event.

She also found that after some practice, children could make changes and expand on these initial formulaic expressions. The implication of this finding for the primary grades is that books, songs, poems, and chants that emphasize patterns are promising tools that teachers can use. The Teacher Note box on page 222 is one example of using pattern books to facilitate early literacy. Although such books cannot serve as the primary source of reading material, and they do not represent the only approach teachers should take to literacy instruction, they provide a great deal of language input for children, help them to role-play being a reader, and typically delight them with their patterns and rhymes.

Teacher Note

Using Pattern Books in Instruction

Pattern books contain stories that make use of repeated phrases, refrains, and rhymes. The predictable patterns allow beginning second-language readers to become involved immediately in the language by discovering and repeating the pattern. They provide a model of word and sentence structure and assist comprehension because of the repeated pattern. Often they also contain pictures that support the learner's understanding. After reading a book with a group or class, students can read the book to one another and create their own stories or books that imitate the pattern (Peregoy & Boyle, 2001).

There are many sources for examples of pattern, or "predictable" books, but Peregoy and Boyle offer the following suggestions as ones that have been used successfully with older and younger English language learners:

Allard, H. (1979). *Bumps in the Night.* Garden City, NJ: Doubleday.

Barrett, J. (1970). *Animals Should Definitely Not Wear Clothing.* New York: Atheneum.

Brown, M. (1947). *Goodnight Moon.* New York: Harper & Row.

Carle, E. (1977). *The Grouchy Ladybug.* New York: Crowell.

Charlip, R. (1971). *Fortunately.* New York: Four Winds Press.

Flack, M. (1932). *Ask Mr. Bear.* New York: Macmillan.

Galdone, P. (1975). *The Gingerbread Boy.* Boston: Houghton Mifflin.

Hoban, R. (1972). *Count and See.* New York: Macmillan.

Hutchins, P. (1968). *Rosie's Walk.* New York: Macmillan.

Keats, E. J. (1971). *Over in the Meadow.* New York: Scholastic Press.

Martin, B. (1967). *Brown Bear, Brown Bear, What Do You See?* New York: Holt, Rinehart & Winston.

Mayer, M. (1968). *If I Had . . .* New York: Dial Press.

Paola, T. de (1978). *Pancakes for Breakfast.* Orlando: Harcourt Brace Jovanovich.

Polushkin, M. (1978). *Mother, Mother, I Want Another.* New York: Crown.

Sendak, M. (1962). *Chicken Soup with Rice.* New York: Scholastic Press.

Tolstoy, A. (1968). *The Great Big Enormous Turnip.* New York: Watts.

The Influence of Culture on Language Learning

Ways in which culture affects language learning are discussed in detail in chapter 2. It is an issue that is often overlooked but is of such importance and relevance that we have mentioned it repeatedly. Social scientists have underscored the relationship among language, culture and learning (Freire, 1970; Quintanar-Sarellana, 1997; Trumbull et al., 2001; Vygotsky, 1962). Paolo Freire, for example, posits the need to teach students to think and question, not only to learn skills. He focuses on the dialectical[2] role of the teacher and the essentiality of making the learning process relevant to the student. At the heart of Freire's pedagogy is the assumption that each student brings a wealth of language, culture, and knowledge to the classroom. The teacher is the facilitator who helps to extend and enrich the existing knowledge of the student. Freire emphasizes the need to integrate the students' background knowledge in the educational process. It is crucial for students to be able to relate their academic knowledge to their immediate and past environment. When we translate this theory into classroom practice, it means we need to start by connecting the home and school culture. Incorporating the child's language and culture into the school curriculum is beneficial to the educational process and provides an advantage to all students (García, 1994; Quintanar-Sarellana, 1991, 1997). Schools are a place to help students expand their minds and gain knowledge of other cultures. Not only cultural content but also culturally based modes of learning and communicating ought to be tapped (Cummins, 2001; Trumbull et al., 2001).

Valdés (1996) and LeVine

Teacher Note

As one European-American teacher related: "My students are all Latinos, and they really like to share and help each other. Yesterday I had asked them to bring art objects from home because we were going to make small collages. When I asked the class to place their objects on their desk, Lourdes looked embarrassed and said she did not have any. The children immediately got up from their desks and gave her one or two objects. I just let them share their materials. At the beginning, I would have stopped them and asked them to sit down, and I would have solved the problem. Now I have learned how much they like helping each other, and I don't interfere as much."

and White (1986) argued that agrarian values can be found in metropolitan areas around the world. These agrarian values are embedded in the lifestyle of immigrants who arrive from rural areas hoping to improve their economic conditions and their children's opportunity to receive an education. These agrarian values include interdependence, security, trust, and continuity. Another word for interdependence is *collectivism*. Many immigrant families value education immensely, and they also want their children to be an integral part of their family and community. Certainly the security of the group is not available to a child in his first days of school. In addition, parents sometimes feel conflict between their home values and the school values. The vignette in the Teacher Note box above presents an example of how a teacher learned to value the approach of children who come from cultures that are more collectivistic.

Often there is an obvious tension between the home values and the school values. All parents want their children to learn and to succeed in life. In fact, many parents migrate to this country because they want their children to have an education. Given this situation, this chapter will continue to explore instruction that accommodates cultural and linguistic differences.

Activating Prior Knowledge

Every time a concept is introduced in the classroom, it is important to find out how much the students know about it and related concepts. Díaz-Rico & Weed (1995) and Chamot (1994) stress that students must link previous knowledge to new concepts. There are a couple of reasons to investigate students' prior knowledge.

First, students come to class with a wealth of experiences. A teacher can facilitate learning by building on a student's experiences. For example, if a teacher is going to talk about budgets in everyday life, she might start by asking the students how many of them receive allowances. She might also ask students what chores they perform to earn some extra money, and similar questions. There are several techniques that help students to bring their knowledge to the forefront. A few of them are discussed in Figure 6-1.

Second, it is imperative that teachers have information on the students' culture(s) in order to make learning relevant. When teachers and students share the same cultural capital (Bourdieu & Passeron, 1977), it is easier to negotiate meaning and to collaborate in the construction of knowledge.

Cultural capital is defined as the set of linguistic patterns, social behavior, and mannerisms of a certain socioeconomic or ethnic group. A teacher does not need to be of the same ethnicity as his students, but he does need to cultivate the ability or willingness to view the world through their eyes.

Figure 6-1. Activating Prior Knowledge

There are several techniques that help students activate their previous knowledge. One is known as KWL and is accomplished by asking students what they *know* about the topic, subject, or concept to be introduced, what they *want to know* as a result of studying the topic, subject, or concept, and at the end of the lesson, emphasizing what they *learned*. In this way, the teacher activates prior knowledge, sets goals for their learning, and captures what they learn on a KWL chart. Brainstorming with a graphic organizer (some sort of visual model or depiction of knowledge or concepts) to depict what students know about the topic, subject, or concept grants students the opportunity to see the links between different ideas and concepts. Such graphic organizers include mind maps and webs. The following is an example of a web.

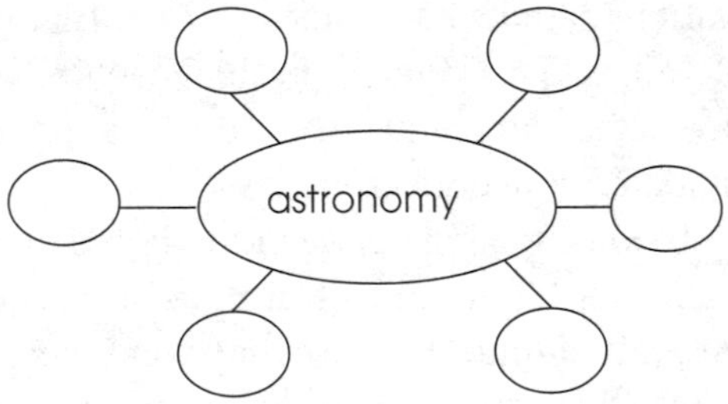

Another strategy is to use a pair or trio share, in which students get together in pairs or small groups and share their past experiences connected with the topic at hand and make notes about everything they know about it.

One way for a teacher to motivate and acknowledge students' prior knowledge is to weave their experiences within a lesson. In addition, the teacher can provide feedback on students' performance in order to validate their contributions and encourage them to continue learning. For example, during a unit on electricity, a high school teacher asked his students if they had fixed an electric appliance at home. Most of the students had experience helping their parents, and they were aware of the principles of how electricity works. Even misconceptions of how electricity works provide a platform for the teacher to explain and expand upon previous knowledge. Chapter 2 reports on the concept *funds of knowledge* (Diaz, Moll, & Mehan, 1986) that exist within ethnic minority communities. This knowledge needs to be highlighted in the curriculum, allowing learning to emerge from a cultural context.

Sociolinguistic Awareness and Socioaffective Factors

Very young bilingual children are capable of inferring which of their two languages is more valued in the social arena (Saville-Troike, 1976). A sense that one's mother tongue is perceived as inferior can lead to feeling unaccepted or devalued. It is important that schools strive to provide equal status to both languages so that children feel their language and culture is validated (Legarreta-Marcaida, 1981). Cummins (2001) suggests that schools use the students' language along with English. Ideally, students' primary language would be used for instruction, school libraries would have bilingual books, and buildings would have signs in different languages. Parents could be invited to their child's classroom to share a story, poem, song, tongue twister, or a riddle, a great way to bring in literature that is relevant to the children.

Students facing an unknown language and culture experience more stress than students who are learning in their native language and are surrounded by cultural phenomena that are familiar and comfortable for them (Valenzuela, 1999). In addition, English language learners may experience an environment that is not supportive of their needs (Faltis & Hudelson, 1994). Thomas and Collier (1997) emphasized the importance of the sociocultural context of schooling of language-minority students. When students think that their language and culture are valued, they feel better about learning another language. The teacher's role in making students feel safe to venture using their English skills cannot be emphasized enough. In his model, Krashen (1982) describes the process of helping students to feel more comfortable as "lowering the affective filter" (see chapter 4), thereby increasing the student's opportunity for developing language proficiency.

Using a Child's First Language as a Resource for Developing the Second Language

Guadalupe Valdés (1996) studied the obstacles faced by ESL students during the middle school years. After observing many classes, she questioned the exclusive use of English in ESL classes to explain concepts and convey information. We take it for granted that our native language can help us to understand a language unknown to us. After analyzing worldwide research, Cummins (1994) found that skills and concepts learned in one language could transfer to another (see discussion of "common underlying proficiency" in chapter 4).

In a recent study, Espinoza-Herold (2003) explored the issues that were relevant to teachers and students. Educators who were interviewed believed that strong language skills were the foundation for students' academic success. On the other hand, students felt deprived of the freedom to use their native language to learn. They thought that their language and identity were devalued at school. Frequently, linguistic minority students are forbidden to use their native language as a source of important support to further their learning. This is extremely unfortunate because it is vital to acknowledge and respect and allow students to use the knowledge base of their native language so that they can more effectively learn a second language.

Understanding Language Disorders and Language Differences

Language Disorders

The American Speech-Language Hearing Association (ASHA, 1993) defines a language disorder as

> impaired comprehension and/or use of spoken, written, and/or other symbol systems. The disorder may involve (1) the form of language (phonology, morphology, or syntax), (2) the content of language (semantics), and/or (3) the function of language in communication (pragmatics in any combination).

The concepts included in this definition have been presented earlier in this book (chapters 1 and 3). We have also emphasized the importance of considering the interrelationships of language with sociocultural factors, and this is no less salient when thinking about children with language disorders:

> Since language is embedded in culture, any definition of a language disorder must be defined by the parameters established by the community of which the child is a member. As culturally defined, a language disorder is impaired comprehension and/or use of a spoken, written, and/or other symbol system used by the child's indigenous culture and language group. (Taylor, 1986)

In a position paper on social dialects, ASHA (1983) also emphasizes the following:

> No dialectal variety of English (or any other language) is a disorder or pathological form of speech or language. Each social dialect is adequate as a functional and effective variety of English. Each serves a communication function as well as a social solidarity function. It maintains the communication network and the social construct of the community of speakers who use it. (pp. 23–24)

Teacher Note

Confusing Learning Disabilities with Normal Second-Language Learning Features

Mercer (1987) and Damico, Oller, and Storey (1983) have suggested some indicators of learning disabilities that may also be characteristics of students learning a second language:

- A discrepancy between verbal and nonverbal performance measures on intelligence tests
- Academic learning difficulty, particularly with the abstract concepts required in upper elementary and secondary grades
- Inability to perceive and organize and remember information when such information is based on different experiences, different cultural values, or different linguistic backgrounds
- Social and emotional difficulties related to difficulty in ability to communicate or to problems related to adjustment to a new culture and cultural expectations in a new academic environment
- The appearance of attention-deficit problems because of difficulty comprehending information presented
- Delays in responding to questions, or silence or not responding, as the result of difficulty understanding the second language rather than a word-finding or expression problem.

Adapted from Bernstein & Tiegerman-Farber (2002)

The identification of language disorders is quite complex and difficult and should not be undertaken by the teacher alone. If a classroom teacher thinks that something unusual is going on with a child's language development, he should contact a speech-language pathologist (SLP) or other specialist to plan a consultation regarding the child. The identification of a language disorder in children who are by definition in the process of learning a language is particularly difficult. Distinctions also have to be made regarding age expectations.

When considering a child from a culturally or linguistically nondominant community, the task is even more challenging. A bilingual speech and language pathologist with special training is needed (Langdon, 1992). Knowledge of both the child's languages and of signs of actual abnormality or delay in development are critical. Because of the morphological contrasts between standard American English and Spanish, for example, children learning English as a second language may be perceived as having a language disorder. The differences involve the placement of noun modifiers, the order of elements in a question, and the placement of negation markers. For instance, in Spanish most adjectives follow the noun they modify, such as, *luna llena*, "moon full." The sequence of subject and verb is also different in English and Spanish. In a Spanish question, the verb tends to go before rather than after the subject. *¿Ya comió Alberto?* ("Already eaten has Albert?") or *¿Dijo ella que es maestra?* ("Has said she that [she] is a teacher?"). In English, the subject in sentences like the first one is interposed between the auxiliary verb and the rest of the verb ("Has Albert already eaten?"). One sees the same order of subject and verb in the second sentence.

Negatives may require two morphemes rather than one, as in *No puedo dar ningún ejemplo*—"Not I can give not any example." *No puedo dar un ejemplo* ("Not I can give an example") is equally acceptable, although the meaning varies slightly. When a child uses the school language as her primary language, development of proficiency in the first language, which may be the language of the home, may be slowed or stopped. The child may be misidentified as having a disorder in the first language or in both languages, since she may not have developed the language proficiency in the second language to be able to use it for complex academic tasks (Bernstein & Tiegerman-Farber, 2002).

Cultural differences can also explain certain nonlinguistic behaviors that may result in the misidentification of language disorders. Eye contact, for example, is culturally determined. Use of averted or indirect eye contact may give the appearance that a child is not paying attention. Children in a new language environment may be hesitant to respond with less than adequate language skills.

Language Differences

Contrasted with a language disorder, a language difference is a rule-governed language style that deviates in some way from the standard usage of the mainstream culture. Some children from culturally different backgrounds have language disorders, and the SLP's job is to provide remediation in a culturally sensitive way. However, many children from culturally different backgrounds are referred for language assessment on the belief that they have language disorders, when what they exhibit are actually language differences. When assessment reveals a difference rather than a disorder, the choice is either to do nothing—simply report it to teacher and parents—or address the difference, as in an educational program (Paul, 1995). (See section below on Ebonics).

Some groups who are native to the United States or who emigrate from countries where languages other than English are spoken exhibit language differences that may be confused with language disorders or disabilities. The use of a nonstandard dialect does not constitute a disorder, but the use of one—such as AAVE, or Ebonics—may be a handicap to users if speakers of the standard dialect see it as inferior or deviant. Many children of Hispanic heritage come to school with what has been referred to as limited English proficiency (LEP): They know a little English but are not fluent communicators and have trouble functioning in a monolingual English classroom. LEP is not a disorder, nor is it permanent. When such children are provided with supportive strategies and abundant opportunities for interaction, they eventually master English and often become bilingual, able to communicate effectively in two languages.

More than 200 distinct languages are spoken by Native Americans in North America today. It is not possible to identify interference points with Standard English for all 200. Harris (1993) and Young (1967) have identified several general differences that are frequently seen between English and Native American languages. For example, the Navajo language does not use consonant clusters in a final-position syllable. Silence is a rule-governed practice denoting respect, thoughtfulness, a question worthy of serious consideration, or an unfamiliar situation.

Like Native American languages, Asian languages that can influence the speech of ELLs are so many and diverse that it is not possible to identify all the points of interference. One feature that

Teacher Inquiry

Dialect Study

Use the charts in Rhea Paul's book, *Language Disorders from Infancy Through Adolescence* (1995), to identify examples of dialectical differences in your own students' (or peers') dialects.

is widely known (and illustrated in countless comedy routines) is that /r/ and /l/ occur in the same phonemic category and are confused in Asian dialects of English. *Be* verbs can be omitted or improperly inflected ("I going" or "I is going"). Plurals may be omitted with quantifiers (*two shoe*) or overgeneralized (*the sheeps*). There may be omission or misuse of prepositions ("She is at room" or "We go car") For some charts of identified features of Black English, Spanish-influenced English, Native American and Asian dialects of English, see Paul (1995). Despite the unfortunate title (nonstandard dialects are not disorders), this book has some very useful information.

Distinguishing Language Difference from Disorder

At times, there will be a need to assess if a real language disorder exists, or there is only the perception that a disorder exists. The initial step is to find out whether the problem is perceived because of a difference in cultural expectations for communication or because the child has a genuine disability. Paul (1995) presents a good exemplar (see Teacher Note box below) of a case referred for assessment. It illustrates both the confusion resulting from observation of a child's overt behavior and the suggested follow-up resulting from the assessment.

Teacher Note

Assessment of Harry

Harry was an American Indian child recently arrived from the reservation to an urban Head Start program. He seemed to the teachers to be inordinately quiet. When asked a question he took an exceedingly long time to answer, causing teachers to question his comprehension skills. He had a great deal of difficulty presenting information during sharing time and did not seem to process teachers' verbal directions. He was referred for speech and language assessment. Ms. Lopez, the SLP, observed his classroom behavior and saw the same problems the teachers had pointed out. Before deciding Harry had a disorder, though, she interviewed Harry's parents. She found that they spoke both English and Navajo in the home. Both were fluent in English and had jobs in which they conversed with English speakers regularly. They believed that Harry was proficient in English; he watched English-language TV and played with English-speaking children in the neighborhood and seemed to get along with them all right. They didn't really understand why he should

cont.

be having so much trouble in school. Ms. Lopez decided to collect a language sample from Harry during a play period with a peer. She analyzed the sample and found that Harry's use of syntax and semantics was generally age appropriate. Receptive language testing, using a standardized picture-pointing test, showed that Harry's receptive vocabulary score was somewhat below the normal range. Ms. Lopez asked the parents about the items Harry failed to identify on the test, and they explained that he was unlikely to have encountered those words in their home or on the reservation. Ms. Lopez assessed Harry's comprehension of classroom directions with some criterion-referenced measures. She found that Harry could follow most directions but was very slow and careful about doing so. When she asked his parents why this might be the case, they explained that he had been taught at home to think carefully before acting. They commented that Harry had once said that the teachers seemed to want him to act like a "show-off" in school. Ms. Lopez concluded that there was a mismatch between the teachers' expectations and Harry's communication style. Although Harry would need some help in developing some of the vocabulary items with which he'd had no previous experience, this could be done by consulting with teachers about some concepts to emphasize in the course of their regular program. Ms. Lopez also shared her nonstandardized assessment results with the teachers and talked with them about Harry's need to consider before answering and his unwillingness to stand out from the group in sharing time. She suggested some ways they could modify their interactions with Harry that could bring their communicative expectations more in line with his and suggested that they also talk with him about some of the different ways people can be expected to act at school and at home, so that some of the school rules might seem less foreign to him.

Paul (1995) notes: "In Harry's case the assessment suggests a difference rather than a disorder of communication. The remedy for this situation is two-pronged. Some work must be done to help Harry adjust to the communicative demands of the classroom. This work, though, should be culturally sensitive; care should be taken not to invalidate the styles of communicating that are appropriate at home. The second prong involves making some adjustments in the classroom's communication requirements. This would include consultation with teachers to make them aware of Harry's communication style, assuring them that it is a difference rather than a disorder and that Harry has the potential to communicate effectively. It would also involve finding ways to accommodate his communication in the classroom setting" (pp. 163–164).

Dialectal Differences: The Case of Ebonics[3]

There are a number of Black scholars who would not agree with the subheading of this section or the alternative labels we have given to Ebonics elsewhere in this book. This is because they think of Ebonics as a different language, not as a dialect of English. Although people tend to think that the term was coined at the time of the controversy over its use and inclusion in a resolution in Oakland, California, in 1998, it actually emerged 24 years earlier. At that time, Dr. Robert Williams reported that the term was created when Black conferees at a Language and the Urban Child conference in St. Louis, Missouri, held a separate caucus and devised the term. For them, it referred to

> linguistic and paralinguistic features which on a concentric continuum represent the communicative competence of the West African, Caribbean, and United States slave descendants of African origin. It includes the various idioms, patois, argots, ideolects, and social dialects of black people, especially those who have been forced to adapt to colonial circumstances. (Williams, 1975, cited in Smitherman, 1998, p. 29)

Smitherman explains that "for this group of scholars, the conceptual framework of 'Ebonics' represented an avenue for decolonization of the African-American mind, a way to begin repairing the psycholinguistically maimed psyche of Blacks in America. As Freire and Macedo (1985) have noted, "language variations (female language, ethnic language, dialects) are intimately interconnected with, coincide with, and express identity. They help defend one's sense of identity and they are absolutely necessary in the process of struggling for liberation" (p. 186).

Smitherman and other Black scholars argue that Ebonics is not based on English. Smith (1998), for example, posits that the grammars of the so-called Black English dialect and the English spoken by Europeans and Euro-Americans are not the same, although there has been extensive borrowing or adoption of English and other European words. He argues further that the grammar of the language of the descendants of Niger-Congo African slaves follows the grammar rules of the Niger-Congo African languages (Alleyne, 1971; Jahn, 1961). He uses other arguments regarding lexical and etymological development to support the proposition that Ebonics is a separate language with roots in Africa, totally unrelated to the Germanic roots of English. On the other hand, despite some African-language features in Ebonics, African-American linguists tend not to agree with Smitherman and others' contention that it is not a dialect of English (Baugh, 1994; Rickford, 1997). By the usual criterion (mutual intelligibility), Ebonics is a dialect of English: English speakers and Ebonics speakers can understand each other, with an occasional misunderstanding or failure to perceive a shade of meaning due to a vocabulary or syntactic difference.

Whether one identifies Ebonics as a dialect or a language, we agree with many linguists and Black scholars about what a teacher's response should be to a child who speaks Ebonics. The first is to respect and appreciate the language he or she brings to school. As Delpit (1998) stresses, "It is the language they heard as their mothers nursed them and changed their diapers and played peek-a-boo with them. It is the language through which they first encountered love, nurturance, hope" (p. 17). Delpit has also emphasized in her writings that we must acknowledge that Standard English is the language of power and that students will be hampered in their life pursuits if they do not learn it. Although having access to the standard language form may not guarantee economic success, not having it will almost certainly guarantee failure.

What else should a teacher do to help students gain access to Standard English? One thing is certain: Constant correction will not produce the desired result. A student who is frequently corrected increases his or her cognitive monitoring of speech, making it difficult to talk. Forcing speakers to monitor their language typically produces silence (Delpit, 1998). A teacher must also be aware that issues of group identity affect production of a different dialect. In a study of the Pima Indian language, Sharon Nelson-Barber (1982) found that in grades 1–3, students' dialect approximated that of the teacher, but by grade 4 their language moved more toward the local dialect, counter to expectations that they would be gaining mastery of standard forms. In addition to teachers being mindful of the sociocultural factors associated with identifying with one's first language (or dialect), there are specific instructional approaches that teachers can use to ensure learning for students. We will discuss these below.

Literacy and English Language Learners

In our opinion, a universal goal for all students who speak more than one language is *biliteracy*, proficiency with the literate forms of both languages. This topic was addressed in chapter 5. Here we focus on ELLs' acquisition of literacy in English.

For students learning English as a second language, learning to read and write in English is almost certainly more of a challenge than for those who speak English as a first language. Achieving nativelike proficiency is often even more difficult (Weber, 1991). The following list contains the most frequently cited factors influencing the development of literacy in a second language:

1. Level of literacy development in first language
2. Background knowledge (degree of match between student's experience and cultural orientation and text demands)
3. Vocabulary
4. Grammatical knowledge
5. Differences in text structure or style between first language and English
6. Speed of processing

The Role of Literacy in the First Language

Research has shown that students who have learned to read in their first language do not need to start from scratch when learning to read in a second language (see reviews in Fitzgerald, 1995; Krashen, 1996). This is because many reading skills transfer from language to language. The student does not have to relearn, for example, that written forms represent oral language or that reading is not simply decoding but also constructing meaning.

The Issue of Transfer

Students who have developed effective reading strategies in their primary language (predicting, confirming, using context) will probably transfer those skills to English text to support their decoding efforts (August, Calderón, & Carlo, 2002; Calero-Breckheimer & Goetz, 1993; Langer, Bartolomé, Vasquez, & Lucas, 1990; Thonis, 1983). It seems clear that the basic cognitive processes that English learners use in reading are the same as those of native English speakers (Fitzgerald, 1995).

Not all literacy skills transfer well across languages, and ELLs are likely to need instruction in certain specific, nontransferable skills: hearing the sounds of

English, linking them to the symbols (letters) they represent, learning English spelling patterns, and understanding the different English terms for concepts they have already developed in the first language. Heubert and Hauser (1999) conclude, "Such transfer is not automatic; it occurs only when conditions for the emergence of the analogous second-language skills exist, and it can be aided by explicit support for the process of transfer" (p. 224).

Marie Altchech, a fourth-grade teacher affiliated with the Bridging Cultures Project mentioned earlier, observed that because many ELLs are mainstreamed into English-only instruction at fourth grade, there are suddenly many referrals for special education evaluations of these students in her district. She suggests that most teachers assume that phonemic awareness skills in Spanish will transfer readily to English (Trumbull et al., in press). Of course, phonological awareness may transfer (Durgunoglu, Nagy, & Hancin-Bhatt, 1993), but the majority of students will likely need some explicit instruction in English orthography (spelling conventions) and word analysis (Beaumont, de Valenzuela, & Trumbull, 2002). Spanish decoding instruction does not provide enough of a basis for transfer of orthographic skills to English, despite many similarities between the two systems. For one thing, the basic orthographic building block in Spanish is the syllable, compared to the phoneme in English (Escamilla, 1999). Spanish is a very rhythmic language, with regular consonant-vowel alternation in most words. There are many fewer possible syllable patterns in Spanish, so children may be taught "syllabic families" like *ma-, me-, mi-, mo-, mu-* or *pa-, pe-, pi-, po-, pu-*. This strategy is very productive for Spanish-reading novices but would be much less so for those learning to read in English (Vernon & Ferreiro, 1999).

One possible sticking point for speakers and readers of languages like Spanish that have fewer vowels is the complex vowel representation system in English: five letters represent approximately 15 vowel sounds, individually or in combination. The letter *A* alone stands for at least four sounds (consider *happy, fate, father, all*). Confusions can arise over differences in the sounds represented by the same letter; in Spanish the letter *H* is silent, unless it is combined as *ch*; and *J* is pronounced roughly like the English *H* in

---

Teacher Note

Strategies of Successful Bilingual Readers

A study involving eight successful native Spanish-speaking readers of English (Jiménez, García, & Pearson, 1996) showed that these sixth- and seventh-grade students used several strategies: (1) they sometimes translated from English to Spanish to understand the meaning better, (2) they looked for cognates (words that have the same root in Spanish and English and look similar, such as, *problema* and *problem, obtener* and *obtain*), and (3) they used both grammatical context (e.g., what part of speech the word must be) and subsequent text to resolve the meaning of unknown words. Like good native English-speaking readers, many of them also (4) monitored their comprehension, (5) connected their own prior knowledge with the text they were reading, and (6) asked themselves questions. Many of these strategies overlap with those discussed by Pressley (1999) and Palincsar and David (1991).

many dialects. In addition, English language learners' vocabularies are not going to be equivalent to those of native English speakers.

Jiménez (1997) found that low-achieving, native Spanish-speaking readers of English tended to focus on decoding and pronunciation of words rather than on comprehension of texts. This may be true, in part, because they have not yet become automatic with the decoding process and need further instruction and practice. Alternatively, literacy instruction in their first language may have overemphasized decoding, leading to underdeveloped comprehension strategies (Kucer & Silva, 1995). In any case, less proficient readers tend to read "by paying excessive attention to the forms and inadequate attention to the developing meanings" (Bialystok, 1991, p. 129).

For students whose first-language's writing system is alphabetic and who have learned read in that language, moving to English orthography represents less of a cognitive step than for those who have learned to read in a syllabic or logographic writing system. In Japanese, for example, a syllable like *ku-* or *ri-* is represented by a single graphic element. In reality, Japanese uses a combination system, with some words being written in symbols that stand for syllables[4] and some written in logograms (*kanji*) that represent whole words. Kanji, which are Chinese in origin, can be very complex, with many pen or brush strokes composing a single one. Such a system places an extremely high demand on visual memory but relatively less demand on phonological and phonemic skills.

Teacher Note

Building Background Knowledge and Vocabulary

The combined factors of vocabulary and prior knowledge are, not surprisingly, a major predictor of success in reading and a primary determinant of reading comprehension for students learning to read English as a second language (August & Hakuta, 1997; García, 1991). Teachers should strive to build the background knowledge and vocabulary necessary to comprehend the reading they assign. This can be accomplished through informal instruction—such as reading aloud to students—and direct step-by-step instructional strategies for teaching key concepts and vocabulary from selected texts in both pre- and post-reading activities, such as semantic mapping (Heimlich & Pittelman, 1986). Group vocabulary development, versus individuals looking words up in the dictionary and writing sentences, has the advantage of promoting students' learning from each other.

The Role of Content and Vocabulary Knowledge

When speakers of other languages encounter a text in English (whether a story, essay, or scientific explanation), they will naturally attempt to draw from their own experiences to make sense of what they are reading. However, their experience may not help them comprehend the content of a text written for students in the United States (Jiménez et al., 1996; Kucer & Silva, 1995). If they have not had prior experience with a concept (e.g., ice fishing, hula dancing, keyboarding, democracy, majority rule, Benedict Arnold), they may also need to learn the ideas behind the new vocabulary. Vocabulary familiar to English speakers may be unknown to students who are still learning English (García, 1991; Nagy, 1997; Wong Fillmore, 1989). Sometimes the least common words carry much of the core meaning of a text, something that is hard on all young readers, but native speakers of English may at least have heard these words spoken and be able to make a tentative identification.

Lewis (2001) cites the example of a short text about Abraham Lincoln and the freeing of the slaves in which the following were the key concept words: *Abe Lincoln, Stephen Douglas, blacks, free* and *freed, slave* and *slavery, speech* and *speeches, argument, elected* and *election, state, nation, Illinois, America, president, Senate*. Students new to the United States may know equivalent words for some of these concepts in their first language, but they may not, depending on their background. Furthermore, according to Lewis, they may not recognize relationships between "tenses, plurals, possessives and other forms of the same word" (p. 11)—relationships that native speakers are more likely to see—never mind the cultural and historical context of the text. These observations are echoed by others (Stoller & Grabe, 1995).

The Role of Grammatical Knowledge

ELLs may have difficulty using grammatical knowledge to monitor their comprehension (Gibbons, 1991). Native English speakers are sensitive to their own mistakes that result in a nongrammatical sentence (Flood & Menyuk, 1983; Vellutino, Scanlon, & Tanzman, 1990), but nonnative speakers are probably much less sensitive to such errors and consequently self-correct less. That is, they don't as readily detect their errors, so they don't use them as a way to monitor their reading. If a native speaker misreads *descent* as *decent*, and the resulting text doesn't make sense in light of the story—or the resulting sentence isn't grammatical—he or she is likely to stop and self-correct. A second-language learner may not hear the error and may continue to read without correcting a misconception regarding the text.

Certainly, English learners have much greater difficulty paraphrasing what they have read, an activity that requires sophisticated language knowledge and considerable flexibility with language (Anderson & Roit, 1996). The same problems arise with assessment when the language of test items paraphrases from the text they are based on instead of using the exact terminology (García, 1991). The fact that second-language readers show much greater understanding of text read in English when allowed to discuss it in their first language suggests that these limitations are not simply a problem of comprehension.

The Role of Knowledge of Text Structures and Literary Styles

We mentioned earlier that ways of structuring text vary around the world, and we described the U.S. school norm for a persuasive essay or argument. Students who have been schooled in many other countries may naturally gravitate to a different organization. An inductive argument, in which facts are presented first and a conclusion drawn, may be laid out (Leki, 1992). The grader or scorer may flinch when he or she fails to see a topic sentence followed by evidence and a conclusion. Nevertheless, the inductive form is neither superior nor inferior to a deductive argument, in which an allegation is made and facts are offered to support it.

Students who have been exposed to different expectations for how text should be structured may not recognize the patterns of the stories or descriptions that are used in the classroom (or expected in their writing). Although this level of literacy knowledge is sometimes overlooked, it should be recognized as important, particularly for English language learners, who may come from different cultural backgrounds.

A related area has to do with literary styles that students may use or recognize in writing. A couple of brief examples will illustrate this issue. Vietnamese narrative style apparently emphasizes the importance of setting, so that a student may expend what a teacher considers a disproportionate amount of time on describing the setting of a narrative and neglect plot or character. For instance, some cultures value a written narrative style that might be considered flowery by U.S. dominant-culture readers. Students coming from an Arabic writing tradition may seem to digress when they use elaborate description. In both cases, students and teachers may find themselves focusing on different text elements. Here is a ripe opportunity for misdiagnosis of a student's literacy skills.

Native-born students may also find their preferred modes of discourse misunderstood or devalued. According to Kochman (1989), African Americans are more likely to follow the classical Greek pattern of including not only logical evidence in an argument but also an appeal to the emotions—revealing how they feel about a topic. Somehow the dominant culture represented in schools has come to regard the emotional appeal as undermining the logic of the argument (which, of course, it does not), wheras African-American regard the elimination of emotion as an insincere move.

Speed of Processing as an Issue

Even when students have mastered concepts in English, they may access them more slowly than they do in their first language (Figueroa & Garcia, 1994; Jiménez et al., 1996). This time factor can become a serious problem when there are requirements to finish tasks within a scheduled block of time or when students are being formally tested (Shaw, 1997).

What About Writing?

Teachers must help students to build a broad basis of oral English, a foundation firm enough to support their understanding of written English. However, *this does not mean that writing instruction must wait until the student is proficient in English* (Leki, 1992). Writing can be developed at the same time as oral language and reading. Often too much attention is paid to oral language and not enough to print literacy in early phases of development in the new language.

Instructional Approaches for English Language Learners

Some Useful Guidelines

In chapter 4, on second-language acquisition, we provided one set of general guidelines regarding instruction that emerged from our knowledge of how individuals acquire a second language and the implications of that knowledge for instruction. It is also useful to think about more specific principles or guidelines to follow when one is planning lessons that will be appropriate for students with language differences and will optimize learning opportunities for them. Here we provide two sets of principles or teaching standards that serve as guidelines for thinking about planning instruction. One set is taken from the work of researchers who have explored many aspects of teaching students from a range of linguistic and cultural communities; the second is from two researchers and practitioners who have also done extensive exploratory work in teaching English learners in order to provide effective professional development for teachers.

CREDE's Five Standards

The researchers at the Center for Research on Education, Diversity, & Excellence (CREDE) at the University of California, Santa Cruz, developed a core document known as the "Five Standards for Effective Teaching and Learning"— a set of principles of effective pedagogy that are appropriate for all students. Although the work contributing to these standards comes from several theoretical systems, they are stated in the language of sociocultural theory—the grounding for this book as well. The standards, which follow below, are applicable to all settings but are particularly important for students from nondominant communities, where there is always the danger of dumbing down the curriculum because of confusions between difference and deficit. The standards are as follows:
- Teachers and students producing together (joint productive activity)
- Developing language across the curriculum (language development)
- Making meaning: connecting school to students' lives (contextualization)
- Teaching complex thinking (cognitive challenge)
- Teaching through interactive discussions (instructional conversation[5])

Not all standards will be reflected in all lessons; however, teachers are often concerned about covering content and curriculum and thus ignore students' language development, which is critical for academic success. In Figure 6-2, Jana Echevarria and Claude Goldenberg (1999) describe a student in a class and the lesson that is planned for the student and others with similar language needs. You may want to use this activity as a basis for discussion with students or colleagues. First discuss what you think is meant by the Five Standards (additional references listed at the end of this chapter). The point of the activity is to discover which of CREDE's five standards are reflected in the lesson.

Figure 6-2. Planning Instruction for
Students with Language Needs

Tommy is a seventh grader enrolled in a neighborhood middle school. He has been in the United States for 9 months and was last in school in the fifth grade in his native country. His family does not speak English at home, but he has basic conversational abilities in English, and in 9 months he has developed rudimentary reading skills in English. His teacher realizes, however, that he would have a difficult time in a mainstream content area classroom taught in English. She recognizes that he is capable of completing many academic tasks if the teacher considers his language needs. In the lesson described, Tommy's teacher sets a content objective *and* a language development objective for Tommy and other students with similar abilities and needs:

- Content Objective: Name, describe, and tell the function of a knight's armor and weaponry. Define key terms and describe how armor and weaponry differed for these purposes and occasions.

- Language Objective: Locate information in a written text and use this information to complete sentences using standard English grammar and spelling.

To facilitate note taking, the teacher distributes a tree diagram graphic organizer:

The teacher makes the reading more accessible to students with limited English skills by copying the material and identifying paragraphs containing the required information by numbering them to correspond with the numbers on the graphic organizer and worksheet. She also modifies the worksheet so that instead of answering questions, the ELLs are given sentence prompts to complete. The concept is the same for all students, but language complexity is reduced for the English learner students.

The teacher begins the lesson by reviewing previous lessons about the Middle Ages and refers to a posted list of key terms. After reviewing the lesson objectives, the teacher then opens a discussion about different types of clothing and their uses. She shows pictures from department store circulars depicting formal, casual, and work clothes. She ties the topic to students' personal experiences by prompting them to discuss the function of different types of clothes. When she feels there is sufficient understanding, she distributes the reading passage and reads the section aloud, paraphrasing as needed and drawing attention to information that may be used to complete the tree diagram. Students are given 10 minutes to complete the diagram, using information from the reading. Pairs of students share their notes, and several report on their notes to the class. After giving instruction for the activity, the teacher calls on two students to model the assignment. Students work in pairs to complete the assignment, with the teacher providing assistance as needed.

Dutro and Moran's Principles

Another set of principles is provided by Susana Dutro and Carol Moran (2003), who believe that "English language instruction should provide not only ample opportunities for meaningful and engaging uses of language for a wide range of social and academic purposes, but necessary instruction in how English works. It should be deliberate, strategic, and purposeful" (p. 14).

Their principles are drawn from the literature in cognitive psychology, language acquisition, and many years of instructional practice.

1. Build on students' prior knowledge of both language and content. It is essential that every lesson take into account what students bring to the lesson and build on that existing knowledge and language skill.

2. Create meaningful contexts for functional use of language. Creating context is essential for students to map new knowledge onto prior knowledge or new forms and labels onto existing concepts. The use of visuals, gestures, graphic organizers, and word banks to reinforce concepts and vocabulary is effective. At the early levels of English proficiency, use of simulations, gestures, realia (real objects or props), and theater are powerful, whereas comparisons, metaphors, and analogies can be useful at higher levels of language functioning. Figure 6-2 shows a lesson that both builds content knowledge and language through a meaningful context that is likely to be of interest to students.

3. Provide comprehensible input and model language use in a variety of ways. Learning occurs when modeling is clear, information is presented in small, comprehensible chunks, and frequent feedback is provided.

4. Provide a range of opportunities for practice and application. Creating situations for focused interaction through debates, theater, interactive writing, and so forth, gives students opportunities to try out new language learning. Cooperative group work around a situational task offers students the chance to use language purposefully and receive feedback on their performance.

5. Establish a positive and supportive environment for practice with clear goals and immediate corrective feedback. Particularly in settings with few English-speaking models, teachers must create many opportunities for English learners to hear, use and receive corrective feedback on academic language for the purpose of building the linguistic competencies required to achieve grade level standards. Although it is important to create an environment where mistakes are seen in a positive light, corrective feedback must be a part of the equation to develop academic language skills to an advanced level.

6. Reflect on the forms of language and the process of learning. This is a principle that is not commonly followed in American classrooms. It is the process of helping students to become metacognitively aware of the language they are using or developing and the processes they use to learn by discussing these processes with them before or after they engage in a learning activity (i.e., with questions like "How did you go about solving that problem?" or "What new vocabulary did you have to learn for this activity or lesson?")

Cummins's Analysis of Linguistic and Cognitive Demands of Tasks

One final set of concepts to keep in mind when planning instruction for students with language differences is their level of proficiency vis-à-vis the level of language processing complexity required to complete assigned tasks. Cummins (1982) theorized that tasks could be identified by the range of contextual support provided and the degree of cognitive involvement required and that teachers could and should adjust their instruction on the basis of the proficiency levels represented in the students in her classroom. Figure 6-3 shows a schema devised by Cummins for classifying tasks with examples suggested by Cuevas (1996). Quadrant. A represents communication tasks that rely on gestures, visuals, and expressive movements and do not require a high degree of cognitive processing. Quadrant B includes communication that is not cognitively demanding but is not supported by visuals, gestures, or hands-on materials. Quadrant C represents verbal or written communication with low cognitive demand but which also has visual cues to provide context. Quadrant D depicts communication that is cognitively demanding and offers no help in the form of gestures or visuals. This classification scheme can be used by teachers to analyze the level of language demand posed in their classrooms by different activities.

Figure 6-3. Contextual Support and Cognitive Demand in Classroom Activities

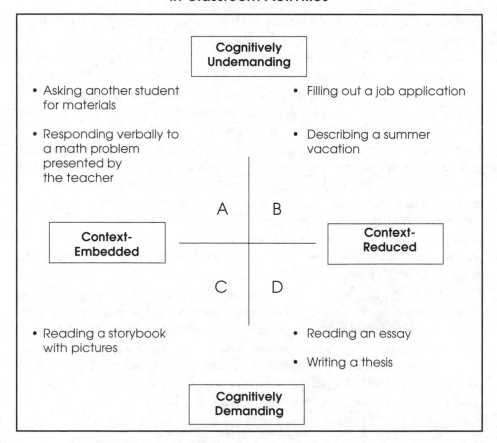

Academic language (discussed in detail in chapter 4) is a powerful device in the acquisition of knowledge. It is the language needed to understand math, science, and social science textbooks. Academic language is often not supported by the contextual clues afforded by daily conversation; therefore, it tends to be more challenging. Teachers can provide context by activating the students' prior experiences, using visual aids, modeling instruction, and emphasizing hands-on learning (Cummins, 2001).

Using English Language Development Standards to Guide Instructional Planning for English Learners

It is important for teachers to understand why a standards-based movement has swept the country and why standards are important. In seeking to reform schools and better prepare students for the 21st century, many educators came to realize that

> without clarity or consensus about what all students should know and be able to do, expectations for learning have been defined by the textbooks and tests used in the overwhelming majority of schools, and many students have left school without ever being challenged to their full potential. (Lachat, 1999a, p. 3)

In chapter 3 we introduced the idea that ELD standards can be used effectively to plan instruction and to assess students' progress in developing proficiency in English. ELD or ESL standards describe the language skills necessary for social and academic success. Such standards should be used in conjunction with content standards (e.g., math, science, social studies) developed by the various professional groups.

Part of the hope of those who have supported the standards-based movement is that the establishment of standards will provide all students with equal access to challenging curricula and learning experiences. Lachat (1999a) identified the following potential benefits of standards for ELLs:

- Raising expectations for student achievement
- Emphasizing authentic learning tasks
- Improving teaching practices

At the same time, she raises some concerns about *how* students with varying levels of English proficiency will be included in the implementation of standards at the classroom level. Setting expectations for all students to achieve rigorous standards means that some children will require some accommodations in assessment to ensure that they are not doomed to failure. The language demands of higher order learning tasks, for example, are often such that specific attention must be given to English learners who are at various proficiency levels to enable them to accomplish the task by adjusting or modifying the task to accommodate their language learning (Abedi et al., 2001; Solano-Flores & Trumbull, 2003). In addition, so-called authentic tasks that are designed to simulate real-life situations may not reflect the realities of second-language students. Finally, scoring rubrics and assessments used to evaluate students' performance on learning tasks should focus on the subject-area knowledge, skills, and abilities being assessed, not on the quality of the language in which the response is expressed (LaCelle-Peterson & Rivera, 1994). Unfortunately, it is not only the language of student responses that must be considered but also the complexity of the language in which test items are cast (see chapter 7).

The set of standards developed by the organization for Teachers of English to Speakers of Other Languages (TESOL) is a prime example that can be very useful to teachers. The standards are grouped by grade-level clusters and provide descriptors, progress indicators, vignettes and discussions for each section. The standards for most content areas (e.g., math, reading, social studies) are sequenced on the assumption that most students will have similar background knowledge based on their grade level. This is not an assumption that can be made for students whose native language is not English. Thus, as stated in the TESOL standards:

> **Teacher Note**
>
> **TESOL Standards**
> **Grades Pre-K–3**
> **Goal 1, Standard 1**
> To use English to communicate in social settings: Students will use English to participate in social interactions
> **Descriptors**
> • Sharing and requesting information
> • Expressing needs, feelings, and ideas
> • Using nonverbal communication in social interactions
> • Getting personal needs met
> • Engaging in conversations
> • Conducting transactions

> The *ESL Standards* have a more difficult task: not only to show growth in knowledge of the English language across proficiency levels, but also to accommodate the language and academic needs of any beginning-level student who might enter the school system at any grade level. This document must reflect that reality and, thus, readers will find classes with beginners at Grade 10 as well as at Grade 1.

Three proficiency levels are identified in the standards: beginning, intermediate, and advanced. They also recognize that some students enter the U.S. school system with limited formal schooling. The standards and other useful information are available at the TESOL Web site (www.tesol.org). In the Teacher Note box on TESOL Standards above, an example of a pre-K–3 standard is provided. TESOL has also published a set of guidebooks designed to help teachers integrate the standards into classroom practice; separate volumes are provided for grades pre-K–2, 3–5, 6–8, and 9–12.

Some states and other organizations have also developed ELD standards. The next section focuses on California's ELD standards. Of all the states, California has worked longest and hardest to craft standards that are both high and realistic.

California's English Language Development Standards

California developed ELD standards as an on-ramp to academic content areas. Therefore, the ELD standards are frequently used in conjunction with other subject matter standards. The California ELD standards are written by grade span—K–2, 3–5, 6–8, and 9–12—and share the domains, strands, and substrands of the English Language Arts (ELA) standards. Table 6-1 shows an overview of an alignment of the domains of listening, speaking, reading, and writing in the ELD standards with the ELA standards (Carr, 2002). (A map that shows the complete alignment of specific ELA and ELD standards across all grade levels is available from WestEd publishers in San Francisco.)

Table 6-1. ELD Standards Aligned with ELA Standards

ELD	ELA
Listening & Speaking	
Strategies for Applications	(Written &) Oral English Language Conventions
Word Analysis	Word Analysis, Fluency & Systematic Vocabulary Development
Fluency & Systematic Vocabulary Development	
Reading	
Reading Comprehension	Reading Comprehension
	Expository Critique (Grade 5 and up)
Literary Response & Analysis	Literary Response & Analysis
Writing	
Strategies & Applications	Strategies
	Applications
Conventions	Written (& Oral) English Language Conventions
	From Carr (2002)

Instructional Programs and Strategies for English Language Learners

Describing and discussing instructional programs or strategies for ESL students requires some consideration of the instructional goals and a sorting of programs, approaches, and strategies based on those goals. Is the goal to promote single-language mastery in English, or is it to promote dual-language mastery? Is it to help students learn to read in the second language, or is it to focus on oral language development? Is the teacher looking for a program or an approach that is comprehensive and will serve as the instructional program, or is she interested in some teaching ideas that can be incorporated in the existing program that will facilitate learning for the second-language learner? Is the teacher focused on developing language or on teaching subject matter content while supporting language development? Is part of the goal of the instructional program to ensure that students can maintain connections with their families and that parents can socialize their children? It will be important to keep these questions in mind as you review the material on instructional strategies presented in the remainder of this chapter.

Second-language Acquisition Programs

Background on Bilingual and ESL Programs

Second-language education in the United States has a history whose rocky course has been strongly influenced by social and educational politics and a dearth of research. Many people are unaware of the fact that second-language and bilingual education programs have existed in the United States since the initiation of the movement to create a public school system—more than 150 years (Cuevas, 1996). Toward the end of the 19th century, Wisconsin, Illinois, Iowa, Kansas, Minnesota, Indiana, and Nebraska adopted laws to protect the use of languages other than English for instruction (Hakuta, 1986). One of the effects of the Depression and the world wars was that public sentiment turned against providing services to immigrants in the form of native language instruction, particularly for German Americans. During the same period, immigration became more regulated, and English fluency became a requirement for American citizenship. As the Civil Rights Movement gained momentum in the mid-1960s, the tide shifted once more, and laws were passed which again permitted instruction in a language other than English. This trend was accelerated with the large number of Cuban refugees arriving in Florida and the need for Dade County Schools to institute a formal English-Spanish language program. The Ford Foundation funded an experimental program designed to create Spanish and English proficiency among native English and Spanish speakers while promoting high academic achievement—engendering the term *bilingual education*. Although the program proved successful, the federal government chose to fund only programs that used the native language as a tool for rapid acquisition of English. That is, they chose to fund programs that would mainstream students as soon as possible rather than promote fluency in two languages (Cuevas, 1996).

President Johnson signed into law Title VII of the Elementary and Secondary Education Act in 1968. This program provided funds for staff and the development of materials to teach students who had limited proficiency in English. However, there were few programs available until a watershed court case—*Lau v. Nichols*—was argued before the Supreme Court in 1974. The court ruled that "there is no equality of treatment merely by providing students with the same facilities, textbooks, teachers, and curriculum, for students who do not understand English are effectively foreclosed from any meaningful education" (Meyer & Fienberg, 1992).

In the 1970s and the 1980s, a variety of bilingual education programs existed across the country, but they varied greatly in goals and approaches, and it was difficult to document their effectiveness due to the absence of standardization. Many of them would really be considered ESL programs, since they did not involve native language instruction. One of the reasons that research on bilingual programs has not consistently proven the value of bilingual education is that programs were often not faithful to their label, and there was a severe shortage of fully qualified bilingual teachers.

> The value of bilingual education was called into question by its critics during the 1980s because of researchers' inability to prove its effectiveness through conclusive large-scale evaluations. By the 1980s, the English-only movement had gained popularity in several states. (Padilla, 1991)

Fueled by two decades of decline in real wages for American workers, anti-immigrant sentiment emerged again in the early 1990s, eroding public support for bilingual education (Cuevas, 1996). This movement resulted in the passage of Proposition 227 in California in 1998 and Proposition 203 in Arizona in 2000—English-only initiatives that passed in those states with substantial margins. A similar measure was passed in Massachusetts but was defeated in Colorado in 2002.

Programs for second-language education have evolved over the years. One way to consider the main thrust of these programs is to think of them on a continuum, as Cuevas (1996) portrayed them (Figure 6-4).

Figure 6-4. Second-Language Education Program Options

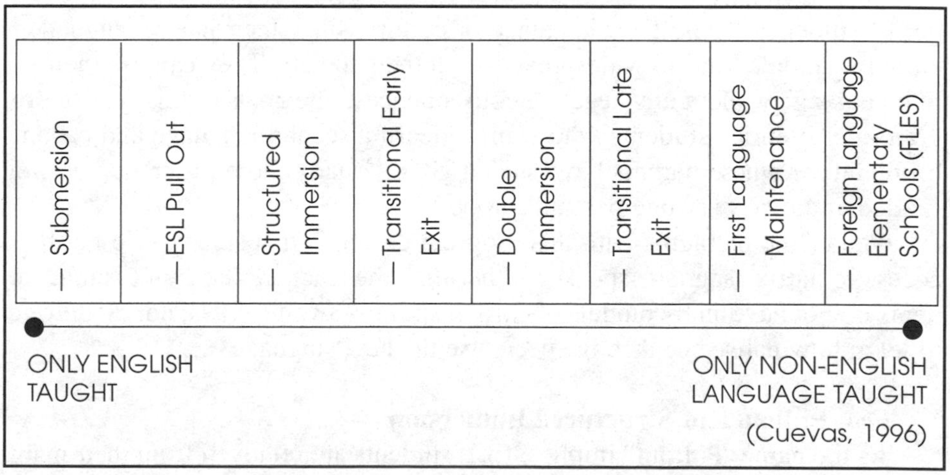

| Submersion | ESL Pull Out | Structured Immersion | Transitional Early Exit | Double Immersion | Transitional Late Exit | First Language Maintenance | Foreign Language Elementary Schools (FLES) |

ONLY ENGLISH TAUGHT   ONLY NON-ENGLISH LANGUAGE TAUGHT

(Cuevas, 1996)

Some programs are designed to immerse children in L2 (second language) instruction that is conducted *only* in L2, or, as you move along the continuum, with varying amounts of support in the children's first language. At the opposite extreme, instruction is provided only in L1.

Submersion Programs—U.S. Model

It is important to draw a distinction between immersion programs in Canada (described below) and submersion programs in the United States. Submersion programs place ELLs in an English-only classroom, offering no instruction or support in the native language. Submersion programs are commonly referred to as "sink or swim" programs, and many children do sink, failing to thrive academically. The teachers are not bilingual and cannot respond adequately to the students' academic and social language needs. Also, since L1 is not supported, the student usually loses his or her native language or at least does not continue to develop it—sometimes referred to as *subtractive bilingualism* (Lambert, 1975). Many educators believe that submersion programs promote subtractive bilingualism. When students lose their native language, they also frequently lose communication with their family (Wong Fillmore, 1991). Parents lose their ability to socialize their children as they might because of the loss of a common language, and they are usually not aware of the different program options for their children. Most often, they are English learners themselves and are still learning how to navigate the school system.

Immersion Programs—Canadian Model

In Canada, English speakers constitute the dominant culture, and French speakers are the linguistic minority. In this program model, most of the students are linguistically and culturally homogeneous (L1 English speakers) and are not interacting with native French speakers. In the primary grades, L2 instruction is specifically designed to advance students' knowledge in different content areas, through visuals and hands-on learning.

Teachers are bilingual and are able to provide support in the native language as well as respond to their students' academic and social needs. There is no danger of students' losing their language or culture, since their native language is already validated and in widespread use in their society. They can use their native language without any negative consequences. The goals of this type of program are to enrich students who want to learn a second language and become bilingual, or whose parents have such a goal. Usually these programs are well funded and receive strong parental support.

One of the problems with this program design is that students do not have access to native language speakers other than the teacher. The result is that students do not have many models of correct speech (Swain, 1991), nor do they get to learn how native speaker age peers use the new language.

ESL Pullout and Structured Immersion

As the name "Pullout" implies, ELL students are removed from their mainstream English-only classrooms for English language instruction by a resource teacher, instructional aide, or volunteer (Cuevas, 1996). They may also be taught separately within the same classroom. For the remainder of the day, their experience would be similar to being in a submersion program. This model is often the choice when there are insufficient numbers of bilingual teachers, low numbers of ELL students, or students from a number of dissimilar language backgrounds. It also occurs in high schools where students must enroll in one to three periods in ESL classrooms to reach an acceptable level of English proficiency.

Students in a structured immersion program are in English-only mainstream classrooms, but with teachers who have had special instruction in language education methods (sometimes called *sheltered*). Teachers in these classrooms occasionally use students' native languages to convey meaning and promote language acquisition by using visual aids, modified speech, and other techniques (Berman et al., 1992).

Transitional Programs (Early and Late Exit)

The main goal of transitional bilingual education is to provide students the opportunity to learn math, science, and social studies in their native language at the same time as they acquire English language proficiency. This kind of instructional program serves as a bridge for students, until they are able to function in English-only classes. Early-exit transitional programs usually last for 3 years, compared to late-exit programs that may last 5–6 years. Early-exit transitional programs are considered subtractive, since biliteracy is not one of the goals, and the students' native language is not fully developed through this kind of model. Moreover, transitional bilingual programs are often perceived as compensatory or remedial (Hernández-Chavez, 1978). The focus is on English acquisition, and L1 is not valued in its own right.

Two-Way (or Dual) Immersion Programs

Two-way bilingual education integrates language minority and language majority students for academic instruction delivered in two languages during separate periods of instruction (Christian, 1994). For example, a classroom of half L1 Spanish speakers and half L1 English speakers would spend the morning hours learning in English and the afternoon hours learning in Spanish. The duration of a two-way bilingual program should be a minimum of 4–6 years, which is the average amount of time required to develop social as well as academic proficiency in a language (Cummins, 2001; Thomas & Collier, 2001). The length of time spent in a two-way bilingual immersion program is a critical factor because the goal of the program is to achieve bilingualism and biliteracy, and this goal cannot be achieved in 2 or 3 years. Language development and academic achievement occur simultaneously in a two-way bilingual immersion program. Academic content is the vehicle for promoting language development in both languages. Subject areas are taught entirely in L1 or L2. Research indicates that students learn more efficiently when the languages are not intermingled during lesson delivery (Legarreta-Marcaida, 1981; Swain, 1983).

Parent involvement is an integral part of dual-immersion bilingual programs. Parents are encouraged to volunteer in the classroom and to work with their children on language skills at home. Valenzuela (1999) and Vásquez (2003) emphasize the need to build on the students' linguistic and cultural background in order to provide a safe and enriched academic environment. Thomas and Collier

(2001) analyzed different instructional program models and reported that students in dual-language immersion programs achieve higher academic competence and a higher degree of bilingualism.

Maintenance Programs

Maintenance programs are similar to transitional bilingual programs. The main and important difference is that in maintenance programs, the learners are transitioned into English content classes, and they continue to read in their native language, enabling them to become biliterate. Maintenance programs are considered more effective programs for linguistic minority students, since they validate the native language (Hakuta & Gould, 1987). In addition, students in late-exit bilingual programs have been shown to score comparably to English speakers in English standardized tests (Ramirez et al., 1991). Therefore, maintenance bilingual programs are considered *additive*, since they add a second language without sacrificing the native language.

Teaching Academic Content while Facilitating the Development of a Second Language

Teachers have found it to be a significant challenge to provide linguistic minority students with a rigorous academic curriculum. In order to achieve this purpose, several instructional approaches have been developed that have helped to minimize the barriers between learning a second language and an enriched academic curriculum. This chapter will address three approaches, as well as some of the strategies that are an integral part of these instructional approaches.

Specially Designed Academic Instruction in English (SDAIE)

The California Commission on Teacher Credentialing (1995) defined Specially Designed Academic Instruction in English (SDAIE) as follows:

> A set of systematic instructional strategies designed to make grade-appropriate or advanced curriculum content comprehensible to English learners with intermediate language proficiency. The purpose of SDAIE (also referred to as "sheltered instruction") is to provide English learners with access to the core curriculum at the same academic level as provided to their native English-speaking counterparts.

Becijos (1997) describes SDAIE with the following key points:

- Instruction in academic classes for nonnative students who (a) speak conversational English and have intermediate proficiency in reading and writing English, and (b) are proficient in their own language
- Content instruction at grade level
- Material presented with contextual clues, such as gestures, visuals, facial expressions, props, maps, graphs, advanced organizers, realia, manipulatives, dramatization, and overheads
- Results: Students learn content material and acquire English at the same time.

Becijos adds that it should not be a watered-down or remedial curriculum. Stated in terms of Cummins's theories of the complexity and demand of classroom tasks, "SDAIE works, not by 'dumbing down' the curriculum, but by moving cognitively demanding curriculum from context reduced to context embedded" (Becijos, 1997). (For an activity designed to help you think about Cummins's categories, see the Teacher Inquiry box.)

Sobul (1994) points out that SDAIE combines the framework of second-language acquisition with teaching that makes a lesson accessible to students. It is important to note that it is not the intent that students replace their native language with the second language as a result of participating in SDAIE. In fact, students should have a minimum of intermediate English fluency before being placed in the SDAIE setting. Students with intermediate fluency need the instructional support to acquire knowledge in the academic areas and advance their literacy skills in their second language.

> ## Teacher Inquiry
>
> Use Cummins's schema for categorizing classroom activities presented in Figure 6-3 to categorize the following activities (Key: A = cognitively undemanding, context embedded; B = cognitively undemanding, context reduced; C = cognitively demanding, context embedded; D = cognitively demanding, context reduced) Discuss your selections.
>
> - Advanced science and math
> - Teacher lectures
> - Talking on the phone
> - Art class
> - Literature class
> - Lab demonstration and experiments
> - Written instructions
> - Mainstream English texts
> - Social science class
> - Standardized tests
> - Audiovisual assisted lessons
> - Basic math computation

Sheltered Instruction Observation Protocol (SIOP)

Another approach that is worth knowing about is the Sheltered Instruction Observation Protocol (SIOP) model, described in detail with abundant examples by Echevarria, Vogt, and Short (2000). SIOP provides a tool for teachers and administrators to evaluate the content and format of sheltered classes. It includes indicators for lesson preparation, building background, instructional strategies, interaction, practice and application, lesson delivery, and review and assessment.

Cognitive Academic Language Learning Approach (CALLA)

Chamot and O'Malley (1994) developed the Cognitive Academic Language Learning Approach (CALLA), which focuses on supporting ELLs to learn academic language. This approach blends cognitive language development and academic content instruction. It is an instructional model that "integrates current educational trends in standards, content-based language instruction, learning strategies, and portfolio assessment" (Chamot, Barnhardt, El-Dinary, & Robbins, 1999, p. 7). CALLA has been applied in ESL, English as a first language (EFL), and foreign-language instruction. Chamot and O'Malley emphasize the importance of being aware of the metacognitive strategies used by students when they are learning different disciplines. When students become aware of different learning strategies that work for them, they can become better learners. The authors integrated the theory on academic language development and learning strategies for different academic areas. The approach they developed is useful for teachers because it can guide instructional planning. CALLA utilizes language as a tool to learn the content of different subjects, such as science, math, and social studies.

Part of CALLA entails building students' schemata[6] by highlighting relations between concepts—through tools such as graphic organizers, clustering concepts, tables, and charts. Graphic organizers aid students' memory and help to systematize their knowledge. A central component in CALLA is the process of helping students to develop an awareness of their own metacognitive strategies. That is, it prompts students to ask themselves questions such as "What helps me to understand this subject?", "Shall I outline the chapter?", "Will a timeline help me to remember and understand the chronology of events?", or "Will a summary of the important ideas help me to systematize the chapter's content?" Frequently students are encouraged to write a plan that will help them to outline the steps required to solve real life problems. It is vital that as educators we explain the cognitive value of these teaching aids.

Both CALLA and SDAIE emphasize the development of academic vocabulary through such strategies as hypothesizing, categorizing, and summarizing. Both approaches also underline the need to explain language that is required in most academic instruction and testing that signals important relationships among ideas—words such as *underlying*, *furthermore*, *nevertheless*, and *therefore*. SDAIE and CALLA are both types of sheltered instruction, which means that they provide instruction and language input that is accessible to students who are learning a second language.

Instructional Approaches for Students Who Speak Ebonics[7]

Teaching Students About Language Diversity

One recommended approach is to make the study of language diversity part of the curriculum for all students. Discussions about the differences in the ways TV characters use language might provide a starting point. Using children's books or taped books that feature dialogue written in the dialects of various cultural groups can provide a basis for furthering a discussion of linguistic diversity. Heath (1983) wrote about a teacher whose students became language detectives—interviewing a variety of individuals and listening to the radio and TV to discover differences and similarities in the way people talk. Another idea is to have students make bilingual dictionaries of their own language form and Standard English. They can also study contrastive grammatical structures, but the teacher must be knowledgeable of the grammatical structures of Ebonics. Asking students to role-play, to participate in dramatic productions or newscasts in which Standard English is used, can support their use of the mainstream dialect or language and allows them to get the feel of a different style of communication without the threat of correction. Younger students can create puppet shows or role-play cartoon characters. The idea is for children to understand that different language forms are appropriate in different contexts (Delpit, 1998; see also chapter 2).

Standard English Proficiency (SEP) Programs

In California, and most notably in Oakland, where the controversy over Ebonics raged in 1996–98, Standard English Proficiency (SEP) programs are often used in schools where there is a sizable population of students who speak Ebonics. The underlying philosophy of the program taught in Oakland is that they are teaching students "a second language, not fixing the home language you bring to school" (Secret, 1998; see also chapter 2). The program is not a grammar and drill program but one that focuses on culture, language, and literacy. It highlights nine cultural aspects that reflect African-American life: spirituality, resilience, emotional vitality, musicality and rhythm, humanism, communalism, orality and verbal expressiveness, personal style and uniqueness, and realness. Carrie Secret is a teacher in Oakland who is considered a master of teaching African-American students. She makes the following recommendations:

- *Encourage* but do not *require* students to practice English most of the instructional time.
- Embrace and respect Ebonics as the home language of the students, and use strategies that will move them to a competency level in English.
- Read literature that has Ebonics patterns in it (e.g., Joyce Hansen's *Yellow Bird and Me* and *The Gift Giver*).
- Develop awareness that when writing in school, students must present finished pieces in English, but when Ebonic structures appear in earlier drafts, simply point them out and ask students to translate them.
- Design opportunities for students to practice English (e.g., role plays or when there are classroom visitors), and tell them what you will be listening for.
- When providing reading instruction, remember that it is not a speech lesson. You are interested in whether they are comprehending what they are reading. Keep anecdotal records of Ebonics features that students must be alerted to for a separate instructional setting.
- Children who speak Ebonics do not hear the features (e.g., dropping off a *T* at the end of a word, such as *lef* for *left*. Hearing the language is a crucial step. Engage them in listening activities and in some overenunciation that allows them to hear and develop an ear for both languages.
- Read to students as often as possible. They need to learn that words are only something that someone else has said and written down. Explore literature with students. Read Black literature for its cultural essence and beauty. Help them understand that their best models for excellent writers wrote fluently in both English and Ebonics. Provide a good deal of adult intellectual language. Address the culture of all the children in a class or others they should learn about (e.g., read *To Destroy You Is No*

Loss by John Criddle or *The Clay Marvel* by Minfong Ho, about Cambodian children).

- For young children, provide many opportunities for word work and phonics instruction. Use dictation, play word and sound pattern games, and work with phrases and sentences. Capitalize on instructional opportunities by using an activity for building one skill to build another, such as in critical thinking. Example: Use the pictures for words in a phonics book or game to teach about categorizing.
- Ask students to take notes in a record-keeping book. Have them write in journals daily about things they are reading or thinking about.
- Encourage parents to visit the classroom and support what you are doing and the philosophy you embrace in respecting children's home language and in teaching them to use Standard English correctly and effectively, as situations require it.

Instructional Approaches for Students with Language Disorders

As special education law (Public Law 99-457) has introduced programming for infants and preschoolers, language development has become a critical component in the evaluation and treatment of young children with disabilities. (Most children with developmental disabilities have language and communicative disorders, or LCD.) The philosophy that generated PL 99-457 supports a family-centered approach that emphasizes that the needs of the child and the needs of the family are interdependent. The SLP has the knowledge, training, and expertise to meet this educational challenge. As changes have occurred in policy, and practice and research has revealed advantages of some approaches over others, interactive teaming approaches such as consultation and collaboration are now used most commonly to provide services to children with disabilities, including language disorders. The SLP has become a teacher consultant, parent trainer, and collaborative team member (Bernstein & Tiegerman-Farber, 2002).

Early Intervention for Language Disorders

It is generally agreed by specialists that earlier is better when it comes to identification and treatment of LCD. What the children learn early on is needed to support the more sophisticated learning that will follow. For a young child, most early learning is mediated through language; therefore, it is important that families participate in an early intervention program. Early intervention allows SLPs as well as other professionals to set up support systems for children and families to avoid the development of secondary or associated disabilities. Another reason for the growing interest in early language intervention is the recognition that individuals identified in the preschool years as having language disorders are often the same students diagnosed as language-learning disabled later on in their academic careers (Aram, Ekelman, & Nation, 1984; King, Jones,

& Lasky, 1982). One of the reasons for this is undoubtedly the connection between a child's oral language competencies and acquisition of literacy skills. The connections are complicated and are not the same all the way through the developmental process (Wallach & Butler, 1994). These differences and the complications with literacy development are detailed in the following section.

Intervention by Speech-Language Pathologists

The role of the teacher of students with language disorders is largely to be alert to the possibility of such disorders and to refer students for assessment. In addition, the teacher can support the students by following the classroom recommendations of the SLP. An SLP or other specialist—either in a clinical setting or within the classroom—will support most students who are found to have a language disorder. Olswang and Bain (1991) have identified three alternatives as the purpose of intervention: facilitation, maintenance, and induction.

Facilitation is intended to accelerate the rate or growth of learning but not to change the final outcome. It can help a child by bringing language to a higher level of awareness, which can influence other aspects of development. Paul (1995) offers this example: A child with a phonological disorder may outgrow his multiple articulation errors without intervention by age 8 or 9. With intervention, articulation can be improved, and it can focus a child's attention on the sound structure of words. This increased awareness will help him as he develops his literacy skills.

Intervention can also change behavior through *maintenance*. Such an approach is designed to preserve a behavior that might otherwise decrease or disappear. A child with a cleft palate, for example, for whom surgery is delayed for medical reasons, would benefit from intervention to maintain babbling and early vocal behaviors, thus providing the articulation behaviors necessary for developing language once the palatal vault is closed by surgery.

Finally, *induction* is intervention that brings about an outcome that would not otherwise have been accomplished. These concepts are presented here to help a teacher understand the different approaches a specialist might use in treating a child with a language disorder.

Fey (1986) described four different types of language-impaired children, a method for identifying these types, and a suggested prescription for planning intervention. As a functionalist approach to identifying language disorders, it may also be useful to teachers as they monitor their students for possible disorders. Fey used two features of conversational participation as his diagnostic variables: *conversational assertiveness*—a child's propensity or ability to take a turn in a conversation even when not solicited—and *conversational responsiveness*—a child's propensity or ability to provide appropriate responses to the requests made by the child's conversation partner. Various combinations of these features are used to identify the type of language impairment. Children who are *active conversationalists* usually need new structures to fulfill them in conversation. *Inactive communicators* need to learn their roles in conversation first, before specific forms are targeted (Bernstein & Tiegerman-Farber, 2002).

Collaborative Models for Intervention

A number of service delivery models have been used to provide services to children with language disorders. These range from a pullout or classroom model to ones labeled *consultation* or *collaborative consultation*. By serving as a consultant to a classroom, an SLP can provide more productive assistance, and both SLPs and teachers can learn more about the other's area of expertise. The SLP can help the teacher to understand the individual needs of children with LCD in a classroom. The SLP can share management techniques, task analysis skills, and instructional procedures that can facilitate language learning for *all* the children in the classroom. A classroom teacher can contribute by sharing her knowledge of instructional strategies and activities. She can provide frequent language learning experiences and make them more relevant to the child's ongoing classroom curriculum. She can also help to pinpoint the situational demands on language during classroom routines and monitor a child's progress in generalizing language features targeted in intervention.

> By periodically changing a child's seating arrangement to promote interactions
> with a variety of classmates (some of whom may be more willing to interact with
> a child who has a language disorder than others), the child may have more oppor-
> tunities to practice and perfect new communication skills. The classroom teacher
> should have expert understanding of the classmates' social dynamics, and this
> information can be used to advantage by those planning language intervention.
> (Bernstein & Tiegerman-Farber, 2002, p. 269)

Collaborative models for providing services have become the modus operandi in recent years. These models work best when teams of parents, teachers, and SLPs start with mutual identification of the problems they will address as a team. When individuals on a team collaborate, each draws on his or her own expertise about the child to build a "comprehensive picture of the family's culture, values, and hopes; aspects of the curriculum or early development that are particularly challenging for the child; and the child's communicative needs and strengths" (Bernstein & Tiegerman-Farber, 2002, p. 107).

Instructional Strategies to Support Second-Language or Second-Dialect Development in General Classroom Instruction

Mapping, graphic organizers, and some of the other strategies described below can be integrated as part of daily instruction in any classroom that includes ELL students, as well as students who are Ebonics speakers or have other language differences. These are basically good teaching techniques that are selected because they make learning easier for students with language development needs. They provide greater access to learning concepts and help students to use what they know to learn new content and develop greater facility with their first or second language or second dialect.

Graphic Organizers

Graphic organizer is a general term for schematic diagrams that help students to identify key concepts and make relationships among them (Muth & Alvermann, 1999; see also chapter 5). They provide ELL students with visual clues that they can relate to the written or spoken words to which they are exposed. They can be used prior to reading or other classroom activity to help students focus their attention and make connections. They can be used, for example, to organize students' knowledge about a topic prior to reading, doing an experiment, or having a discussion. Prior to reading, they can be a guide and build background, especially for difficult or dense text. After reading (or whatever classroom activity), they can be used for recording understandings or knowledge gained. Graphic organizers include story or text structure charts, Venn diagrams, story maps, timelines, discussion webs, word webs, clusters, and thinking maps. (Echevarria et al., 2000; see also chapter 5).

Modeling and Scaffolding

Effective teaching requires modeling at every stage and at every grade level. All students, especially ELLs, require the modeling of academic language. The teacher is the expert in the classroom and can help students to practice their newly acquired vocabulary, utilize it in different contexts, and provide feedback (O'Malley & Chamot, 1990). It is important for teachers to rephrase their questions and explanations, as well as expand on students' input. Effective modeling also provides students with access to examples of finished products, such as solved problem sets. For example, the teacher can explain a problem in trigonometry and then have different examples of problems that clearly demonstrate the various steps involved in solving the problem. The idea of providing models and representations to

---

Teacher Note

Adjusting Instruction for English Language Learners

In this classroom, all the students are beginning to advanced beginning speakers of English, and they have varying levels of literacy in their native languages. The teacher has been teaching a unit on *buoyancy*—the ability to float. The science text tells why some objects float while others sink and reviews the concepts of *mass* and *volume*. The goal is for students to understand that objects float as long as the mass doesn't exceed the object's capacity or volume.

Mr. Lew first draws his students' attention to the objective written on the board. As he says the word *float*, he points to an orange floating in an aquarium at the front of the room. As he says the word *sink*, he drops an orange peel into the water, and it sinks to the bottom. The words *float*, *sink*, *calculate*, *predict*, and *buoyant* are written in a word list for students to see. Both content vocabulary (*float*, *sink*) and functional words (*predict*, *calculate*) are included.

Throughout the lesson, Mr. Lew uses language structures and vocabulary that he believes his students can understand. He slows his normal rate of speech and enunciates clearly. He avoids the use of idioms and paraphrases when he thinks that his students do not appear to understand. He repeats important words and writes them for students to see.

students is not new. Knowledge has always been imparted through direct modeling, such as through apprenticeships in skilled craftsmanship. At home, parents teach their children by showing them how to cook, sew, or play through direct physical engagement. Bruner (1985) recommended the use of charts, models of cells, and illustrated books.

Teachers are often cognizant of the need to provide scaffolding for students to be successful in academic tasks. Scaffolding helps the student to perform successfully just beyond an independent level, in Vygotsky's zone of proximal development (ZPD). According to Vygotsky (1978), the ZPD can be defined as "the distance between the actual developmental level as determined by independent problem solving and the level of potential development as determined through problem solving" (p. 86). Teachers need to assess what students know in order to help them reach the next level of development. The ZPD, then, is the difference between what children can accomplish alone and what they can accomplish with the assistance of someone more experienced. Vygotsky recommended challenging students at the same time that academic and affective support are provided in order for them to achieve their potential. Just as construction workers or window washers use scaffolding on a building to bring them closer to where their task needs to be accomplished, teachers can provide scaffolding by teaching or reviewing concepts or skills needed by students prior to having them engage in the assigned task—the one for which they will demonstrate what they have learned. *Scaffolding* also refers to the contextual supports embedded in instruction to make it comprehensible.

Echevarria et al. (2000) identify two types of scaffolding that can be used with ELLs. One is *verbal scaffolding*, in which teachers use prompting, questioning, and elaboration to facilitate students' progress to high levels of language use, comprehension, and thinking. They offer three examples of verbal scaffolding:

- Paraphrasing—restating a student's response to model correct English usage
- Using think-alouds—providing carefully structured models of how effective learners think and monitor their understandings (Baumann, Jones, & Seifert-Kessell, 1993)
- Reinforcing contextual definitions—pointing out where appositives or contextual definitions are presented within text

The other form of scaffolding they describe is *procedural scaffolding*, or showing someone how to do something. Figure 6-5 shows how these authors view the scaffolding model.

Figure 6-5. Scaffolding Model
Increasing Independence

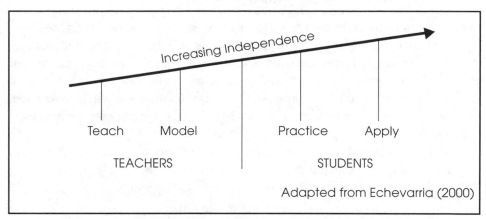

Adapted from Echevarria (2000)

Some writers have described scaffolds that can be used when teaching certain skills or certain groups of students. Peregoy and Boyle (2001), for example, describe scaffolding techniques applied to first- and second-language acquisition—responding to a child's simple response with an elaborated form that provides a linguistic model; allowing children to use gestures or pictures to indicate a choice or need before they have the words to do so; setting up predictable patterns and routines so that children know what to expect in the learning situation, freeing them to focus on language development. They also discuss *literacy scaffolds*, in which the teacher makes use of language and discourse patterns that make texts more predictable, sets up written conversations with students, or provides models for comprehending or producing written language patterns.

Aída Walqui (2002) has written extensively about scaffolding and has designed professional development materials to help teachers understand the complexity and power of this technique. She states the following:

> It is true that these strategies have long been recognized as excellent pedagogy. What's different is that for our English learners we need to use them more extensively, continuously building scaffolds as the need arises, and we need to communicate their purpose and uses to students. While for the native speaker two tasks may be sufficient to understand and practice a concept, the English learner may need four or five different tasks to achieve similar competence. (p. 10)

She identifies five main types of instructional scaffolding:

Modeling. Walk students through an interaction or first do it together as a class activity. Show examples of student work. Model appropriate language use to perform specific functions.

Bridging. Build on previous knowledge and understandings. Activate students' previous knowledge. Use anticipatory guides to get students to predict and infer. Establish personal links between the student and content, showing how new material is relevant to the student's life.

Contextualization. Embed language in sensory context by using manipulatives, pictures, film clips, and other types of authentic objects and sources of information to make language accessible and engaging. Use analogies and metaphors to bring complex ideas closer to the students' world experience.

Schema building. Prepare for reading assignments by having students preview the text, noting heads and subheads, illustrations and captions, and titles of charts, to get a general sense of the topic. Use an advance organizer to walk students through the most important pieces of information that will be discussed. Use tools such as a Compare and Contrast Matrix to bridge students' prior knowledge and build their schema for the target content.

Text re-presentation. Have students transform linguistic constructions that they find modeled in one genre into forms used in another genre.

> It has been argued (see, for example, Moffet, 1983) that there is a progression in the ability of language users to use different genres within academic discourses. In terms of language use, this continuum starts with asking students to say what is happening (as in drama or dialogue), then what has happened (narratives, reports), then what happens (generalizations in exposition), and, finally, what may happen (tautological transformations, theorizing). (Walqui, 2002, p. 18)

Students may re-present an article as a play, with students of different ability levels contributing as they are able.

Metacognitive Development

A number of researchers and educators have also written about the importance of supporting the metacognitive development of all students, but particularly those with language development needs. As Walqui (2002) states, it refers to the ways in which students manage their thinking and includes at least three aspects:

1. Conscious application of strategies while engaging in activities
2. Knowledge and awareness of strategic options and the ability to choose the most effective one for a particular activity
3. Monitoring and the ability to evaluate and adjust during performance and to plan for future performance based on evaluation after an activity

Helping students to develop strategies or "plans of attack" and engaging them in making their thinking public allows them to become more metacognitively aware of their learning strategies and to gain autonomy in the process.

Hands-On Activities

We have seen a radical shift in how educators view teaching and learning over the last decade. The shift in emphasis from behavioral to cognitive psychology has been accompanied by a view of students as active participants in the learning process. As we have discussed throughout this book, a constructivist view of learning is one in which students are seen as constructing meaning through experience and developing personal theories about the physical and social world

(Osborne & Wittrock, 1983; Piaget, 1928). We have also emphasized that socio-cultural learning theorists have gone beyond constructivism to argue that accom-modating students' social and cultural experience is another important key to student learning. Whether one assumes a constructivist or sociocultural position, it is clear that we need to reconceptualize how we provide instruction for ELLs.

The new national science standards, for example, emphasize hands-on in-quiry designed to promote students' conceptual knowledge by building on prior knowledge, active engagement in science learning, and application to real-world situations. Drawing from the corresponding Professional Practice Standards (Danielson, 1996), many districts are developing teaching standards to increase the expectation for a teacher's capacity to establish a learning environment and to use performance-based assessment to inform instruction. Hands-on activities give students another way of expressing their understanding of information and concepts when they may have learned the lesson's information but have diffi-culty expressing their understanding in English. Such activities can also be used to reinforce concepts (Echevarria et. al, 2000).

Language Experience Approach

The language experience approach was conceptualized many years ago as a strategy for teaching reading, and it has been used successfully with ELLs for many years (Herrell, 2000). The basic idea is to provide instruction that helps students see the relationships among thinking, speaking, reading, and writing. Students respond to a recently experienced event (usually one devised by the teacher—a science experiment, cooking lesson, dramatization, or the like). The students watch or participate, and subsequently, the teacher asks them to recall what happened and records their responses as a group story. The story is read aloud by the teacher and then as a choral reading by the students (Cuevas, 1996). Follow-up activities may include copying the story (younger learners), writing a new version (older learners), practicing the story by sequencing sentence strips from the story, or completing cloze (fill-in-the-blank) exercises.

Cooperative Learning

Small-group interaction allows students more time to discuss and solve prob-lems with their peers. In most classrooms, when the teacher talks, the students have to listen, and time constraints are not conducive to asking questions or shar-ing personal experiences. Cooperative learning involves much more than placing students in groups to accomplish a task. Kagan (1986) states that such groups must be *positively interdependent* so that the success of any one team member contrib-utes to the success of the whole group. Slavin (1983) adds that a well-designed task structure guarantees that students are encouraged to share information and responsibility and are supported in doing so (Cuevas, 1996). Elizabeth Cohen and Rachel Lotan (1994) developed a form of cooperative learning, *complex instruc-tion*, which specifically targets heterogeneous groups and addresses differences in status by providing tasks and rotating roles so that access to materials and control over how work is accomplished are not regulated by a small number of dominant students. Complex instruction includes a multiple-ability curriculum that requires students to cooperate in order to solve problems.

Participation is a key factor in learning and especially in developing a second language (Losey, 1995). The more students talk together and the more feedback they receive, the more advanced is their learning. In a classroom with different levels of English proficiency, it is important to encourage everybody to participate. A unique aspect of complex instruction is that it helps students to broaden their perception of intelligence and the different ways in which a student can contribute to the group. Due to the different levels of language proficiency that exist in the classroom, it is important to have heterogeneous groupings, in order to expose students to different language models (Cohen, 1994). Other research on cooperative learning supports it as a powerful instructional strategy with second-language learners (Calderón, Hertz-Lazarowitz, & Slavin, 1998; Sharan, Raviv, Kussell, & Hertz-Lazarowitz, 1984).

Thematic Instruction

Thematic instruction is appropriate for any content area and grade level. It can be especially effective with ELLs because it

> creates a meaningful conceptual framework within which students are invited to use both oral and written language for learning content. The meaningful context established by the theme supports the comprehensibility of instruction, thereby increasing both content learning and second-language acquisition. (Peregoy & Boyle, 2001)

In addition, thematic instruction can increase motivation, engagement, and a sense of purpose. Working together on projects, students use language to ask questions, inform, solve problems, negotiate, and interact with and report to their peers. The best themes around which to build units are universal ideas, rather than merely topics. Cuevas (1996) suggests "the interdependence of all life forms of earth" or "the role of children in families throughout the world." Interdisciplinary or integrated thematic units combine two or more subjects such as math and reading or social studies and science. One should be cautious, however, about forcing the inclusion of a subject area when the connections are fairly thin. A teacher can judge the power of a link to a content area by evaluating whether it addresses an important content area standard.

Some educators promote the use of thematic instruction because of the possibility of involving students in making decisions about the content and direction of a unit. This is sometimes referred to as a *theme cycle*, in which students and the teacher negotiate certain choices—topics, selection of materials and resources, organization of projects, grouping, and manner of presenting final products of learning (Peregoy & Boyle, 2001). Engaging in such planning strengthens students' sense of self-efficacy, an important benefit for English learner students. Literature-based thematic units are another way to explore learning thematically. Themes such as cooperation and courage are found in many children's books, and teachers can gather a collection that covers the theme from different cultural perspectives.

Teacher Note

Planning Thematic Instruction
The following are some criteria for planning thematic instruction to promote language development and critical thinking.

- **Set meaning and purpose.** The content should be interesting and relevant to the students. Allow students to participate in decision making and make sure the purpose and goals are clear.

- **Build on prior knowledge.** The unit should build on prior in-class as well as out-of-class experiences. The teacher and students can pool their knowledge of what they know about the topic and what they want to know more about.

- **Integrate opportunities to use oral and written language.** The teacher should incorporate different forms and functions of print according to goals and student interests and skill needs.

- **Scaffold for support.** The teacher should support students' efforts by using sheltering techniques and various types of scaffolds to assist students in participating successfully. Students should be given various opportunities to display and share their learning.

- **Allow for collaboration.** Students should have many opportunities to work together on theme-related projects and activities. Collaboration in pairs or small groups allows students to process complex information in a low-risk, low-anxiety situation.

- **Vary everthing.** Variety should permeate the unit—in topics of study, in the ways that learning is shared, in the functions of oral and written language used, in roles and responsibilities, and in task difficulty. Varying activities on all these levels promotes and sustains a high level of interest and allows all students to participate.

Adapted from Peregoy & Boyle (2001)

Questioning Strategies and Wait Time

Asking questions is by far the most common strategy used by teachers in classrooms. Educators have given far too little thought to questioning strategies, but the following questions about questions are worth asking:

- Does the set of questions include ones that probe higher order thinking, that start with "What do you think . . . ?" or "How do you know . . . ?"
- Are the questions designed to teach students a comprehension or interpretation skill, or are they just a test of what they know?
- Are the questions framed to accommodate different levels of language proficiency?
- Do the responses that the questions require reflect a sensitivity to sociocultural aspects of displaying knowledge?
- Are questions used in the classroom framed in a variety of ways to allow responses through various modalities?

- Are students given the opportunity to respond to questions in different settings? (e.g., one at a time, pairs, small groups, whole group)

Díaz-Rico and Weed (1995) propose that the third and fourth questions above are critical to consider if the perils with which typical questioning strategies are fraught are to be avoided. They suggest that the teacher apply a hierarchy of question types depending on the language proficiency of the students in the group.

> For students in the "silent period," a question requiring a nonverbal response—a head movement, pointing, manipulating materials—will elicit an appropriate and satisfactory answer. Once students are beginning to speak, either/or questions provide the necessary terms, and the student needs merely to choose the correct word or phrase to demonstrate understanding: "Is the water evaporating or condensing?" (p. 78)

As students gain language proficiency, questions that begin with *wh-* become more appropriate.

The second area of concern for these authors has to do with sociocultural issues. Everyone is familiar with the scene of students' waving their hands in the classroom, essentially to "bid" to answer the teacher's question, in response to which a teacher calls on an individual to provide his or her answer or guess at the answer. This can be a problem for language-minority students, who may be reluctant to draw attention to themselves "either because they see such an action as incompatible with group cohesiveness and cultural norms, or because they may be reluctant to display knowledge in front of others." In such cases, teachers need to explore other ways to have students demonstrate their language and their content knowledge (Díaz-Rico and Weed, 1995). Teachers should be cautious about awarding grades on the basis of direct questioning in the group or having such responses count toward a grade (Trumbull & Farr, 2000).

When an adult asks a question, usually there is a period of waiting for the child to answer. When a child is slow to respond, teachers are faced with the dilemma of offering clues, waiting silently, or moving on to another student. Teachers often mention that waiting too long becomes embarrassing to the student. On the other hand, one might call on another student and not give the initial student time to think and respond. Otto (2002) affirms the importance of wait time in the use of questioning strategies. Wait time is a vital aspect in a classroom with students who are learning a second language. Echevarria and Graves (1998) corroborate the significance of wait time when they cite a teacher's comment:

> "I found that my expectations of what the students could produce and the kinds of ideas that they could come up with are very different than they used to be. Allowing them wait-time and asking them to explain why they feel the way they do and to relate it to something we have read, I am more willing to give them more opportunities to speak and explain themselves in a variety of situations." (p. 62)

Instructional Conversation

Instructional conversation is a method recommended for use with culturally and linguistically diverse learners (Tharp, 1997; Tharp & Gallimore, 1991). This instructional strategy, which is discussed in the context of literacy instruction in chapter 5, is closely associated with researchers involved with the Kamehameha Elementary Education Project (KEEP) project in Hawaii and the Rough Rocks project in Arizona (Au & Jordan, 1981b; McCarty, 1989). It is a process of questioning and sharing ideas and knowledge that provides a means by which teachers and students relate formal, schooled knowledge to the student's individual, community, and family knowledge.

> "Teachers who use it, like parents in natural teaching, assume that the student has something to say beyond the known answers in the head of the adult. The adult listens carefully, makes guesses about the intended meaning, and adjusts responses to assist the student's efforts—in other words, engages in conversation." (Ochs, 1982)

Such conversation reveals the knowledge, skills, values, and the culture of the learner, enabling the teacher to contextualize teaching to fit the learner's experience base (Tharp, 1997).

Instructional conversation is grounded in the Vygotskian notions discussed earlier: That higher order cognitive activities are developed on the basis of "interactions with more competent others" (Rueda, Goldenberg, & Gallimore, 1992). Key elements include responsivity and assisted performance. As common as instructional conversations are in the interactions of parents and children, they are uncommon in most classrooms. There is evidence, however, that the art of instructional conversations can be fostered (Goldenberg & Gallimore, 1991; Tharp & Gallimore, 1991). The developers caution, however, that learning experiences that allow teachers to develop an understanding of the conceptual framework, observe effective practitioners, practice and receive feedback, and receive coaching are necessary. Through the efforts of a research team, in particular, Claude Goldenberg, who conducted extensive collaborative work with teachers in classrooms with high percentages of bilingual or ELL students, an instructional conversation scale was developed as a tool for examining responsive teaching (Rueda et al., 1992). The scale provides ratings (not shown) for each of the elements as displayed in the following list. The rating scale in this case would be used to rate an instructional conversation that is conducted in response to a text that students read.

1. *Challenging but non-threatening atmosphere.* Teacher creates a zone of proximal development where a challenging atmosphere is balanced by a positive affective climate.
2. *Responsiveness to student contributions.* Though having an initial plan and focus, teacher is responsive to students' statements and the opportunities provided.
3. *Promotion of discussion.* Discussion centers on questions for which there might be more than one answer.

4. *Connected discourse.* Discussion is characterized by multiple, interactive, connected turns; succeeding utterances build on previous ones.

5. *General participation, including self-selected turns.* Teacher encourages general participation and does not hold exclusive right to determine who talks; students are encouraged to volunteer or otherwise influence the selecting of speaking turns.

6. *Thematic focus.* Teacher selects a theme or idea as a starting point and has a general plan for how it will unfold.

7. *Activation and use of background knowledge and relevant schemata.* Teacher provides students with pertinent background information necessary for understanding a text.

8. *Direct teaching.* When necessary, teacher provides direct teaching of a skill or concept.

9. *Promotion of more complex language and expression.* Teacher elicits more extended student contributions by using a variety of elicitation techniques.

10. *Promotion of bases for statements or positions.* Teacher promotes students' use of text, pictures, and reasoning to support an argument or position (known in some literacy approaches as "accountable talk."

Complete information about procedures used in instructional conversations, research on them, training, and professional development, examples, and the rating form can be obtained from the National Center for Research on Cultural Diversity and Second Language Learning (http://www.crede. ucsc.edu/). (See also discussion in chapter 5.)

Promoting Oral Language Development in the Classroom

Teachers have an overabundance of things to think about in order to design and carry out instruction for diverse groups of students, including managing the classroom. The current mandate to teach to a wide variety of content standards presents a daunting challenge in and of itself. In the midst of all the needs demanding attention, teachers should also remember that there are numerous opportunities to help students develop their oral language. We have already alluded to several opportunities in the course of this chapter and other chapters. Some of the opportunities to develop oral language do not require a great deal of additional time, only a slight adjustment in how classroom activities are designed or carried out. In addition to the basic classroom routines—roll call, recess, snack, lunch, special classes, field trips—there are also some routine instructional events that are ideal opportunities for developing oral language: circle time, journal writing, literature study circles, process writing, projects, cooperative groups.

To the extent that these activities maintain a routine structure over time, students can become familiar with the activity as an interactional format that supports their oral language use and development (Peregoy & Boyle, 2001). For example, literature study circles may routinely serve as forums for discussions of plot, characters, setting, problem, theme, lesson, genre, and so on. In this context, ELL students would become familiar with the vocabulary common to such discussions and the meanings attached to them as they relate to a text being read.

Many resources are available with suggestions of ways to build oral language opportunities into learning activities (see Teacher Note box). It is also important for teachers to review their own instructional delivery to determine if there are opportunities that are being missed—for providing meaning cues, prompts, and well-placed questions; for using dramatization, visuals, graphics, or concrete objects; for adjusting the input to ensure understanding; or to check for understanding before proceeding with a lesson or activity. As one's awareness increases, it is a good idea to keep a log of strategies that work or even to videotape lessons for later analysis.

> ### Teacher Note
>
> **Learning Activities That Promote Oral Language Development**
>
> - Songs, drama, poetry
> - Show and tell (Charlie Brown used to say, "Bring and Lie")
> - Describing to partners ("One Looks, One Doesn't") – one member of a pair describes something that the other one hasn't seen and attempts to draw.
> - Tape recording children's re-creations of wordless picture books
> - Taping and dubbing a television show
> - Choral reading
> - Riddles and jokes
> - Describing how a math problem was solved or a science experiment conducted
> - Presenting simulations or reenactments of historical events
>
> Adapted from Peregoy & Boyle (2001)

Reflections

This chapter could easily expand to book length, because there is so much to know about so many different types of students with specific language learning needs, and there are many good ideas for instructional strategies. We hope that we have provided enough of a selection of ideas that a teacher will be able to select and devise many of his or her own. The guidelines that were presented before the programs and strategies are important to use in framing an instructional program and approach to teaching ELLs and other students with language differences, and standards such as the ones TESOL provides can likewise help to outline a program that is comprehensive.

In summarizing this chapter, there are a few principles we want to emphasize:

Respect the native or home language of the students. It is integral to their identity, and any rejection of their language is a rejection of them. Use it as a tool and a foundation on which to build the additional language knowledge they need to be successful academically and in life.

Build on what students bring to the classroom in terms of the structural and strategic knowledge they have developed in learning their first (and second or third) language(s). Engage them in metacognitive discussions about language and how they learn and use it so they become more keenly aware of what they know and how to draw on that knowledge.

Language mediates all learning. It is with language that one explains, directs, conceptualizes, infers, predicts, synthesizes, assesses, conveys emotions, understands, propounds, and so on. Enrich the classroom with a wealth of linguistic opportunities to learn. Aída Walqui (2002) says, "Amplify, don't simplify." It is through rich and powerful language that students learn the most.

Learning occurs through interaction, through "an engagement with other learners and teachers in joint activities that focus on matters of shared interest and that contain opportunities for learning" (Walqui, 2002, p. 1). Think here, too, about two of CREDE's teaching principles: (1) teachers and students producing together (joint productive activity) and (5) teaching through interactive discussions (instructional conversation).

Vygotsky's concept of the zone of proximal development is an extraordinarily powerful one. Providing the scaffolding needed by each individual learner in each teaching situation is not an easy task, but it has enormous payoff. If a teacher understood scaffolding (or the process of "spiraling" instruction) and perfected no other strategy than its use, his or her students would almost never fail to learn.

Know (or become familiar with) programs or practices that have proven to be effective with ELL students or students with language differences or disorders. Teachers should be given comprehensive information about the resources available to them to help plan appropriate instruction or intervention for such students. This would include information about (a) school or district policies, programs, and practices, (b) specialists available to help teachers address the language needs of students, (c) professional literature to help teachers build their knowledge base, and (d) opportunities for teacher inquiry or other professional development.

Notes

1. We use the terminology of the Bureau of the Census.
2. *Dialectical* refers to the process of negotiation between two opposing forces, such as oppressor and oppressed (as discussed in Freire's *Pedagogy of the Oppressed* (1970). Another dialectical relationship Freire explores is that of the world and human consciousness.
3. This topic is also discussed at some length in chapter 2.
4. In fact, there are two syllabaries: *hiragana*, for native Japanese words, and *katakana*, for words borrowed from other languages.
5. See description of instructional conversation as a teaching strategy later in this chapter, and in chapter 5 on literacy strategies.
6. Plural of *schema*, meaning an organizing framework for understanding a set of relationships. For instance, a student may have a schema for understanding the features of mammals or for how to go about a particular kind of science experiment.

7. Chapter 2 describes some specific strategies for promoting awareness of the differences between Ebonics and Standard English. We use the term *Ebonics* because it is the term used in much of the educational intervention literature. African-American venacular English (AAVE) is used more in the linguistics literature.

For Further Reading

Bialystok, E. (2001). *Bilingualism in development: Language, literacy, and cognition.* New York: Cambridge University Press.

Chamot, A., Barnhardt, S., El-Dinary, P. B. & Robbins, J. (1999). *The learning strategies handbook.* White Plains, NY: Longman.

Delpit, L. (1995). *Other people's children: Cultural conflict in the classroom.* New York: New Press.

Delpit, L. (1998). Ebonics and culturally responsive instruction. In T. Perry & L. Delpit (Eds.) *The real Ebonics debate* (pp. 160–161). Boston: Beacon Press.

Gutierrez, K., Baquedano-López, P., & Tejeda, C. (1999). Rethinking diversity: Hybridity and hybrid language practices in the third space. *Mind, Culture and Activity,* 6 (4), 286–303.

Hayes, C. W., Bahruth, R., & Kessler, C. (1998). *Literacy con cariño.* Portsmouth, NH: Heinemann.

Herrell, A. (2000). *Fifty strategies for teaching English language learners.* Upper Saddle River, NJ: Merrill.

Langdon, H. W. (1992), *Hispanic children and adults with communication disorders* (With L. Cheng). Gaithersburg, MD: Aspen.

Power, B. M., & Hubbard, R. S. (1996). *Language development: A reader for teachers.* Englewood Cliffs, NJ: Prentice-Hall.

Wallach, G., & Butler, K. (1994). *Language learning disabilities in school age children and adolescents.* New York: Macmillan.

Wolfram, W., Adger, C. T., & Christian, D. (1999). *Dialects in schools and communities.* Mahwah, NJ: Lawrence Erlbaum Associates.

Chapter 7

Language and Assessment

Elise Trumbull

How can we truly know what our students know and can do? This is an age-old dilemma for teachers. Back in the time of the ancient Greeks, assessment took the form of the teacher's sitting by the student—observing and conversing with the student. In fact, the word assess *comes from the Latin word* (assidere) *meaning "to sit beside." Classes were small in those days, and we in the United States are at another extreme, faced with assessing many students from a range of cultural and linguistic backgrounds in many subjects. We hope that this chapter will give readers support to approach the task with confidence and strategies for maximizing the utility and validity of assessment.*

Assessing a student without depending on language in any way would be a challenge indeed! Of course, a swimming instructor may need to rely on very little language to convey what he or she expects students to do on a final exam. The students can demonstrate how well they have mastered the butterfly stroke without resorting to any overt language at all. However, nearly all assessments rely on language in some way—and most often in a big way. This chapter examines the role of language in assessment, the language demands of various kinds of assessments, and particular issues that arise when English is used as the language of assessment for English language learners (ELLs).

Any time students are assessed through their second language one cannot be sure if their performance represents what they really know and can do or if it is largely an index of proficiency with English. Standardized tests present well-known problems, but so can classroom assessment. There are ways, however, that teachers can anticipate language-based demands of assessments and make their assessment practices fairer for all their students.

Classroom teachers who have responsibility for ELLs are also responsible for assessing their language skills, particularly what have been called *content-obligatory language skills* (Genesee & Hamayan, 1994, p. 213)—the specialized language of each academic content area. This chapter will review some basic ways a teacher can monitor a student's developing language proficiency. (See chapter 3 for a description of the language acquisition process and stages of development.)

Because language is the primary medium of reasoning, its influence is found everywhere, both in the classroom and in activities of daily life. Even tasks that appear to be primarily visual (e.g., following a map or solving a jigsaw puzzle) are often mediated by language. People translate visual information into verbal in order to remember it (Oller, 1991). How often do we find ourselves looking at a map muttering something like, "Okay, let's see . . . if I go east for about a mile, I should come to Oak Street, and then I'll need to take a right"?

Russian psychologist Alexander Luria showed through his research that for children at an early stage of development, successful performance of many motor tasks depended on verbal skills as well (Oller, 1992). Small children who are trying to figure out how to put together a Three Little Pigs puzzle are probably relying on mental or spoken language to help themselves figure out where to put the wolf's head relative to its body ("Here goes his head on top") or the roof of the house relative to the house ("The roof goes on top of the house").

One cannot go directly from visual perception to problem solution even with a test such as *Raven's Progressive Matrices* (Raven, 1983), which is often used as a nonverbal index of intelligence. On this test, the test taker is asked to determine which of a number of visual designs should logically follow in a progression. In order to figure out what design comes next, one needs to mentally represent to oneself the designs and their relationship to each other, whether using such terms as *square*, *circle*, *dot*, or some others (Oller, 1991, p. 54). We know from research that language proficiency is related to mathematics achievement (MacGregor & Price, 1999; Secada, 1992), though somewhat less on tasks that are strictly computational (Kiplinger, Haug, & Abedi, 2000).

Once again, it is almost impossible to discuss language in any context without bringing up the topic of culture. Assessment is a cultural event, a process that may look quite different, depending on the culture at hand. For instance, even the idea of using language to assess is by no means a cultural universal. In some indigenous communities, for example, a great deal of learning that takes place outside school is typically assessed directly: A learner performs the actual criterion task—shearing a sheep, for instance, something that may not entail any spoken or written language such as questions or directions from an adult. (Mental use of language, of course, may be taking place.) Such a learner may not quickly take to the extremely linguistic forms of informal and formal assessment in the classroom. Given the increasing diversity of the United States, a great many teachers will at some time in their careers have students from ethnolinguistic groups that have orientations to teaching, learning, and assessment that are different from those of the dominant culture of the United States. Assessing those students will be more challenging than assessing those whose language and experience are as expected and who are socialized to be comfortable with the assessment norms of U.S. schools (see also chapter 2).

Defining Terms and Perspective

For the purposes of this book, the term *assessment* is used to mean "the process by which teachers go about determining how well students have learned the standards-based knowledge and skills associated with their curricula." It can, of course, also refer to "an individual activity that contributes to understanding a student's learning and learning processes." Learning is construed broadly—to include the social skills, values, and dispositions supported by parenting and schooling. One goal of good assessment, in this author's opinion, is that the student gain understanding of his or her own learning processes and engage in setting goals for further learning. Thus, assessment is focused not just on products but also on processes. Foremost among the purposes of classroom assessment is feedback to teachers so they can ensure that their instruction is successful. Good classroom assessment is contextualized in a way that externally developed tests are not: It is curriculum-linked and mirrors appropriate instructional strategies. It can reflect the language and ways of communicating that are usual in the classroom.

> ### Teacher Note
>
>
> **What Is "Common Knowledge"?**
> Testing expert James Popham examined all the items on two national tests in five content areas at a single grade level and counted the items he judged to be more easily answered by students from middle or high socioeconomic status (SES). By his tally, 15% of reading items, 65% of language arts items, 45% of science items, 45% of social studies items, and 5% of mathematics items fell into this category. Popham gives as an example this sixth-grade science item:
> A plant's fruit always contains seeds. Which of the items below is *not* a fruit?
> A.   orange
> B.   pumpkin
> C.   apple
> D.   celery
> Popham suggests that a middle-class child's parents are more likely to purchase fresh celery and a pumpkin to carve at Halloween than parents depending on food stamps. Note also that use of the negative (*not*) is considered by testing experts to introduce a linguistic demand unrelated to the concept being tested.
> Popham (2001a, p. 62)

Formal standardized achievement tests typically sample small segments of learning and usually serve the purpose of monitoring student learning in comparison to other students. They are arguably unfair because many items are easier for students from higher socioeconomic strata (Popham, 2001a). (See Teacher Note box on "Common Knowledge."). In addition, to the degree that formal, standardized tests developed outside the classroom cannot reflect the language forms and uses common in the classroom, they introduce additional problems in determining when a student response error is a problem in learning versus a problem with proficiency in English, or test language.

Testing Culture Distinguished from Assessment Culture

There are philosophical distinctions between what has been called a testing culture and an assessment culture (Wolf, Bixby, Glenn, & Gardner, 1991). The *testing culture* has focused on measuring learning and is associated with efforts to control for context (whether sociocultural context or the specific curriculum a student has had) by selecting items that are (presumably) not particular to any context (Taylor, 1994). An *assessment culture* is focused on informing teachers and students about student learning and using all that is known about context to understand how a student learns best. Teachers use their judgment as they critically examine evidence (student performance) to come to conclusions about students' proficiency in various areas. The assessment culture is more harmonious with a standards-based approach to education and a constructivist view of learners: It assumes that students' learning potential is more strongly influenced by experience than destiny and that students are active participants in their own learning.

The assessment culture is also more compatible with a sociocultural approach to learning—one that recognizes that all learning is grounded in social and cultural contexts. Instead of sorting and ranking students in relation to each other (e.g., through norm-referenced, standardized tests), teachers assess students in terms of agreed-upon standards, using agreed-upon criteria that are known to students. Many believe that norm-referenced standardized tests should not be used at all, but because of recent legislation (such as *The No Child Left Behind Act of 2001*) and the fact that some school funding is dependent on such tests, it is virtually impossible for public schools to avoid them.

Recent Assessment Trends

States and districts across the country have stepped up their use of norm-referenced standardized tests in the wake of increased demands for public accountability for student achievement, even though educators are acutely aware of the limitations of such tests—especially for ELLs and other minority students. Of course, these tests are vastly easier to administer and score than the kinds of assessments associated with an assessment culture.

A promising countertrend in assessment reform that began during the late 20th century has promoted multi-intelligence and performance assessments, sup-

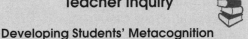

Teacher Inquiry

Developing Students' Metacognition
Interview selected students to find out what situations are comfortable for them to reflect on their learning and progress—teacher-student, student-student, small group, or private written reflection in a journal. Ask them what kind of feedback helps them improve their learning. Younger students may have a harder time identifying what works for them; direct experimentation may be the only way to determine this—but the teacher can help them to acquire the language of metacognition in the process, talking about "what helps you think about your own learning" and "how do you learn best?"

porting use of modalities other than language (Mitchell, 1992; Wiggins, 1993; Wolf et al., 1991).[1] This movement has led to a proliferation of assessments that are intended to promote the expression of student creativity, high-level thinking, and construction of knowledge within students' own contexts. Portfolios are among the most promising tools, particularly when students are meaningfully engaged in evaluating their own work, choosing portfolio entries, and annotating the portfolio with their own reflections. Portfolios are valuable also because they can contextualize learning by including information about student experience and language history.

Pros and Cons of Alternative Assessments

Overall, these alternative assessments offer what might be called cognitive advantages, and they are considered by many to be more valid than norm-referenced standardized tests for judging student achievement for that reason and because they tend to be better linked to the curriculum and grade-level standards (Wiggins, 1993; Wolf, et al., 1991).[2] Nevertheless, because they nearly always rely on advanced levels of language proficiency (usually in English) and may rely on dominant culture norms of communication, they can penalize the same students for whom standardized tests seem unfair.

Language is inevitably used in the directions and assessment prompts of assessment tasks, and a student must process this language accurately enough to figure out how to proceed in solving the problem at hand. Research has shown, not surprisingly, that the ability to conceptualize a problem accurately is a major factor in solving it (Durán, 1985). ELLs are likely disadvantaged by these assessments even more than by multiple choice and short-answer tests (August & Hakuta, 1997; Farr & Trumbull, 1997).

The kinds of communication required for the portfolio process may put some students off-kilter because of cultural differences. Expectations to evaluate one's own work may conflict with home-culture notions of the teacher as the ultimate arbiter of student progress. Taking a somewhat egalitarian stance vis-à-vis the teacher could be considered arrogant. Giving critical feedback to peers (as is often done in the process-writing approach, for example) can be a tricky requirement as well, depending on a student's cultural background. This is not to say that students cannot become more comfortable with such processes, but when we suggest that some process is universally good, we need to examine its differential impact on the students we are teaching.

The Teacher Note box at the top of page 274 shows a performance assessment that is typical of many newer assessment tasks in that it integrates multiple skills and modalities and is open-ended in terms of how it can be completed. It is useful to examine some of the language demands of this task, but first let's explain why teachers might want to use a task like this one instead of the one shown in the Teacher Note box at the bottom of page 274.

Teacher Note

A Multiday Performance Assessment on Volume

Background: Manufacturers naturally want to spend as little as possible, not only on the product but also on packing and shipping it to stores. They want to *minimize* the cost of production of their packaging, and they want to *maximize* the amount of what is packaged inside (to keep handling and postage costs down—the more individual packages you ship, the more it costs).

Setting: Imagine that your group of two or three people is one of many in the packing department responsible for M&Ms candies. The manager of the shipping department has found that the cheapest material for shipping comes as a flat piece of rectangular paperboard (the piece of poster board you will be given). She is asking each work group in the packing department to help solve this problem: What completely closed container, built out of the given piece of poster board, will hold the largest volume of M&Ms for safe shipping?

To Do: 1. Prove, in a convincing written report to company executives, that both the shape and the dimensions of your group's container maximize the volume. In making your case, supply all important data and formulas. Your group will also be asked to make a 3-minute oral report at the next staff meeting. Both reports will be judged for accuracy, thoroughness, and persuasiveness.

2. Build a model (or multiple models) out of the poster board of the container shape and size that you think solves the problem. The models are not proof; they will illustrate the claims you offer in your report.

Wiggins (1993)

Assessment expert Grant Wiggins, who has used the performance assessment above many times with middle and high school students, says that it is extremely engaging to students. He believes that because students can tackle a real problem and use creativity to do so, they are likely to be more motivated to perform than they would be on a less interesting task. In addition, Wiggins speculates, they probably deepen their understanding of the concepts assessed when they engage in active, direct solving of a problem than when simply applying a formula, and they are using a combination of skills to do so. This sounds like an ideal assessment.

This assessment is, however, almost as much an assessment of language as of mathematics. It probably relies on language

Teacher Note

Standardized Test Questions on Volume

1. What is the volume of a cone that has a base area of 78 square centimeters and a height of 12 centimeters?

   a. 30 cm³

   b. 312 cm³

   c. 936 cm³

   d. 2808 cm³

2. A round and a square cylinder share the same height. Which has the greater volume?

Wiggins (1993)

skills as much as mathematical skills—as do many mathematics assessments, which reflect not only mathematics standards of competence with solving problems but also with communicating about how they were solved.

It has been known for some time that performance on mathematics tests is influenced by students' language skills. High reading skills are correlated with successful problem-solving ability (Aiken, 1971). Comprehending the problem is, of course, the first step toward solving it, as mentioned. Researchers say that the "large gap between the performance of English language learners (ELLs) and native English speakers on math items with high language demand strongly suggests that factors other than mathematical skill contribute to success in solving word problems" (Kiplinger et al., 2000, p.1; see also Cocking & Chipman, 1988; Cummins, Kintsch, Reusser, & Weimer, 1988). Linguistic variables that affect the difficulty of a test question are length of the prompt, words per sentence (an index of syntactic complexity), number of syllables per word, word ambiguity, and word frequency (Kiplinger et al., 2000).

Language Demands of the Performance Task on Volume

What *are* the language demands of this performance task? In traditional language arts terms, they are extensive. Students have to be proficient readers. They have to wade through a lot of text in order to understand the task and the questions. Students also have to be proficient writers and presenters to do well. They have to exercise good listening skills as members of a collaborative group. We might also look at the range of language uses demanded by this task: following directions, obtaining and conveying information (explaining), and narrating.

The language itself is potentially quite difficult to understand. Terms like *minimize* and *maximize, dimensions*, and perhaps even *illustrate* (for which students need to distinguish between presenting an example as proof versus giving mathematical evidence to support a claim) could cause problems for ELLs. Beyond vocabulary, sentence length and complexity present a considerable demand. Just look at the sentence, "They want to *minimize* the cost of production of their packaging, and they want to *maximize* the amount of what is packaged inside (to keep handling and postage costs down—the more individual packages you ship, the more it costs)."

>
>
> **Teacher Inquiry**
>
> **Postassessment Interviews**
>
> Interview a sample of students after an assessment to find out how they construed the problems they were given. Ask them why they did what they did and what they were thinking. What caused trouble? What was easy? Ask how they would explain the problem to a friend.

Here we have four clauses, including a complex parenthetical statement, in which the first part is explained by the second after a dash. "The amount of what is packaged" is a complex noun phrase that includes a passive form ("is packaged"). Passive forms are considered harder to process than active ("The company packaged the M&Ms") (Horgan, 1978; Tager-Flusberg, 1985). In addition, what is in the parentheses, is syntactically and cognitively complex. Now let's look at another sentence: "What completely closed container, built out of the given piece of poster board, will hold the largest volume of M&Ms for safe shipping?" The question format makes this a difficult sentence to understand. To what does the "what" refer? Moreover, it is quite separated from the verb "will hold" by a very complex noun phrase with another passive structure ("built out of"), making the sentence unnecessarily complex (Lagunoff, personal communication).

We could probably discover additional potential language demands if we continued looking at this task. It should also be emphasized that it is not only ELLs who may struggle with these language-heavy assessments but also students whose academic language proficiency (oral or written) is low (Kiplinger et al., 2000; MacGregor & Price, 1999). However, recent research with large numbers of ELLs and native English speakers suggests that "the higher the English 'language load' in the assessment, the larger the gap between performance of LEP [limited English proficient] and non-LEP students" (Abedi, 2003. p. 4).[3]

Assessing English Language Learners

This section focuses primarily on assessing ELLs' academic or subject-matter learning through the medium of English. Of course, teachers are inevitably assessing students' language proficiency on an ongoing basis, and not just their performance in English and language arts. From kindergarten on, teachers are helping students to learn what counts as appropriate communication in school and acquire the specialized language of different domains. Science has its own vocabulary, as does every other subject area. In this regard, content area assessment and language proficiency assessment overlap, as do content area teaching and language teaching. Currently, perhaps the most accepted way to build language proficiency and maintain an ELL's academic progress is to integrate the two—to teach language through content (Met, 1994; Short, 1991, 1994). For these reasons, it makes sense to begin with a very brief discussion of assessing language proficiency itself (see chapters 3 and 4 for a thorough treatment of first- and second-language acquisition and how to monitor students' language development).

Assessing Students' Language Proficiency

Understanding students' language proficiency, both in English and in their home languages, is a key factor in being able to make decisions about their learning needs. It is also necessary for making decisions about how to assess them academically and interpret their performance on assessments. As mentioned, teachers are assessing students' language on a constant basis, whether through informal or formal means. Most classroom teachers assess reading, writing, listening and speaking—and not through the kinds of tests or methods used by speech and language specialists, but through a range of classroom methods. Indeed, teachers are, in many ways, in a much better position to evaluate students' mastery of the language forms and uses required for educational success (Saville-Troike, 1991) than are specialists. The field of assessment of language proficiency has moved toward a communicative competence perspective (see chapters 1 and 4), meaning that rather than focusing on isolated grammatical and vocabulary skills, assessments focus on use of language in meaningful contexts for real purposes (Bachman, 1990b; Rivera, 1983).

Many of the methods mentioned later in this chapter under classroom assessment are excellent for learning not only about students' academic progress but also about their language proficiency in communicative competence terms—including how they communicate under different conditions and about different topics. This participation of teachers in assessing the language proficiency of ELLs is of crucial importance. As Genesee and Hamayan (1994) say:

> Grade level teachers who share responsibility for the overall development
> of these students must be able to assess both their language development
> and their academic achievement. In particular, it is important that grade-
> level teachers be able to assess these students' content-obligatory language
> skills in order to devise effective strategies for teaching content that take
> into account the students' academic language skills at the same time as
> they extend students' acquisition of these skills. (p. 214)

"Grade-level teachers" can be interpreted as including not only elementary but also secondary school teachers who teach single subjects.

Teachers may not be in a position to assess an ELL's first language proficiency, however, and this is absolutely necessary for developing a true picture of his or her total language proficiency. This is particularly important with regard to literacy in students who have begun schooling in another country. They may have academic language and literacy skills in their home language but not yet in English. Formal assessment by a speaker of the student's home language (which should be done, if at all possible) can be complemented with parent interviews to find out the parents' perceptions of the student's proficiency as well as when and how he or she prefers to use the home language. An interpreter may be needed. Teacher observation of the student in various settings can help to establish the student's preferences for using English or the home language and proficiency with English under various conditions.

Even if a teacher does not speak the home language of students, students should be encouraged to use their home languages in the classroom, as they deem necessary with other students who speak the language. Use of a home language need not detract from acquiring English and can support academic development. Because a student may have acquired different vocabulary in each language, he or she should be allowed to *code-switch* (use either or both languages) while completing a task (Heubert & Hauser, 1999). It may be counterintuitive to monolingual speakers, but "bilingual students frequently produce more comprehensive recalls of text written in their second language when they are permitted to use their first language" (Garcia, 1992, p. 5). In real life, bilingual speakers code-switch frequently in order to communicate most effectively (Crystal, 1997; Skiba, 2003; see also chapter 4). A teenage girl, for example, may sprinkle her largely Chinese-language conversation with a friend with English names of clothing items.

As acknowledged, assessing a student in his or her home language may not be feasible in many cases, but we should keep in mind that it may be the only true way to actually find out what a student knows. Without allowing a student to use all of his cognitive resources, we are constraining the range of learning that he can demonstrate. If a student's English vocabulary is limited, we need not assume that her total vocabulary is limited or that she has difficulty learning.

Assessing Learning Through a Second Language

The *Standards for Educational and Psychological Tests*, developed jointly by the American Educational Research Association, the American Psychological Association, and the National Council on Measurement in Education (1999) state bluntly that every assessment is an assessment of language. As has already been discussed, this is even more the case with language-heavy assessments. Moreover, we compound the problem of separating content knowledge from language proficiency when we evaluate ELLs with assessments designed for native English speakers. Consider the number of possible meanings a simple word like *field* has (see Teacher Note box). English learners cannot be assumed to have had the experience necessary to distinguish so many common meanings.

As noted bilingual education researchers Guadalupe Valdés and Richard Figueroa (1994) state:

> When a bilingual individual confronts a monolingual test, developed by monolingual individuals, and standardized and normed on a monolingual population, both the test taker and the test are asked to do something that they cannot. The bilingual test taker cannot perform like a monolingual. The monolingual test cannot "measure" in the other language. (p. 87)

We can hardly state this fact too strongly: A bilingual student will never perform just like a monolingual student, and comparisons between the two on the basis of a test created for the monolingual student are always of questionable validity.[4]

Teacher Note

What Does *Field* Mean?

An ELL's English vocabulary may not be as elaborate as that of a native speaker. Consider the fourth-grade reading test item below, which James Popham identifies as SES-linked. An ELL student might know the equivalent meanings of the word *field* and how to match them to a word in her home language but not yet be able to do so in English. Consider also the cultural knowledge required, such as about baseball.

My father's *field* is computer graphics.

In which of the sentences below does the word *field* mean the same thing as in the sentence above?

A. The shortstop knew how to *field* his position.
B. We prepared the *field* by plowing it.
C. What *field* do you plan to enter when you graduate?
D. The nurse examined my *field* of vision.

Popham (2001b, p. 60)

Types of Bias

Standardized tests may be invalid on many counts (García & Pearson, 1994, synthesized in August & Hakuta, 1997):

1. *Norming bias*: Tests are typically tried out with populations that include only a small number of students from any given minority group so that knowledge about how different items work for such students is limited.
2. *Content bias*: The nature of the knowledge being tested favors some students, and assessment procedures and ways of using language are more familiar to students from the dominant culture.
3. *Linguistic and cultural biases*: Factors such as timed administration, certain English vocabulary, and failure to tap knowledge that a student may have in his or her first language combine to give an advantage to some students over others.

It could be argued that language is really at the heart of all of these sources of bias.

Educators' concerns about the validity of assessing students in their second language have historically centered around students' proficiency with that language. As with any student, it is almost impossible to separate language proficiency from academic proficiency. With ELLs, the problem is greatly amplified. First, we know that we are assessing them quite possibly through their second- or third-best language. Second, language differences are always associated with differences in experience and, frequently, differences in access to curriculum (opportunities to learn). Third, the special kinds of knowledge such students do have may go largely untapped. Thus ELLs are faced with competing on unequal grounds from many perspectives.

Different Implications for Different Students

Having made the very strong statement that tests designed for monolingual speakers are not valid for bilingual students, we need to acknowledge two issues. First, *different* performance does not always mean *inferior* performance. We know from research discussed in earlier chapters that bilingualism can confer cognitive advantages, particularly in terms of language awareness that is associated with higher literacy skill.

Many bilingual students may do extremely well on tests designed for native English monolingual speakers. Pragmatically, in such cases, our concerns for validity are reduced. We assume that if students do well, we can fairly test them in English. However, if we tested them in another language, we might see different patterns of performance that would be informative as well, and there is always the question of whether a student might do even better if somehow an assessment's dependence on language were reduced.

In general, students who have developed strong academic language proficiency in English and not in their home language are probably better served by being tested in English (see section on assessing in the home language below). The greatest concerns about validity—the accuracy of the inferences we make about a student's ability on the basis of test performance—are related to students who have not reached an advanced level of proficiency with English.

Classroom Academic Assessment of English Language Learners

The examples used here are mainly with regard to language arts assessment, but many of the points made apply across subject-matter domains. With integrated language arts instruction (in which reading, writing, speaking, and listening are not taught separately) come assessments that combine all four areas. There is a concomitant move away from tests that focus on isolated skills (although, as we know, for accountability purposes norm-referenced standardized multiple-choice tests are often still used), because these are not seen as valid indicators of what we have come to think of as true reading and writing. Tests developed by basal reader publishers are also in some disfavor because of their tendency to focus too heavily on skills over comprehension (Garcia, 1992).

Informal assessment activities such as story retelling, classroom observation, running records, tape recordings, reading logs, writing samples, reading response logs, storytelling, teacher-student conferences, and think-alouds may be used by the teacher in conjunction with building a student portfolio throughout the year (Garcia, 1992; Genesee & Hamayan, 1994; Navarrete, Wilde, Nelson, Martinez, & Hargett, 1990). Most of these tools transcend the language arts arena and can be used with mathematics, science, and social studies. Garcia cautions as follows:

> Informal assessment relies on the teacher's expertise. Teachers who are interested in informal assessment have to be knowledgeable about the literacy process. Informal assessment provides one means for teachers to find out the strengths and weaknesses of their students' ongoing literacy development. However, teachers must know how to interpret this data. If they work with second-language children, then they need to make a concerted effort to become knowledgeable about first- and second-language acquisition and literacy processes. (p. 14)

Teacher Note

Samples of ELL Student Writing

He geib ibriting hi had hi dident kip nating.

(*He gave everything he had. He didn't keep nothing*)

I help some homeless people the was slipping in the estrits.
(*I help some homeless people they was sleeping in the streets.*)

Yo yahto know way I don't gibb many bicas wen I diden habe many they !deden Helpmy!

(*You ought to know why I don't give money because when I didn't have money they didn't help me!*)

!Stil you so posto gib many the piople in this vilig are yor famali!

(*Still, you supposed to give money the people in this village are your family!*)

Based on Beaumont et al. (2002, p. 250)

Part of understanding these processes is being able to interpret assessment performance by students at different developmental levels of English acquisition. In a collaborative assessment development project with elementary school teachers in the Sequoia Valley District[5] in California, assessment consultants saw many examples of student writing in English that were hard to decipher without reference to students' native Spanish (Beaumont et al., 2002). (Reading comprehension was measured largely through written responses to readings.) The Teacher Note on page 280 shows four examples of student writing and researchers' interpretations of them, based on knowledge of Spanish. Teachers who know Spanish will recognize immediately that most of the errors are phonetic confusions between Spanish and English spelling and pronunciation (and in some cases grammar). Vocabulary limitations were evident in students' responses as well. When asked to describe characters, they often used general positives or negatives (*nice, bad, mean*) rather than more explicit terms (*generous, selfish, cruel*). One way to support teachers who do not know the home languages of students is through collaborative scoring or grading with teachers who are familiar with those languages. Failing that, the assistance of a paraprofessional from a student's community may be helpful.

Depending on how an assessment is framed to the student, it may take the form of an examination, an interview, or a conversation, all of which have different levels of formality and different sorts of expectations of the role of student vis-à-vis the adult. Therefore, "the importance of the role taken by the adult in eliciting language from students for language proficiency assessment cannot be overemphasized" (Bennett & Slaughter, 1983, p. 9). This is to say that the teacher needs not only subject matter expertise but also knowledge of these pragmatic, communicative aspects of assessment in order to choose valid assessment practices.

Informal assessment in the classroom is intimately tied to expectations about what counts as normal communication patterns between teacher and students and among students.

> ### Teacher Inquiry
>
>
> **Monitoring Student Performance**
>
> Note which students shine or fade, depending on the kind of language use required or the degree of language involved in completing an assessment. Choose two or three focal students and note how they perform depending on which way they are assessed. Consider group discussion, oral questioning, oral presentation, collaborative problem solving, written essay, short-answer questions, multiple-choice format, demonstration, diagram, pictorial illustration, and other forms of assessment used in the classroom.

Informal assessment often takes the form of questioning within the whole group. Again, we have to ask ourselves if an accurate picture of student learning can be developed when some students will quite likely be extremely uncomfortable with individual questioning in front of peers. Some of the new assessments would appear to demand participant structures that are probably new to students, such as the instructional conversation (IC) (Tharp & Gallimore, 1988).

In the instructional conversation approach (discussed in greater depth in chapters 5 and 6), students take a much more active role in classroom discourse. The teacher facilitates discussion, poses questions, encourages students to respond to each other, and introduces important information at key moments but does not regulate student talk as much as is typical. In other words, the communication does not always go through the teacher as in the traditional pattern of teacher asks question, student responds, teacher evaluates response—what Mehan (1979) has called the *recitation script*. The instructional conversation is a promising strategy for both instruction and assessment. However many students will need time and support to participate in it successfully. (Goldenberg, 1991; Tharp & Gallimore, 1991).

Assessing in the Home Language versus the School Language: Dilemmas

If students can show what they know better through their first or home language, why not assess or test them in that language? First of all, this is a big *if*. Doing so would depend on how well developed their home language is and whether they have the academic language necessary to show subject matter knowledge through that language. The standard wisdom among educators is that it is unwise to test in a language that is not being used for instruction, so students who are not learning mathematics, science, and other academic subjects through the medium of their home languages ought not to be tested in those languages (Abedi et al., 2000). However, sometimes students do better on an assessment in their home language, even when instruction has been in English (Cocking & Chipman, 1988). In fact, even within a domain such as science, ELLs may do better in English on one item and better in their home language on another. It may therefore be necessary to give bilingual students more options and more test items than monolingual English speakers in order to get an accurate picture of their learning (Solano-Flores & Trumbull, 2003). The apparent contradiction in the research is a reminder that many contextual factors influence how various educational practices affect students: level of language proficiency, length of time in the United States, amount of prior schooling, socioeconomic status, and grade level, among others.

Suppose the student has been in a bilingual Spanish-English program for 3 years and is still receiving mathematics instruction in Spanish. It would probably be a better choice to assess in Spanish. This can be fine if the classroom teacher is able to construct assessments in Spanish—in the dialect of Spanish used in the classroom—or use locally or commercially developed tests approved by the district for periodic evaluation of student progress. The latter may not be matched to the curriculum or the student's particular dialect of Spanish, however, and thus may be of limited utility. If students are required to be tested for statewide or districtwide accountability purposes, and their primary academic language is not English, then certainly it is preferable to use tests in their home language if they are available. In California, the *SABE* (2000) and *Aprenda* (1997) tests have been used by districts to gauge the achievement of Spanish-speaking students in bilingual education programs.

As suggested, if the student has transitioned to English-only instruction, the logical language of assessment would be English. As any teacher who has dealt with these issues knows, the whole matter is less simple than it can be made to sound. Teachers of bilingual students in a California school district who had just transitioned to English-only instruction worked to develop an alternative to the fifth-grade performance assessment in reading (Trumbull & Koelsch, 2000). They were concerned that the districtwide assessment painted an unrealistically negative picture of their students. They knew their students could read, but according to the assessment they were virtually nonreaders. In this case, a test of reading in Spanish would have undoubtedly shown their reading skill more accurately.

However, creating an assessment in Spanish would have been politically and perhaps practically impossible. So the teachers did the next best thing: They persuaded the district to hire consultants to help them design an English reading assessment that was parallel to classroom instruction in format and based on culturally appropriate texts. Some of the assessment strategies these teachers used are described in the section below on reducing language demands of assessments. We can see from this brief example that decisions about how to assess ELLs are complicated. We don't always get the best information from assessments, even when we try to observe research-based guidelines. Individual contexts must always be considered.

Translating the Assessments

Whenever we go from one language to another, we are really interpreting: there is no such thing as pure translation, and new ways of thinking get interjected into the process. Meaning is almost inevitably changed when assessments or tests are translated, because language and meaning (and culture) are inextricably linked (Greenfield, 1997; Van de Vivjer & Poortinga, 1997). When meaning is changed, we are no longer assessing exactly what we were assessing in the original test and are, hence, jeopardizing construct validity.

An equally serious problem is that the second-language version of an assessment does not receive as much time and attention in development as the original. Typically, the first version is gone over with a fine-tooth comb, revised, piloted at least once, and revised again. Rarely does a translated test get such careful treatment. When the original assessment and its translation are developed using such different procedures, they cannot be considered equivalent (Solano-Flores, Trumbull, & Nelson-Barber, 2002).

The following illustration will demonstrate how translation can cause problems. In a statewide reading assessment in a western state, high school students were to read and answer some questions about a short humorous essay by former syndicated columnist Russell Baker. The essay was about how Baker had been a somewhat lackadaisical and undirected young man (at around the same age as the readers of the essay). Baker described himself as a "bump on a log" without much "gumption."

These words were probably placed in proximity because of their repeated sound pattern. *Bump on a log* is an idiom familiar to most American speakers of English, and *gumption* is an old-fashioned word that conjures up the pioneer spirit.

It isn't hard to imagine how much the subtle humor of this piece, with its particular use of language, was completely lost in the Spanish translation, and it didn't help that those in charge of the translation were given a very short time frame in which to complete it. "Bump on a log" was translated literally into something like *un chichón en un tronco*. "Gumption" was translated as *motivación*—a word that does not have the same "oomph" at all. Here we see an example of inexact word equivalencies from one language to the next that resulted in a completely different literary effect. How could students whose first language is Spanish be expected to respond to this text in the same way as native English speakers? Perhaps with enough advance notice, bilingual educators could have chosen a humorous text in Spanish of similar difficulty and developed sensible questions to accompany it. Such an alternative would not have been equivalent to the original test question, but it would have been more likely to succeed in providing an index of students' ability to respond to literature.

Another well-known problem created by the translation process is alteration in text length. A test translated from English to Spanish is likely to be longer than the original. The inability to find exact equivalents for words poses an even larger threat to validity, however, and the greater the difference between cultures, the more difficult it is likely to be to find equivalents. This problem is illustrated once again in the Teacher Note box "Collaborating in Chuuk."

Teacher Note

Collaborating in Chuuk

A Micronesian educator from the island of Chuuk speaking at the annual Pacific Educational Conference, held in Guam in July 2001, detailed the multiple elements of meaning associated with the concept of *collaboration* in Pacific Island societies. He explained that there are several related words that capture different aspects of collaboration. According to the speaker, *ekichu* is roughly translated as "to think or plan together." *Angechu* means "cooperate, aim, or labor together"; *tipechu* is "common honesty or sensitivity." *Iechu* means "lead or be charitable together; and *techu* is "oneness or the whole, everyone belongs to each other." In the Chuukese language, these terms entail the following values and expectations:

1. Everyone pitches in (no need to be encouraged to do so)
2. Everyone is accountable for (sense of belonging)
3. Everyone is responsible (feeling of interdependence)
4. Everyone has joy
5. Everyone has gain.

The culture's emphasis on the well-being of the group as primary over that of the individual is clearly reflected in the language, and one can only imagine the difficulty of translating from Chuukese to English. What important meanings must be obscured because of the paucity of appropriate vocabulary in English!

Reducing Language Demands

Language demands of assessments can be reduced directly by simplifying the language of directions or of test prompts. (Sometimes the directions and the prompts are one and the same; sometimes there are general instructions, followed by one or more prompts.) Researchers have shown that linguistic modification of linguistically complex test questions does narrow the gap in performance between ELLs and native English speakers (Abedi et al., 2000). Offering students a glossary to clarify possibly confusing terms used in each test item can also be helpful.

In one study, researchers modified mathematics test items from the *National Assessment of Education Progress* (Kiplinger et al., 2000) to see whether those modifications would make a difference in student performance. The study involved fourth graders from three groups: ELLs, native English speakers, and native English speakers with learning disabilities. One set of students from each of the three groups was given a version of the items in which the language had been simplified (see Teacher Note box below). Another set of students was given a glossary that explained key terms in each item; these same students were also allowed to spend extra time completing the items.[6] Students benefited most from linguistic simplification of the items, and the ELLs benefited the most.

Teacher Note

Linguistic Modification of a Mathematics Test Question

Original version:

> A certain reference file contains approximately six billion facts.
> About how many thousands is that?

Simplified version:

> Mack's company sold six billion hamburgers.
> About how many thousands is that?

Glossary version:

> A certain reference file contains approximately six billion facts.
> About how many thousands is that?
>
> a certain reference file = a folder for papers
>
> contains = holds
>
> approximately = about

Abedi, Lord, & Plummer (1997, p. 41)

One needs to be cautious about drawing sweeping conclusions from this research because *over*simplification of language can actually result in text that is harder to read. Revising a wonderful story, whose sentences are perhaps complex but rich with information, to a series of staccato subject-verb-object sentences tends to reduce the meaning—not to mention the appeal—of the story. In such a case, it may be much better to provide additional background information to help readers process the story better (Saville-Troike, 1991).

A study of high school ELLs who were completing science performance assessments suggested that they were unduly penalized because they could not finish in the time expected. The researcher, Jerome Shaw (1997), surveyed students about where they had problems. A Filipina sophomore commented, "I don't like the test because I don't finish the experiment, then the bell will ring!" The assessments took longer because students needed assistance with understanding the tasks, at least in part because they could not fully understand the language of instructions. A Vietnamese sophomore wrote, "Sometimes I don't understand what did the test want to talk?" Another responded to one of the researcher's questions with a heartbreaking sentence, "The test was explein with secretly words." The writing portions were laborious for many students, causing anxiety. A Vietnamese senior said, "I don't like take the test have much writing because it very difficult for me when I writing" (Shaw, p. 336).

The effects of time most likely depend on the assessment, and some studies have shown that both ELLs and native English speakers benefit from additional time, so that the gap in performance between the two groups is not narrowed by adding time alone (e.g., Abedi et al., 2000; García, 1991). In the study by Kiplinger et al. (2000), ELLs benefited more than native English speakers from the glossary combined with extra time, but both modifications (including the linguistic simplification) produced higher scores in all fourth graders. The glossary alone, without extra time, did not improve ELL performance. Time was needed, apparently, for reading the glossaries. It was not only ELLs who did disproportionately better with these modifications, but also—not surprisingly—students who had received Ds or Fs in reading the previous semester. In fact, in the study conducted by Abedi et al. (2000), performance of both ELLs and native English speakers in the eighth grade on math tests was highly correlated with reading ability (as measured by an independent test). This research illustrates how easy it is to confuse subject area proficiency with language proficiency. We should also note that the effectiveness of modifications may vary not only with language status but also with age and other student factors. Kiplinger et al. (2000) conclude as follows:

> These data suggest that linguistic simplification or clarification of the vocabulary of mathematics word problems can benefit *virtually all students*. Thus we believe that unnecessarily complex linguistic structures or difficult vocabulary in a mathematics assessment introduces non-construct-related variance that can be removed by careful attention to construction of the assessment to measure the construct of math knowledge—not reading ability. (p. 13)

Making Assessment Culturally Responsive

The next Teacher Note box offers an example of another performance assessment activity. It is an interdisciplinary fifth-grade task designed at T'saile Elementary School, part of the Chinle Public School District on the Navajo Nation in Arizona. This task is designed to be completed over a period of several weeks. It addresses skills related to three content area standards established by the district: environmental and cultural awareness and responsibility, life skills, and communication.

Teacher Note

The Deforestation Task

Prompt to student:
In this task you will collect data and information regarding one aspect of deforestation (such as erosion, endangered animals, economics, values, and effect on the biosystem and sacred places) to become an expert in one or more areas. You will conduct an interview about the issues and values of deforestation. You will work in small groups to present your material in a variety of ways, including a debate in which you take a pro or con position.

Re-explanation for student:
You will find out more about deforestation by reading, interviewing, and sharing. You will work in a small group to present your information. To accomplish this task, you will need to:
1. Research one area of deforestation
2. Write interview questions
3. Complete the interview
4. Keep a notebook of your information and data collected, a record of research problems and solutions, and personal reflections.
5. Work with a group to present information about deforestation

Adapted from Farr & Trumbull (1997, pp. 307–308)

The T'saile teachers have identified ways to connect this task to other classroom activity, such as through literature studies, role-playing, drama, and various other kinds of written and oral presentations and products. The language demands of this rich, lengthy task are quite evident; many are directly listed. Any one of the activities, such as preparing for and conducting an interview, entails a whole constellation of language skills. Interviews require a real sense of what one wants to know, how a question must be posed to elicit that information, what sequence of questions makes most sense, and how to phrase questions so that they will be considerate (e.g., not too intrusive). Carrying out the interview requires an equally complex set of language skills. Students have to learn how to manage the multiple tasks involved in keeping an interviewee engaged while taking notes, monitoring whether the desired information is forthcoming, and reasking or rephrasing questions if it is not.

If we go back to the list of language uses in chapter 1 (Teacher Note box, "Functions of Language in the Classroom"), we would certainly identify the following as part of the assessment: describing (uses of special terminology will be required), following directions, recounting (eliciting accounts from interviewees and giving recounts of what they say), obtaining and giving information (researching and recording information), narrating (giving a report of some kind). The heuristic function of language is prominent here; that is, language is being used as a tool for learning and developing one's thinking about a topic. We could add *arguing* and *persuading* (using information to take a position for a debate), although it is not clear whether the debate is a choice or a required activity. All language arts components are involved: listening, speaking, reading, writing, and performing.[7]

The Deforestation Task has the advantage of being culturally congruent for the students who will be carrying it out. Since the Chinle Public Schools' curriculum is based on the cultural values and knowledge of the Navajo community to which students belong, tasks associated with it are likely to be meaningful and contextualized. Concern for the local environment is paramount in this community, and much of the research students are required to do can be accomplished firsthand, not least by interviewing Navajo elders. The task is designed so that students do some independent work and then come together to present to the class, pooling their expertise as students do on the M&Ms task. The task directions are largely an outline for students to follow. Students and teachers interact many times during the course of students' completing this multifaceted task, so there is considerable support or scaffolding throughout the process.

Mirroring Instruction in Assessment

The Sequoia Valley teachers identified specific strategies for mediating assessments for ELLs. They used principles of exemplary ESL instruction as a basis for developing appropriate assessments for their students who had just transitioned to English-only instruction. They spoke of scaffolding their students' participation in the new, alternative performance assessment of reading by using the following:

- Preassessment activities that activated prior knowledge and introduced vocabulary in context
- Graphic organizers such as a cartoon sequence, thought bubble, matrix, and partially completed charts to be filled in (see Figure 7-1)
- Opportunities to both write and draw (multimodality assessment)
- Open-ended questions focused on main concepts in the texts and not on hard-to-locate details
- Comprehension questions that built knowledge across items on the assessment (linked rather than isolated questions)
- Simplified, relatively short instructions
- Culturally appropriate texts that reflected the values of their primarily Mexican-American immigrant students (Trumbull & Koelsch, 2000).

Figure 7-1. Graphic Organizers Used
in a Reading Performance Assessment

Here is a picture of the Rich Señora dropping into the sea of darkness. In the thought bubble coming from her head, write what she is thinking about the things she did in her life.

1. Trevor did many things when he began to help the homeless. Using your pencil, underline four different things that Trevor did for the homeless after he saw the news report on television. Be sure to underline the entire sentence in your article.

2. Think about what you have read about Trevor and complete the chart.

Draw Trevor	Give three words that describe the way Trevor is	Copy a sentence from the article that tells what Trevor did that shows the way he is.

Adapted from the Sequoia Valley Transitional
Performance-Based Assessment

The resulting 10-item assessment (which took three 50-minute periods to complete) was engaging for students and resulted in a large output of student work. Students showed what they knew and could do, in contrast to how comparable students had performed on the district's performance assessment the previous year. They apparently understood the instructions and the tasks, and even though their performance averaged somewhat below grade-level expectations, a much more realistic picture of their progress emerged. Some students were able to perform at a very high level, giving sophisticated and elaborate responses to thought questions. Even those who were clearly in trouble with English reading could partially complete some of the tasks. Although students' drawing was not scored, it allowed some struggling students to express themselves and remain involved with the assessment. No one gave up in the middle, as appeared to happen with the previous year's district assessment.

A Caveat Regarding Modifications

It is important to clarify the difference between scaffolding or supporting students, so that they can tackle an assessment, and overexplaining the assessment to the extent that the task itself is made too easy. Shaw (1997) says:

> Such guidance needs to be provided with care. Teachers may take liberty to clarify instructions or questions for students to the extent that the assessment is still able to perform its measurement function. What needs to be avoided is explaining a concept or procedure whose possession, comprehension, or use is intended to be measured by the assessment. This is akin to the difference between helping a student understand a question versus giving away the answer. (p. 337)

Similarly, ESL and bilingual educators are leery of simplifying language too much, particularly in instruction, because in the past that has been associated with providing a dumbed-down curriculum and taking a remedial approach. Students need rich linguistic input if they are to acquire language at high levels. Nevertheless, it is hard to argue with the suggestion to provide simple and clear language on assessments. As Shaw says, "Performance assessments should be designed to maximize student comprehension of what the task is asking them to do" (p. 337). Infact the recommendation should be extended to include all forms of assessment and testing.

Assessment as a Cultural Practice: The Relationship Between Language and Culture

As has been said all along, assessment itself is a cultural practice, as is every element in education or any other aspect of society. Assessment researcher Richard Durán (1989) has noted:

> Contemporary cross-cultural research suggests that there are intimate connections among the ways people perceive the nature of problem-solving situations, problem-solving tasks, the language surrounding tasks, and sociocultural experiences. Thus, analysis of issues affecting the testing of language-minority persons is not totally reducible to consideration solely of how lack of familiarity with a language affects test performance. (p. 574)

This observation extends beyond students who are learning English as a second or third language to those who could be considered "language minority" by virtue of speaking a nonstandard dialect of English or who grow up in homes where another language in addition to English is spoken.

In many indigenous cultures, children are taught complex skills at home (e.g., weaving, fishing, sailing, sewing, dancing) largely through modeling by adults. In that case, the natural form of assessment is through direct demonstration of a skill. Language may play a very minor role in the teaching and learning process. When students from these and other cultures enter formal schooling, the transition to more language-based learning and individual assessment may be a major one for them. Traditional cultures in Micronesia share similar values, and those values affect common assessment practices. For example, concerns that assessment must yield an individual grade are not paramount, even in schools based on the U.S. system like those on the island of Rota in the Commonwealth of the Northern Marianas Islands (Nelson-Barber et al., 2000).

A fifth-grade teacher at Rota Elementary School, discussing evaluating students' basket making during a 2-week focus on local culture in the schools, said, "Group discovery is important. It doesn't matter who did what. It sounds silly to examine who did what strand of the weaving. Ask them, 'What did you learn from that experience?'" Assessment in Rota is often conducted by teachers in the whole group or in small groups. The group structure of assessment (in Rota) reflects the values of the culture, just as the individualized structure of assessment in U.S. schools does.

Such group-oriented values may be evident even in formal testing situations. Chadwick Fleck, a visiting American educator in Nepal, was shocked when his seventh graders openly "cheated" on their final science exams (Fleck, 2000). Students were talking with each other about test questions, and even students outside the classroom in the schoolyard were holding conversations with his students through the open windows—apparently offering their ideas of how to answer certain questions. He had reminded them in advance to pay attention to their own papers, and they had all nodded compliantly. Now he was having to intervene with

> ### Teacher Inquiry
>
> **Cheating vs. Helping**
> Do a survey in your classroom to find out what students think cheating is. You could have them write a paragraph in response to the question "What is the difference between cheating and helping?" Or, students could discuss this question in small groups or pairs first and then write or draw their thoughts.

constant instances of outright defiance of the rules. What was going on? What Fleck learned was that the definition of cheating in Nepal is more like "stealing" than "getting help with answers"—as it is in the United States. Getting help on a test question is acceptable, and offering help is laudable. What is not okay is actually completing the assessment for another person or taking someone else's assessment and passing it off as your own.

Some of the examples used in this chapter are from cultures one might consider distant from the dominant culture of the United States, but U.S. schools have students from all over the world. These examples raise points that are completely relevant to U.S. classrooms. Research shows that students from many minority groups in the United States have different ideas from their teachers about where the line between helping and cheating is drawn (Nelson-LeGall & Resnick, 1998; Rothstein-Fisch et al., 2003). Several teachers in the Bridging Cultures Project described how they tapped their immigrant Latino students' culture-based value of helping in order to prepare them for standardized tests. The next Teacher Note box shows how one teacher approached test preparation. Although students take practice tests individually, as they might in any classroom, the practice described here draws upon students' willingness and ability to cooperate for the good of the group.

Teacher Note

Test Preparation in Mrs. Amada Pérez's Third-Grade Classroom

"I also use a lot of collectivistic activities to prepare the students for individual standardized testing. When we practice multiple-choice tests . . . all the children take the tests individually in silence, with privacy screens. They take their tests and then we correct them in a group, orally. Each table or cooperative group is responsible for one question. So they can discuss it together, about what the best answer is, then all the members of the table stand, and everyone has a role. Person No. 1 reads the question, Person No. 2 reads all the possible answers, Person No. 3 selects the worst answer or answers—the throw-away items and why to reduce the options to two. Person No. 4 selects the right answer and says why. Everyone gets to hear and participate.

"When the right answer comes out—and it almost always is the right answer—that's very interesting. Rarely do they get it wrong because they have had the power of the group. Everybody applauds for the whole table. They tackled it together. They leave with good positive feelings, almost like it's been a game show, so they look forward to taking an individual test because they have a paired association with the group.

"(We) sit on the floor in a circle with the test and debrief it . . . most of the time in groups. Nobody gets bored, and everyone is completely attentive. If someone got it wrong, they now understand WHY they got it wrong. They say why they selected that answer. They look back to make sure the answer looks right. If they say there are three toss-away questions and only one makes sense, just say why. So they are developing some test savvy."

From Rothstein-Fisch et al. (2003, pp. 19–20)

Very few communities have completely homogeneous groups of students, and all can benefit from exploring differences and how they may interfere with student success. We seem to have moved somewhat afield from the topic of language, but actually we are confronting a whole interaction among ideas of what constitutes knowledge (Is it group constructed or individually constructed?), appropriate times for communicating what one knows (during a formal test?), and what constitutes learning (If the group jointly knows something, does that count for each student?).

Once again it must be stressed that it is often the *uses of language* that students are called on to engage in and that cause problems. Students whose communities do not use language in ways parallel to those of the classroom cannot help but require additional time and support to expand their repertoire of language uses—something they will have to do if they are to succeed. At the same time, teachers need resources to support their own ability to recognize their students' ways of using language, for example (as mentioned in chapter 2), to hear a nonlinear narrative as actually having a structure, rather than concluding that a child has no sense of story structure.

One feature of the more open-ended assessments is that they present a problem in context. This is thought to increase a student's ability or motivation to engage with the problem or problems at hand. What kinds of context are useful to which students? Take the bird feeder problem shown in Figure 7-2. This is a sample task from the *Washington Assessment of Student Learning* (WASL) (Washington State Commission on Student Learning, 1998). For the large population of migrant students who have come to Washington from the state of Michoacán in Mexico, building a birdhouse may not be a meaningful or particularly interesting task. This is not to say that the students will not be able to solve the problem, but we may be deluding ourselves to think that the context offered here motivates better participation than a problem that states "You need to build a box using the materials provided."

Current research on what has been called culturally valid assessment attempts to get below the surface of student performance by interviewing students about how they understood an assessment item and why they responded as they did (Solano-Flores & Nelson-Barber, 2001). Such research promises to help us understand why students' assessment performance varies: Is it because of linguistic misunderstanding? Is it because of cultural differences in ways of understanding the world and going about solving a problem? Is it because of differences in experience and access to curriculum? If the student is an immigrant, how are these elements related to the length of time he or she has been in the United States or what kind of education he or she had prior to coming to the United States?

Figure 7-2. The Bird Feeder Problem

Your class project is to build a bird feeder.

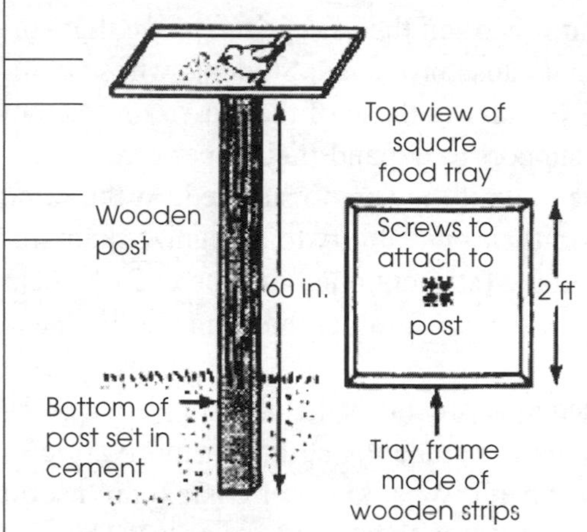

Wooden post

60 in.

Bottom of post set in cement

Top view of square food tray

Screws to attach to post

Tray frame made of wooden strips

2 ft

Item	Cost per Unit
wooden post	2.50 per foot
wooden strips for tray frame	$1.00 per foot
tray bottom	$6.00
tools, screws, nails, wood glue and cement mix	Loaned or donated by parents

Explain how you could use the information given to find the total cost of materials. Use words, numbers, or pictures.

Adapted from Washington State Commission on Student Learning
(1998, pp. 106–107)

Reflections

It can be almost overwhelming to think of the numbers of changes that would have to be made to make assessment and testing equitable and more valid for the widely varying population of students we now have in our schools. Some say that we don't have the resources to do what we need to do: How could we possibly provide assessments in every student's language or account for every important element of a student's background in order to perfectly understand why he or she performs a certain way on a given assessment? Others say we simply don't have the will to do what is ethically and educationally imperative or that current policies and systems are designed to maintain a social status quo, with some groups of students privileged over others. Wherever the truth lies, there are certainly steps that teachers can take to improve assessment practices in their own schools.

A good grasp of the issues is a powerful tool in the hands of a committed teacher. Many teachers have had a single course in tests and measurements and may not believe that they are qualified to critique assessment practices and make recommendations for change, even though they intuitively understand the limitations of current practice. An informed and confident teacher will make better decisions and wield stronger influence than a less-informed one. The final Teacher Note box offers recommendations for improving assessment. They are, naturally, largely from the perspective of recognizing the role of language in assessment. These recommendations are linked to the examples presented throughout the chapter to illustrate how language, culture, and assessment intersect.

It is easy to sit outside the classroom and make suggestions, some of which may not be practical or even useful in many schools. Thus, it is left to the reader to construct a vision of what is desirable and realistic in his or her own setting. At the very least, perhaps this chapter will have stimulated some thinking about possibilities.

Teacher Note

Recommendations for Increasing the Equity and Validity of Assessment

1. Be conscious of the kinds of language proficiency (including uses) that your assessments demand of students.

2. Ensure that directions and assessment prompts are written or given orally in simple language—not so as to simplify the task, but to make it clear.

3. Check with students about their understanding of what they are expected to do on an assessment.

4. Provide some variety in assessment formats so that all students have a chance to show what they know and can do.

5. Be wary of judging a student's ability on the basis of his or her participation in group discussions. Observe the student in other situations, such as peer conversations and small-group work.

6. Assess students in the language of instruction if possible, bearing in mind that assessing a bilingual student in *both* languages may well reveal more about what a student really knows and can do.

7. Work closely with bilingual and ESL specialists to keep track of a student's language development, ideally in all of his or her languages. If students are lagging academically, investigate whether English language proficiency is holding them back and seek intensive ESL support for them.

8. Be conservative in interpreting the results of mandated tests designed for populations different from the students you teach. Do not make important decisions on the basis of these test scores, if at all possible.

cont.

9. If you do not know the home languages of your students, enlist the support of other adults who do (whenever possible) to help interpret their language behavior in the classroom and their writing.

10. Learn, if you can, about the most salient differences between the student's home language and the school language. Is the home language a written language, or has it been for quite a while? Is it alphabetic? How is the sound system different? What are the norms of literacy and oral language use in the student's culture? Are young people expected to initiate conversation with elders?

11. Help students to be conscious of how they can best show what they know and can do and what helps them to do well on various kinds of assessments.

12. Make clear to students what counts as cheating and what is acceptable as helping. Capitalize on students' willingness to help each other whenever possible, even in preparing for or debriefing formal tests.

Notes

1. Performance assessments require the student to demonstrate the same behavior that the teacher wants to evaluate (e.g., writing an essay, when the teacher wants to know how well a student can write an essay) (Meyer, 1992). Some use the term to mean any open-ended, complex assessment task.

2. Psychometricians would argue that norm-referenced standardized tests are often used for purposes for which they are not intended. Note, also, that many states such as Arizona, Connecticut, and California have tried at various times to develop standardized performance assessment systems to be used on a large scale. Such assessment systems are standards-referenced rather than norm-referenced.

3. *LEP* and *non-LEP* are terms used in federal legislation and hence in some research using national tests.

4. We all know adults who learned English as a second or third language and who speak it extremely well, but who would never be mistaken for native speakers. The ways they use language and see the world are going to be somewhat different from those of native English monolingual speakers. A monolingual speaker will almost certainly not have the level of language awareness or the potential for multiple perspective–taking that a bilingual or multilingual speaker has.

5. Not the district's real name

6. Extra time is thought to be important because it has long been argued that processing in a second language moves more slowly (Mestre, 1984; Rincón, 1980).

7. Many current conceptualizations of language arts components do not include performing, but we use Moffett's & Wagner's (1991) scheme here because the performance aspect of using language can vary so much cultur-

ally. Some students will be much more comfortable with the demand to present a report than others will.

For Further Reading

Abedi, J. (2001). *Assessment and accommodations for English language learners: Issues and recommendations.* (Policy Brief No. 4). Los Angeles: National Center for Research on Evaluation, Standards, and Student Testing. Available online at www.cse.ucla.edu/products/policybriefs_set.htm.

August, D., & Hakuta, K. (Eds.) (1997). *Improving schooling for language-minority children* (Chap. 5: Student assessment). Washington, DC: National Academy Press.

Farr, B. P., & Trumbull, E. (1997). *Assessment alternatives for diverse classrooms.* Norwood, MA: Christopher-Gordon.

Genesee, F., & Hamayan, E. (1994). Classroom-based assessment. In F. Genesee (Ed.), *Educating second language children: The whole child, the whole curriculum, the whole community* (pp. 212–239). Cambridge, UK: Cambridge University Press.

Hood, S. (1998).Culturally responsive performance-based assessment: Conceptual and psychometric considerations. *Journal of Negro Education, 67* (3), 187–197. Available online at www.iaaec.com/projects/etcd/etcd2.html

Popham, W. J. (2001). *The truth about testing.* Alexandria, VA: Association for Supervision and Curriculum Development.

Stiggins, R. J. (2001). *Student-involved assessment* (3rd ed.). Upper Saddle River, NJ: Merrill Prentice-Hall.

Tinajero, J. V., & Hurley, S. R. (Eds.). (2001). *Literacy assessment of second language learners.* Boston: Allyn & Bacon.

Glossary

Academic English: language used in formal contexts for academic subjects.

Accent: the collection of features of pronunciation associated with regional or social differences.

Accommodation: the process of reorganizing cognitive structures or schemata in response to external stimuli that do not fit into any available schema.

Acquisition-learning hypothesis: one of Krashen's hypotheses that attempts to explain how second-language knowledge is processed, how it is stored, and how it is used; unconscious internalization that results from participation in natural communication in which the focus is on meaning.

Additive bilingualism: building on what a child brings to the classroom and adding to it, rather than neglecting or rejecting the student's language and culture.

Affective filter: a metaphor for the interaction of personality and emotional factors with other factors that serves to make a second-language learner more or less open to second-language input. When the "filter" is down, the learner engages with new language input at a deeper level, according to Krashen (1982).

African-American Vernacular English (also known as Black English, Black language, Black dialect, Ebonics, Negro nonstandard dialect): the variety of English spoken by many African Americans, variable in terms of which features are maintained in different communities. It is contested by some as a variety of English and labeled a "language."

Ambiguity (semantic or syntactic): the property of having two or more possible meanings, either because of vocabulary (e.g.,*sanction*, has two opposite meanings) or syntax ("the husband of the chef, who was smiling" can mean that the husband or the chef was smiling).

Arbitrariness: an important feature of language, usually referring to the lack of relationship between the physical form of a word or morpheme and the thing to which it refers.

ASL (American Sign Language): the manual and visual-spatial linguistic system that is the primary means of communication for most deaf Americans, different from sign language systems that developed in other countries.

Assessment: the process of gathering information about student learning; a test, an example of student work, or another indicator of student learning.

Basal reader: a book (typically containing a number of stories) within a graded series of books that are designed to increase predictably in level of difficulty.

BICS (Basic Interpersonal Communication Skills): conversational fluency, including mastery of pronunciation, vocabulary, and grammar; language used in everyday activities.

Bicultural: proficient in the norms and practices of two different cultures.

Bidialectal: proficient with two dialects and able to selectively use each dialect appropriately.

Bidirectional bridging: adapting classroom practices to harmonize with norms of students' home cultures while supporting students to adapt to common school-culture practices.

Biliteracy: proficiency with two linguistic and cultural systems and the ability to communicate the messages and intentions meaningful in both systems.

Black English. *See* African-American Vernacular English

Black language. *See* African-American Vernacular English

Bound morpheme: a morpheme that cannot stand alone (e.g., *-ful*, *pre-*, *-s*).

CALLA (Cognitive Academic Language Learning Approach): an instructional model developed by Chamot and O'Malley (1994) for content and language learning that incorporates student development of learning strategies.

CALP (Cognitive Academic Language Proficiency): language proficiency associated with schooling and the abstract language abilities required for academic work.

Choral reading: students reading aloud together in a group.

Circumstantial bilingualism: learning a second language when it is essential due to circumstances pertaining to group membership outside the learner's control (e.g., movement of peoples, conquest, colonization, immigration).

Clause: a syntactic unit that has a subject and verb but may or may not stand alone as a sentence.

Code-based: (in literacy instruction) focused on the nature of the alphabetic code—that is, how sounds of the language are represented by letters and letter combinations.

Code-switching: the practice of moving back and forth between two or more languages in a single conversational event.

Cognitive: pertaining to cognition (mental processes entailed in learning and knowing).

Collectivistic: pertaining to a value system that emphasizes the group over the individual.

Common underlying proficiency: the foundational linguistic knowledge and skills on which a learner can draw to learn a new language (Cummins, 1984). Once a learner has acquired one language, he or she does not start from scratch but has a basis (common underlying proficiency) for learning any additional language.

Communication: the transfer of information from one person (or animal) to another, entailing both transmission and reception.

Communicative competence: the ability to use all linguistic systems to effectively exchange information with another.

Comprehensible input: understandable messages through which students are better able to acquire language. According to Krashen (1982), such input ensures that the learner understands the communication.

Comprehension: (in literacy) the process of making sense of what one reads or hears, constructing understanding on the basis of old and new information.

Construct validity: the degree to which a test actually evaluates what it purports to evaluate (e.g., that a math test evaluates math skills and knowledge and does not rely so heavily on reading skill as to become a test of reading proficiency).

Constructivism: a philosophy or theory that holds that knowledge is not objective or neutral but actively constructed by a learner on the basis of what he or she already knows.

Content area assessment: assessment focused on subject matter such as history social studies, language arts, mathematics, or science.

Content-obligatory: pertaining to the specialized core skills and knowledge associated with a particular content area.

Content validity: the degree to which a test's items adequately represent the content area being tested (math, reading, and so forth).

Contextualized: surrounded by meaningful information.

Contrastive analysis: a method by which two languages are compared to discover in what respects they are similar and in what respects they differ.

Creole: a language developed from a pidgin, which becomes the native language of children in a speech community.

Criterion-referenced: (in tests) scored on the basis of actual performance against specified standards, rather than relative to how others perform (norm-referenced).

Critical literacy: the ability to use language in all of its forms as a tool for thinking and communicating; the ability to identify hidden meanings and biases in written texts and other media.

Critical period: the time between early childhood and puberty during which a child can acquire language easily, swiftly, and without external intervention.

Culture: a system of values and practices associated with a group, passed from generation to generation but modified in interaction with the social, physical, and historical environment.

Decoding: using knowledge of the alphabetic code to translate a string of letters into a pronounceable word.

Decontextualized: having little or no supporting context (in the physical or linguistic setting) language between people who do not share a social context; (in written text) requiring the reader to supply background knowledge in order to comprehend.

Dependent clause: a clause that cannot stand alone as a sentence (e.g., *in order that she get well, because koalas cannot live without eucalyptus, when the sun was setting*).

Dialect: a regional or social variety of a language, entailing distinctive pronunciation, vocabulary, syntax, and discourse conventions.

Discourse: a stretch of language (oral or written) consisting of two or more sentences.

Discourse convention: an accepted way of engaging in stretches of spoken or written language (conversation, speech, text), variable according to culture or speech community.

Discourse structure: an organizational pattern of stretches of spoken or written language, such as the turn-taking pattern in conversation or the episodic structure of narrative.

Dominant culture: in the United States, the culture based on Western European values and history.

Ebonics: another term for African-American Vernacular English (AAVE); a method of teaching language arts that draws upon AAVE.

ELL (English language learner): a person who is learning English as a second or third language.

Ellipsis: the omission of part of a sentence without jeopardizing comprehensibility (*Where are you going? Memphis* [elliptical response]).

Ethnicity: membership in or identification with a group with a common history, culture, and often language and religion.

Ethnography: the study of a group or culture.

Ethnolinguistic group: a group sharing a common linguistic and cultural history.

Expansion: a response to the utterance of a language-acquiring child that enlarges or extends the child's expression.

Fast-mapping: a strategy used by a child learning a language to connect a word with its referent after only one exposure.

Formalist theory: a theory of language acquisition that holds that there is a singular mechanism and a set of parameters—that is, an underlying abstract structure of language—that children must acquire (*see* Functionalist theory).

Fossilization: a characteristic of second-language learning in which the learner reaches a plateau and seems unable to acquire some aspects of the second language.

Function word (also **functor**): a word that serves a grammatical purpose but has little independent meaning (e.g., *for*, *the*, *a*, *also*).

Functionalist theory: a theory of language acquisition that differentiates the sequence and timing of simultaneous and sequential second-language acquisition because social interaction and previous knowledge play such a major role.

Generativity: (in language) the quality of being able to generate an infinite number of sentences on the basis of a finite number of linguistic rules and morphemes.

Grammar: the set of rules governing language in general or a particular language; the syntax and morphology of a language.

Heuristic: serving as a tool to stimulate thinking to help one understand a concept or approximate a solution to a problem; the method or tool itself.

Holophrase: an utterance composed of a single word, which could stand for a whole sentence.

Iconic: the form of a thing represented (e.g., drawing a circle in the air to represent a ring).

Iconicity: the feature of being iconic.

Immersion: a teaching approach for limited-English proficient students that does not involve using a student's native language. Immersion bilingual education programs have bilingualism as their goal and may vary the amount of time spent in immersion during a day, such as total immersion with 100% involvement in the second language, or partial immersion, with 50% involvement in the second language.

Independent clause: a clause that can stand alone as a sentence (e.g., *David slew Goliath*).

Indirect speech: speech in which much of the message is left implicit rather than overtly expressed.

Individualistic: pertaining to a value system that emphasizes the individual over the group.

Innateness hypothesis: a theory that the human species is genetically equipped with a universal grammar (*see entry*) that provides the basic design for all human languages.

Interlanguage: a transitional system in which a person uses rules from two or more languages simultaneously.

Kinesic: pertaining to movement or gesture to communicate meaning; pertaining to a system of representation based on movement and gesture.

Language: the primary means of human communication; the most widely used system for representing thought.

LAD (Language Acquisition Device): a term coined by Noam Chomsky to refer to an innate or inborn language acquisition mechanism.

Language experience method: an approach to teaching literacy skills in which students write or dictate their own stories or expository texts and read them back, often with the aid of a teacher or parent.

Language variety: *See* Dialect, Register.

LEP (limited English proficient): a term often used in legal documents to refer to students who are learning English, but not preferred by educators because of its negative connotation.

Lexicographer: one who composes a dictionary.

Literacy: proficiency with reading and writing; proficiency with the full range of oral and written language forms and purposes valued by one's society.

Logogram (also **logograph**): a written symbol representing a morpheme or word.

Media literacy: proficiency with critical analysis of messages associated with written language, television, film, and other means of communication.

Mediate: to intervene so as to influence the outcome of some process.

Metacognitive: pertaining to the ability to examine and guide one's own cognitive processes.

Metalinguistic: pertaining to the language of language (metalanguage); having to do with the ability to regard language as an object, to remove oneself from the automatic use of language.

Modality: one of the primary forms of sensation—touch, vision, taste, smell, hearing.

Monitor: a construct developed to refer to the mechanism by which learners of a second language process, store, and retrieve conscious language rules.

Morpheme: the smallest unit of language that bears grammatical or semantic information.

Morphology: the study of word structure, related to morphemes, not phonemes.

Morphophonemic: pertaining to the interaction between morphemic structure and phonological (sound) structure of a word, e.g., electric/electricity, legal/legalistic, mendacity/mendacions.

Motherese: the language used by an infant's mother or other caretaker that is systematically modified; characterized by short utterance length and simple syntax.

Multi-intelligence assessment: an assessment that does not rely only on paper and pencil skills or language, for example, but draws upon many facets of intelligence (such as visuo-spatial, logico-mathematical, interpersonal).

Multi-morphemic: composed of more than one morpheme (e.g., *blueberry* = two unbound morphemes; *tasteful* = one unbound and one bound morpheme; *distasteful* = two bound morphemes and one unbound morpheme)

Narrative: a story (true or fictional); pertaining to a story or the art of storytelling.

Nativist theory: a theory that asserts that at least some aspects of language are innate.

Nativization: a second-language learner's internal processing, entailing assimilation and accommodation. The learner simplifies the learning task by forming hypotheses based on innate, language-specific knowledge and adjusts the internalized system to fit the input.

Natural approach: a method for fostering second-language acquisition that focuses on teaching communicative skills, both oral and written.

Natural order hypothesis: a theory (from Krashen) that holds that grammatical structures will be acquired by learners in a predictable order.

Negro nonstandard dialect. *See* African-American Vernacular English

Neonate: a newborn.

Neurofunctional theory: a theory of second-language acquisition that asserts a connection between language function and neural anatomy. Some parts of the brain contribute more to language function than others.

Nonliteracy: a term preferred by members of some oral cultures to mean a consciously chosen lack of literacy.

Norm-referenced: (in tests) scored on the basis of statistics, relative to how a large (norm) group has scored previously on the same test.

Oral tradition: the handing down of customs, beliefs, and practices from generation to generation by word of mouth.

Orthography: the study of the spelling rules or patterns of a language; the spelling system of a language.

Overextension: the use of a word for a class of referents, some of which are outside adult categories, such as *doggie* as a reference to any four-legged animal.

Paralinguistic variation: a change in pitch, volume, rhythm, and/or timing of speech.

Paraphrase: restatement of a spoken or written passage; to restate a passage.

Passive: the grammatical form (voice) in which the direct object of a sentence becomes the subject (*Vicki was kissed by Dan*, versus the active voice, *Dan kissed Vicki*.)

Patois: a rural or provincial dialect, sometimes specifically a French rural dialect.

Peer-oriented: pertaining to a culture-based tendency for children to attend to the behaviors, needs, and language of their peer group or to instruction that fosters interaction among students rather than between teacher and student.

Performance assessment: a measure of educational achievement in which students produce a response, create a product, or apply knowledge in ways similar to instructional tasks; analysis and interpretation according to preset criteria.

Phoneme: the smallest unit of sound in a language that makes a difference to meaning (e.g., the difference between /b/ and /p/ but not between the /b/ at the beginning of *bib* and the /b/ at the end of *bib*, even though they are pronounced differently).

Phonetics: the science of speech sounds, addressing how they are produced and perceived.

Phonics: a method of teaching reading that focuses on sound-letter relationships; the skills and knowledge associated with how letters represent sounds.

Phonology: the branch of linguistics concerned with the study of the sound systems (patterns) of language.

Phrase: a group of words modifying another sentence element.

Pidgin: the reduced language system that develops when groups who speak different languages need to communicate on a continuing basis.

Portfolio: an assessment tool; typically a collection of student work in one or more subject areas, selected by teacher and student to illustrate progress vis-à-vis designated standards.

Pragmatics: the branch of linguistics concerned with how language is used in social interactions to accomplish different goals.

Prompt: the portion of a test item that poses a question or instructs the student on what to do.

Prosody: the pitch, loudness, and rhythm of speech.

Proto-conversation: the response of children at around 3 months of age that seems to reflect a communicative intention.

Psycholinguistic: pertaining to the mental processes associated with learning or using language.

Psychometrician: a professional designer of tests related to intelligence or learning.

Race: a socially constructed category based on perceived physical differences between groups of people.

Rapid automatized naming: the process of labeling, without any apparent hesitation, familiar pictures or symbols (letters, numbers) presented visually.

Ratify: (in linguistic terms) to acknowledge, in positive terms, what someone has said in a conversation, either by nonverbal vocalization or actual words.

Raven's Progressive Matrices: a test used to evaluate visual reasoning skills.

Recitation script: the common classroom discourse pattern in which the teacher initiates a question, a student responds to it, and the teacher evaluates the student's response.

Register: a variety of speech (formal or informal) associated with a particular social context or group (e.g., religions; doctor-patient; legal).

Representational: standing for something else, as in the sensorimotor, kinesic, and linguistic systems of representation.

Rule-governed: systematic, not random.

Scaffolding: the process of support offered by a teacher in order to move a student toward a more advanced skill or cognitive process by presenting information that is just above the student's proficiency level.

Script: a basic pattern for a familiar event, such as going to the park.

SDAIE (Specially Designed Academic Instruction in English): an instructional method used to provide limited-English-proficient students with content instruction in the core curriculum while developing their English language. The term was coined in California in conjunction with setting standards for teachers of ELLs..

Second-order symbolism: a representation of a primary form of representation, such as written language in relation to oral language.

Semantic bootstrapping hypothesis: a theory that children develop understanding of grammatical categories before they have labels for them.

Semantic map: a graphic organizer used in teaching vocabulary or relationships among concepts.

Semantics: the branch of linguistics concerned with the study of meaning.

Semiotics: the study of signs or representational systems.

Sensorimotor: the representational system through which we have mental images of physical objects and how they can be expected to behave under certain circumstances; the earliest stage of cognitive development, according to Piaget, in which young children build up mental images of how objects and people operate in the physical world.

Sentence: a syntactic unit consisting at minimum of a subject (or noun phrase) and predicate (or verb phrase).

Sign: a unit of the manual language of the deaf that may be equivalent to a word, phrase, or sentence; an element of language or behavior that conveys meaning (a word is a special form of sign called a *symbol*).

Signifying: an African-American oral language game in which speakers engage in ritual insult and language play.

Slang: the jargon of a social group, frequently changing.

Social: pertaining to humans or animals living in a community.

Sociocultural: pertaining to the interaction of social (interpersonal or group) and cultural (values and practices guiding daily life) factors.

Sociolinguistics: the study of language in society, or the interaction of social factors with linguistic usage.

Standard English: the privileged dialect of English, the dialect spoken by the dominant cultural group (variable, depending upon the English-speaking nation concerned).

Standards-based: linked to explicit statements of expected performance.

Story grammar: the structure of narrative, commonly entailing a series of episodes and often a problem and its solution.

Submersion program: an organized curriculum designed for native speakers of a language but often used with language-minority students in which there is no special instructional approach focused on the needs of language minority students.

Subtractive bilingualism: learning a new language at the expense of the first or native language.

Syllable: a unit of language consisting of a vowel or a set of sounds with a single vowel center, which may or may not be a morpheme (e.g., *oh*, *-o* [as in *okay*], *slow*).

Symbol: a sign that has an arbitrary relationship with the thing to which it refers (e.g., a word other than a sound that imitates what the word stands for); a character or set of characters used to represent something, such as a letter that stands for one or more sounds, or the numerals 2 and 4, which combined as 24 stand for a particular quantity.

Syntax: the branch of linguistics concerned with the study of word combinations and sentence structure.

Text structure: the organizational pattern of an oral or written text.

TPR (Total Physical Response): an approach to teaching a second language that emphasizes the use of physical activity for increasing meaningful learning opportunities. It involves a set of actions performed by students in response to a set of commands given by the teacher.

Transfer: (in language) the application of rules from one's first language to a second language that one is attempting to acquire.

Unbound morpheme: a morpheme that can function alone as a word (a "free" morpheme), e.g., hot, table, green, with.

Universal grammar: the innate principles and properties that pertain to the grammars of all human languages.

Whole language: a whole-to-part approach to literacy instruction in which meaning-making is central, and skills are typically taught within a meaningful context (such as reading literature or writing one's own stories)

Word: an unbound morpheme; the smallest grammatical unit of language that can stand as a complete utterance; in written English, separated from other words by a space.

Zone of proximal development: the difference between the developmental level at which a learner can complete a task independently and the level at which he or she can complete it with the support of a more competent other, such as a teacher (Vygotsky, 1978).

References

Abedi, J. (2003). *Impact of students' language background on content-based performance: Analyses of extant data*. (CSE Technical Report No. 603). Los Angeles: University of California, Center for the Study of Evaluation/National Center for Research on Evaluation, Standards, and Student Testing.

Abedi, J., Lord, C., Hofstetter, C., & Baker, E. (2000). Impact of accommodation strategies on English language learners' test performance. *Educational Measurement: Issues and Practice, 19* (3), 16–26.

Abedi, J., Lord, C., & Plummer, J. R. (1997). *Final report of language background as a variable in NAEP mathematics performance*. (CSE Technical Report No. 429). Los Angeles: University of California, Center for the Study of Evaluation/National Center for Research on Evaluation, Standards, and Student Testing.

Adams, B. C., Bell, L. C., & Perfetti, C. A. (1995). A trading relationship between reading skill and domain knowledge in childrens' test performance. *Discourse Processess, 20*, 307–323.

Adams, M. (1990). *Beginning to read: Thinking and learning about print*. Cambridge, MA: MIT Press.

Adams, M. J., Foorman, B. R., Lundberg, I., & Beeler, T. (1998). *Phonemic awareness in young children*. Baltimore: Brookes.

Adger, C. T., Snow, C., & Christian, D. (2002). *What teachers need to know about language*. Washington, DC: Center for Applied Linguistics.

Aiken, L.R. (1971). Verbal factors and mathematics learning: A review of research. *Journal for Research in Mathematics Education, 2*, 304–313.

Albert, M. L., & Obler, L. K. (1978). The bilingual brain: Cerebral representation of languages. *Brain and Language, 79*, 211–222.

Alleyne, M. (1971). Linguistic continuity of Africa in the Caribbean. In R. J. Henry (Ed.), *Topics in Afro-American studies*. New York: Black Academy Press.

Allington, R. L. (2001a). Research on reading/learning disability interventions. In S. J. Samuels & A. Farstrup (Eds.), *What research says about reading instruction*. Newark, DE: International Reading Association.

Allington, R. L. (2001b). *What really matters for struggling readers: Designing research-based programs*. New York: Longman.

Allington, R. L., & Woodside-Jiron, H. (1999). The politics of literacy teaching: How "research" shaped educational policy. *Educational Researcher, 28* (8), 4–12.

American Educational Research Association, American Psychological Association, & National Council on Measurement in Education (1999). *Standards for educational and psychological testing*. Washington, DC: Authors.

American Speech-Language Hearing Association (ASHA). (1983). Position paper on social dialects. *ASHA, 25* (9), 23–24.

American Speech-Language Hearing Association (ASHA). (1993). Definitions of communication disorders and variations. *ASHA, 35* (10), 40–41.

Anderson, J. R., Greeno, J. G., Reder, L. M., & Simon, H. A. (2000). Perspectives on learning, thinking and activity. *Educational Researcher, 29* (4), 11–13.

Anderson, J. R., Reder, L. M., & Simon, H. A. (n.d.). Applications and misapplications of cognitive psychology to mathematics education [Online.] Available: http://act-r.psy.cmu.edu/papers/misapplied.html.

Anderson, R. (1983). Introduction: A language acquisition interpretation of pidginization and creolization. *Pidginization and creolization as language acquisition.* Rowley, MA: Newbury House.

Anderson, R. C., & Pearson, P. D. (1984). A schema-theoretic view of basic processes in reading. In P. D. Pearson (Ed.), *Handbook of reading research* (vol. 1, pp, 255–291.) White Plains. NY: Longman.

Anderson, V. (1992). A teacher development project in transactional strategy instruction for teachers of severely reading-disabled adolescents. *Teaching and Teacher Education, 8,* 391–403.

Anderson, V., & Roit, M. (1996). Linking reading comprehension instruction to language development for language-minority students. *Elementary School Journal, 96* (3), 295–309.

Aram, D., Ekelman, B., & Nation, J. (1984). Preschoolers with language disorders: Ten years later. *Journal of Speech and Hearing Research, 27,* 232–244.

Au, K., & Jordan, C. (1981a). Teaching reading to Hawaiian children: Analysis of a culturally appropriate instructional event. *Anthropology and Education Quarterly, 11,* 91–115.

Au, K., & Jordan, C. (1981b). Teaching reading to Hawaiian children: Finding a culturally appropriate solution. In H. Trueba, G. P. Guthrie, & K. H. Su (Eds.), *Culture in the bilingual classroom: Studies in classroom ethnography* (pp. 139–152). Rowley, MA: Newbury House.

August, D., Calderón, M., & Carlo, M. (2002). *Transfer of skills from Spanish to English: A study of young learners.* Report for practitioners, parents, and policy makers. Washington, DC: Center for Applied Linguistics.

August, D., & Hakuta, K. (1993). *Federal education programs for limited-English-proficient students: A blueprint for the second generation.* Stanford, CA: Stanford Working Group.

August, D., & Hakuta, K., (Eds.). (1997). *Improving schooling for language-minority children: A research agenda.* Washington, DC: National Academy Press.

Azuma, H. (1991). Continuities and discontinuities in the cognitive socialization of minority children. In P. M. Greenfield & R. R. Cocking (Eds.), *Proceedings of a workshop.* Washington, DC: Department of Health and Human Services.

Bachman, L. (1990a). Assessment and evaluation. *Annual Review of Applied Linguistics, 10,* 210–226.

Bachman, L. (1990b). *Fundamental considerations in language testing.* Oxford, UK: Oxford University Press.

Bachman, L., & Palmer, A. S. (1982). The construct validation of some components of communicative proficiency. *TESOL Quarterly, 16* (4), 449–465.

Ball, A. (1997). Expanding the dialogue on culture as a critical component when assessing writing. *Assessing Writing, 4* (2), 169–202.

Bambara, T. C. (1998). My man Bovanne. In T. McMillan (Ed.). *Breaking ice: An anthology of contemporary Afro-American fiction* (pp. 33–38). New York: Penguin.

Banks, J. A. (1988). *Multiethnic education: Theory and practice.* Boston: Allyn & Bacon.

Barnhardt, C. (1982). Tuning-in: Athabaskan teachers and Athabaskan students. In R. Barnhardt (Ed.), *Cross-cultural issues in Alaskan education* (Vol. 2). Fairbanks, AK: University of Alaska, Centers for Cross-Cultural Studies.

Barrett, M. (Ed.). (1999). *The development of language.* Fairbanks, East Sussex, UK: Psychology Press.

Barthes, R. (1982). *Empire of signs* (R. Howard, Trans.). New York: Hill and Wang.

Bartlett, F. C. (1932). *Remembering.* Cambridge, UK: Cambridge University Press.

Bates, E., Bretherton, I., & Snyder, L. (1988). *From first words to grammar: Individual differences and dissociable mechanisms.* New York: Cambridge University Press.

Bates, E. & Goodman, J. (1999). On the emergence of grammar from the lexicon. In B. MacWhinney (Ed.), *The emergence of language* (pp. 29–79). Mahwah, NJ: Erlbaum.

Baugh, J. (1994). New and prevailing misconceptions of African American English for logic and mathematics. In E. Hollins, J. King, & W. Hayman (Eds.), *Teaching diverse populations* (pp. 191–205). Albany, NY: SUNY Press.

Baumann, J., Jones, L., & Seifert-Kessell, N. (1993). Using think-alouds to enhance children's comprehension monitoring abilities. *The Reading Teacher, 47* (3), 184–193.

Beaumont, C., de Valenzuela, J., & Trumbull, E. (2002). Alternative assessment for transitional readers. *Bilingual Research Journal, 26* (2), 241–268.

Becijos, J. (1997). *SDAIE: Strategies for teachers of English language learners.* Bonita, CA: Torch.

Beck, I., & McKeown, M. (1991). Conditions of vocabulary acquisition. In R. Barr, M. I. Kamil, P. Mosenthal, & P. D. Pearson (Eds.), *Handbook of reading research* (Vol. 2, pp. 789–814). White Plains. NY: Longman.

Beck, I., McKeown, M. G., & Kucan, L. (2002). *Bringing words to life.* New York: Guilford Press.

Beck, I., Perfetti, C. A., & McKeown, M. G. (1982). Effects of long-term vocabulary instruction on lexical access and reading comprehension. *Journal of Educational Psychology, 74,* 506–521.

Beebe, L. M. (1988). Five sociolinguistic approaches to second language acquisition. In L. M. Beek (Ed.), *Issues in second language acquisition: Multiple perspectives* (pp. 43–77). Rowley, MA: Newbury House.

Beers, J. W., & Henderson, E. H. (1977). A study of developing orthographic concepts among first graders. *Research in the Teaching of English, 11*, 133–148.

Bennett, A., & Slaughter, H. (1983). A sociolinguistic/discourse approach to the description of the communicative competence of linguistic minority children. In C. Rivera (Ed.), *An ethnographic sociolinguistic approach to language proficiency assessment* (pp. 2–26). Clevedon, UK: Multilingual Matters.

Ben-Zeev, S. (1977). The influence of bilingualism on cognitive strategy and cognitive development. *Child Development, 48*, 1009–1018.

Berdiansky, B., Cronnell, B., & Koehler, J. (1969). *Spelling-sound relations and primary form-class descriptions for speech-comprehension vocabularies of 6–9-year-olds* (Technical Report No. 15). Austin, TX: Southwest Educational Regional Development Laboratory.

Berko, J. (1958). The child's learning of English morphology. *Word, 14*, 150–177.

Berman, P., Chambers, J., Gandara, P., McLaughlin, B., Minicucci, C., Nelson, B., Olsen, L., & Parrish, T. (1992). *Meeting the challenge of language diversity: An evaluation of programs for pupils with limited proficiency in English.* Berkeley, CA: BW Associates.

Bernstein, D. K., & Tiegerman-Farber, E. (2002). *Language and communication disorders in children.* Boston: Allyn & Bacon.

Bialystok, E. (1988). Levels of bilingualism and levels of linguistic awareness. *Developmental Psychology, 24*, 560–567.

Bialystok, E. (1991). Metalinguistic dimensions of bilingual language proficiency. In *Language processing in bilingual children* (pp. 113–140). Cambridge, UK: Cambridge University Press.

Bialystok, E. (1997). Effects of bilingualism and biliteracy on children's emerging concepts of print. *Developmental Psychology, 33*, 429–440.

Bialystok, E. (2001). *Bilingualism in development: Language, literacy, and cognition.* New York: Cambridge University Press.

Bialystok, E., & Hakuta, K. (1994). *In other words: The science and psychology of second-language acquisition.* New York: Basic Books.

Bickerton, D. (1995). *Language and human behavior.* Seattle, WA: University of Washington Press.

Biemiller, A. (1977–78). Relationships between oral reading rates for letters, words, and simple text in the development of reading achievement. *Reading Research Quarterly, 13*, 223–253.

Biemiller, A. (2001). Teaching vocabulary: Early, direct, and sequential. *American Educator, 25*, 24–28, 47.

Birdsong, D. (1989). *Metalinguistic performance in interlinguistic competence.* New York: Springer-Verlag.

Bissex, G. L. (1980). *GNYS AT WRK: A child learns to read and write.* Cambridge, MA: Harvard University Press.

Blachman, B. (1983). On the interaction between phonological awareness and reading acquisition: It's a two-way street. *Annals of Dyslexia, 43*, 125–148.

Blachowitz, C. Z., & Fisher, P. (2004). Vocabulary lessons. *Educational Leadership*, *61* (6), 60–69.

Bley-Vroman, R. (1989). What is the logical problem of second language learning? In S. Gass & J. Schachter (Eds.), *Linguistic perspectives on second language acquisition* (pp. 41–68). Cambridge, UK: Cambridge University Press.

Bloom, L. (1970). *Language Development: Form and Function in Emerging Grammars*. Cambridge, MA: MIT, Press.

Bloome, D., Champion, T., Katz, L., Morton, M., & Muldrow, R. (2000). Spoken and written narrative development: African American preschoolers as storytellers and storymakers. In J. E. Harris, A. G. Kamhi, & K. E. Pollock (Eds.), *Literacy in African American communities* (pp. 45–75). Mahwah, NJ: Erlbaum.

Bloomfield, L. (1933). *Language*. New York: Holt.

Bohannon, J. N. III, & Warren-Leubecker, A. (1985). Theoretical approaches to language acquisition. In J. B. Gleason (Ed.), *The development of language* (pp. 174–226). Columbus, OH: Merrill.

Bourdieu, P., & Passeron, J. C. (1977). *Reproduction in education, society and culture*. Beverly Hills, CA: Sage.

Bowerman, M. (1974). Discussion summary: Development of concepts underlying language. In R. Schiefelbusch & L. Lloyd (Eds.), *Language perspectives: Acquisition, retardation, and intervention*. Baltimore: University Park Press.

Bowerman, M. (2000). Where do children's word meanings come from? Rethinking the role of cognition in early semantic development. In L. P. Nucci, G. B. Saxe, & E. Turiel (Eds.), *Culture, thought, and development* (pp. 199–230). Mahwah, NJ: Erlbaum.

Bowers, P. G. (1995). Tracing symbol naming speed's unique contributions to reading disabilities over time. *Reading and Writing: An Interdisciplinary Journal*, *7*, 189–216.

Bowey, J. A. (1986). Syntactic awareness in relation to reading skill and ongoing reading comprehension monitoring. *Journal of Experimental Child Psychology*, *41*, 282–299.

Bowey, J. A., & Tunmer, W. E. (1984). Word awareness in children. In W. E. Tunmer (Ed.), *Metalinguistic awareness in children: Theory, research and implications* (pp. 73–92). New York: Springer.

Bowman, C. (2000). Creating connection: Challenging the text and student writers. *English Journal*, *89* (4), 78–84.

Bradley, L., & Bryant, P. (1985). *Rhyme and reason in reading and spelling*. (International Academy for Research in Learning Disability Monograph Series, No. 1). Ann Arbor, MI: University of Michigan Press.

Branch, C. (1999). Racial identity and human development. In R. H. Sheets & E. R. Hollins (Eds.), *Racial and ethnic identity in school practices: Aspects of human development* (pp. 7–28). Mahwah, NJ: Erlbaum.

Bransford, J. D., Brown, A. L., & Cocking, R. R. (Eds.). (2000). *How people learn: Brain, mind, experience and school*. Washington, DC: National Academy Press.

Braunger, J., & Lewis, J. (1998). *Building a knowledge base in reading.* Newark, DE: International Reading Association.

Bredecamp, S. A. (n.d.). Commentary on "What teachers need to know about language." Washington, DC: Center for Applied Linguistics.

Briggs, P., Austin, S., & Underwood, G. (1984). The effects of sentence context in good and poor readers: A test of Stanovich's interactive-compensatory model. *Reading Research Quarterly, 20,* 54–61.

Brown, R. (1973). *A first language: The early stages.* Cambridge, MA: Harvard University Press.

Brown, D. (1987). *Principles of language learning and teaching* (2nd ed.). Englewood Cliffs, NJ: Prentice-Hall.

Brown, R., & Hanlon, C. (1970). Derivational complexity and the order of acquisition in child speech. In J. Hayes (Ed.), *Cognition and the development of language* (pp. 155–207). New York: Wiley.

Brown, R., Pressley, M., Van Meter, P., & Schuder, T. (1996). A quasi-experimental validation of transactional strategies instruction with low-achieving second grade readers. *Journal of Educational Psychology, 88,* 18–37.

Bruck, M. (1985). The adult functioning of children with specific learning disabilities. In I. Siegel (Ed.), *Advances in applied developmental psychology* (pp. 91–129). Norwood, NJ: Ablex.

Bruck, M., & Treiman, R. (1992). Learning to pronounce words: The limitations of analogies. *Reading Research Quarterly, 27,* 375–388.

Bruer, J. T. (1999). Education and the brain: A bridge too far. *Educational Researcher, 26* (8), 4–16.

Brumfit, C. (1997). The teacher as educational linguist. In L. van Lier & D. Corson (Eds.), *Encyclopedia of language and education*: Vol. 6. *Knowledge about language* (pp. 163–172). Dordrecht, Netherlands: Kluwer.

Bruner, J. (1966). *Toward a theory of instruction.* Cambridge, MA: Harvard University Press.

Bruner, J. (1973). *Going beyond the information given.* New York: Norton.

Bruner, J. (1977). *The process of education.* Cambridge, MA: Harvard University Press.

Bruner, J. (1985). Vygotsky: A historical and conceptual perspective. In J. Wertsch (Ed.), *Culture, communication, and cognition: Vygotskian perspectives.* Cambridge, UK: Cambridge University Press.

Bruner, J. (1986). *Actual minds, possible worlds.* Cambridge, MA: Harvard University Press.

Bruner, J. (1996). *The culture of education.* Cambridge, MA: Harvard University Press.

Bruner, J., & Sherwood, V. (1976). Peekaboo and the learning of rule structures. In J. S. Bruner, A. Jolly, & K. Sylva (Eds.), *Play: Its role in development and evolution* (pp. 277–285). Harmondsworth, UK: Penguin Books.

Bus, M. H., van IJzendoorn, M. H, & Pellegrini, A. D. (1995). Joint book reading makes for success in learning to read: A meta-analysis on intergenerational transmission of literacy. *Review of Educational Research, 65* (1), 1–21.

Butler, F. A., & Bailey, A. L (2002). Equity in the assessment of English language learners K–12, *Idiom* [New York State TESOL newsletter], *32*, 1.

Cairns, H. S. (1986). *The acquisition of language*. Austin, TX: Pro-Ed.

Calderón, M.E., Hertz-Lazarowitz, R., & Slavin, R. (1998). Effects of bilingual cooperative integrated reading and composition on students making the transition from Spanish to English reading. *Elementary School Journal, 99* (2), 153–164.

Calero-Breckheimer, A., & Goetz, E. T. (1993). Reading strategies of biliterate children for English and Spanish texts. *Reading Psychology, 14*, (3), 177–204.

Calfee, R. C. (1988). *The book*. Unpublished manual for Project READ, Stanford University, Stanford, CA.

Calfee, R., & Curley, R. (1984). Structures of prose in the content areas. In J. Flood (Ed.), *Understanding reading comprehension: Cognition, language, and the structure of prose* (pp. 161–180). Newark, DE: International Reading Association.

Calfee, R., & Nelson-Barber, S. (1991). Diversity and constancy in human thinking: Critical literacy as amplifier of intellect and experience. In E. Hiebert, *Literacy for a diverse society: Perspectives, practices, and procedures* (pp. 44–57). New York: Teachers College Press.

Calkins, L. (1994). *The art of teaching writing*. Portsmouth, NH: Heinemann.

Cambourne, B. (1988). *The whole story: Natural learning and the acquisition of literacy in the classroom*. Auckland, New Zealand: Ashton Scholastic.

Canale, M. (1983). From communicative competence to communicative language pedagogy. In J. C. Richards & R. Schmidt (Eds.), *Language and communication* (pp. 2–27). London: Longman.

Canale, M., & Swain, M. (1980). Theoretical bases of communicative approaches to second language teaching and testing. *Applied Linguistics, 1* (1), 1–47.

Carlisle, J. F. (1987). The use of morphological knowledge in spelling derived forms by learning disabled and normal students. *Annals of Dyslexia, 37*, 90–108.

Carlo, M. S., August, D., McLaughlin, B., Snow, C. E., Dressler, C., Lippman, D.N., Lively, T.J., & White, C. E. (2004). Closing the gap: Addressing the vocabulary needs of English-language learners in bilingual and mainstream classrooms. *Reading Research Quarterly, 39* (2), 188–215.

Carney, E. (1998). English spelling is kattastroffik. In L. Bauer & P. Trudgill (Eds.), *Language myths* (pp. 32–40). London: Penguin Books.

Carr, J. (2002). *The map of standards for English learners*. San Francisco: WestEd.

Carroll, J. B. (1971), Current issues in psycholinguistics and second language teaching. *TESOL Quarterly, 5*, 101–114.

Carroll, J. (1974). *Research in language comprehension*. Paper presented at the Interdisciplinary Institute on Child Development and Reading, Newark, DE.

Carroll, J. B. (1981). Conscious and automatic processes in language learning. *Canadian Modern Language Review, 37* (3), pp 462–474.

Carroll, J. B., & Sapon, S. M. (1959). *Modern language aptitude est*. New York: Psychological Corporation.

Carroll, J. B., & Sapon, S. M. (1967). *Elementary Modern Language Aptitude Test*. New York: Psychological Corporation.

Caspe, M. (2003). Family literacy: A review of programs and critical perspectives [Online]. Available: www.gse.harvard.edu/hfrp/projects/fine/resources/research/literacy.html

Catts, H. W., & Kamhi, A. G. (1999). *Language and reading disabilities*. Needham Heights, MA: Allyn & Bacon.

Cazden, C. B. (1968). The acquisition of noun and verb inflections. *Child Development, 39*, 433–448.

Cazden, C. (1974). Play with language and metalinguistic awareness: One dimension of language experience. *Urban Review, 1*, 28–39.

Cazden, C. B. (1988). *Classroom discourse: The language of teaching and learning*. Portsmouth, NH: Heinemann.

Chafe, W. (1985). Linguistic differences produced by differences between speaking and writing. In D. R. Olson, N. Torrance, & A. Hildyard (Eds.), *Literacy, language, and learning: The nature and consequences of reading and writing* (pp. 105–123). Cambridge, UK: Cambridge University Press.

Chaika, E. (1982). How shall a discourse be understood? *Discourse Processes, 4* (1), 71–88.

Chall, J. S. (1983). *Stages of reading development*. New York: McGraw-Hill.

Chamot, A.U. (1994). A model for learning strategy instruction in the foreign language classroom. In J. E. Alatis (Ed.), *Georgetown University round table on languages and linguistics* (pp. 323–336). Washington, DC: Georgetown University Press.

Chamot, A. U., Barnhardt, S., El-Dinary, P. B., & Robbins, J. (1999). *The learning strategies handbook*. White Plains, NY: Longman/Pearson.

Chamot, A. U., & O'Malley, J. M. (1994). *The CALLA handbook: Implementing the cognitive academic language learning approach*. Reading, MA: Addison-Wesley.

Chaney, C. (1994). Language development, metalinguistic awareness, and emergent literacy of 3-year-old children in relation to social class. *Applied Psycholinguistics, 15* (4), 371–394.

Chastain, K. (1975). Affective and ability factors in second language acquisition. *Language Learning, 25*, 153–161.

Chen, Y. P., & Allport, A. (1995). Attention and lexical decomposition in Chinese word recognition: Conjunctions of form and position guide selective attention. *Visual Cognition, 2* (2/3), 235–268.

Chesterfield, R., & Chesterfield, K. (1985). Natural order in children's use of second language learning strategies. *Applied Linguistics, 6*, 45–59.

Chomsky, N. (1959). A review of B. F. Skinner's *Verbal Behavior. Language, 25*, pp. 26–58.

Chomsky, N. (1965). *Aspects of the theory of syntax*. Cambridge, MA: MIT Press.

Chomsky, N. (1972). *Language and mind*. New York: Harcourt Brace Jovanovich.

Chomsky, N. (1975). *Reflections on language*. New York: Pantheon.

Chomsky, N. (1988). *Language and problems of knowledge: The Managua lectures*. Cambridge, MA: MIT Press.

Chomsky, N. (1993). *Language and thought*. Wakefield, RI: Moyer Bell.

Chomsky, N., & Halle, M. (1968). *The sound patterns of English*. New York: Harper & Row.

Christian, C. C. (1972). Language functions in the maintenance of socioeconomic hierarchies. In R. W. Ewton, Jr., & J. Ornstein (Eds.), *Studies in language & linguistics, 1972–1973* (pp. 181–191). El Paso: Texas Western Press.

Christian, D. (1987). Vernacular dialects in U.S. schools [Online]. Available: http: //ericae.net/db/digs/ed289364.htm (ERIC Documentation Reproduction Service No. ED 289 364).

Christian, D. (1994). *Two-way bilingual education: Students learning through two languages* (Educational Practice Report No. 12). Santa Cruz, CA: National Center for Research on Cultural Diversity and Second Language Learning.

Christie, F. (1985). Language and schooling. In S. Tchudi (Ed.), *Language, schooling, and society* (pp. 21–40). Upper Montclair, NJ: Boynton/Cook.

Clark, E. V. (1979). Building a vocabulary: Words for objects, actions and relations. In P. Fletcher & M. Garman (Eds.), *Language acquisition: Studies in language development* (pp. 149–160). Cambridge, UK: Cambridge University Press.

Clark, E. V. (1993). *The lexicon in acquisition*. Cambridge, UK: Cambridge University Press.

Clark, K., & Holquist, M. (1984). *Mikhail Bakhtin*. Cambridge, MA: Harvard University Press.

Clay, M. (1975). *What did I write?* Portsmouth, NH: Heinemann.

Clay, M. (1989). *The early detection of reading difficulties* (3rd ed.). Portsmouth, NH: Heinemann.

Coady, J., & Huckin, T. (Eds.). (1997). *Second language vocabulary acquisition*. Cambridge, UK: Cambridge University Press.

Cobb, P. (1994). Where is the mind? Constructivist and sociocultural perspectives on mathematical development. *Educational Researcher, 23* (7), 13–20.

Cocking, R. R., & Chipman, S. (1988). Conceptual issues related to mathematics achievement of language minority children. In R. R. Cocking & J. P. Mestre (Eds.), *Linguistic and cultural influences on learning mathematics* (pp. 17–46). Hillsdale, NJ: Erlbaum.

Cohen, E. G. (1994). *Designing groupwork: Strategies for the heterogeneous classroom* (2nd ed.). New York: Teachers College Press.

Cohen, E. G., & Lotan, R. A. (1994). Producing equal-status interaction in the heterogeneous classroom. *American Educational Research Journal, 32*, 99–120.

Cole, M., & Scribner, S. (1974). *Culture and thought: A psychological introduction*. New York: Wiley.

Collier, V. P. (1987). Age and rate of acquisition of second language for academic purposes. *TESOL Quarterly, 21* (4), 617–641.

Collier, V. P. (1992). A synthesis of studies examining long-term language-minority student data on academic achievement. *Bilingual Research Journal, 16* (1, 2), 187–212.

Collins, C. (1991). Reading instruction that increases thinking abilities. *Journal of Reading, 34,* 510–516.

Commission on Teacher Credentialing of the State of California. (1995). *California code of regulations: Guidelines for staff development programs for teachers of English learners.* Sacramento, CA: Author.

Cope, B., & Kalantzis, M. (Eds.). (2000). *Multiliteracies: Literacy learning and the design of social futures.* London: Routledge.

Corder, S. P. (1967). The significance of learners' errors. *International Review of Applied Linguistics, 5,* 161–170.

Corson, D. (1994). Towards a comprehensive language policy: The language of the school as a second language. *Education Canada, 35* (2), 48–54, 60.

Crawford, J. (1997). Best evidence: Research foundations of the bilingual education act [Online]. Available: http://www.ncbe.gwu.edu/ncbepubs/reports/bestevid.html.

Cromer, R. F. (1991). *Language and thought in normal and handicapped children.* Oxford, UK: Basil Blackwell.

Cross, W. E., Jr., Strauss, L., & Fhagen-Smith, P. (1999). African American identity development across the life span: Educational implications. In R. H. Sheets & E. R. Hollins (Eds.) *Racial and ethnic identity in school practices: Aspects of human development* (pp. 108–123). Mahwah, NJ: Erlbaum.

Crystal, D. (1987). *The Cambridge encyclopedia of language.* Cambridge, UK: Cambridge University Press.

Crystal, D. (1997). *The Cambridge encyclopedia of language.* (2nd ed.). Cambridge, UK: Cambridge University Press.

Cuevas, J. A. (1996). *Educating limited-English-proficient students: A review of the research on school programs and classroom practices.* San Francisco: WestEd.

Cummins, D. D., Kintsch, W., Reusser, K., & Weimer, R. (1988). The role of understanding in solving word problems. *Cognitive Psychology, 20,* 405–438.

Cummins, J. (1979). Cognitive/academic language proficiency, linguistic interdependence, the optimum age question and some other matters. *Working Papers on Bilingualism, 19,* 121–129.

Cummins, J. (1980a). The cross-lingual dimensions of language proficiency: implications for bilingual education and the optimal age issue. *TESOL Quarterly, 14,* 175–187.

Cummins, J. (1980b). Psychological assessment of immigrant children. Logic or intuition? *Journal of Multilingual and Multicultural Development, 1,* 97–111.

Cummins J. (1981a). Age on arrival and immigrant second language learning in Canada: A reassessment. *Applied Linguistics, 2,* 132–149.

Cummins, J. (1981b). The role of primary language development in promoting educational success for language minority students. In *Schooling and language minority students: A theoretical framework* (pp. 16–62). Los Angeles:

California State University, Evaluation, Dissemination and Assessment Center.

Cummins, J. (1982). Tests, achievement, and bilingual students. Wheaton, MD: National Clearinghouse for Bilingual Education.

Cummins, J. (1983). *Policy report: Language and literacy learning in bilingual instruction.* Austin, TX: Southwest Educational Development Laboratory.

Cummins, J. (1984). *Bilingualism and special education: Issues in assessment and pedagogy.* Clevedon, UK: Multilingual Matters.

Cummins, J. (1989). Language and literacy acquisition in bilingual contexts. *Journal of Multilingual and Multicultural Development, 10,* 17–29.

Cummins, J. (1991a). Interdependence of first and second-language proficiency in bilingual children. In E. Bialystok (Ed.), *Language processing in bilingual children* (pp. 70–89). New York: Cambridge University Press.

Cummins, J. (1991b). Language development and academic learning. In L. M. Malave & G. Duquette (Eds.), *Language, culture, and cognition* (pp. 161–175). Clevedon, UK: Multilingual Matters.

Cummins, J. (1993). Empowering minority students: A framework for intervention. In L. Weis & M. Fine (Eds.), *Beyond silenced voices: Class, race, and gender in United States schools* (pp. 101–117). Albany, NY: SUNY Press.

Cummins, J. (1994). Knowledge, power, and identity in teaching English as a second language. In F. Genessee (Ed.), *Educating second language children: The whole child, the whole curriculum, the whole community* (pp. 33–58). Cambridge, UK: Cambridge University Press.

Cummins, J. (2001). *Negotiating identities: Education for empowerment in a diverse society.* Ontario, CA: California Association for Bilingual Education.

Cummins, J., Harley, B, Swain, M., & Allen, P. (1990). Social and individual factors in the development of bilingual proficiency. In B. Harley, P. Allen, J. Cummins, & M. Swain (Eds.), *The development of second language proficiency* (pp. 119–133). Cambridge, UK: Cambridge University Press.

Cummins, J., & Swain, M. (1986). *Bilingualism in education.* London: Longman.

Cunningham, A. E., & Stanovich, K. E. (1997). Early reading acquisition and its relation to reading experience and ability 10 years later. *Developmental Psychology, 33,*. 934–945.

Cunningham, P. M. (1999). What should we do about phonics? In L. B. Gambrell, L. M. Morrow, S. B. Neuman, & M. Pressley (Eds.), *Best practices in literacy instruction* (pp. 69–89). New York: Guilford Press.

Curtiss, S. (1977). *Genie: A psycholinguistic study of a modern day wild child.* New York: Academic Press.

Damico, J. S., Oller, J. W., & Storey, M. E. (1983). The diagnosis of language disorders in bilingual children: Surface-oriented and pragmatic criteria. *Journal of Speech and Hearing Disorders, 46,* 385–394.

Danielson, C. (1996). *Enhancing professional practice: A framework for teaching.* Alexandria, VA: Association for Supervision and Curriculum Development.

DeCasper, A. J., & Fifer, W. P. (1980). Of human bondage: Newborns prefer their mothers' voices. *Science, 208,* 1174–1176.

DeCastell, S., & Luke, A. (1983). Defining "literacy" in North American schools: Social and historical conditions and consequences. *Journal of Curriculum Studies, 15*, 373–389.

DeLemos, C. (1981). Interactional processes in the child's construction of language. In W. Deutsch (Ed.), *The child's construction of language* (pp. 57–76). New York: Academic Press.

Delgado-Gaitan, C. (1994a). Socializing young children in Mexican-American families: An intergenerational perspective. In P. M. Greenfield & R. R. Cocking (Eds.), *Cross-cultural roots of minority child development* (pp. 55–86). Hillsdale, NJ: Erlbaum.

Delgado-Gaitan, C. (1994b). Sociocultural change through literacy: Toward the empowerment of families. In B. M. Ferdman, R. M. Weber, & A. G. Ramirez (Eds.), *Literacy across languages and cultures* (pp. 143–169). Albany, NY: SUNY Press.

Delpit, L. (1988). The silenced dialogue: Power and pedagogy in educating other people's children. *Harvard Educational Review, 58* (3), 280–298.

Delpit, L. (1995). *Other people's children: Cultural conflict in the classroom.* New York: New Press.

Delpit, L. (1998). Ebonics and culturally responsive instruction. In T. Perry & L. Delpit (Eds.), *The real Ebonics debate* (160–161). Boston: Beacon Press.

Denckla, M. B., & Rudel, R. G. (1976). Rapid automatized naming (R.A.N.): Dyslexia differentiated from other learning disabilities. *Neuropsychologia, 14*, 471–479.

deVilliers, P. A., & deVilliers, J. G. (1972). Early judgment of semantic and syntactic acceptability by children. *Journal of Psycholinguistic Research, 1*, 11–22.

Díaz, R. (1983). Thought and two languages: The impact of bilingualism on cognitive development. *Review of Research in Education, 10*, 23–34.

Díaz, S., Moll, L., & Mehan, H. (1986). Sociocultural resources in instruction: A context specific approach. In *Beyond language: Social and cultural factors in schooling language minority children* (pp. 187–230). Los Angeles: California State Department of Education and California State University.

Díaz-Rico, L., & Weed, K. (1995). *The crosscultural, language, and academic development handbook.* Boston: Allyn & Bacon.

Dickinson, D. K., & Tabors, P. O. (2001). *Beginning literacy with language.* Baltimore: Brookes.

Dickson, S. V., Simmons, D. C., & Kameenui, E. J. (n.d.). *Text organization and its relation to reading comprehension: A sysnthesis of the reseach* [Online]. Available: http://idea.uoregon.edu/~ncite/documents/techrepo/tech17.html.

Diebold, A. R., Jr. (1968). The consequences of early bilingualism in cognitive development and personality formation. In E. Norbeck, D. P. Williams, & W. McCord (Eds.), *The study of personality: An interdisciplinary approach* (pp. 218–245). New York: Holt, Rinehart & Winston.

Donahue, P. L., Voelkl, K. E., Campbell, J. R., & Mazzeo, J. (1999). *The NAEP 1998 reading report card for the nation and the states.* Washington, DC: National Center for Education Statistics.

Donald, M. (2000). The central role of culture in cognitive evolution: A reflection on the myth of the "isolated mind." In L. P. Nucci, G. B. Saxe, & E. Turiel (Eds.), *Culture, thought, and development* (pp. 19–38). Mahwah, NJ: Erlbaum.

Dore, J. (1983). Feeling, form, and intention in the baby's transition to language. In R. M. Golinkoff (Ed.), *The transition from prelinguistic communication* (pp. 234–253). Hillsdale, NJ: Erlbaum.

Downing, J., & Oliver, P. (1974). The child's concept of a word. *Reading Research Quarterly, 9,* 568–582.

Driver, R., Asoko, H., & Leach, J. (1994). Constructing scientific knowledge in the classroom. *Educational Researcher, 23* (7), 5–12.

Dromi, E. (1999). Early lexical development. In B. Martyn (Ed.), *The Development of Language* (pp. 99–129). Hove, East Sussex, UK: Psychology Press.

Dulay, H., & Burt, M. (1973). Should we teach children syntax? *Language Learning 23,* 245–258.

Dulay, H., & Burt, M. (1974). Errors and strategies in child second language acquisition. *TESOL Quarterly, 8,* 129–138.

Dulay, H., Burt, M., & Krashen, S. (1981). *Language two.* New York: Oxford University Press.

Dulay, H., Hernández-Chavez, E., & Burt, M.K. (1978). The process of becoming bilingual. In S. Singh & J. Lynch (Eds.), *Diagnostic procedures in hearing, language and speech* (pp. 305–326). Baltimore: University Park Press.

Dumont, R., Jr. (1979). Learning English and how to be silent: Studies in Sioux and Cherokee classrooms. In C. Cazden, V. John, & D. Hymes (Eds.), *Classroom discourse* (pp. 344–369). New York: Teachers College Press.

Duncan, S. E., & DeAvila, E. A. (1979). Bilingualism and cognition: Some recent findings. *NABE Journal, 4,* 15–50.

Durán, R. P. (1985). Influences of language skills on bilinguals' problem solving. In S. F. Chipman, J. W. Segal, & R. Glaser (Eds.), *Thinking and learning skills* (pp. 187–207). Hillsdale, NJ: Erlbaum.

Durán, R. P. (1989). Testing of linguistic minorities. In R. Linn, (Ed.), *Educational measurement* (3rd ed.). New York: Macmillan.

Durgunoglu, A. Y., Nagy, W. E., & Hancin-Bhatt, B. J. (1993). Cross-language transfer of phonological awareness. *Journal of Educational Psychology, 85,* 453–465.

Dutro, S. (2001). *A focused approach for English language development.* Unpublished manuscript.

Dutro, S., & Moran, C. (2003). Rethinking English language instruction: An architectural approach. In G. Garcia (Ed.), *English learners: Reaching the highest level of English literacy,* (pp. 227–258). Newark, DE: International Reading Association.

Dutro, S., Prestridge, K., & Herrick, J. (2001). Examples of ELD language structures by proficiency level. Oakland, CA: California Reading and Literature Project.

Dworin, J. E. (2003). Insights into biliteracy development: Toward a bidirectional theory of bilingual pedagogy. *Journal of Hispanic Higher Education, 2* (2), 171–186.

Dyson, A. H. (1993). *Social worlds of children learning to write in an urban primary school.* New York: Teachers College Press.

Echevarria, J., & Goldenberg, C. (1999). *Teaching secondary language minority students* (Research Brief No. 4). Santa Cruz, CA: Center for Research on Education, Diversity, and Excellence.

Echevarria, J., & Graves, A. (1998). *Sheltered content instruction: Teaching English-language learners with diverse abilities.* Boston: Allyn & Bacon.

Echevarria, J., Vogt, M. E., & Short, D. (2000). *Making content comprehensible for English language learners.* Needham Heights, MA: Allyn & Bacon.

Eggen, P., & Kauchak, D. (1997). *Educational psychology: Windows on classrooms* (3rd ed.). Upper Saddle River, NJ: Merrill/Prentice-Hall.

Ehri, L. C., Nunes, S. R., Willows, D. M., Schuster, B. V., Yahgoub-Zadeh, Z., & Shanahan, T. (2001). Phonemic awareness instruction helps children learn to read: Evidence from the national reading panel's meta-analysis. *Reading Research Quarterly, 36* (3), 250–287.

Ehri, L. C., & Wilce, L. (1985). Movement into reading: Is the first stage of printed word learning visual or phonetic? *Reading Research Quarterly, 20,* 163–179.

Ehri, L. C., & Robbins, C. (1992). Beginners need some decoding skill to read words by analogy. *Reading Research Quarterly, 27,* 12–26.

Eimas, P. D., Siqueland, E. R., Juscyk, P., & Vigorito, J. (1971). Speech perception in infants. *Science, 270,* 305–306.

Eisenberg, R. B. (1975). *Auditory competence in early life: The roots of communicative behavior.* Baltimore: University Park Press.

Elbro, C., Borstrom, I., & Petersen, D. K. (1998). Predicting dyslexia from kindergarten: The importance of distinctness of phonological representations of lexical items. *Reading Research Quarterly, 33* (1), 3–60.

Elley, W. B. (1997). *In praise of incidental learning: Lessons from some empirical findings on language acquisition.* Albany, NY: National Research Center on English Learning and Achievement.

Ellis, R. (1984). Communication strategies and the evaluation of communicative performance. *ELT Journal, 38* (1), 39–44.

Ellis, R. (1986). *Understanding second language acquisition.* Oxford, UK: Oxford University Press.

Elman, J. L., Bates, E. A., Johnson, N. H., Karmiloff-Smith, A., Parisi, D., & Plunkett, K. (1996). *Rethinking innateness.* Cambridge, MA: MIT Press.

Epstein, J. L. (1998). *Sharing the role of expert in the national network of partnership schools.* Baltimore: Johns Hopkins University.

Erickson, F. (1991). Foreword. In E. H. Hiebert (Ed.), *Literacy for a diverse society: perspectives, practices, and policies* (pp. vii–ix). New York: Teachers College Press.

Ervin-Tripp, S,. & Miller, W. (1964). The development of grammar in child language. *Monographs of the Society for Research in Child Development, 92*, 9–34.

Escamilla, K. (1999). Teaching literacy in Spanish. In J. Tinajero & R. DeVillar (Eds.), *The power of two languages* (pp. 126–141). New York: Macmillan/McGraw-Hill.

Esling, J. H. (1998). Everyone has an accent except me. In L. Bauer & P. Trudgill (Eds.), *Language myths* (pp. 169–175), London: Penguin Books.

Espinoza-Herold, M. (2003). *Issues in Latino education: Race, school culture, and the politics of academic success.* Boston: Allyn & Bacon.

Estrin, E. T., & Chaney, C. (1989). Developing a concept of the *word. Childhood Education, 65* (2), 78–82.

Evans, N. (1998). Aborigines speak a primitive language. In L. Bauer, & P. Trudgill (Eds.), *Language myths* (pp. 159–168). London: Penguin Books.

Faltis, C. J., & Hudelson, S. J. (1994). *Bilingual education in elementary and secondary school communities.* Boston: Allyn & Bacon.

Fantini, A. (1985). *Language acquisition of a bilingual child: A sociolinguistic perspective.* San Diego: College Hill Press.

Farr, B., & Trumbull, E. (1997). *Assessment alternatives for diverse classrooms.* Norwood, MA: Christopher-Gordon.

Feldman, C. F. (1971a). The interaction of sentence characteristics and mode of presentation in recall. *Language and Speech, 14* (1), 18–25.

Feldman, C. F. (1971b). The role of underdeterminacy and reference in the sentence recall of young children. *Language and Speech, 14* (1), 26–33.

Ferdman, B. M. (1990). Literacy and cultural identity. *Harvard Educational Review, 60*, 181–203.

Ferguson, C. (1977). Baby-talk as a simplified register. In C. Snow & C. Ferguson (Eds.), *Talking to children: Language input and acquisition* (pp. 209–235). Cambridge, UK: Cambridge University Press.

Fetterman, D. M. (1989). *Ethnography step by step* (Applied Social Research Methods Series, 17). Newbury Park, CA: Sage.

Fey, M. (1986). *Language intervention with young children.* Boston: Allyn & Bacon.

Figueroa, R. A., & Garcia, E. (1994). Issues in testing students from culturally and linguistically diverse backgrounds. *Multicultural Education, 2* (1), 10–19.

Fischer, B., & Fischer, L. (1979). Styles of teaching and learning. *Educational Leadership, 36* (4), 245–251.

Fishman, J. (1964). Language maintenance and language shift as a field of inquiry. *Linguistics, 9*, 32–70.

Fishman, J. A. (1989). *Language and ethnicity in minority sociolinguistic perspective.* Clevedon, UK: Multilingual Matters.

Fishman, J. A. (1996). What do you lose when you lose your language? In G. Cantoni (Ed.), *Stabilizing indigenous languages* (pp. 80–91). Flagstaff, AZ: Northern Arizona University.

Fitzgerald, J. (1995). English-as-a-second-language learners' cognitive reading processes: A review of research in the United States. *Review of Educational Research, 65*, 145–190.

Fleck, C. (2000). Understanding cheating in Nepal. *Electronic Magazine of Multicultural Education* [Online]. *2* (1). Available: http://www.eastern.edu/publications/emme.

Flood, J. E. (1977). Parental styles in reading episodes with young children. *The Reading Teacher, 30*, 864–867.

Flood, J. E., & Menyuk, P. (1979). *Detection of ambiguity and production paraphrase in written language*. Washington, DC: National Institute of Education.

Flood, J., & Menyuk, P. (1983). The development of metalinguistic awareness and its relation to reading achievement. *Journal of Applied Developmental Psychology, 4*, 65–80.

Francis, N. & Reyhner, J. (2002). *Language and literacy teaching for indigenous education: A bilingual approach*. Clevedon, UK: Multilingual Matters.

Frederiksen, J. R. (1981). Sources of process interactions in reading. In A. M. Lesgold & C. A. Perfetti (Eds.), *Interactive processes in reading* (pp. 361–386). Hillsdale, NJ: Erlbaum.

Freebody, P., & Luke, A. (1990). Literacies programs: Debates and demands in cultural contexts. *Prospect, 5*, 7–17.

Freedman, S. W., Simons, E. R., Kalnin, J. S., Casareno, A., & the M-Class Teams. (1999). *Inside city schools: Investigating literacy in multicultural classrooms*. New York: Teachers College Press.

Freeman, D., & Freeman, Y. (1994). *Between worlds: Access to second language acquisition*. Portsmouth, NH: Heinemann.

Freeman, Y. S., & Freeman, D. E. (1998). *ESL/EFL teaching: Principles for success*. Portsmouth, NH: Heinemann.

Freeman, Y. S., & Freeman, D. E. (2000). *Teaching reading in multilingual classrooms*. Portsmouth, NH: Heinemann.

Freire, P. (1970). *Pedagogy of the oppressed*. New York: Seabury Press.

Freire, P. (1985). *The politics of education: Culture, power, and liberation* (D. Macedo, Trans.). South Hadley, MA: Bergin & Garvey.

Freire, P., & Macedo, D. (1987). *Literacy: Reading the word and the world*. South Hadley, MA: Bergin & Garvey.

Friedlander, B. (1970). Receptive language development in infancy. *Merrill Palmer Quarterly, 16*, 7–51.

Gagné, E. D. (1985). *The cognitive psychology of school learning*. Boston: Little, Brown.

Galambos, S., & Goldin-Meadow, S. (1990). The effects of learning two languages on metalinguistic development. *Cognition, 34*, 1–56.

Gambrell, L. B., & Mazzoni, S. A. (1999). Principles of best practice: Finding the common ground. In L. B. Gambrell, L. M. Morrow, S. B. Neuman, & M. Pressley (Eds.), *Best practices in literacy instruction* (pp. 11–21). New York: Guilford Press.

Garan, E. M. (2001). Beyond the smoke and mirrors: A critique of the national reading panel report on phonics. *Phi Delta Kappan, 82* (7), 500–506.

García, E. (1994). *Understanding and meeting the challenge of student cultural diversity*. Boston: Houghton Mifflin.

García, G. E. (1991). *Factors influencing the English reading test performance of Spanish-speaking Hispanic children* (Technical Report No. 539). Urbana-Champaign, IL: University of Illinois Center for the Study of Reading.

García, G. E. (1992). *The literacy assessment of second-language learners* (Technical Report No. 559). Urbana-Champaign, IL: University of Illinois Center for the Study of Reading.

García, G. E. (2000). Bilingual children's reading. In M. L. Kamil, P. B. Mosenthal, P. D. Pearson, & R. Barr (Eds.), *Handbook of reading research* (Vol. 3, pp. 813–834). Mahwah, NJ: Erlbaum.

García, G. E., & Pearson, P. D. (1994). Assessment and diversity. *Review of Research in Education, 20,* 337–391.

García, O. (2002). Writing backwards across languages: The inexpert English/Spanish biliteracy of uncertified bilingual teachers. In M. J. Schleppegrell & C. Colombi (Eds.), *Developing advanced literacy in first and second languages* (pp. 245–260). Mahwah, NH: Erlbaum.

Gardner, H. (1983). *Frames of mind: The theory of multiple intelligences*. New York: Basic Books.

Gardner, R. C., & Lambert, W. C. (1972). *Attitudes and motivation in second language learning*. Rowley, MA: Newbury House.

Gass, S. (1988). Integrating research areas: A framework for second language studies. *Applied Linguistics, 9,* 198–217.

Gass, S. M., & Selinker, L. (1994). *Second-language acquisition: An introductory course*. Hillsdale, NJ: Erlbaum.

Gee, J. P. (1989). Two styles of narrative construction and their linguistic and educational implications. *Discourse Processes, 12,* 287–307.

Gee, J. P. (1990). *Social linguistics and literacies: Ideology in discourses*. New York: Falmer Press.

Gee, J. P. (1999). Reading versus reading something: A critique of the National Academy of Sciences' report on reading. *American Reading Forum Yearbook, 19,* 1–12.

Geller, L. G. (1981). Linguistic consciousness-raising: Child's play. *Language Arts, 50* (1), 120–125.

Genesee, F., & Hamayan, E. (1994). Classroom-based assessment. In F. Genesee (Ed.), *Educating second language children: The whole child, the whole curriculum, the whole community* (pp. 212–239). Cambridge, UK: Cambridge University Press.

Geschwind, N. (1972). Language and the brain. *Scientific American, 226,* 76–83.

Gibbons, P. (1991). *Learning to read in a second language*. Portsmouth, NH: Heinemann.

Giles, H., Bourhis, R., & Taylor, D. (1977). Toward a theory of language in ethnic group relations. In H. Giles (Ed.), *Language, ethnicity, and intergroup relations*. New York: Academic Press.

Gillet, J. H., & Temple, C. (1994). *Understanding reading problems* (4th ed.). Glenview, IL: Scott, Foresman.

Gleason, J. B. (1977). Talking to children: Some notes on feedback. In C. E. Snow & C. A. Ferguson (Eds.), *Talking to children: Language input and acquisition* (pp. 199–205). Cambridge, UK: Cambridge University Press.

Gleitman, H., & Gleitman, L. R. (1979). Language use and language judgment. In C. Fillmore, D. Kempler, & D.S.Y. Wang (Eds.), *Individual differences in language ability and language behavior* (pp. 103–126). New York: Academic Press.

Gleitman, L. R., Gleitman, H., & Shipley, E. F. (1972). The emergence of the child as grammarian. *Cognition, 1*, 137–164.

Glenn, C., & Stein, N. (1980). *Syntactic structures and real world themes in stories generated by children.* Urbana, IL: University of Illinois, Center for the Study of Reading.

Goffman, E. (1967). *Interaction ritual: Essays on face-to-face behavior*. Garden City, NY: Anchor Books.

Goldenberg, C. (1991). *Instructional conversations and their classroom application* (Educational Practice Report No. 2). Santa Cruz, CA: National Center for Research on Cultural Diversity and Second Language Learning.

Goldenberg, C., & Gallimore, R. (1991). Local knowledge, research knowledge, and educational change: A case study of first-grade Spanish reading improvement. *Educational Researcher, 20* (8), 2–14.

Golinkoff, R. M. (1993). When is communication a "meeting of the minds"? *Journal of Child Language, 20*, 199–207.

Gonzalez, R. D. (1982). Teaching Mexican-American students to write: Capitalizing on the culture. *English Journal, 71*, 20–24.

Goodman, K. (1976). Behind the eye: What happens in reading. In H. Singer & R. R. Ruddell (Eds.), *Theoretical models and processes of reading* (pp. 470–496). Newark, DE: International Reading Association.

Goodman, K. (1986). *What's whole in whole language?* Portsmouth, NH: Heinemann.

Goodman, K. (1992). Whole language research: Foundations and development. In S. J. Samuels & A. E. Farstrup (Eds.), *What research has to say about reading instruction* (2nd ed., pp. 46–69). Newark, DE: International Reading Association.

Goodman, K. (1994). Deconstructing the rhetoric of Moorman, Blanton, and McLaughlin: A response. *Reading Research Quarterly, 29* (4), 340–346.

Goodman, Y. (1986). Children coming to know literacy. In W. Teale & E. Sulzby (Eds.), *Emergent literacy* (pp. 1–14). Norwood, NJ: Ablex.

Goswami, U. (1995). Phonological development and reading by analogy: What is analogy and what is not? *Journal of Research in Reading, 18*, 139–145.

Gough, P. (1983). Context, form, and interaction. In K. Rayner (Ed.), *Eye movements in reading* (pp. 331–358). Cambridge, MA: MIT Press.

Graves, D. H. (1991). *The reading/writing teacher's companion: Building a literate classroom*. Portsmouth, NH: Heinemann.

Greenfield, P. (1966). On culture and conservation. In J. S. Bruner, R. R. Olver, & P. M. Greenfield (Eds.), *Studies in cognitive growth* (pp. 225–256). New York: Wiley.

Greenfield, P. (1972). Oral or written language: The consequences for cognitive development in Africa, the United States and England. *Language and Speech, 15*, 169–178.

Greenfield, P. (1994). Independence and interdependence as developmental scripts: Implications for theory, research, and practice. In P. M. Greenfield & R. R. Cocking, (Eds.) (1994). *Cross-cultural roots of minority child development* (pp. 1–37). Mahwah, NJ: Erlbaum.

Greenfield, P. (1997). You can't take it with you: Why ability assessments don't cross cultures. *American Psychologist, 52* (10), 1115–1124.

Greenfield, P., Brazelton, T. B., & Childs, C. P. (1989). From birth to maturity in Zinacantan: Ontogenesis in cultural context. In V. Bricker & G. Gossen (Eds.), *Ethnographic encounters in southern Mesoamerica: Celebratory essays in honor of Evon Z. Vogt* (pp. 177–216). Albany, NY: Institute of Mesoamerican Studies.

Greenfield, P., & Bruner, J. S. (1969). Culture and cognitive growth. In D. Goslin (Ed.), *Handbook of socialization theory* (pp. 653–657). Chicago: Rand McNally.

Greenfield, P., & Lave, J. (1982). Cognitive aspects of informal education. In D. Wagner & H. Stevenson (Eds.), *Cultural perspectives on child development* (pp. 181–201). San Francisco: Freeman.

Greenfield, P. M., Quiroz, B., & Raeff, C. (2000). Cross-cultural conflict and harmony in the social construction of the child. In S. Harkness, C. Raeff, & C. M. Super (Eds.), *The social construction of the child: Nature and sources of variability. New directions in child psychology* (pp. 93–108). San Francisco: Jossey-Bass.

Greenleaf, C. L., Schoenbach, R., Cziko, C., & Mueller, F. L. (2001). Apprenticing adolescent readers to academic literacy. *Harvard Educational Review, 71* (1), 79–129.

Gregg, K. (1984). Krashen's monitor and Occam's razor. *Applied Linguistics*, 5, 79–100.

Grosjean, F. (1989). Neurolinguists, beware! The bilingual is not two monolinguals in one person. *Brain and Language, 36*, 3–15.

Grossen, B. (1997). A synthesis of research on reading from the National Institute of Child Health and Human Development [Online]. Available: www.nrrf.org/synthesis_research.htm.

Guerrero, M. (1997). Spanish academic language proficiency: The case of bilingual education teachers in the U.S. *Bilingual Research Journal, 21* (1), 25–43.

Gumperz, J. J., & Hymes, D. (Eds.). (1972). *Directions in sociolinguistics: The ethnography of communication*. New York: Holt, Rinehart & Winston.

Gutiérrez, K. (1993). Biliteracy and the language minority child. In B. Spodek & R. N. Saracho, (Eds.), *Yearbook of early childhood education:* Vol. 4. *Lan-*

guage and literacy in early childhood education (pp. 82–101). New York: Teachers College Press.

Gutiérrez, K., Baquedano-López, P., & Tejeda, C. (1999). Rethinking diversity: Hybridity and hybrid language practices in the third space. *Mind, Culture, and Activity, 6* (4), 286–303.

Gutiérrez, K., Stone, L., & Larson, J. (in press). Hypermediating in the urban classroom: When scaffolding becomes sabotage in narrative activity. In C. D. Baker, J. Cook-Gumperz, and A. Luke (Eds.), *Literacy and Power.* Oxford, UK: Blackwell.

Hakes, D. (1980). *The development of metalinguistic abilities in children.* Berlin: Springer-Verlag.

Hakuta, K. (1974). Prefabricated patterns and the emergence of structure in second language learning. *Language Learning, 24,* 287–297.

Hakuta, K. (1986). *Mirror of language: The debate on bilingualism.* New York: Basic Books.

Hakuta, K., & Cancino, H. (1977). Trends in second language acquisition. *Harvard Educational Review, 47,* 294–316.

Hakuta, K., & Díaz, R.M. (1985). The relationship between degree of bilingualism and cognitive ability: A critical discussion and some new longitudinal data. In K. Nelson (Ed.), *Children's language* (pp. 319–345). Hillsdale, NJ: Erlbaum.

Hakuta, K., & Gould, L. J. (1987). Synthesis of research on bilingual education. *Educational Leadership, 44,* 38–45.

Hall, W. S., & Guthrie, L. F. (1980). On the dialect question and reading. In R. J. Spiro, B. C. Bruce, & W. F. Brewer (Eds.), *Theoretical issues in reading comprehension: Perspectives from cognitive psychology, linguistics, artificial intelligence, and education* (pp. 439–450). Hillsdale, NJ: Erlbaum.

Halliday, M.A.K. (1970). Language structure and language function. In J. Lyons (Ed.), *New horizons in linguistics* (pp. 140–165). Harmondsworth, UK: Penguin.

Halliday, M.A.K. (1975a). Learning how to mean. In E. H. Lenneberg & E. Lenneberg (Eds.), *Foundation of language development: A multidisciplinary approach* (pp. 239–265). New York: Academic Press.

Halliday, M.A.K. (1975b). *Learning how to mean: Explorations in the development of language.* New York: Arnold.

Halliday, M.A.K. (1980). Three aspects of children's language development: Learning language, learning through language, learning about language. In Y. M. Goodman, M. M. Hausser, & D. S. Strickland (Eds.), *Oral and written language development: Impact on schools* (pp. 7–19). Newark, DE: International Reading Association & National Council of Teachers of English.

Halliday, M.A.K., & Hasan, R. (1976). *Cohesion in English.* London: Longman.

Halliday, M.A.K., & Hasan, R. (1989). *Language, context, and text: Aspects of language in a social semiotic perspective.* Oxford, UK: Oxford University Press.

Hamayan, E. (1990). Preparing mainstream classroom teachers to teach potentially English proficient students. In *Proceedings of the first research symposium on limited English proficient students' issues* (pp. 1–21). Washington, DC: U.S. Department of Education, Office of Bilingual Education and Minority Language Affairs.

Hamayan, E. (1994). Language development of low literacy children. In F. Genesee (Ed.), *Educating second language children: The whole child, the whole curriculum, the whole community* (pp. 278–300). Cambridge, UK: Cambridge University Press.

Hamayan, E., & Perlman, R. (1990). *Helping language minority students after they exit from bilingual/ESL programs: A handbook for teachers.* Washington, DC: National Clearinghouse for Bilingual Education.

Hammett, L. A., Van Kleeck, A., & Huberty, C. J. (2003). Patterns of parents' extratextual interactions during book sharing with preschool children: A cluster analysis study. *Reading Research Quarterly, 38* (4), 442–468.

Hanzlik, J., & Stevenson, (1986). Mother-infant interaction in families and infants who are mentally retarded, mentally retarded with cerebral palsy or nonretarded. *American Journal of Mental Deficiency, 90,* 513–520.

Harris, G. (1993). American Indian cultures: A lesson in diversity. In D. E. Battle (Ed.), *Communication disorders in multicultural populations* (pp. 78–113). Boston: Andover Medical.

Harris, V. J. (1993). *Teaching multicultural literature in grade K–8.* Norwood, MA: Christopher-Gordon.

Hart, B., & Risley, T. R. (1995). *Meaningful differences in the everyday experiences of young American children.* Baltimore: Brookes.

Hatch, E. (1978). *Second language acquisition: A book of readings.* Rowley, MA: Newbury House.

Heath, S. B. (1983). *Ways with words: Language, life, and work in communities and classrooms.* New York: Cambridge University Press.

Heath, S. B. (1986). Sociocultural contexts of language development. In *Beyond language: Social and cultural factors in schooling language minority students* (pp. 143–186). Los Angeles: California State University Evaluation, Dissemination and Assessment Center.

Heimlich, J. E., & Pittelman, S. D. (1986). *Semantic mapping: Classroom applications.* Newark, DE: International Reading Association.

Henderson, A. T., & Berla, N. (1994). *A new generation of evidence: The family is critical to student achievement.* Washington, DC: National Committee for Citizens in Education.

Henderson, A. T., & Mapp, K. L. (2002). *A new wave of evidence: The impact of school, family, and community connections on student achievement.* Austin, TX: National Center for Family & Community Connections with Schools. Southwest Educational Development Laboratory.

Hernández-Chavez, E. (1978). Language maintenance, bilingual education, and philosophies of bilingualism in the United States. In J. E. Alatis (Ed.), *Inter-*

national dimensions of bilingual education (pp.527–550). Washington, DC: Georgetown University Press.

Herrell, A. (2000). *Fifty strategies for teaching English language learners.* Upper Saddle River, NJ: Merrill.

Heubert, J. P., & Hauser, R. M. (Eds.), (1999). *High stakes testing for tracking, promotion, and graduation.* Washington, DC: National Academy Press.

Higgs, T. (1991). Research on the role of grammar and accuracy in classrooms-based foreign language acquisition. In B. Freed (Ed.), *Foreign language acquisition research and the classroom* (pp. 46–53). Lexington, MA: Heath.

Hinton, L. (1994). *Flutes of fire.* Berkeley, CA: Heyday Books.

Hirsh, D., & Nation, P. (1992). What vocabulary size is needed to read unsimplified texts for pleasure? *Reading in a Foreign Language, 8* (2), 689–696.

Ho, S. H., & Bryant, P. (1997).Learning to read Chinese beyond the logographic phase. *Reading Research Quarterly, 32* (3), 276–289.

Hobbs, R., & Frost, R. (1999). Instructional practices in media education and their impact on students' learning. *New Jersey Journal of Communication, 6* (2), 123–148.

Hobbs, R., & Frost, R. (2003). Measuring the acquisition of media-literacy skills. *Reading Research Quarterly, 38* (3), 330–355.

Hockett, F. (1963). The problem of universals in language. In J. H. Greenberg (Ed.), *Universals of language* (2nd ed, pp. 1–29). Cambridge, MA: MIT Press.

Hofstede, G. (1983). National cultures revisited. *Behavior Science Revisited, 18,* 285–305.

Hogaboam, T. W., & Perfetti, C. A. (1978). Reading skill and the role of verbal experience in decoding. *Journal of Educational Psychology, 70* (5), 717–729.

Hoge, W. (2001, March 18). Inside the Arctic Circle, an ancient people emerge. *New York Times*, [Online]. Available: www.arch.columbia.edu/gsasp/3109.

Hollins, E. R. (1996). *Culture in school learning: Revealing the deep meaning.* Mahwah, NJ: Erlbaum.

Holzman, M. (1984). Evidence for a reciprocal model of language development. *Journal of Psycholinguistic Research, 13,* 119–146.

Horgan, D. (1978). The development of the full passive. *Journal of Child Language*, *5*, 65–80.

Hsueh-chao, M. H., & Nation, P. (2000). Unknown vocabulary density and reading comprehension. *Reading in a Foreign Language* [Online], *13* (1). Available: http://nf/rc.hawaii.edu/rfl/PastIssues/volume.html.

Hurston, Z. N. (1990). *Their eyes were watching God.* New York: Harper & Row. (Original work published 1937)

Hymes, D. (1971). Competence and performance in linguistic theory. In R. Huxley and E. Ingram (Eds.), *Language acquisition: Models and methods.* New York: Academic Press.

Hymes, D. (1972a). Introduction. In C. Cazden, V. John, & D. Hymes, (Eds.), *Functions of language in the classroom* (pp. xi–lvii). New York: Teachers College Press.

Hymes, D. (1972b). On communicative competence. In J. B. Pride & J. Holmes (Eds.), *Sociolinguistics* (pp. 269–293). Harmondsworth, UK: Penguin Books.

Hymes, D. (1985). Toward linguistic competence. *AILA Review, 2*, 9–23.

Imel, S., & Grieve, S. (1985). *Adult literacy education: Overview.* Columbus, OH: ERIC Clearinghouse on Adult Career and Vocational Education.

Irvine, J. J., & York, D. E. (1995). Learning styles and culturally diverse students: A literature review. In A. Banks & C. Banks (Eds.), *Handbook of research on multicultural education* (pp. 484–497). New York: Simon & Schuster Macmillan.

Isaac, A. R. (1999). *How teachers' cultural ideologies influence children's relations inside the classroom: The effect of a cultural awareness teacher training program in two classrooms.* Unpublished thesis, University of California, Los Angeles.

Jackendoff, R. (1994). *Patterns in the mind: Language and human nature.* New York: Basic Books.

Jahn, J. (1961). *Muntu: An outline of the new African culture.* New York: Grove Press.

Jansky, J., & de Hirsch, K. (Eds.). (1972). *Preventing reading failure.* New York: Harper & Row.

Jenkins, J. R., Stein, M., & Wysocki, K. (1984). Learning vocabulary through reading. *American Educational Research Journal, 21*, 767–787.

Jiménez, R. T. (1997). The strategic reading abilities and potential of five low-literacy Latina/o readers in middle school. *Reading Research Quarterly, 32* (3), 224–243.

Jiménez, R. T., García, G. E., & Pearson, P. D. (1996). Three children, two languages, and strategic reading: Case studies in bilingual/monolingual reading. *American Education Research Journal, 32*, 67–97.

Johnson, D. D., & Pearson, P. D. (1984). *Teaching reading vocabulary* (2nd ed.). New York: Holt, Rinehart & Winston.

Johnson, J. S., & Newport, E. L. (1989). Critical periods effects in second-language learning: The influence of maturational state on the acquisition of English as a second language. *Cognitive Psychology, 21*, 60–69.

Juel, C., & Minden-Cupp, C. (2000). Learning to read words: Linguistic units and instructional strategies. *Reading Research Quarterly, 35* (4), 458–492.

Kaderavek, J., & Justice, L. M. (2000). Children with learning disabilities as emergent readers: Bridging the gap to conventional reading. *Intervention in School and Clinic, 36*, 82–93.

Kaestle, C., Damon-Moore, H., Stedman, L. C., Tinsley, K., & Trollinger, W. V. (1991). *Literacy in the United States: Readers and reading since 1880.* New Haven, CT: Yale University Press.

Kagan, S. (1986). Cooperative learning and sociocultural factors. In Bilingual Education Office (Ed.), *Beyond language: Social and cultural factors in schooling language minority students* (pp. 231–298). Los Angeles: California State University, Evaluation, Dissemination and Assessment Center.

Kaplan, R. (1988). Contrastive rhetoric and second language learning: Notes toward a theory of contrastive rhetoric. In A. Purves (Ed.), *Writing across languages and cultures: Issues in contrastive rhetoric* (pp. 275–304). Newbury Park, CA: Sage.

Kemper, S., & Edwards, L. (1986). Children's expression of causality and their construction of narratives. *Topics in Language Disorders, 7* (1), 11–20.

Kim [Yoon], Y. H., & Goetz. E. T. (1994). Context effects on word recognition and reading comprehension of poor and good readers: A test of the interactive-compensatory hypothesis. *Reading Research Quarterly, 29* (2), 179–187.

King, R., Jones, C., & Lasky, E. (1982). In retrospect: A fifteen-year follow-up report of speech-language disorders in children. *Language, Speech and Hearing Services in Schools, 13*, 24–32.

Kintsch, W. (1988). The role of knowledge in discourse comprehension: A construction-integration model. *Psychological Review, 95*, 163–182.

Kiplinger, V. L., Haug, C. A., & Abedi, J. (2000, April). *Measuring math—not reading—on a math assessment: A language accommodations study of English language learners and other special populations.* Paper presented at the Annual Meeting of the American Educational Research Association, New Orleans.

Kleinfeld, J. S. (1979). Intellectual strengths of culturally different groups: An Eskimo illustration. *Review of Educational Research, 43* (3), 341–359.

Knapp, M. S., Shields, P. M., & Turnbull, B. J. (1995). Academic challenge in high-poverty classrooms, *Phi Delta Kappan, 76* (10), 770–776.

Kochman, T. (1989). Black and white cultural styles in pluralistic perspective. In B. Gifford (Ed.), *Test policy and test performance: Education, language, and culture* (pp. 259–296). Boston: Kluwer.

Kochman, T. (1990). Force fields in Black and White. In D. Carbaugh (Ed.). *Cultural communication and intercultural contact* (pp. 193–194). Hillsdale, NJ: Erlbaum.

Koelsch, N., Estrin, E. T., & Farr, B. (1995). *Guide to analyzing linguistic and cultural assumptions in assessment.* San Francisco: Far West Laboratory for Educational Research and Development.

Krashen, S. (1981). *Second language acquisition and second language learning.* Oxford, UK: Pergamon Press.

Krashen, S. (1982). *Principles and practice in second language acquisition.* Oxford, UK: Pergamon Press.

Krashen, S. (1991). *Bilingual education: A focus on current research.* Washington, DC: National Clearinghouse for Bilingual Education.

Krashen, S. (1996). A gradual exit, variable threshold model for limited English proficient children. *NABE News, 19*, 1–17.

Krashen, S., & Biber, D. (1998). *On course: Bilingual education's success in California.* Sacramento: California Association of Bilingual Education.

Krashen, S., Long, M., & Scarcella, R. (1979). Age, rate, and eventual attainment in second language acquisition. *TESOL Quarterly, 13*, 573–582.

Krashen, S. & Terrell, T. (1983). *The natural approach: Language acquisition in the classroom.* Oxford, U.K.: Pergamon Press.

Kucer, S. B., & Silva, C. (1995). Guiding bilingual students "through" the literacy process. *Language Arts, 72* (1), 20–29.

Kwachka, P. (1994). Comments on what we mean by literacy. In J. Harvey-Morgan (Ed.), *Native literacy and language roundtable proceedings* (pp. 8–9). Philadelphia: National Center on Adult Literacy and the Native Education Initiative of the U.S. Department of Education Regional Educational Laboratories.

Laberge, D., & Samuels, S. J. (1974). Toward a theory of automatic information processing in reading. *Cognitive Psychology, 6*, 293–323.

Labov, W. (1972). *Language in the inner city: Studies in the Black English vernacular.* Philadelphia: University of Pennsylvania Press.

LaCelle-Peterson, M., & Rivera, C. (1994). Is it real for all kids? A framework for equitable assessment policies for English language learners. *Harvard Educational Review, 64* (1), 55–75.

Lachat, M. A. (1999a). *Standards, equity and cultural diversity.* Providence, RI: Brown University, Northeast and Islands Regional Educational Laboratory.

Lachat, M. A. (1999b). *What policymakers and school administrators need to know about assessment reform and English language learners.* Providence, RI: Brown University, Northeast and Islands Regional Educational Laboratory.

Lambert, W. E. (1975). Culture and language as factors in learning and education. In A. Wolfgang (Ed.), *Education of immigrant students.* Toronto, Ontario, Canada: OISE.

Lamendella, J. (1977). General principles of neurofunctional organization and their manifestations in primary and non-primary acquisition. *Language Learning, 27*, 155–196.

Langdon, H. W. (1992). *Hispanic children and adults with communication disorders* (with L. Cheng). Gaithersburg, MD: Aspen.

Langer, J. (1991). Literacy and schooling: A sociological perspective. In E. Hiebert (Ed.), *Literacy for a diverse society: Perspectives, practices, and policies* (pp. 9–27). New York: Teachers College Press.

Langer, J. A., Bartolomé, L., Vasquez, O., & Lucas, T. (1990). Meaning construction in school literacy tasks: A study of bilingual students. *American Educational Research Journal, 27*, 427–471.

Larsen-Freeman, D. (1985). State of the art on input in second language acquisition. In S. Gass & C. Madden (Eds.), *Input in second language acquisition* (pp. 433–444). Cambridge, MA: Newbury House.

Larsen-Freeman, D., & Long, M. H. (1991). Explanations for differential success among second language learners. In *Introduction to second language acquisition research* (pp.153–167). New York: Longman.

Leap, W. L. (1991). Pathways and barriers to Indian language literacy-building on the Northern Ute reservation. *Anthropology & Education Quarterly, 22*, 21–41.

Lebra, T. S. (1994). Mother and child in Japanese socialization: A Japan-U.S. comparison. In P. M. Greenfield & R. R. Cocking (Eds.), *Cross-cultural roots of minority child development* (pp. 259–274). Hillsdale, NJ: Erlbaum.

Lee, C. (1993). *Signifying as a scaffold for literary interpretation: The peda-gogical implications of an African American discourse genre*. Urbana, IL: National Council of Teachers of English.

Lee, C. (1995). A culturally based cognitive apprenticeship: Teaching African American high school students skills in literary interpretation. *Reading Research Quarterly, 30* (4), 608–630.

Lee, C. (2000, April). *Culture as a resource: Scaffolding literacy with low achieving African American adolescents*. Paper presented at the Annual Meeting of the American Educational Research Association, New Orleans.

Legarreta-Marcaida, D. (1981). Effective use of the primary language in the class-room. In *Schooling and language minority students: A theoretical framework*. (p. 83–116. California Department of Education; Los Angeles: Evaluation, Dissemenation and Assessment Center, California State University.

Leki, I. (1992). *Understanding ESL writers: A guide for teachers*. Portsmouth, NH: Boynton/Cook.

LeMoine, N. (2001). Language variation and literacy acquisition in African American students. In J. L. Harris, A. G. Kamhi, & K. E. Pollock (Eds.), *Literacy in African American communities* (pp. 169–194). Mahwah, NJ: Erlbaum.

Lenneberg, E. (1967). *Biological foundations of language*. New York: Wiley.

LeVine, R., & White, M. (1986). *Human conditions: The cultural basis of educational development*. New York: Routledge.

Lewis, J. (2001). One story's words. *Context: Newcomers in California's classrooms, 22* (148), 10–11.

Lewontin, R. C., Rose, S., & Kamin, L. J. (1984). *Not in our genes*. New York: Pantheon Books.

Liberman, I. Y., & Shankweiler, D. (1985). Phonology and the problems of learning to read and write. *Remedial and Special Education, 6*, 8–17.

Liberman, I. Y., Shankweiler, D. S., Fisher, F. W., & Carter, B. (1974). Explicit syllable and phoneme segmentation in the young child. *Journal of Experimental Child Psychology, 18*, 201–212.

Liberman, I. Y., Shankweiler, D., Liberman, A. M., Fowler, C., & Fischer, F. W. (1977). Phonetic segmentation and recoding in the beginning reader. In A. S. Reber & D. Scarborough, (Eds.), *Toward a psychology of reading: The proceedings of the CUNY Conference* (pp. 207–225). Hillsdale, NJ: Erlbaum.

Lilja, L. D. (1980). Measuring the effectiveness of language education. In G. S. Pinnell (Ed.), *Discovering language with children* (pp. 105–108). Urbana, IL: National Council of Teachers of English.

Linden, E. (1986). *Silent partners: The legacy of the ape language experiments*. New York: Times Books.

Linguistic Institute for Native Americans. (n.d.). *Native language communities: A descriptive study of two community-based efforts to preserve their native language*. Albuquerque, NM: Author.

Linguistics Society of America. (1998). Resolution on Ebonics. In T. Perry & L. Delpit (Eds.) *The real Ebonics debate* (pp. 160–161). Boston: Beacon Press.

Lipka, J., & the Ciulistet Group. (1998). *Transforming the culture of schools* with G. Mohatt. Mahwah, NJ: Erlbaum.

Lipson, M. Y., & Wixson, K. K. (1986). Reading disability research: An interactionist perspective. *Review of Educational Research, 56*, 111–136.

Lipson, M. Y., & Wixson, K. K. (2003). *Assessment and instruction of reading and writing disabilities: An interactive approach.* (3rd ed.). New York: Pearson, Allyn & Bacon.

Locke, R. F. (1989). *The book of the Navajo.* Los Angeles: Mankind.

Lodge, A. (1998). French is a logical language. In L. Bauer & P. Trudgill (Eds.), *Language myths* (pp. 23–31). London: Penguin Books.

Ludwig, C. (2003, February). Making sense of literacy. *Newsletter of the Australian Literacy Educators' Association*, 1–4.

Luke, A., & Freebody, P. (1999). A map of possible practices, *Practically Primary, 4* (2), 5–8.

Lustig, M. W., & Koester, J. (1999). *Intercultural competence: Interpersonal communication across cultures* (3rd ed.). New York: Longman.

MacGregor, M., & Price, E. (1999). An exploration of aspects of language proficiency and algebra learning. *Journal for Research in Mathematics Education, 30* (4), 449–467.

Macias, R. F. (2000). The flowering of America: Linguistic diversity in the United States. In S. L. MacKay and S. L. C. Wong (Eds.), *New immigrants in the United States* (pp. 11–57). Cambridge, UK: Cambridge University Press.

MacWhinney, B. (1999). The emergence of language from embodiment. In *The emergence of language* (pp. 213–256). Mahwah, NJ: Erlbaum.

Mahiri, J., & Godley, A. J. (1998). Rewriting identity: Social meanings of literacy and "re-visions" of self. *Reading Research Quarterly, 33* (4), 416–433.

Malakoff, M., & Hakuta, K. (1991). Translation skill and metalinguistic awareness in bilinguals. In E. Bialystok (Ed.), *Language processing in bilingual children* (pp. 141–167). Cambridge, UK: Cambridge University Press.

Malcolm, I. (1982). Speech events of the Aboriginal classroom. *International Journal of Sociology of Language, 36*, 115–134.

Mandler, J. M., & Johnson, N. S. (1977). Remembrance of things parsed: Story structure and recall. *Cognitive Psychology, 9*, 111–151.

Martin, J. R. (1989). *Factual writing.* Oxford, UK: Oxford University Press.

Martin, J. R. (1992). *English text: System and structure.* Philadelphia: Benjamins.

Marzano, R. J. (2003). Direct vocabulary instruction: An idea whose time has come. In B. Williams (Ed.), *Closing the achievement gap: A vision for changing beliefs and practices* (2nd ed., pp. 48–66). Alexandria, VA: Association for Supervision and Curriculum Development.

Mathis, J. B. (2001). Respond to stories with stories: Teachers discuss multicultural literature. *Social Studies, 92* (4), 155.

Matthews, P. H. (1997). *Oxford concise dictionary of linguistics.* Oxford, UK: Oxford University Press.

Mattingly, I. (1972). Reading, the linguistic process, and linguistic awareness. In J. P. Kavanagh & I. Mattingly (Eds.), *Language by ear and by eye* (pp. 133–

147). Cambridge, MA: MIT Press.

McCarty, T. L. (1989). School as community: The Rough Rock demonstration. *Harvard Educational Review, 59* (4), 484–503.

McCarty, T. L. (2002). *A place to be Navajo*. Mahwah, NJ: Erlbaum.

McCarty, T. L., & Schaffer, R. (1992). Language and literacy development. In J. Reyhner (Ed.), *Teaching American Indian students* (pp. 115–131). Norman, OK: University of Oklahoma Press.

McCollum, P. (1991). Cross-cultural perspectives on classroom discourse and literacy. In E. H. Hiebert (Ed.), *Literacy for a diverse society: Perspectives, practices, and policies* (pp. 108–121). New York: Teachers College Press.

McCormick, S. (1992). Disabled readers' erroneous responses to inferential comprehension questions: Description and analysis. *Reading Research Quarterly, 27* (1), 54–77.

McCormick, S. (1994). A nonreader becomes a reader: A case study of literacy acquisition by a severely disabled reader. *Reading Research Quarterly, 29* (2), 156–76.

McLaughlin, B. (1978). *Second-language acquisition in childhood*. Hillsdale, NJ: Erlbaum.

McLaughlin, B. (1985). *Second language acquisition in childhood* (Vol. 2). Hillsdale, NJ: Erlbaum.

McLaughlin, B. (1987). *Theories of second language acquisition*. London: Arnold.

McLaughlin, B. (1990). "Conscious" versus "unconscious" learning. *TESOL Quarterly, 19* (4), 617–634.

McLaughlin, B. (1992). *Myths and misconceptions about second language learning: What every teacher needs to unlearn*. (Educational Practice Report No. 5). Santa Cruz, CA: National Center for Research on Cultural Diversity and Second Language Learning.

McLaughlin, B. (1995). *Fostering second language development in young children: Principles and practices*. Santa Cruz, CA: National Center for Research on Cultural Diversity and Second Language Learning.

McWhorter, J. (1998). *The word on the street: Debunking the myth of a "pure" standard English*. Cambridge, MA: Perseus.

Mehan, H. (1979). *Learning lessons*. Cambridge, MA: Harvard University Press.

Meier, T. (1999). The case for Ebonics as part of exemplary teacher preparation. In C. T. Adger, D. Christian, & O. Taylor (Eds.), *Making the connection: Language and academic achievement among African American students* (pp. 97–114). Washington, DC: Center for Applied Linguistics.

Menyuk, P. (1976). Relations between acquisition of phonology and reading. In J. T. Guthrie (Ed.), *Aspects of reading acquisition* (pp. 89–111). Baltimore: Johns Hopkins University Press.

Menyuk, P. (1977). *Language and maturation*. Cambridge, MA: MIT Press.

Menyuk, P. (1995). Language development and education. *Journal of Education, 177* (1), 39–62.

Mercer, C. D. (1987). *Students with learning disabilities* (3rd. ed.). New York: Merrill.

Merino, B. J. (1993, Fall). Language minority native Spanish speakers at the secondary level and the role of the foreign language teacher. *Peabody Journal of Education, 69* (1), 152–171.

Mestre, J. P. (1984). The problem with problems: Hispanic students and math. *Bilingual Journal, 32,* 15–19.

Met, M. (1994). Teaching content through a second language. In F. Genesee (Ed.), *Educating second language children: The whole child, the whole curriculum, the whole community* (pp. 159–182), Cambridge, UK: Cambridge University Press.

Meyer, B. (1975). *The organization of prose and its effects on memory.* Amsterdam: North-Holland.

Meyer, B.J.F., Brandt, D. M., & Bluth, G. J. (1978, March). *Use of authors' schema: Key to ninth graders' comprehension.* Paper presented at the Annual Meeting of the American Educational Research Association, Toronto.

Meyer, C. (1992). What's the difference between authentic and performance assessment? *Educational Leadership, 49,* 39–40.

Meyer, M. M., & Fienberg, S. E. (1992). *Assessing evaluation studies: The case of bilingual education strategies.* Washington, DC: National Academy Press.

Michaels, S. (1981). "Sharing time": Children's narrative styles and differential access to literacy. *Language in Society, 10,* 423–442.

Michaels, S., & Cazden, C. (1986). Teacher-child collaboration on oral preparation for literacy. In B. Schieffelin & P. Gilmore (Eds.), *Acquisition of literacy: Ethnographic perspective* (pp. 132–154). Norwood, NJ: Ablex.

Michaels, S., & Collins, J. (1984). Oral discourse styles: Classroom interaction and the acquisition of literacy. In D. Tannen (Ed.), *Coherence in spoken and written discourse* (pp. 219–244). Norwood, MA: Ablex.

Mitchell, R. (1992). *Testing for learning.* New York: Free Press.

Moffett, J., & Wagner, B. J. (1991). *Student-centered language arts, K–12.* Portsmouth, NH: Boynton/Cook.

Moll, L. C. (1992). Bilingual classroom studies and community analysis: Some recent trends. *Educational Researcher 21* (2), 20–24.

Montaño-Harmon, M. L. (1991). Discourse features of written Mexican Spanish: Current research in contrastive rhetoric and its implications. *Hispania, 74* (2), 417–425.

Morais, J., Cary, L., Alegria, J., & Bertelson, P. (1979). Does awareness of speech as a sequence of phonemes arise spontaneously? *Cognition, 7,* 323–331.

Moskowitz, G. (1978). *Caring and sharing in the foreign language class.* Cambridge, MA: Newbury House.

Muma, J. (1978). *Language handbook.* Englewood Cliffs, NJ: Prentice-Hall.

Muth, K. D., & Alvermann, D. E. (1999). *Teaching and learning in the middle grades.* Needham Heights, MA: Allyn & Bacon.

Nagy, W. E., Herman, P. A., & Anderson, R. C. (1985). Learning words from context. *Reading Research Quarterly, 20,* 233–253.

Nagy, W. E., & Scott, J. A. (2000). Vocabulary processes. In M. L. Kamil, P. B. Mosenthal, P. D. Pearson, & R. Barr (Eds.), *Handbook of reading research*

(Vol. 3, pp. 269–284). Mahwah, NJ: Erlbaum.

Naiman, N., Frohlich, M., Stern, H. H., & Todesco, A. (1978). *The good language learner.* Toronto, Ontario, Canada: Ontario Institute for Studies in Education.

Nathensen-Mejía, S., & Escamilla, K. (2003). Connecting with Latino children: Bridging cultural gaps with children's literature. *Bilingual Research Journal, 27* (1), 101–116.

National Council of Teachers of Mathematics (NCTM). (1989a). *Principles and standards for school mathematics.* Reston, VA: Author.

National Council of Teachers of Mathematics (NCTM). (1989b). *Curriculum and evaluation standards for school mathematics.* Reston, VA: Author.

National Reading Panel. (2000). *Teaching children to read.* Bethesda, MD: National Institute of Child Health and Human Development.

National Research Council. (1996). *National science education standards.* Washington, DC: National Academy Press.

Navarrete, C., Wilde, J., Nelson, C., Martinez, R., & Hargett, G. (1990). *Informal assessment in educational evaluation: Implications for bilingual education programs* (Program Information Guide No. 13). Washington, DC: National Clearinghouse for Bilingual Education.

Navarro, M. (2003, November 9). Going beyond Black and White, Hispanics in census pick "other." *New York Times,* pp. 1, 21.

Neisser, U. (1967). *Cognitive psychology.* Englewood Cliffs, NJ: Prentice-Hall.

Nelson-Barber, S. (1982). Phonological variations of Pima English. In R. St. Clair & W. Leap (Eds.), *Language renewal among American Indian tribes: Issues, problems and prospects* (pp. 115–131). Rosslyn, VA: National Clearinghouse for Bilingual Education.

Nelson-Barber, S., Trumbull, E., & Wenn, R. (2000). *The coconut wireless project: Sharing culturally responsive pedagogy through the World Wide Web.* Honolulu: Pacific Resources for Education and Learning.

Nelson-LeGall, S., & Resnick, L. (1998). Help seeking, achievement motivation, and the social practice of intelligence in school. In S. A. Karabenick (Ed.), *Strategic help seeking: Implications for learning and teaching* (pp. 39–60). Mahwah, NJ: Erlbaum.

Neuman, S. B. (1995). Reading together: A community-supported parent tutoring program. *The Reading Teacher, 49,* 120–129.

Neuman, S. B., & Celano, D. (2001). Access to print in low-income and middle-income communities: An ecological study of four neighborhoods. *Reading Research Quarterly, 36* (1), 8–26.

Neuman, S., Copple, C., & Bredekamp, S. (2000). *Learning to read and write: Developmentally appropriate practices for young children.* Washington, DC: National Association for the Education for Young Children.

Neuman, S. B., & Roskos, K. (1997). Literacy knowledge in practice: Contexts of participation for young writers and readers. *Reading Research Quarterly, 32* (1), 10–32.

Newport, E. L. (1976). *Motherese: The speech of mothers to young children* (Technical Report No. 53). San Diego: University of California, Center for Human Information Processing.

Newport, E., Gleitman, H., & Gleitman, L. R. (1977). Mother, I'd rather do it myself: Some effects and non-effects of maternal speech style. In C. E. Snow & C. A. Ferguson (Eds.), *Talking to children: Language input and acquisition* (pp. 109–149). Cambridge, UK: Cambridge University Press.

Nickolaisen, D. (n.d.). *Specially designed academic instruction in English (SDAIE)*. Unpublished training manual.

Ninio, A., & Snow, C. (1988). Language acquisition through language use: The functional sources of children's early utterances. In Y. Levy, I. Schlesinger, & M. Braine (Eds.), *Categories and processes in language acquisition* (pp. 11–30). Hillsdale, NJ: Erlbaum.

No Child Left Behind Act (2001). Washington, DC: U.S. Department of Education.

Nsamenang, A. B., & Lamb, M. E. (1994). Socialization of Nso children in the Bamenda Grassfields of Northwest Cameroun. In P. M. Greenfield and R. R. Cocking (Eds.), *Cross-cultural roots of minority child development* (pp. 133–146). Hillsdale, NJ: Erlbaum.

Nunan, D. (1993, April). Exploring perceptions of the teaching process. Symposium at Twenty-seventh Annual Teachers of English to Speakers of Other Languages Convention, Atlanta, GA.

Ochs, E. (1982). Talking to children in Western Samoa. *Language and Society, 11*, 77–104.

Ogbu, J. U. (1992). Understanding cultural diversity and learning. *Educational Researcher, 21* (8), 5–14.

Oller, J. W., Jr. (1991). *Language and bilingualism: More tests of tests* (With S. Chesarek & R. Scott). Lewisburg, PA: Bucknell University Press.

Oller, J. W., Jr. (1992). Language testing research: Lessons applied to LEP students and programs. In *Proceedings of the second national research symposium on limited English proficient student issues: Focus on evaluation and measurement* (Vol. 2, pp. 123–126). Washington, DC: U.S. Department of Education, Office of Bilingual Education and Minority Language Affairs.

Olson, D. R. (1985). Introduction. In D. R. Olson, N. Torrance, & A. Hildyard (Eds.), *Literacy, language, and learning: The nature and consequences of reading and writing* (pp. 1–15). Cambridge, UK: Cambridge University Press.

Olson, L. (2000a). Minority groups to emerge as a majority in U.S. schools. *Education Week Online, 20* (4), 34–35.

Olson, L. (2000). Mixed needs of immigrants pose challenges for schools. *Education Week Online, 20* (4), 38, 39.

Olswang, L. B., Bain, B. A. (1991). Clinical forum: Treatment of efficacy, when to recommend intervention. *Language, Speech, and Hearing Services in Schools, 22*, 255–263.

O'Malley, J. J., & Chamot, A. U. (1990). *Learning strategies in second language acquisition*. Cambridge, UK: Cambridge University Press.

O'Neil, W. (1998). If Ebonics isn't a language, then tell me, what is? In T. Perry & L. Delpit (Eds.), *The real Ebonics debate* (pp. 38–48). Boston: Beacon Press.

Osborne, J., & Lehr, F. (n.d.). *A focus on fluency* (With E. H. Hiebert). Honolulu: Pacific Resources for Education and Learning.

Osborne, R., & Wittrock, M. C. (1983). Learning science: A generative process. *Science Education, 67*, 489–508.

Otto, B. (2002). *Language development in early childhood*. Upper Saddle River, NJ: Pearson Education.

Owens, R. (2001). *Language development: An introduction*. Boston: Allyn & Bacon.

Oxford, R. (1990). *Language learning strategies*. New York: Newbury House.

Oyama, S. (1976). A sensitive period for the acquisition of a nonnative phonological system. *Journal of Psycholinguistic Research, 5*, 261–285.

Padilla, A. (1991). Bilingual education: Issues & perspectives. In A. Padilla, H. Fairchild, & C. Valadez (Eds.), *Bilingual Education: Issues and Strategies* (pp. 15–26). Newbury Park, CA: Sage.

Palincsar, A. S., & David, Y. M. (1991). Promoting literacy through classroom dialogue. In E. H. Hiebert (Ed.), *Literacy for a diverse society: Perspectives, practices, and policies* (pp. 122–140). New York: Teachers College Press.

Papandropoulou, I., & Sinclair, H. (1974). Experimental study of children's ideas on grammar. *Human Development, 17*, 241–258.

Parker, F., & Riley, K. (2000). *Linguistics for non-linguists*. Boston: Allyn and Bacon.

Paul, R. (1995). *Language disorders from infancy through adolescence*. St. Louis: Mosby.

Peal, E., & Lambert, W. E. (1962). The relation of bilingualism to intelligence. *Psychological Monographs, 76* (27), entire issue.

Pearson, P. D. (2002). Thinking about the reading/writing connection with David Pearson. National Writing Project [Online]. Available: http://nwp.edgateway.net/pub/nwpr/voice/2002no2/staff4.html.

Pearson, P. D. (2003). Facilitating comprehension [Online]. Available: http://www.ciera.org/library/presos/2002/2002csi/2002csipearson/02csidpf.pdf.

Pearson, P. D. & Camperell, K. (1981). Comprehension of text structures. In J. T. Guthrie (Ed.), *Comprehension and teaching: Research reviews* (pp. 27–55). Newark, DE: International Reading Association.

Pearson, P. D., & Fielding, L. (1991). Comprehension instruction. In R. Barr, M. L. Kamil, P. Mosenthal, & P. D. Pearson (Eds.), *Handbook of reading research* (Vol. 2, pp. 815–860). White Plains, NY: Longman.

Pearson, P. D., & Raphael, T. E. (1999). Toward an ecologically balanced literacy curriculum. In In L. B. Gambrell, L. M. Morrow, S. B. Neuman, & M. Pressley (Eds.), *Best practices in literacy instruction* (pp. 22–33). New York: Guilford Press.

Pease, D. M., & Gleason, J. B. (1985). Gaining meaning: Semantic development. In J. B. Gleason (Ed.), *The development of language* (pp. 103–138).

Columbus, OH: Merrill.

Pei, M., & Gaynor, F. (1969). *Dictionary of linguistics*. Totowa, NJ: Littlefield, Adams.

Peñalosa, F. (1980). *Chicano linguistics: A brief introduction*. Rowley, MA: Newbury House.

Peregoy, S., & Boyle, O. (2001). *Reading, writing, & learning in ESL*. New York: Addison Wesley Longman.

Pérez, B., & Torres-Guzmán, M. (1996). *Learning in two worlds: An integrated Spanish/English biliteracy approach*. White Plains, NY: Longman.

Perez, S. A. (1999). Using Ebonics or Black English as a bridge to teaching standard English. *Classroom Leadership Online, 2* (7), 1–5.

Perfetti, C. A., Goldman, S. R., & Hogaboam, T. W. (1979). Reading skill and the identification of words in discourse context. *Memory and Cognition, 7*, 273–282.

Perfetti, C. A., & Lesgold, A. (1977). Discourse comprehension and sources of individual differences. In M. A. Just & P. A. Carpenter (Eds.), *Cognitive processes in comprehension* (pp. 141–183). Hillsdale, NJ: Erlbaum.

Perry, T. (1998). "I 'on know why they be trippin": Reflections on the Ebonics debate. In T. Perry & L. Delpit (Eds.), *The real Ebonics debate* (pp. 3–15). Boston: Beacon Press.

Perry T., & Delpit, L. (Eds.). (1998). *The real Ebonics debate: Power, language, and the education of African-American children*. Boston: Beacon Press.

Philips, S. U. (1983). *The invisible culture: Communication in classroom and community on the Warm Springs Indian Reservation*. New York: Longman.

Philipson, R. (1992). *Linguistic imperialism*. Oxford, UK: Oxford University Press.

Piaget, J. (1928). *Judgment and reasoning in the child*. New York: Harcourt, Brace.

Piaget, J. (1954). *The construction of reality in the child*. New York: Basic Books.

Piaget. J. (1967). *Six psychological studies*. New York: Vintage Books.

Piestrup, A. M. (1973). *Black dialect interference and accommodation of reading instruction in first grade* (Monograph of the Language-Behavior Research Laboratory, No. 4). Berkeley, CA: University of California.

Pimsleur, P. (1966). *Pimsleur language aptitude battery*. New York: Harcourt Brace Jovanovich.

Pinker, S. (1984). *Language learnability and language development*. Cambridge, MA: Harvard University Press.

Pinker, S. (1989). *Learnability and cognition*. Cambridge, MA: MIT Press.

Pinker, S. (1994). *The language instinct*. New York: Morrow.

Pinker, S. (1997). *How the mind works*. New York: Norton.

Pinnell, G. S. (1975). Language in primary classrooms. *Theory into Practice, 14* (5), 318–327.

Pinnell, G. S. (1980). *Discovering language with children*. Urbana, IL: National Council of Teachers of English.

Pinnell, G. S. (1996). Ways to look at the functions of children's language. In B. M. Power & R. S. Hubbard (Eds.), *Language development: A reader for teachers*. Englewood Cliffs, NJ: Merrill.

Piper, T. (2003). *Language and learning: The home and school years*. Upper Saddle River, NJ: Merrill/Prentice-Hall.

Plunkett, K., & Schafer, G. (1999). Early speech perception and word learning. In M. Barrett (Ed.), *The development of language* (pp. 51–68). East Sussex, UK: Psychology Press.

Popham, W. J. (2001a, September 19). Standardized achievement tests: misnamed and misleading. *Education Week* on the Web [Online]. Available: http://www.edweek.com/ew/newstory.cfm?slug=03pophem.h21.

Popham, W. J. (2001b). *The truth about testing: An educator's call to action*. Alexandria, VA: Association for Supervision and Curriculum Development.

Power, B. M., & Hubbard, R. S. (1996). *Language development: A reader for teachers*. Englewood Cliffs, NJ: Prentice-Hall.

Pressley, M. (n.d.). *Comprehension instruction: What works* [Online]. Available: http://www.readingrockets.org.

Pressley, M. (1998). *Reading instruction that works: The case of balanced teaching*. New York: Guilford Press.

Pressley, M. (1999). Self-regulated comprehension processing and its development through instruction. In L. B. Gambrell, L. M. Morrow, S. B. Neuman, & M. Pressley (Eds.), *Best practices in literacy instruction* (pp. 90–97). New York: Guilford Press.

Pressley, M., Wood, E., Woloshyn, V. E., Martin, V., King, A., & Menke, D. (1992). Encouraging mindful use of prior knowledge: Attempting to construct explanatory answers facilitates learning. *Educational Psychologist, 27*, 91–110.

Purcell-Gates, V. (1995). *Other people's words: The cycle of low literacy*. Cambridge, MA: Harvard University Press.

Purcell-Gates, V. (1996). Stories, coupons, and the *TV Guide*: Relationships between home literacy experiences and emergent literacy knowledge. *Reading Research Quarterly, 31* (4), 406–428.

Purcell-Gates,V., & Dahl, K. (1991). Low-SES children's success and failure at early literacy learning in skills-based classrooms. *Journal of Reading Behavior, 23*, 1–34.

Quintanar-Sarellana, R. (1991). Teachers' perceptions of the language and culture of linguistic minority students. Unpublished dissertation, Stanford University, Stanford, CA.

Quintanar-Sarellana, R. (1997). Teachers' perceptions of the language and culture of linguistic minority students. In J. King, E. Hollins, & W. Hayman (Eds), *Preparing teachers for cultural diversity* (pp. 40–52). New York: Teachers College Press.

Quintanar-Sarellana, R., Huebner, T., & Jensen, A. (1993). Tapping a natural resource: Language minority students as foreign language tutors. In B. Merino & H. Trueba (Eds.), *Language and culture in learning: Teaching Spanish to native speakers of Spanish* (pp. 208–221). Washington, DC: Falmer Press.

Quintanar-Sarellana, R., Huebner, T., & Jensen, A. (1997). La utilización de nuestros recursos linguísticos: Estudiates hispanohablentes como tutores en clases de Español como secundo idioma. In C. Columbi & F. Alarcón, (Eds.), *Español para hispanohablantes* (pp. 308–326). Boston: Houghton Mifflin.

Raeff, C., Greenfield, P. M., & Quiroz, B. (2000). Conceptualizing interpersonal relationships in the contexts of individualism and collectivism. In S. Harkness, C. Raeff, & C. Super (Eds.), *Variability in the cross-cultural construction of the child* (New Directions in Child Development, No. 87, pp. 59–74). San Francisco: Jossey-Bass.

Rafferty, C. D. (1999). Literacy in the information age. *Educational Leadership*, *57* (2), 22–25.

Ramírez, A. G. (1985). *Bilingualism through schooling*. Albany, NY: SUNY Press.

Ramírez, J. D. (1991). *Longitudinal study of structured English immersion strategy, early-exit and late-exit transitional bilingual education programs for language minority children*. Washington, DC: U.S. Department of Education, Office of Bilingual Education.

Ramírez, J. D., Yuen, S. J., Ramey, D. R., Pasta, D. J., & Billings, D. K. (1991). *Final report: Longitudinal study of structured immersion strategy, early-exit, and late-exit transitional programs for language-minority children*. San Mateo, CA: Aguirre International.

Ramírez M., & Casteñeda, A. (1974). *Cultural democracy, biocognitive development, and education*. New York: Academic Press.

Rabinski, T. (2004). Creating fluent readers. *Educational Leadership*, *61* (6), 46–51.

Ratner, N., & Bruner, J. S. (1978). Games, social exchange and the acquisition of language. *Journal of Child Language, 5*, 391–401.

Raven, J. C. (1983). *Raven's Standard Progressive Matrices*. London: Raven.

Read, C. (1971). Preschool children's knowledge of English phonology. *Harvard Educational Review*, *41* (1), 1–34.

Reddy, V. (1999). Prelinguistic communication. In M. Barrett (Ed.), *The Development of Language* (pp. 25–47). Hove, East Sussex, UK: Psychology Press.

Reder, S. (1994). Practice-engagement theory: A sociocultural approach to literacy across languages and cultures. In B. M. Ferdman, R. M. Weber, & A. G. Ramírez (Eds.), *Literacy across languages and cultures* (pp. 33–74). Albany, NY: SUNY Press.

Reder, S., & Green, K. (1983). Contrasting patterns of literacy in an Alaska fishing village. *International Journal of the Sociology of Language, 42*, 9–39.

Resnick, D. P., & Resnick, L. (1988). The nature of literacy: A historical exploration. In E. R. Kingten, B. M. Kroll, & M. Rose (Eds.), *Perspectives on literacy* (pp. 190–204). Carbondale, IL: Southern Illinois University Press.

Reyes, B. J. (2001). *A portrait of race and ethnicity in California: An assessment of social and economic well-being*. San Francisco: Public Policy Institute.

Richardson Bruna, K. (2002). *Manufacturing dissent: The new economy of power relations in multicultural teacher education.* Unpublished dissertation, University of California, Davis.

Richardson Bruna, K., Eaton, M., & Smith, J. (2003). *Evaluation of the English language development California professional development institutes: Final report.* Oakland, CA: University of California Office of the President, Teacher Education and Professional Development Division.

Rickford, J. R. (nd). The Ebonics controversy in my backyard: A sociolinguist's experiences and reflections. [Online]. Available: http://www.stanford.edu/~rickford/papers/EbonicsInMyBackyard.html.

Rickford, J. R. (1997). Unequal partnership: Sociolinguistics and the African American Speech Community. *Language in Society, 26,* 161–197.

Rincón, E. (1980). Test speededness, test anxiety, and test performance: A comparison of Mexican American and Anglo American high school juniors (Doctoral dissertation, University of Texas at Austin, 1979). *Dissertation Abstracts International, 40,* 5772A.

Rivera, C. (Ed.). (1983). *An ethnographic sociolinguistic approach to language proficiency assessment* (pp. 2–26). Clevedon, UK: Multilingual Matters.

Rivers, W. (1980). Foreign language acquisition: Where the real problems lie. *Applied Linguistics 1* (1), 48–59.

Robb, L. (2000). *Teaching reading in middle school.* New York: Scholastic Professional Books.

Rogoff, B. (2003). *The cultural nature of human development.* Oxford, UK: Oxford University Press.

Rogoff, B., & Lave, J. (Eds.). (1984). *Everyday cognition: Its development in social context.* Cambridge, MA: Harvard University Press.

Rogoff, C. (1990). *Apprenticeship in thinking: Cognitive development in social context.* New York: Oxford University Press.

Rondal, J., & Cession, A. (1990). Input evidence regarding the semantic bootstrapping hypothesis. *Journal of Child Language, 17,* 711–717.

Rosenblatt, L. (1976). *Literature as exploration.* New York: Modern Language Association. (Original work published 1938)

Rothstein-Fisch, C., Trumbull, E., & Greenfield, P.M. (in press). *Reconceptualizing classroom organization and management: Building on students' cultural strengths.* New York: Sage Foundation.

Rothstein-Fisch, C., Trumbull, E., Isaac, A., Daley, C., & Pérez, A. (2003). When "helping someone else" is the right answer: Bridging cultures in assessment. *Journal of Latinos and Education, 2* (3), 123–140.

Routman, R. (1996). *Literacy at the crossroads: Crucial talk about reading, writing and other teaching dilemmas.* Portsmouth, NH, Heinemann.

Rowe, D. W., & Harste, J. C. (1986). Metalinguistic awareness in writing and reading: The young child as curricular informant. In D. B. Yaden, Jr., & S. Templeton (Eds.), *Metalinguistic awareness and beginning literacy: Conceptualizing what it means to read and write* (pp. 235–256). Portsmouth, NH: Heinemann.

Rubin, A. (1980). A theoretical taxonomy of the differences between oral and written language. In R. J. Spiro, B. C. Bruce, W. F. Brewer (Eds.), *Theoretical issues in reading comprehension.* Hillsdale, NJ: Erlbaum.

Rubin, H., & Liberman, I. (1983). Exploring the oral and written language errors made by language disabled children. *Annals of Dyslexia, 33,* 110–120.

Rueda, R., Goldenberg, C., & Gallimore, R. (1992). *Rating instructional conversations: A guide.* Santa Cruz, CA: National Center for Research on Cultural Diversity and Second Language Learning.

Rumelhart, D. E. (1980). Schemata: The building blocks of cognition. In R. J. Spiro, B. C. Bruce, W. F. Brewer (Eds.), *Theoretical issues in reading comprehension* (pp. 33–58). Hillsdale, NJ: Erlbaum.

Sachs, J., Bard, B., & Johnson, M. L. (1981). Language learning with restricted input: Case studies of two hearing children of deaf parents. *Applied Psycholinguistics 2* (1), 33–54.

Salzmann, Z. (1993). *Language, culture, and society: An introduction to linguistic anthropology.* Boulder, CO: Westview Press.

Sapir, E. (1921). *Language.* New York: Harcourt, Brace, and World.

Saussure, F. de (1959). *Course in general linguistics.* New York: McGraw-Hill. (Original work published 1916)

Saville-Troike, M. (1976). *Foundations for teaching English as a second language: Theory and method for multicultural education.* Englewood Cliffs, NJ: Prentice-Hall.

Saville-Troike, M. (1980). Discovering what children know about language. In G. S. Pinnell (Ed.), *Discovering language with children* (pp. 109–112). Urbana, IL: National Council of Teachers of English.

Saville-Troike, M. (1991*). Teaching and testing for academic achievement: The role of language development* (Occasional Papers in Bilingual Education, No. 4). Washington, DC: National Clearinghouse for Bilingual Education.

Saxe, G. (1990). *Culture and cognitive development: Studies in mathematical understanding.* Hillsdale, NJ: Erlbaum.

Scarcella, R. (1996). Secondary education in California and second language research: Instructing ESL students in the 1990s. *The CATESOL Journal, 9* (1), 129–151.

Schachter, J. (1992). A new account of language transfer. In S. M. Gass & L. Selinker (Eds.), *Language transfer in language learning.* Philadelphia: Benjamins.

Schieffelin, B. B., & Ochs, E. (Eds.). (1986). Language socialization across cultures. Cambridge, UK: Cambridge University Press.

Schleppegrell, M. J. (1998). Grammar as resource: Writing a description. *Research in the Teaching of English, 32* (2), 182–211.

Schleppegrell, M. J. (2001). Linguistic features of the language of schooling. *Linguistics and Education 12* (4), 431–459.

Schleppegrell, M. J., & Achugar, M. (2002). *Working with English language learners in the history classroom.* Unpublished manuscript.

Schmida, M. (1996). *"I don't understand what she be saying": Reconsidering the interlanguage and semilingual theories and explanations for first language loss and limited SLA.* Unpublished manuscript, University of California at Berkeley.

Schoenbach, R., Greenleaf, C., Cziko, C., & Hurwitz, L. (1999). *Reading for understanding: A guide to improving reading in middle and high school class-rooms.* San Francisco: Jossey-Bass.

Scholl, D., & Ryan, E. B. (1980, April–June). Development of metalinguistic performance in the early school years. *Language and Speech, 23* (2), 199–211.

Schumann, J. (1978). The acculturation model for second-language acquisition. In R. Gringas (Ed.), *Second language acquisition and foreign language teaching.* Washington, DC: Center for Applied Linguistics.

Scollon, R., & Scollon, S. W. (1981). *Narrative, literacy, and face in interethnic communication.* Norwood, NJ: Ablex.

Scollon, R., & Scollon, S. W. (1995). *Intercultural communication: A discourse approach.* Oxford, UK: Blackwell.

Scribner, S., & Cole, M. (2001). Literacy without schooling: Testing for intellectual effects. In. S. W. Beck & L. N. Oláh (Eds.), *Perspectives on language and literacy: Beyond the here and now* (pp. 187–199). Cambridge, MA: Harvard Educational Review. (Original work published 1978)

Secada, W. (1992). Race, ethnicity, social class, language, and achievement in mathematics. In D. A. Grouws (Ed.), *Handbook of research on mathematics teaching and learning* (pp. 623–660). New York: Macmillan.

Secret, C. (1998). Embracing Ebonics and teaching standard English: An interview with Oakland teacher Carrie Secret. In T. Perry & L. Delpit (Eds.), *The real Ebonics debate* (pp. 79–88). Boston: Beacon Press.

Seliger, H. (1977). Does practice make perfect?: A study of interaction patterns and L2 competence. *Language Learning, 27,* 263–278.

Selinker, L. (1972). Interlanguage. *International Review of Applied Linguistics, 10,* 209–230.

Senechal, M. (1997). The differential effect of storybook reading on preschoolers' acquisition of expressive and receptive vocabulary. *Journal of Child Language, 24,* 123–138.

Sharan, S., Raviv, S., Kussell, P., & Hertz-Lazarowitz, R. (1984). Cooperative and competitive behavior. In *Cooperative learning in the classroom: Research in desegregated school* (pp. 73–102). Hillsdale, NJ: Erlbaum.

Share, D. L., & Stanovich, K. E. (1995). Cognitive processes in early reading development: Accommodating individual differences into a model of acquisition. *Issues in Education, 1,* 1–57, 101.

Sharwood-Smith, M. (1981). Consciousness raising and the second language learner. *Applied Linguistics, 2* (2), 159–168.

Shaw, J. (1997). "The test was explein with secretly words": Reflections on performance assessment of English language learners. In B. Farr & E. Trumbull, *Assessment alternatives for diverse learners* (pp. 334–342). Norwood, MA: Christopher-Gordon.

Shaywitz, S. S., Shaywitz, B., Pugh, K., Fulbright, R., Constable, T., Mencl, W., Shankweiler, D., Liberman, A., Skudlarski, P., Flether, J., Katz, L., Marchione,

K., Lacadie, C., Gatenby, C., & Gore, J. (1998). Functional disruption in the organization of the brain for reading in dyslexia. *Proceedings of the National Academy of Science, 95*, 2636–2641.

Sheets, R. H. (1999a). Human development and ethnic identity. In R. H. Sheets & E. R. Hollins (Eds.), *Racial and ethnic identity in school practices: Aspects of human development* (pp. 91–105). Mahwah, NJ: Erlbaum.

Sheets, R. H. (1999b). Relating competence in an urban classroom to ethnic identity development. In R. H. Sheets & E. R. Hollins (Eds.), *Racial and ethnic identity in school practices: Aspects of human development* (pp. 157–178). Mahwah, NJ: Erlbaum.

Sheets, R. H., & Hollins, E. R. (Eds.). (1999). *Racial and ethnic identity in school practices: Aspects of human development*. Mahwah, NJ: Erlbaum.

Shipley, E. F., Smith, C. S., & Gleitman, L. R. (1969). A study in the acquisition of language: Free response to commands. *Language, 45*, 322–342.

Short, D. (1991). *How to integrate language and content instruction: A training manual*. Washington, DC: Center for Applied Linguistics.

Short, D. (1994). Expanding middle school horizons: Integrating language, culture, and social studies. *TESOL Quarterly, 28* (3), 581–608.

Shu, H., Anderson, R. C., & Zhang, H. (1995). Incidental learning of word meanings while reading: A Chinese and American cross-cultural study. *Reading Research Quarterly, 30* (1), 76–95.

Siegel-Causey, E., & Ernst, B. (1989). Theoretical orientation and research in nonsymbolic development. In E. Siegel-Causey & D. Guess (Eds.), *Enhancing nonsymbolic communication interactions among learners with severe disabilities* (pp. 15–47). Baltimore: Brookes.

Skiba, R. (2003). Code switching as a countenance of language interference [Online]. Available: http://iteslj.org/Articles/Skiba-CodeSwitching.html

Skinner, B. F. (1957). *Verbal behavior*. New York: Appleton-Century-Crofts.

Slavin, R. E. (1983). *Cooperative learning*. New York: Longman.

Slobin, D. (1970). Universals of grammatical development in children. In G. B. Flores D'Arcais & W. J. M. Levelt (Eds.), *Advances in psycholinguistics* (pp. 174–186). Amsterdam: North-Holland.

Slobin, D. (1982). Universal and particular in the acquisition of language. In E. Wanner & L. R. Gleitman (Eds.), *Language acquisition: The state of the art* (pp. 128–170). Cambridge, UK: Cambridge University Press.

Slobin, D. (1985). Introduction: Why study acquisition crosslinguistically? In *The crosslinguistic study of language acquisition*: Vol. 1. *The data* (pp. 3–24). Hillsdale, NJ: Erlbaum.

Smagorinsky, P. (2001). If meaning is constructed, what is it made from? Toward a cultural theory of reading. *Review of Educational Research, 71* (1), 133–169.

Smiley, P., & Huttenlocher, J. (1995). Conceptual development and the child's early words for events, objects, and persons. In M. Tomasello & W. Merriman (Eds.), *Beyond names for things: Young children's acquisition of verbs* (pp. 21–61). Hillsdale, NJ: Erlbaum.

Smith, C. B. (1997). Vocabulary instruction and reading comprehension. Bloomington, IN: Indiana University. (ERIC Documentation Reproduction Service No. ED CS 9707)

Smith, E. (1998). What is Black English? What is Ebonics? In T. Perry & L. Delpit (Eds.), *The real Ebonics debate* (pp. 49–58). Boston: Beacon Press.

Smith, F. (1973). *Psycholinguistics and reading*. New York: Holt, Rinehart & Winston.

Smith, F. (1985). A metaphor for literacy: Creating worlds or shunting information? In D. R. Olson, N. Torrance, & A. Hildyard (Eds.), *Literacy, language, and learning: The nature and consequences of reading and writing* (pp. 195–213). Cambridge, UK: Cambridge University Press.

Smitherman, G. (1998). Black English/Ebonics: What it be like? In T. Perry & L. Delpit (Eds.), *The real Ebonics debate* (pp. 49–58). Boston: Beacon Press.

Snow, C. E. (1977). Mothers' speech research: From input to interaction. In C. E. Snow & C. Ferguson (Eds), *Talking to children: Language input and acquisition* (pp. 31–49). New York: Cambridge University Press.

Snow, C. (1983). Literacy and language: Relationships during the preschool years. *Harvard Educational Review, 53*, 165–189.

Snow, C. (1990a). The development of definitional skills. *Journal of Child Language, 17,* 697–710.

Snow, C. (1990b). Rationales for native language instruction: Evidence from research. In A. M. Padilla, H. H. Fairchild, & C. M. Valadez, (Eds.), *Bilingual education: Issues and strategies* (pp. 60–74). Newbury Park, CA: Sage.

Snow, C. E., Burns, M. S., & Griffin, P. (Eds.). (1998). *Preventing reading difficulties in young children*. Washington, DC: National Academy Press.

Snow, C., Cancini, H., Gonzalez, P., & Shriberg, E. (1989). Giving formal definitions: An oral language correlate of school literacy. In D. Bloome (Ed.), *Classrooms and literacy* (pp. 233–249). Norwood, NJ: Ablex.

Snow, C., & Hoefnagel-Hohle, M. (1978). The critical period for language acquisition: Evidence from second language learning. *Child Development, 49,* 1114–1118.

Snow, C. E., & Tabors, P. O. (1993). Language skills that relate to literacy development. In B. Spodek & O. N. Saracho (Eds.), *Language and literacy in early childhood education* (pp. 1–20). New York: Teachers College Press.

Sobul, D. (1994, February). *Strategies to meet the goals of SDAIE*. Paper presented at the California Association of Bilingual Education Conference, San Jose, California.

Solano-Flores, G., & Nelson-Barber, S. (2001). On the cultural validity of science assessments. *Journal of Research in Science Teaching, 38* (5), 553–573.

Solano-Flores, G., & Trumbull, E. (2003). Examining language in context: The need for new research and practice paradigms in the testing of English language learners. *Educational Researcher, 32* (2), 313.

Solano-Flores, G., Trumbull, E., & Nelson-Barber, S. (2002). Concurrent development of dual language assessments: An alternative to translating tests for linguistic minorities. *International Journal of Testing, 2* (2), 107–129.

Söter, A. O. (1988). The second language learner and cultural transfer in narration. In A. C. Purves (Ed.), *Writing across language and cultures: Issues in contrastive rhetoric,* pp 177–205. Thousand Oaks, CA: Sage.

Spanos, G., Rhodes, N. C., Dale, T. C., & Crandall, J. (1988). Linguistic features of mathematical problem solving: Insights and applications. In R. R. Cocking & J. P. Mestre (Eds.), *Linguistic and cultural influences on learning mathematics* (pp. 221–241). Hillsdale, NJ: Erlbaum.

Stahl, S. A., & Fairbanks, M. M. (1986). The effects of vocabulary instruction: A model-based meta-analysis. *Review of Educational Research, 56* (1), 72–110.

Stanovich, K. (1984). The interactive-compensatory model of reading: A confluence of developmental, experimental, and educational psychology. *Remedial and Special Education, 5* (3), 11–19.

Stanovich, K. E. (1994). Romance and reality. *The Reading Teacher, 47,* 280–291.

Stanovich, K., Cunningham, A. E., & Cramer, B. B. (1984). Assessing phonological awareness in kindergarten children: Issues of task comparability. *Journal of Experimental Child Psychology, 38,* 175–190.

Stanovich, K., & Stanovich, P. (1995). How research might inform the debate about early reading acquisition. *Journal of Research in Reading, 18* (2), 87–105.

Stanovich, K., West, R. F., & Freeman, D. J. (1981). A longitudinal study of sentence context effects in second-grade children: Tests of an interactive-compensatory model. *Journal of Experimental Child Psychology, 32,* 185–199.

Stanton-Salazar, R. D., Vásquez, O. A., & Mehan, H. (1995). *Engineering success through institutional support.* Berkeley, CA: University of California Latino Eligibility Project.

Stein, N. (1982), What's in a story: Interpreting the interpretations of story grammar. *Discourse Processes, 5,* 319–335.

Stevick, E. (1980). *Teaching languages: A way & ways.* Rowley, MA: Newbury House.

Stockwell, R. P., Bowen, J. D., & Martin, J. W. (1965). *The grammatical structures of English and Spanish.* Chicago: University of Chicago Press.

Stoller, F., & Grabe, W. (1995). Implications for L2 vocabulary acquisition and instruction from L1 vocabulary research. In T. Huckin, M. Haynes, & J. Coady (Eds.), *Second language reading and vocabulary learning* (pp. 24–45). Norwood, NJ: Ablex.

Strickland, D. S., & Morrow, L. M. (1989). *Emerging literacy: Young children learn to read and write.* Newark, DE: International Reading Association.

Subrahmanyam, K., & Greenfield, P. M. (1994). Effect of video game practice on spatial skills in girls and boys. *Journal of Applied Developmental Psychology, 15,* 13–32.

Suina, J. H., & Smolkin, L. B. (1994) From natal culture to school culture to dominant society culture: Supporting transitions for Pueblo Indian students. In P. M. Greenfield & R. R. Cocking (Eds.), *Cross-cultural roots of minority child development* (pp. 115–130). Hillsdale, NJ: Erlbaum.

Sulzby, E. (1980, December). *The development and validation of metalinguistic tasks assessing the child's concept of word.* Paper presented at the 30th Annual Meeting of the National Reading Conference Symposium, San Diego.

Sulzby, E. (1986). Children's elicitation and use of metalinguistic knowledge about words during literacy interactions. In D. B. Yaden, Jr., & S. Templeton (Eds.), *Metalinguistic awareness and beginning literacy: Conceptualizing what it means to read and write* (pp. 219–233). Portsmouth, NH: Heinemann.

Suter, R. (1976). Predictors of pronunciation accuracy in second language learning. *Language Learning, 26,* 155–176.

Sutter, J., & Johnson, C. (1990). School-age children's metalinguistic awareness of grammaticality in verb form. *Journal of Speech and Hearing Research, 33,* 84–95.

Swain, M. (1983). Bilingualism without tears. In M. A. Clarke & J. Handscombe (Eds.), *On TESOL '82: Pacific perspectives on language learning and teaching* (pp. 35–46). Washington, DC: TESOL.

Swain, M. (1985). Communicative competence: Some roles of comprehensible input and comprehensible output in its development. In S. M. Gass and C. G. Madden (Eds.), *Input in second language acquisition* (pp. 235–253). Rowley, MA: Newbury House.

Swain, M. (1991). French immersion and its offshoots: Getting two for one. In B. F. Freed (Ed.), *Foreign language acquisition research and the classroom* (pp. 91–103). Lexington, MA: Heath.

Swain, M., & Burnaby, B. (1976). Personality characteristics and second language learning in young children. *Working Papers on Bilingualism, 3,* 68–79.

Swales, J. M. (1990). *Genre analysis: English in academic and research settings.* Cambridge, UK: Cambridge University Press.

Swan, M., & Smith, B. (1987). *Learner English: A teacher's guide to interference and other problems.* Cambridge, UK: Cambridge University Press.

Swisher, K., & Deyhle, D. (1992). Adapting instruction to culture. In J. Reyhner (Ed.), *Teaching American Indian students* (pp. 81–95). Norman, OK: University of Oklahoma Press.

Tager-Flusberg, H. (1985). Putting words together: Morphology and syntax in the preschool years. In J. B. Gleason (Ed.), *The development of language* (pp. 139–171). Columbus, OH: Merrill.

Tager-Flusberg, H., & Calkins, S. (1990). Does imitation facilitate the acquisition of grammar? Evidence from a study of autistic, Down's syndrome and normal children. *Journal of Child Language, 17* (3), 591–606.

Tannen, D. (1985). Relative focus on involvement in oral and written discourse. In D. R. Olson, N. Torrance, & A. Hildyard (Eds.), *Literacy, language, and learning: The nature and consequences of reading and writing,* (pp. 124–147). Cambridge, UK: Cambridge University Press.

Tartter, V. C. (1986). *Language processes.* New York: Holt, Rinehart & Winston.

Taylor, C. (1994). Assessment for measurement or standards: The peril and promise of large-scale assessment reform. *American Educational Research Journal, 32* (2), 231–262.

Taylor, L. L., Catford, J. C., Guiora, A. Z., & Lane, K. L. (1971). Psychological variables and ability to pronounce a second language. *Language and Speech*, *14*, 146–157.

Taylor, O. (1986). *Nature of communication disorders in culturally and linguistically diverse populations*. San Diego: College Hill.

Teale, W. H. (1986). Home background and young children's emergent literacy development. In W. H. Teale & E. Sulzby (Eds.), *Emergent literacy: Writing and reading* (pp. 173–206). Norwood, NJ: Ablex.

Teale, W., & Sulzby, E. (Eds.). (1986). *Emergent literacy*. Norwood, NJ: Ablex.

Teale, W. H., & Sulzby, E. (1991). Emergent literacy. In R. Barr, M. L. Kamil, P. B. Mosenthal, & P. D. Pearson (Eds.), *Handbook of reading research* (Vol. 2, pp. 418–452). New York: Longman.

Tharp, R. (1997). *From at-risk to excellence: Research, theory, and principles for practice* (Research Report No. 1). Washington, DC: Center for Research on Education, Diversity, & Excellence.

Tharp, R., & Gallimore, R. (1988). *Rousing minds to life: Teaching, learning and schooling in social context*. Cambridge, UK: Cambridge University Press.

Tharp, R., & Gallimore, R. (1991). *The instructional conversation: Teaching and learning in social activity* (Research Report No. 2). Santa Cruz, CA: National Center for Research on Cultural Diversity and Second Language Learning.

Tharp, R. G., Jordan, C., Speidel, G. E., Au, K.H.P., Klein, T. W., Calkins, R. P., Sloat, K.C.M., & Gallimore, R. (1984). Product and process in applied developmental research: Education and the children of a minority. In M. E. Lamb, A. L. Brown, & B. Rogoff (Eds.), *Advances in developmental psychology* (Vol. 3, pp. 91–141). Hillsdale, NJ: Erlbaum.

Thomas, W. P., & Collier, V. P. (1996). *Language minority student achievement and program effectiveness*. Fairfax, VA: George Mason University, Center for Bilingual/Multicultural/ESL Education.

Thomas, W. P., & Collier, V. (1997). *School effectiveness for language minority students*. Washington, DC: National Clearinghouse on Bilingual Education.

Thomas, W. P., & Collier, V. P. (2001). *A national study of school effectiveness for language minority students' long-term academic achievement*. Santa Cruz, CA: Center for Research on Education, Diversity, and Excellence.

Thonis, E. W. (1983). Reading instruction for language minority students. In *Schooling and language minority students: A theoretical framework* (pp. 147–181). California Department of Education, Los Angeles: Evaluation, Dissemination, and Assessment Center: California State University.

Tiberghien, E., Jossem, L., & Barojas, G. (Eds.). (1997). *Making the results of research in physics education available to teacher educators*. College Park, MD: International Commission on Physics Education.

Tierney, R. J., & Cunningham, J. W. (1984). Research on teaching reading comprehension. In P. D. Pearson (Ed.), *Handbook of reading research* (Vol. 1, pp. 609–655). New York: Longman.

Tierney, R. J., & Pearson, P. D. (1981). *Learning to learn from text: A framework for improving classroom practice* (Reading Education Report No. 30). Urbana, IL: Center for the Study of Reading.

Tierney, R. J., & Shanahan, T. (1991). Research on the reading-writing relationship: Interactions, transactions, and outcomes. In R. Barr, M. L. Kamil, P. B. Mosenthal, & P. D. Pearson (Eds.), *Handbook of reading research* (Vol. 2, pp. 246–280). White Plains, NY: Longman.

Tinbergen, N. (1952). The curious behavior of the stickleback. *Scientific American, 187*, 22–26.

Tinbergen, N. (1984). *The curious naturalists* (Rev. Ed.). Amherst, MA: University of Massachusetts Press.

Tomasello, M., & Brooks, P. J. (1999). Early syntactic development: A constructive grammar approach. In M. Barrett (Ed.), *The development of language* (pp. 161–190). Hove, UK: Psychology Press.

Torgesen, J., & Bryant, B. (1994). *Test of phonological awareness*. Austin, TX: Pro-Ed.

Trevarthen, C., & Aitken, K. J. (2001). Infant intersubjectivity: Research, theory, and clinical applications. *Journal of Child Psychology and Psychiatry, 42* (1), 3.

Triandis, H. C. (1989). The self and social behavior in differing cultural contexts. *Psychological Review, 96*, 506–520.

Trueba, H. T. (1993). The relevance of theory on language and culture with pedagogical practices. In B. J Merino, H. T. Trueba, & F. A. Samaniego (Eds.), *Language and culture in learning: Teaching Spanish to native speakers of Spanish (pp. 259–267).* Washington, DC: Falmer Press.

Trumbull, E. (1984). *Metalinguistic skills: Can they be taught?* Unpublished dissertation, Boston University.

Trumbull, E. (2000). Avoiding bias in grading systems. In E. Trumbull & B. Farr (Eds.) *Grading and reporting student progress in an age of standards* (pp. 105–127). Norwood, MA: Christopher-Gordon.

Trumbull, E., Diaz-Meza, R., & Hasan, A. (in press). Using cultural knowledge to inform literacy practices: Teacher innovations from the bridging cultures project. In P. M. Greenfield, A. Isaac, E. Trumbull, C. Rothstein-Fisch, & B. Quiroz (Eds.), *Bridging cultures in U.S. classrooms*. New York: Sage Foundation.

Trumbull, E., & Farr, B. (2000). *Grading and reporting student progress in an age of standards*. Norwood, MA: Christopher-Gordon.

Trumbull, E., & Koelsch, N. (2000, January). *Developing a district-wide reading assessment for students in transition*. Paper presented at the RACE 2000 Conference, Tempe, AZ.

Trumbull, E., Nelson-Barber, S., & Mitchell, J. (2002). Enhancing mathematics instruction for Indigenous American Students (pp.1–18). In J. Hankes (Ed.), *Changing the faces of mathematics: Perspectives on Indigenous people of North America.* Reston, VA: National Council of Teachers of Mathematics.

Trumbull, E., Rothstein-Fisch, C., Greenfield, P. M., & Quiroz, B. (2001). *Bridging cultures between home and school: A guide for teachers*. Mahwah, NJ: Erlbaum.

Trumbull, E., Rothstein-Fisch, C., & Hernandez, E. (2003). Parent involvement—according to whose values? *School Community Journal, 13* (2), 45–72.

Tse, L. (2001). *"Why don't they learn English?": Separating fact from fallacy in the U.S. language debate*. New York: Teachers College Press.

Tunmer, W. E., & Bowey, J. A. (1984). Metalinguistic awareness and reading acquisition. In W. E. Tunmer, C. Pratt, & M. L. Herriman (Eds.), *Metalinguistic awareness in children* (pp. 144–168). NewYork: Springer-Verlag.

Tunmer, W. E., & Chapman, J. W. (1993). To guess or not to guess, that is the question: Metacognitive strategy training, phonological recoding and beginning reading. *Reading Forum, 1*, 3–14.

Tyack, D. (1974). *The one best system*. Cambridge, MA: Harvard University Press.

Tyner, K. (1998). *Literacy in a digital world: Teaching and learning in the age of information*. Mahwah, NJ: Erlbaum.

Uchida, Y. (1986). *The dancing kettle and other Japanese folktales*. Berkeley, CA: Creative Arts.

U.S. Bureau of the Census. (2000). *Profiles of general demographic characteristics*. Washington, DC: U.S. Department of Commerce.

Valdés, G. (1996). *Con respeto*. New York: Teachers College Press.

Valdés, G., & Figueroa, R. A. (1994). *Bilingualism and testing: A special case of bias*. Norwood, NJ: Ablex.

Valdés-Fallis, G. (1978). *Code switching and the classroom teacher*. Washington, DC: Center for Applied Linguistics.

Valenzuela, A. (1999). *Subtractive schooling: U.S.-Mexican youth and the politics of caring*. Albany, NY: SUNY Press.

Van de Vivjer, F., & Poortinga, Y. H. (1997). Towards an integrated analysis of bias in cross-cultural assessment. *European Journal of Psychological Assessment, 13* (1), 29–37.

Vandervelden, M. C., & Siegel, L. S. (1995). Phonological recoding and phoneme awareness in early literacy: A developmental approach. *Reading Research Quarterly, 30*, 854–875.

Varonis, E. M., & Gass, S. M. (1985). Non-native/non-native conversations: A model for negotiation of meaning. *Applied Linguistics, 6* (1), 71–90.

Vásquez, O. A. (2003). *La clase mágica: Imagining optimal possibilities in a bilingual community of learners*. Mahwah, NJ: Erlbaum.

Vellutino, F., & Scanlon, D. (1996). Cognitive profiles of difficult-to-remediate and readily remediated poor readers: Early intervention as a vehicle for distinguishing between cognitive and experiential deficits as basic causes of specific reading disability. *Journal of Educational Psychology*, (8), 601–638.

Vellutino, F., Scanlon, D., & Tanzman, M. (1990). Differential sensitivity to the meaning and structural attributes of printed words in poor and normal readers. *Learning and Individual Differences, 2*, 19–43.

Vernon, S., & Ferreiro, E. (1999). Writing development: A neglected variable in the consideration of phonological awareness. *Harvard Educational Review, 69* (4), 395–415.

Vygotsky, L. (1962). *Thought and language*. Cambridge: MIT Press. (Original work published 1934)

Vygotsky, L. (1978). *Mind in society: The development of higher psychological processes*. (M. Cole, V. John-Steiner, S. Scribner, & E. Souberman, Eds.). Cambridge, MA: Harvard University Press. (Original work published in 1930.)

Wade, S. E., & Moje, E. B. (2000). The role of text in classroom learning. In M. L. Kamil, P. B. Mosenthal, P. D. Pearson, & R. Barr (Eds.), *Handbook of reading research* (Vol. 3, pp. 609–627). Mahwah, NJ: Erlbaum.

Wallace, K. R. (2001). *Relative/outsider: The art and politics of identity among mixed heritage students*. Norwood, NJ: Ablex.

Wallach, G., & Butler, K. (1994). *Language learning disabilities in school age children and adolescents*. New York: Macmillan.

Walqui, A. (2002). Conceptual framework: Scaffolding instruction for English learners. In *Quality teaching for English learners*. San Francisco: WestEd.

Walqui, A., & Galguera, T. (2002). The adaptation of written texts for English learners. *Quality teaching for English learners.* San Francisco: WestEd.

Washington State Commission on Student Learning. (1998*). Grade 4 Mathematics Assessment Sampler*. Olympia, WA: Author.

Watson, I. (1991). Phonological processing in two languages. In. E. Bialystok (Ed.), *Language processing in bilingual children* (pp. 25–48). Cambridge, UK: Cambridge University Press.

Weber, R. M. (1991). Linguistic diversity and reading in American society. In R. Barr, M. L. Kamil, P. Mosenthal, & P. D. Pearson (Eds.), *Handbook of reading research* (Vol. 2, pp. 97–119). White Plains, NY: Longman.

Webster's encyclopedic unabridged dictionary of the English language. (1989). New York: Portland House.

Weir, R. (1962). *Language in the crib*. The Hague, Netherlands: Mouton.

Wells, G. (1986). *The meaning makers: Children learning language and using language to learn*. Portsmouth, NH: Heinemann.

Werker, J. F., & Tees, R. C. (1984). Cross-language speech perception: Evidence for perceptual reorganization during the first year of life. *Infant Behavior and Development, 7,* 49–63.

Whatley, E. (1981). Language among Black Americans. In C. A. Ferguson & S. B Heath (Eds.), *Language in the U.S.A.* (pp. 92–107). Cambridge, UK: Cambridge University Press.

Whorf, B. L. (1956). *Language, thought, and reality: Selected writings of Benjamin Lee Whorf* (J. B. Carroll, Ed.). Cambridge, MA: MIT Press.

Wiggins, G. P. (1993). *Assessing student performance: Exploring the purpose and limits of testing*. San Francisco: Jossey-Bass.

Wijk, A. (1966). *Rules of pronunciation for the English language*. London: Oxford University Press.

Williams, J. D., & Snipper, G. C. (1990). *Literacy and Bilingualism*. New York: Longman.

Williams, L. (1980). Phonetic variation as a function of second-language learning. In G. H. Komshian, J. F. Cavanaugh, & C. A. Ferguson, (Eds.), *Child Phonology*: Vol 2. *Perception* (pp. 185–215). New York: Academic Press.

Williams, R. L. (1975). *Ebonics: The true language of Black folks.* St. Louis: Institute of Black Studies.

Witkin, H., Dyk, R., Faterson, H., Goodenough, D., & Karp, S. (1962). *Psychological differentiation.* New York: Wiley.

Witkin, H. A., & Goodenough, D. R. (1981). *Cognitive styles, essence, & origins; Field dependence and field independence.* New York: International Universities Press.

Wolf, D., Bixby, J., Glenn, J. III, & Gardner, H. (1991). To use their minds well: Investigating new forms of student assessment. In G. Grant (Ed.), *Review of research in education.* Washington, DC: American Educational Research Association.

Wolfram, W. (1993). Speaking of prejudice. *The Alumni Magazine of North Carolina State University, 65* (3), 44.

Wolfram, W., Adger, C. T., & Christian, D. (1999). *Dialects in schools and communities.* Mahwah, NJ: Erlbaum.

Wolk, R. A., & Rodman, B. H. (Eds.). (1994). *Classroom crusaders: Twelve teachers who are trying to change the system.* San Francisco: Jossey-Bass.

Wollman, N., & Estrin, E. T. (1990, August). *Logic and emotion: Orthogonal factors in argumentation.* Paper presented at the Annual Meeting of the American Psychological Association, Boston.

Wong Fillmore, L. (1976). *The second time around: Cognitive and social strategies in second language acquisition.* Unpublished dissertation, Stanford University, Stanford, California.

Wong Fillmore, L. W. (1985). When does teacher talk work as input? In S. Gass & C. Madden (Eds.), *Input for second language acquisition.* Cambridge, MA: Newbury House.

Wong Fillmore, L. (1989). Language learning in social context: The view from research in second language learning. In R. Dietrich & C. F. Graumann (Eds.), *Language processing in social context* (pp. 277–301). North-Holland: Elsevier.

Wong Fillmore, L. W. (1991). When learning a second language means losing the first. *Early Childhood Research Quarterly, 6,* 323–346.

Wong Fillmore, L., & Snow, C. (2000). *What teachers need to know about language.* Washington, DC: U.S. Department of Education, Office of Educational Research and Improvement.

Yaden, D., Rowe, D., & MacGillivray, L. (2000). Emergent literacy: A matter (polyphony) of perspectives. In M. L. Kamil, P. B. Mosenthal, P. D. Pearson, & R. Barr (Eds.), *Handbook of reading research* (Vol. 3, pp. 425–454). Mahwah, NJ: Erlbaum.

Young, R. (1967). *English as a second language for Navajos: An overview of certain cultural and linguistic factors.* Albuquerque, NM: , Bureau of Indian Affairs, Navajo Area Office Division of Education.

Zentella, A. C. (1997). *Growing up bilingual, Puerto Rican children in New York.* Malden, MA: Blackwell.

Index

About the Authors

 Beverly Farr is now Director of Research at ROCKMAN ET AL in San Francisco, an independent evaluation, research, and consulting firm. Current projects include an evaluation of cultural competency training in California and a study of a distance Spanish class in West Virginia. As a Managing Director at the American Institutes for Research, Farr conducted studies of innovative literacy programs, statewide accountability initiatives, and professional development. Prior to her career move to an emphasis on research work, Farr spent 15 years supporting Title I programs in districts and states across the country. She has specialized in curriculum and instruction, assessment and accountability, and the needs of English language learners. She has published numerous articles, contributed to the development of a range of standardized assessments, and, with Elise Trumbull, written two other books, *Assessment Alternatives for Diverse Classroom* and *Grading and Reporting in an Age of Standards*. Farr completed her Ph.D. in Reading Education at Indiana University in 1975.

Elise Trumbull is an educational consultant specializing in sociocultural influences on learning and schooling. A former teacher, Trumbull completed her doctorate in education in the area of applied psycholinguistics at Boston University in 1984. She has studied five languages other than English and has conducted applied research in cultural settings ranging from California and Arizona to Micronesia.

As a senior research associate at WestEd, a federally-funded educational laboratory based in San Francisco, Trumbull directed a teacher collaborative action research called "Bridging Cultures" from 1996-2004. Trumbull has co-authored numerous articles and book chapters, as well as six books. Among them are *Assessment Alternatives for Diverse Classrooms* (with Beverly Farr; Christopher-Gordon, 1997), *Bridging Cultures between Home and School: A Guide for Teachers* (with Carrie Rothstein-Fisch, Patricia M. Greenfield, & Blanca Quiroz; Lawrence Erlbaum, 2001), and *Grading and Reporting in an Age of Standards* (with Beverly Farr; Christopher-Gordon, 2000).

Katherine Richardson Bruna is an assistant professor of Multicultural and International Curriculum Studies in the Department of Curriculum and Instruction, College of Education, Iowa State University. Prior to receiving her doctorate in education with a sociocultural studies specialization from the University of California at Davis in 2002, she worked as a bilingual instructional aide and ESL teacher. She speaks and has taught Spanish, having lived in San José, Costa Rica and Madrid, Spain.

Before taking a position at ISU, Richardson Bruna was a research scientist at the American Institutes for Research in Palo Alto, California. There she was involved in evaluations of the implementation and effects of Proposition 227, California's "English-Only" initiative and of California's professional development institutes for teachers of English learners. She also helped design the Language Survey and Background Questionnaire for the Spanish NAEP (the National Assessment of Education Progress). A former United States Department of Education Bilingual Education Fellow, Richardson Bruna is deeply interested in issues related to the education of language minority children in U.S. schools. Her current grant-supported research examines the nature of explicit academic language instruction for English learners in science. This is her first book chapter.

Rosalinda Quintanar-Sarellana obtained both her Master's in International Education and her Ph.D. in Language, Literacy and Culture from Stanford University. Currently, she is a professor in the College of Education at San José State University (California). She teaches courses on pedagogy in diverse school settings, language acquisition, and the needs of language minority students in English and Spanish to students in both the credential and master's program.

Dr. Quintanar-Sarellana has also taught at Universidad Metropolitana in México City, the University of California at Davis, and Stanford University. She has published on the topics of diversity, equity, first and second language acquisition, and successful educational projects for linguistic minority students. She has been active in forging partnerships between the university and school districts and between the U.S. and other countries. In 2003, Dr. Quintanar-Sarellana received the Teacher Scholar Award from San José State University as well as Professor of the Year Award from Dìa Del Maestro, a Santa Clara County Organization.